D0675002

TRUE STORIES

Medill School of Journalism
VISIONS *of the* AMERICAN PRESS

⬖

GENERAL EDITOR
David Abrahamson

TRUE STORIES
A CENTURY OF
LITERARY JOURNALISM

Norman Sims

Foreword by Ted Conover

MEDILL SCHOOL OF JOURNALISM

Northwestern University Press
Evanston, Illinois

"The Long Fall of One-Eleven Heavy" by Michael Paterniti from *Esquire* magazine, July 2000, pp. 92–134. Copyright (c) 2000 by Michael Paterniti. Used by permission of Michael Paterniti.

"Red Caucasus" from *Orient Express* by John Dos Passos, pp. 32–38. New York and London: Harper and Brothers. Copyright (c) 1922, 1927 by John Dos Passos. Used by permission of Lucy Dos Passos Coggin.

"The Jumping-Off Place" from *The American Earthquake* by Edmund Wilson. Originally published in *The New Republic,* December 23, 1931, and reprinted in *The American Jitters: A Year of the Slump,* pp. 253–260. New York and London: C. Scribner's Sons, 1932. Reprinted also in *The American Earthquake: A Documentary of the Twenties and Thirties,* pp. 414–420. London: W. H. Allen, 1958. Copyright (c) 1958 by Edmund Wilson. Copyright renewed 1986 by Helen Miranda Wilson. Reprinted by permission of Farrar, Straus & Giroux, LLC.

"The Old House at Home" from *Up in the Old Hotel* by Joseph Mitchell. Originally published in *The New Yorker,* April 13, 1940, and reprinted in *McSorley's Wonderful Saloon,* pp. 3–39. New York: Duell, Sloan and Pearce, 1943. Copyright (c) 1992 by Joseph Mitchell. Used by permission of Pantheon Books, a division of Random House, Inc.

"Family Journeys" from *Random Family: Love, Drugs, Trouble, and Coming of Age in the Bronx* by Adrian Nicole LeBlanc, pp. 139–142, 159–162, 188–194. New York: Scribner, 2003. Copyright (c) 2003 by Adrian Nicole LeBlanc. Used by permission of Adrian Nicole LeBlanc.

Northwestern University Press
www.nupress.northwestern.edu

Printed in the United States of America

10 9 8 7 6 5 4 3 2 1

ISBN 978-0-8101-2469-1

Library of Congress Cataloging-in-Publication Data

Sims, Norman.
   True stories : a century of literary journalism / Norman Sims ;
foreword by Ted Conover.
      p. cm. — (Visions of the American press)
"Medill School of Journalism"
   Includes bibliographical references and index.
   ISBN-13: 978-0-8101-2469-1 (pbk. : alk. paper)
   ISBN-10: 0-8101-2469-6 (pbk. : alk. paper)
   1. Reportage literature, American—History and criticism. 2. American prose literature—20th century—History and criticism. 3. American prose literature—21st century—History and criticism. 4. Journalism—United States—History—20th century. 5. Journalism—United States—History—21st century. I. Medill School of Journalism. II. Title. III. Series.
PS366.R44S56 2008
818.50809—dc22

                                    2007028619

For my mentor and friend, Dr. James W. Carey

CONTENTS

◈

FOREWORD

◈

Ted Conover

What a great job! To go out into the world, to poke into things that matter, to ask, to talk, to look, to see. And maybe not just for a few days—ideally, long enough to leave one's own world behind and to enter into another's. And finally, to come back home and tell (i.e., write).

The model for a number of the journeys I've written about was probably an experience that began during high school and re-sumed during college. Lots of students have done it: spent a sum-mer studying abroad. Under the auspices of a small nonprofit based in my hometown of Denver, some fellow students and I lived with families in Pamplona, Spain. The Pamplona families had never done this sort of thing before, and they treated us like royalty. Still, it took me about a week to realize that I was occupying the mas-ter bedroom of a two-bedroom apartment. The *señora,* Felisa, was missing a tooth, and she was a bit hard to understand. Her hus-band, Carmelo, who worked for the power company, took my difficulty with Spanish as a sign of low intelligence and, during the rare times when he was around, spoke to me SLOWLY and LOUDLY. They took me crawfish-fishing and, back in the apart-ment, kept the catch in a state of suspended animation until it was time to make the *paella:* when you opened the refrigerator, you could sometimes hear the crawfish clawing, very slowly, down in the vegetable drawer as they awaited their destiny. The lunch table was set with tall, stoppered bottles of fizzy lemonade and red wine, which I was encouraged to mix: it was about the best drink I'd had in my life, and perfect preparation for an after-lunch siesta.

Another guy from my group stayed down the block in an apartment that doubled as a busy hairdressing salon, so we met lots of girls who offered to show us around. The program bought us summer memberships at the local swim club, and most days found us in the water, or sunbathing on the grass. There were frequent festivals, including one in which small bonfires were lit in a vacant lot at night and teenagers jumped over them; in the process, I singed my eyebrows. The same night, after much singing of Navarran songs, we Americans were asked to sing a couple of songs typical of our land. All we could think of was "Yankee Doodle" and "This Land Is Your Land," which petered out pathetically in the middle of the second verse. Some of the best times were Saturday afternoons in the discos with the kids of our local families and their friends—I remember these occasions as far superior to any other Saturday afternoons I had ever had. There was one young woman in particular, Alicia, who was active in the Basque separatist cause and whose family owned a bar/restaurant in the old section of town. I enjoyed dancing with Alicia very much.

One great excitement of the summer was the arrival of *sanfermines,* or the Festival of San Fermín, Pamplona's patron saint. The most famous part of this is the eight-day running of the bulls, which we watched but, on pain of excommunication from the program, did not participate in. Except for one guy, who may or may not have: he was cagey about it. Either way, I immediately concluded that I was a wimp and should have. It would have been a great rite of passage, and I was looking for a rite of passage. By the end of our stay in Pamplona I was imagining another kind of rite of passage with Alicia, but it all ended too quickly, and before we knew it we were back home in Denver.

Where this story intersects with the idea of literary journalism, I hope, is here: I wanted to go back and so, by hook and by crook, I did. Two years later, on my own, I wrote to the bank clerk who had been our local coordinator in Pamplona—his wife ran the hair salon—to see if he could find me a temporary job. He was something of a fixer and we had liked each other. Still, it seemed like a miracle when he said he had found me employment, not as a waiter or bicycle mechanic (my suggestions) but as a *peón* at a Pamplona sausage factory. During part of a year that I took off from college, I worked forty-six hours a week in the factory. I dated Alicia. I ran with the bulls. And the next summer, when a new crew of foreign-study students from Denver arrived, I was to them the seasoned, quasi-local whose Spanish was really good.

I loved that status, just as I had loved the process of acquiring it. It seemed to me that I had a privileged perspective, one that had been there for the asking. After I returned to school, I hoped it wouldn't be the last time in my life I was in that insider-outsider place that was at once so marginal and so central, that place in which you could know so much.

Back at college I was snagged by cultural anthropology, a discipline devoted to the exploration of other peoples' ways of looking at the world. And I quickly became fascinated by the anthropological field method, participant observation. It was like what journalists do, only you stayed longer, got in deeper, and didn't have to chase breaking news. There seemed to be more space for—and possibility of—insight and contemplation. The *observer* role that the journalist typically occupied was modified and transformed by the realization, practically codified in anthropology, that you also learn things by joining a group and doing them yourself. And that the best place to be, if you want to learn about somebody else, is somewhere in between those poles of participant and observer . . . though it was the participant side of things that really intrigued me. I wanted to be not the observer nor the critic but what Teddy Roosevelt in his famous speech referred to as the "man in the arena, whose face is marred by dust and sweat and blood . . . who at the best knows in the end the triumph of high achievement, and who at the worst, if he fails, at least fails while daring greatly, so that his place shall never be with those cold and timid souls who neither know victory nor defeat." That quote made me think of the bull ring in Pamplona. And yet I also wanted to be a writer, an observer almost by definition. A statue of Ernest Hemingway, who wrote about bulls and Pamplona in *The Sun Also Rises,* stands outside the *plaza de toros.* He had found his own way to do it.

So I proposed to my college advisers some fieldwork: I would ride freight trains with hoboes, about whom I would write an ethnography as a senior thesis. The cost was low, and access seemed possible: friends who had hopped trains told me it was not hard to talk to the hoboes. Unfortunately, freight hopping was also dangerous and against the law. My adviser said no ("You could lose your legs! You could be raped!") but whispered that if I went ahead anyway, left college again, and returned with notes worthy of the task, maybe they would let me write the paper. Long story short, I did, and they did. I rode the rails—twenty-four hours a day, for five months, all around the West. It was an adventure but a *deliberate* adventure, self-aware: my aim was to produce notes by getting to know the "professionals" who rode rails full time, and I did; I learned as much about them as I could stand. And when I got back, people asked me not only *what was it like?* but *what was it like for you?*

That second question, the more personal one, wasn't really what my professors were after, so I largely had to leave that part out of my thesis. But I wanted to describe it—at length!—and people (even my professors) were endlessly asking, so after graduation, instead of taking an internship at a newspaper in Indianapolis as planned, I went home and wrote a book about the experience, in the first person. And got it published.

Experiences like the ones I had in Pamplona, or on the rails—practically any of them, come to think of it—can be very lonely. Susan Orlean once told an interviewer, "Everybody's nightmare is being the complete odd one out. When I was working on another book, I saw a survey in which Americans were asked what activities they feared the most. First was swimming and second was going to a party with strangers. I thought, *That's what I do.*" But that very aloneness is what guarantees you'll be eager for the company of other people, and more approachable than if you were in a group.

Still, even when solo, I've been aware of shadow companions. Out there on the rails, some of them were writers who were my mentors and models. One, I suppose, was Herman Melville, whose own youth, filled with sailing and whaling, exemplified the idea that writers must pursue experience—must fill some well of it—in order to have something to write about. I was also traveling with John Steinbeck, whose *The Grapes of Wrath* was my favorite book and whose *Travels with Charley* suggested how to tell a story in which the narrator was a character. I felt the company of Jack London as well, another writer from the American West with a strong social conscience—and a biography that included tramping of all sorts. George Orwell's novels *1984* and *Animal Farm* I knew from high school, but when a professor pointed me toward *Down and Out in Paris and London,* I had an example before me of how the narrative craft could be put to use in a class-boundary-crossing adventure. I read Jack Kerouac's *On the Road* just before I left because, well, didn't every student before a road trip? Soon I also took up Nels Anderson on the non-folkloric hobo, John Reed on Mexico during the revolution, and short pieces by Joan Didion, Tom Wolfe, and Hunter S. Thompson.

Was I thinking of them all the time? No. In fact, I've always been fascinated by something Jack London wrote to his publisher, Houghton Mifflin, in January 1900: "In the main I am self-educated; have had no mentor but myself." In his case the claim was essentially true; in mine it was not but I fancied it was, that I was sui generis, without forebear or debt. Part of this probably had to do with growing up in a place with as brief a history as Denver, with a public school education that was minimally *belles-lettres.* These were in some ways impediments, but in others—like the experience of being bused, by court order, to a high school where I was in the racial minority—they helped me dare to think differently, to aspire to originality.

And of course we have other influences. One for me was the older brother of a friend on my block who had ridden freights up into the mountains. (I had no older brother, and such stories were potent to me.) Another was the romance of the hobo and the rails, as expressed in folk songs and country songs and movies and probably even Gertrude Chandler Warner's *Boxcar Children* books. Another enabler was parents who, after a certain point, gave me a long leash in a culture that encouraged male independence, expressible in things like solo travel and adventure.

• • •

Most of us work essentially alone, but a book like *True Stories: A Century of Literary Journalism* by Norman Sims can make us feel a part of something bigger. One of the lessons of this volume is that there is no one way to do this work—on the contrary, a distinctive approach is often an advantage, and may even be required. You think of a story that seems to need telling, and you go where it's happening: a living room, a railroad yard, a street, a high school, a doctor's office, Peru. You find somebody there to talk with, and then you meet their friends. You follow a traveler or someone on a mission; you are attentive to difficulty; you are mindful of the difference your presence makes. You acknowledge that a lot happened before you arrived. You think about how this might amount to a story, how it would look on paper. You buy a new pen and notebook. You sit at a table, lean against a counter, or turn the light back on after you lay down and the idea came. You write.

PREFACE

◈

Literary journalism holds an attraction for many writers that at one level surprises me and at another level seems perfectly natural.

My surprise comes from the fact that very few writers have the opportunity to produce literary journalism. It requires a greater investment of time and resources than most employers can afford, and only under rare circumstances can writers use their own time to create a book-length work of literary journalism.

John McPhee once told me that his extended literary journalism in *The New Yorker* had almost no relationship to standard journalism. He could spend a year and a half working on one story, whereas a daily newspaper reporter might write four hundred stories in the same time and a magazine journalist might do a dozen pieces or more. That's correct, of course, but the recent rebirth of narrative journalism at several newspapers shows how attractive the form is to daily news reporters, and magazine writers for the past century have been invested in narrative styles that, at times, became literary journalism.

The natural attraction to literary journalism comes from the fact that reporters are, after all, writers. They can admire and emulate the techniques used by gifted writers like McPhee, Tracy Kidder, Susan Orlean, Michael Paterniti, and Adrian Nicole LeBlanc.

This book provides a history of literary journalism for those who are new to the form, and also for those writers and scholars who are familiar with it but are not aware of its ancestry. The focus is on several themes that began in the nineteenth century and on a limited number of extraordinary individual writers from the past hundred years, rather than on theory or external forces. In part, this comes from my own belief that the writers do the real work and should be given credit for their innovations. I cannot talk about literary journalism without talking about the writers—who they are, what experiences they had, how they wrote, and the times in which they lived. The times mattered because changes and innovations have come in response to events and in some cases in response to personal relationships.

Writers today are still engaged in a struggle to describe reality that has been carried on for more than a century. Two persistent perspectives have characterized journalists since at least the rise of mass-circulation newspapers in the 1890s. One perspective sought to use verifiable facts to grasp reality. This "scientific" journalism since the turn of the twentieth century has reported secondhand information and statistics in search of active social and economic trends. Very little direct experience was involved; a reporter more frequently wrote what someone else said about the trends. The scientific or bureaucratic perspective has been countered by an impulse to describe the quality of ordinary life, consciousness, culture, feelings and sentiments of individuals. Literary journalists are caught in the same bind, of course, and need to rely on what people tell them. But they use special techniques to get closer to direct experience. Participant observation reporting of the kind that Ted Conover uses today is one example, wherein the writer lives with the subjects whether they be hobos, prison guards, or immigrants picking oranges in Arizona. Both approaches have their debatable merits, but it remains fairly clear that literary journalists lean toward the humanistic approach that values immersion with the participants in a cultural world.

• • •

I first became interested in something we now call literary journalism when I was a college undergraduate in the sixties and the New Journalism was blossoming. I remember finding a copy of Tom Wolfe's *Electric Kool-Aid Acid Test* in the journalism library of the University of Illinois, opening it, starting to read, and becoming stuck until I finished it the next day. This was something exciting, something different, something real.

But within a few years the New Journalism faded away, although it had profoundly influenced a generation of writers. It became discredited in the 1970s because of accusations that writers made up details and because of a conflict within the literary community that I will describe in Chapter 6.

It's often impossible to recall when we were touched by things that influenced our lives. Sometimes the events may be a relationship with a professor, an atmosphere around home, or something vague that simply excites us. Not only can I remember the moment I discovered Tom Wolfe, but I can also recall the exact moment that I *rediscovered* literary journalism. I was at my in-laws' house and picked up a *New Yorker* "Profile" by Jane Kramer about Henry Blanton (not his real name), a cowboy in the Texas Panhandle.[1] I happened to pick up the second half of the article and read it first. Once again, as when reading Wolfe's *Acid Test,* I was inspired. Kramer's "Cowboy" (1977) opened my eyes to the possibilities in literary journalism. I was then a graduate student studying a similar literary impulse held by newspaper reporters in Chicago at the turn of the twentieth century. At the time, I did not recognize the intimate connection between the two eras.

As a young college professor in the 1980s, I discovered that there was a second generation of New Journalists writing for the magazines and book publishers. I met several of them—including

Tracy Kidder, Mark Kramer, Richard Rhodes, Sara Davidson, Richard West, and Mark Singer—and began a series of interviews with writers, asking them about how they worked and what motivated them. My approach was largely sociological and historical in nature, rather than guided by literary theory. Eventually, I identified some characteristics that these writers shared, which I labeled the identifying qualities of literary journalism.

In this book, I deal with several related definitions of literary journalism in Chapters 1, 6, and 7. Written descriptions of literary journalism may be abstract or theoretical, but they generally share a vision. Reading examples of literary journalism, however, can give one a better sense of the form than definitions can. I have therefore included five examples of literary journalism, ranging from John Dos Passos in 1922 to Adrian Nicole LeBlanc in 2003, which I believe are representative of the genre's development in different eras. Space limits the number of selections that can be reprinted in a book like this one; thus, in the appendix I have provided a bibliography listing examples of literary journalism from more than a century's worth of the form's development. Even a quick glance at the bibliography and the appendix will show how many other writers have made contributions to the development of literary journalism during the past hundred years and more.

The history of literary journalism shows a progression from the nineteenth century until today. I have highlighted the role played by the "sketch" in nineteenth-century literary journalism as well as several other themes, including the close connection between travel writing and literary journalism. Even before literary journalism had a name, writers were arrayed along boundaries between standard and literary journalistic work and between fiction and journalism. Not until *The New Yorker* arrived did a group of writers find themselves in one place at the same time and able to pursue a vision of literary journalism, even though they did not have a special name for it. The work done by these writers as well as by several others early in the century paved the way for the New Journalists of the sixties, who had a name but did not have something as new as it seemed. Since then, two more generations of literary journalists have continued exploring a form that has provided one of the most important ways for us to understand our times.

A few years ago, when I started talking about this project with David Abrahamson, editor of the Medill School of Journalism series on Visions of the American Press, I did not expect to write a book with a chapter on the New Journalism that talks primarily about the "usual suspects" of Tom Wolfe, Truman Capote, Norman Mailer, Joan Didion, and Hunter S. Thompson. As Tom Connery once complained, "this group of writers has been the focus of just about all of the extended discussion of contemporary literary journalism."[2] I decided, however, that in writing a history, it was necessary to take note of the leading figures. Each chapter deals with writers who were among the most prominent of their time. Others contributed in every era. Along with the "famous" writers, I have included discussions of less well-known literary journalists who have made significant contributions to the genre, including George Ade, Finley Peter Dunne, John Dos Passos, Martha Gellhorn, and contemporary writers Doug Whynott and Adrian Nicole LeBlanc. Students and readers who are new to the form should become familiar with the usual suspects, but I do not intend to slight the many literary journalists who have not become household names.

This book tells stories about writers in action and is meant to serve as a popular survey for those who are new to the history of literary journalism, both students and writers. Alongside the requirements of a history, I have included some new research, interviews, and analysis, particularly on literary journalism's origins in the nineteenth century and on current practitioners such as Whynott, Paterniti, and LeBlanc.

A number of excellent historians are working on literary journalism, including John Hartsock, Tom Connery, Daniel Lehman, Michael Robertson, and John Pauly. My goal in this book is to establish a historical foundation for American literary journalism. In shaping a narrative about the development of the genre over the past hundred years and more, I avoid the terminology of literary theory and the social sciences, except for the term "culture," which came from my studies with Dr. James Carey, my dissertation adviser at the University of Illinois, before the word was adopted in the critical disciplines.

I owe a debt of thanks to many generous people who helped me in various ways during the preparation of this book. First, my thanks to Diane deGroat, without whose support I could not have traversed the past eight years, let alone have written a book. Thanks also to David Abrahamson, who is not only a scholar of literary journalism but also a great editor who has taken on a massive and important project at Northwestern University. My thinking about literary journalism has been shaped by years of conversations with several scholars and colleagues, including Madeleine Blais, Jim Boylan, Tom Connery, David Eason, John Hartsock, John Pauly, Jim Rogers, Patsy Sims, and Howard Ziff. David Hayes in Toronto, whose knowledge of history and practice are superb, and Walt Harrington at the University of Illinois and formerly of the *Washington Post,* have both introduced me to new ideas that play a role in this volume.

I have conducted interviews with a number of literary journalists since 1981, and I owe thanks to all of them. Some of the research for this book first appeared in *Literary Journalism in the Twentieth Century* and my other books, mainly as a result of interviews with writers. For this book, I am especially indebted to Ted Conover; Nick Lemann of *The New Yorker* and dean of the Graduate School of Journalism at Columbia University; Michael Paterniti of *GQ* magazine; Adrian Nicole LeBlanc; and Doug Whynott. Joseph Mitchell was generous beyond all expectations, and Sheila McGrath, his literary executor, has continued that generosity over many years. I also owe thanks to Lucy Dos Passos Coggin for permission to use her father's work.

For making themselves available at a moment's notice during times of panic, I especially want to thank Jack Hart of *The Oregonian,* Mike Deehan for comments on graphic journalism, Jon Hite for his political savvy, Corey Flintoff of National Public Radio for comments on narrative and voice in nonfiction, David Badger for help with the New Journalism, and Frank Faulkner for his knowledge of Irish history. Special thanks go to Kathy Streckfus and Deborah Lynes for their careful editing. Jon and Lynn Franklin are owed a genuine thank-you from writers everywhere for their daily listserv, WriterL, running since 1994 and devoted to literary journalism and narrative.

Of course, any errors of fact, interpretation, or omission are mine alone, but I do want to thank my friends and colleagues who read drafts of the manuscript and made helpful suggestions.

NORMAN SIMS

ONE

A TRUE STORY

What a word is truth—slippery, tricky, unreliable.
—Lillian Hellman

"It reads like a novel."

This statement has been used to compliment and unintentionally to insult literary journalism.

Novels, by definition, are invented prose narratives. The creative invention of characters, events, plot, dialogue, and details has defined the realistic novel since Aphra Behn's *Oroonoko,* which was labeled "A True History" on the cover of the first edition in 1688. The early 1700s saw an upsurge of books whose authors claimed their stories were true, such as Daniel Defoe's *Robinson Crusoe.* Labels became tricky after readers started distinguishing between the novel and nonfiction. Defoe's *The Tempest* was long taken as fiction, and his *Journal of the Plague Year* as fact, but the reverse was closer to reality. Defoe used plain vernacular language and often employed a bumbling style that looped back on itself and forced his narrator to make self-corrections. His ordinary language seemed free of guile. Readers reacted by helping out, by believing.

Reading a nonfiction book that tells gripping stories with emotional complexity may be an experience similar to reading a novel. Stephen Crane, one of the most celebrated journalists at the turn of the twentieth century, wrote on both sides of the great fact-fiction divide. Michael Robertson argued in an excellent book, *Stephen Crane, Journalism, and the Making of Modern American Literature,* that our modern distinctions between journalism and fiction "have distorted our readings of many of Crane's works." Robertson described a literary world where the newspaper and novels "were covering the same terrain." As Robertson explained, departmentalization and sharp distinctions have become much more rigid today than they were in the nineteenth century.[1]

The border guards are much stricter today. The invention of details destroys journalism, and it can be damaging to forms that typically have looser standards, such as memoir and autobiography. The greatest controversies in the history of literary journalism—particularly during the New Journalism era of the 1960s—have involved the accuracy of reports.

Since 1981, I have been interviewing literary journalists about their craft. Not one of those writers ever said it was all right to make up anything. Accuracy is the foremost requirement for them.

Several writers have revealed their annoyance when their literary journalism is confused with the novel.

Tracy Kidder had just won the general nonfiction Pulitzer Prize for *The Soul of a New Machine* when I interviewed him in the cramped office of his rural New England home. Tall and slim, he had the build of a tight end in football, which he had been. Kidder always displays a no-nonsense intensity. A few days before our first interview, a local newspaper piece about the Pulitzer Prize mistakenly had called his book a "novel." Kidder was bemused. "If the story's true, if the dialogue's not invented, then it's journalism," he said. "I don't know what you call the stuff that appears to be hybrid. To me there's journalism and there's fiction. I say it has to be true. Sometimes you have to change names but that's risky."[2]

A few years later, Richard Todd, the former executive editor of *The Atlantic* who edits Kidder's books, said that literary journalism "holds the promise of taking us to worlds we don't ordinarily visit and to make them real," which is increasingly something the novel does not do.[3] Unlike the realistic novel, literary journalism has to be factual.

"I don't see why it's so hard to understand, yet it's a constant source of confusion and curiosity," Susan Orlean, a *New Yorker* staff writer and author of *The Orchid Thief,* told another interviewer. "I find it really funny. I very often will have *The Orchid Thief* referred to as a novel, and it drives me crazy."[4]

John McPhee—noted for more than thirty carefully crafted books that range among topics as widespread as airplanes, oranges, geology, Alaska, efforts to control nature, nuclear weapons, shad fishing, trains, trucks, and canoes—takes great care, along with *The New Yorker* fact-checkers, to assure that everything in his books is accurate. McPhee and Kidder could be related—except that McPhee is about a foot shorter—in that they both have a precise and articulate manner of speaking, and oftentimes they write in a similar style. The separate realms of fiction and journalism were on McPhee's mind when I first met him in his Princeton University office.

"There are things you don't do, things you can do, and things you can't do," McPhee told me.

> What you don't do, for example, is make a composite character. Where I came from, a composite character was a fiction. So when somebody makes a nonfiction character out of three people who

are real, that is a fictional character in my opinion. And you don't get inside their heads and think for them. You can't interview the dead. You could make a list of the things you don't do. Where writers abridge that, they hitchhike on the credibility of writers who don't. And they blur something that ought to be distinct. When people talk about "the line is blurring between fiction and nonfiction," what I see in that image is that we don't know where fiction stops and fact begins. That violates a contract with the reader.[5]

Presumed contracts with readers have been broken or challenged several times in recent history. Some examples:

- An "autobiography" called *The Education of Little Tree* by Forrest Carter was on the *New York Times* paperback nonfiction bestseller list in 1991. The presumed contract in autobiography permits some recollections and even quotations that might never be confirmed, such as what your mother said to you when you were eight years old, as well as some inevitable self-promotion. This went beyond the contract. Supposedly the autobiography of a Cherokee boy, *The Education of Little Tree* was actually written by Asa Earl Carter, who was white, the founder of the Ku Klux Klan of the Confederacy, and a racist speechwriter for former Alabama Governor George Wallace. After the *New York Times* found out about the hoax, the book moved from the nonfiction bestseller list to the fiction list without comment.[6]
- Michael Finkel's cover article, "Is Youssouf Malé a Slave?" in the *New York Times Magazine* of November 18, 2001, told the story of a fifteen-year-old boy in West Africa who sold himself into servitude believing he might acquire a pair of shoes.

Finkel's impressionistic feature contained not a single quotation. David Hayes, a Canadian literary journalist, said he had the article at a copy shop preparing to hand it out to a magazine class when the scandal broke. It turned out that Finkel, under pressure from *Times* editors to write a more dramatic piece, created a composite character named Youssouf Malé—a real person, one of many Finkel interviewed, but Malé did not have the experiences related in the article. An aid worker with Save the Children Canada identified the boy pictured on the cover of the magazine as another child, not Malé, and that was how Finkel was caught. The article, while based on actual reporting, was fictionalized, breaking several contracts with *New York Times* readers and with its editors. Finkel lost his job.

- Dave Eggers published *What Is the What: The Autobiography of Valentino Achak Deng—A Novel* in 2006. Eggers labeled the book a novel, which violates no presumed contract, but it blurs the line between fiction and nonfiction. The main character is a Sudanese refugee whose experiences were the starting point for a fictionalized work. In the end, the main character says he understands that people are listening to him. "How can I pretend that you do not exist? It would be almost as impossible as you pretending that I do not exist." But, of course, he existed no more than Finkel's Youssouf Malé. "Novel, autobiography, whatever," said a *New York Times* reviewer.[7]

- A "memoir" titled "The Blood Runs Like a River through My Dreams," by a Native American writer named Nasdijj, ran in the June 1999 issue of *Esquire*. It recounted the death of a child from fetal alcohol syndrome. Nasdijj followed his initial story with three memoirs of family problems. But Nasdijj was later revealed to be Tim Barrus, whose family history is Scandinavian, not Native American. *Esquire* revealed the fraud in 2006.[8]

- James Frey's "nonfiction memoir" *A Million Little Pieces,* the story of the author's life as a drug addict, alcoholic, and criminal, was endorsed by Oprah Winfrey for her blockbuster-making book club in 2005. Although Frey said the book was straight nonfiction, several examinations disproved his claims about jail terms and other details. Winfrey confronted him on air and withdrew her recommendation.[9]

Unlike Oprah and the editors of the *Times* and *Esquire,* apparently readers did not much care when writers broke the rules of the presumed contracts. *The Education of Little Tree* has sold 2.5 million copies in its long lifespan, and *A Million Little Pieces* has sold some 3.5 million copies.

Memoir, autobiography, the genre known in English departments at universities as "creative nonfiction," literary journalism, and even history and science have had similar embarrassing moments. In the world of journalism, accuracy reigns as the supreme clause in the symbolic contract with readers, and the same is true among literary journalists. Some violations by literary journalists of the presumed contract with readers will be noted in this book—including Truman Capote's *In Cold Blood*—but overall I have always found that literary journalists talk about writing true stories as their primary obligation.

The nature of literary journalism has evolved during the past several decades, and, at best, definitions have always been a bit vague.

Among the shared characteristics of literary journalism are immersion reporting, complicated structures, character development, symbolism, voice, a focus on ordinary people—if for no other reason than that celebrities rarely provide the necessary access—and accuracy. Literary journalists recognize the need for a consciousness on the page through which the objects in view are filtered.

A list of characteristics can be an easier way to define literary journalism than a formal definition or a set of rules. Well, there are some rules, but Mark Kramer used the term "breakable rules" in an anthology we edited. Among those rules, Kramer included:

- Literary journalists immerse themselves in subjects' worlds. . . .
- Literary journalists work out implicit covenants about accuracy and candor. . . .
- Literary journalists write mostly about routine events.
- Literary journalists develop meaning by building upon the readers' sequential reactions.[10]

In his edited volume of presentations from the Nieman Conference on Narrative Journalism, Kramer suggests tips for reporting narrative:

- Pinpoint your subjects' emotional experience, not your own.
- Rigorously research your story's context.
- Cherish the structural ideas and metaphors that come to you while you are reporting.[11]

The journal *Creative Nonfiction* in 2006 gave a list of "The ABCs of CNF" where the use of composite characters was supported, but only with the very important sub-rule: "The key is to let readers know what you are doing and why."[12]

The kind of writing often labeled as literature—meaning fiction—usually departs from the actual details of time and place, and characters are imaginary or injected with made-up thoughts and feelings. Journalism ties itself to the actual, the confirmed, that which is not simply imagined. In the past century and a half, however, literary journalism has developed as a creature with parents in both camps. Literary journalists have adhered to the rules of accuracy—or mostly so—precisely because their work cannot be labeled as journalism if details and characters are imaginary.

In the history of literary journalism that runs from Daniel Defoe in the early 1700s until today, an unusual thing happened in the 1930s. This genre of writing gained a name. A couple of names, to be exact.

In 1937, Edwin H. Ford, who taught in the Department of Journalism at the University of Minnesota, published *A Bibliography of Literary Journalism in America.* Although the term had been used a couple of times earlier in the century, Ford seems to be the first to use *literary journalism* with its contemporary scholarly meaning as a form of journalism and not as the product of a journalist who wrote about literature.[13]

"Literary Journalism as conceived for the purpose of this bibliography might be defined as writing which falls within the twilight zone that divides literature from journalism," Ford wrote. "It has the interpretative caste of literature as well as the contemporary interest of journalism." According to Ford, literary journalists create artistic literature that moves beyond political and social trends. "Through the medium of the sketch or essay, of the literary or humorous column, of verse, or of critical comment, he refashions and evaluates the world about him."[14]

Ford's topic was so broad that his bibliography could only "suggest possibilities inherent in a study of literary journalism." He did a pretty good job. He listed Sherwood Anderson, William Bolitho, Malcolm Cowley, H. L. Mencken, Opie Read, Henry David Thoreau, and Brand Whitlock as writers who combined journalism and literature in books. Among humorists, he mentioned Mark Twain, Eugene Field, Finley Peter Dunne, George Ade, and Ring Lardner. He included novelists Richard Harding Davis, David Graham Phillips, Frank Norris, and Theodore Dreiser, who were also leading journalists of the century. The term *literary journalism* did not catch on in Ford's time, but the period before World War II produced a great deal of literary journalism as well as considerable innovation in the form.

The massive unemployment and suffering of the Great Depression created fertile ground for literary journalism. Ford was correct in saying, "More than ever today is there a need for the literary journalist; for the writer who is sufficiently journalistic to sense the swiftly changing aspects of this dynamic era, and sufficiently literary to gather and shape his material with the eye and the hand of the artist. The theory that a great work of literature takes years to accomplish has yet to be disproved, but such a conception does not imply that the future Titans of literature may not today be writing for magazines, or for newspapers."[15] In the twentieth century, real events were so fantastic as to challenge fiction. The slaughter in the killing fields of Europe during World War I, massive social disruption caused by the Depression, and the atomic bomb and holocaust of World War II challenged writers to portray real events with passion and emotion. It was an equally formidable task for literary journalists as for novelists. Writers would increasingly have difficulty choosing between the two genres.

Ford's term *literary journalism* was joined at the time by another term: *reportage*. Literary journalism and reportage overlapped and tended to refer to the same works. Joseph North, editor of *New Masses* in 1935, defined *reportage* as "three-dimensional reporting. The writer not only condenses reality, he helps the reader feel the fact. The finest writers of reportage are artists in the fullest sense of the term. They do their editorializing through their imagery."[16] In 1973, William Stott described in his book *Documentary Expression and Thirties America* "the techniques of documentary reportage," which he noted was called the New Journalism in the seventies. The term *reportage* was widely used in the thirties and is still used today. In 2003, the Lettre Ulysses Award for the Art of Reportage was established in France. The award's documentation says the art of reportage is "based upon personal experience, perception, and anecdotal evidence, representing a combination of the best of journalism and of creative nonfiction. Outstanding works in this genre have an effect far beyond the situation from which they arose, achieving importance as works of literature."[17] The term *reportage* has not been popular with everyone. Lillian Ross said in her 2002 memoir, "And the fancy word 'reportage' actually gives me the creeps. The appropriate word is 'reporting.' The word 'reportage' seems to have been taken up in the last century by people who wanted to be thought of more highly. The finest practitioners of reportorial writing are 'writers.'"[18]

Lillian Ross was one of the literary journalists who assembled at *The New Yorker* magazine under the editorship of Harold Ross (no relation) and William Shawn in the years between the Great Depression and the rise of the New Journalism in the sixties. The group also included Joseph Mitchell, A. J. Liebling, and John Hersey, but they did not give themselves a special name. Many of their works foreshadowed the rise of New Journalism a generation later. Lillian Ross started at the magazine in 1945 and created wonderfully drawn portraits of Ernest Hemingway and filmmaker John Huston, among others, as well as a visit to New York City by a group of high school students from Indiana.

Tom Wolfe later used the term *New Journalism* and said its power came from devices such as the use of scene-by-scene construction, saturation reporting, the use of dialogue to establish character, third-person point of view, and the recording of everyday details within a scene that might be symbolic of a character's "status life."[19]

In 1980, Sarah R. Shaber made one of the first contemporary uses of *literary journalism* in a scholarly article on Ernest Hemingway's Spanish Civil War dispatches. She said he "was an accomplished literary journalist" and added that "Hemingway's journalism can be called literary because it sought to tell a story, to communicate a slice of real life to his readers, rather than detail facts, interpretations, or descriptions for their own sake."[20]

Literary journalism can be seen as part of a broader sensibility toward telling stories in journalism, or simply a narrative impulse. Mark Kramer, founding director of the Nieman Program on Narrative Journalism at Harvard University, said: "At a minimum, narrative denotes writing with set scenes, characters, action that unfolds over time, the interpretable voice of a teller—a narrator with a somewhat discernable personality—and some sense of relationship to the reader, viewer or listener, which, all arrayed, lead the audience toward a point, realization or destination."[21] Barbara Lounsberry in her book *The Art of Fact* emphasized polished language and fine writing as necessary characteristics, alongside coverage of persistent themes in the American imagination. Paul Many wrote, "Literary journalism focuses on the exterior world in the same referential way that garden variety journalism does. But in doing so, it uses literary techniques that, by their very nature, beg for the inclusion of a wider sort of reality. The usual language and, with it, the content of journalism, thus becomes stretched past what newspaper editors would normally consider factual or objective. And this may be the source of its acceptance problems."[22]

In 1984, after interviewing a number of writers, I listed literary journalism's shared characteristics as including immersion reporting, complicated structures in the prose, accuracy, voice, responsibility, and attention to the symbolic realities of a story.[23] Today, I would add access, attention to ordinary lives, and the special qualities of a writer's connection to the subjects.

It may be obvious, but behind all such lists of characteristics and definitions stand simple qualities in literary journalism. It tells true stories that engage readers in the subject's life and culture. Sometimes literary journalism shows characters engaged in action and brings their feelings and the drama of everyday life to the surface of the report. Literary journalism stands as a humanistic approach to culture as compared to the scientific, abstract, or indirect approach taken by much standard journalism. Richard Todd said the mass-culture mob, so feared by the elite in the fifties, is now closer than we believe. One purpose of literary journalism, Todd said, is to cut some people out of the mob and make them seem human.[24] We can experience reality as it is created, maintained, and repaired by the people Todd mentioned, and we can appreciate their lives as being like our own. Readers use literary journalism in somewhat the same way as realistic fiction, yet it maintains a firm attachment to journalistic accuracy.

The form has been influenced less by definitions and more by the innovations and experiments of dozens of writers over more than a hundred years in North America, including Mark Twain, George Ade, Finley Peter Dunne, several naturalist novelists such as Frank Norris and Theodore Dreiser around 1900, W. E. B.

DuBois, Jack London, John Reed, John Dos Passos, Ernest Hemingway, Martha Gellhorn, James Agee, A. J. Liebling, Joseph Mitchell, John Hersey, Lillian Ross, and Joan Didion. The list of writers goes on and on even without the inclusion of European writers such as Charles Dickens and George Orwell, who influenced generations of American writers.

Agee—a writer who had probably never heard the term *literary journalism*—pointed to a valuable quality of the form in 1941. His book *Let Us Now Praise Famous Men* represents literary journalism struggling to pull itself free from the bedrock of standard journalism. Agee never completely succeeded but he had an artistic vision. He made disparaging remarks about standard journalism, saying he'd never seen a journalism "which conveyed more than the slightest fraction of what any even moderately reflective and sensitive person would mean and intend by those inachievable words,"—meaning the words *who, what, where, when, why,* and *how*—"and that fraction itself I have never seen clean of one or another degree of patent, to say nothing of essential, falsehood."[25] What he was trying to do in his monumental Depression-era book reached beyond the terms "naturalism" and "realism." He described the goal of realism as a beautiful but heavy task that no one had yet mastered:

> Trying, let us say, to represent, to reproduce, a certain city street, under the conviction that nothing is as important, as sublime, as truly poetic about that street in its flotation upon time and space as the street itself. Your medium, unfortunately, is not a still or moving camera, but is words. You abjure all metaphor, symbol, selection and above all, of course, all temptation to invent, as obstructive, false, artistic. As nearly as possible in words (which, even by grace of genius, would not be very near) you try to give

the street *in its own terms:* that is to say, either in the terms in which you (or an imagined character) see it, or in a reduction and depersonalization into terms which will as nearly as possible be the "private," singular terms of that asphalt, those neon letters, those and all other items combined, into that alternation, that simultaneity, of flat blank tremendously constructed chords and of immensely elaborate counter-point which is the street itself. You hold then strictly to materials, forms, colors, bulks, textures, space relations, shapes of light and shade, peculiarities, specializations, of architecture and of lettering, noises of motors and brakes and shoes, odors of exhausts: all this gathers time and weightiness which the street does not of itself have: it sags with this length and weight: and what have you in the end but a somewhat overblown passage from a naturalistic novel: which in important ways is at the opposite pole from your intentions, from what you have seen, from the fact itself.[26]

Lincoln Steffens, when he was the city editor of the *New York Commercial Advertiser* in the 1890s, sometimes sent new reporters out with the assignment Agee mentioned—write about a street, or a corner. In his own overblown way, Agee pointed to the common quest of literary journalists: the rendering of real life *in its own terms,* in a language and style that would allow the participants to recognize their own feelings and experiences in print. If the task is impossibly weighty under the conditions Agee described, it gets lighter as literary journalists adopt metaphor, symbolism, and selection, but not invention.

This book avoids the language of theory, yet with "true stories" in the title, philosophical questions necessarily arise.[27] Relativism shapes our belief in truth today. We recognize that what is true for one person may not be true for another—at least that's what we say. It's a reasonable argument if we're talking about cultural mores or political beliefs, although we might all agree that the speed of light is true for all of us. Michael P. Lynch noted a cynicism about truth that came from postmodernism and the loss of faith in objective truth and knowledge. "Roughly speaking," Lynch said, "the attitude is that objective truth is an illusion and what we call truth is just another name for power. Consequently, if truth is valuable at all, it is valuable—as power is—merely as means." Lynch said he had personally experienced the same beliefs as other left-leaning intellectuals and postmodern thinkers and had sympathy for relativism, but he had come back to a belief in objectivity: "Caring about truth means that you have to be open to the possibility that your own beliefs are mistaken. It is a consequence of the very idea of objective truth."[28]

Our feelings about lies and truth apparently vary from situation to situation. Robert Feldman, a University of Massachusetts psychology professor, once did a study of unacquainted undergrads who met for ten minutes of casual conversation and lied an average of three times while getting to know one another. Feldman said the number of lies told by ordinary people in conversation was probably substantial, but not consistently that high. Another researcher found that "college students lie to their mothers in every other conversation." Men and women lie differently. But apparently no one lies like business people and politicians.[29] When we read novels, watch television dramas, and go to the movies or the theater, we accept the convention that the author is lying about the existence of the characters. When it comes to journalism, however, our standards are much tighter than for ordinary conversation.

Standard journalism brings us apparently factual information about the world. We are left to our own devices in determining its truth. "But the facts themselves are no guarantee of the truth of the interpretation," said John Pauly, dean of the Marquette University College of Communication, "and appeals to the facts often seem a rhetorical strategy for shoring up one's faith either in newsroom routines (our process is so careful that it guarantees factual accuracy) or fighting off the fears we have about the necessary uncertainties of our interpretations (I was so careful about gathering the facts that if I made a huge mistake in the interpretation no one can blame me because it surely was not intentional)."[30] Daily news reporters are not able to evaluate the truth of all statements, but it is factual to report that someone said something.

In his book *The Post-Truth Era,* Ralph Keyes wondered why writers make things up and then call their work nonfiction—why don't they follow Philip Roth's example and admit that mixing fact and fiction has produced a novel? "For two reasons (at least)," Keyes answered. "One has to do with the marketplace: on average, works of nonfiction sell better than ones of fiction. The other is more intangible. Nonfiction writers who fictionalize, then wrap themselves in the mantle of 'narrative truth' or 'larger truth' or 'emotional truth,' get to have it both ways. They enjoy the freedom to make things up while retaining the credibility that comes from calling their work nonfiction."[31]

Literary journalists, as compared with standard journalists, frequently spend more time with their subjects, get to know them, and can crosscheck and evaluate. They triangulate differing stories, sort through participants' memories, make judgment calls, calculate the structure of the story, adopt a point of view, and decipher the symbolism of details. The writer, according to the *Creative Nonfiction* journal's set of ABCs, "is bound by an implicit and sometimes explicit contract with the reader, to make sure the architecture of his story is based on authentic and reasonably verifiable experience."[32] Discovering and revealing the truth in reporting is not easy. But for professional journalists it is easy to know when you are making something up, when you do not know the truth, or when you need to do more work.

The writers whose experiences are described in this book, including former street urchins such as Jack London and Harvard graduates such as John Reed, John Dos Passos, and Tracy Kidder, have paid attention to the same knotty philosophical debates about truth as everyone else. When writers compose their articles or books, however, the nagging fundamental questions about truth always reappear—and not in a relativistic fashion. Are my facts accurate? Can the descriptions of feeling and motivation be confirmed from statements made by the participants? Have I cut corners in my reporting? Is anything unconfirmed? Would the participants themselves agree that the text is accurate? Complicated questions all, but the answers are not difficult philosophical conundrums.

As Kidder mentioned, even the truth can seem unpersuasive, depending on the authority and presentation of the writer. Those with an institution standing behind them hold an advantage. When a story has passed through the editing systems at the *New York Times* or *The New Yorker,* readers know the material is not infallible but at least has been checked. As was once again admitted after James Frey's fictionalized memoir *A Million Little Pieces* was exposed, book publishers do not independently fact-check. Nor do some magazines. Persuading the reader that this material is accurate, and that the author's perspective on the subject is reliable, ultimately depends on the author. Even someone in possession of the facts can seem misguided to the reader, while the wildest fictions can be made to seem realistic.

Rather than speaking from behind a masthead and relying on it for authority, literary journalists put themselves squarely in front of the reader. Through their choices, their interpretations, and most importantly their voices, they show us that we can measure their words on our own scale of accuracy. Kramer said, "The defining mark of literary journalism is the personality of the writer, the individual and intimate voice of a whole, candid person not representing, defending, or speaking on behalf of any institution, not a newspaper, corporation, government, ideology, field of study, chamber of commerce, or travel destination."[33] Whether they are writing in a newspaper, magazine, or book, literary journalists must convince us that their stories are true, and they must do this to a greater degree than even our friends do when relating their own stories of existence in ordinary conversation.

Ben Yagoda, in *The Sound on the Page: Style and Voice in Writing,* wrote that *what* a writer says is information and ideas, or story and characters, but "*how* they say it is style." Yagoda used Hemingway, Dickens, and Didion as examples of writers with distinctive styles that can be identified on sight—interesting choices in that all three are literary journalists. Their styles are as recognizable as a friend's voice on the phone, Yagoda said, and the same could be argued about John Reed, John Dos Passos, Lillian Ross, John McPhee, and many other writers covered in this book.[34] If, as Kramer said, voice is the defining mark of literary journalism, then voice is also the core of a writer's style.

Yagoda said the content of a piece is not as important as the style; that even mundane topics can be enlivened by voice. "Everyone understands that the content is constant, frequently ordinary, and sometimes banal; that the (wide) variation, the arena for expression and excellence, the fun, the art—it's all in the individual style."[35] Literary journalism has been devoted to content ranging from the nature of windows in Scotland to the building of computers, from life in a Mafia family to the disruption of human lives following an airplane crash, from oranges to the creation of a medical facility in Haiti. It can deal with any topic.

Voice distinguishes literary journalism from the standard modern forms of journalism, at least the kind of voice that permits the writer to express a personality and to advance the story by taking a role on the page. Standard journalism—meaning the ordinary forms of fact-based and objective reporting found in newspapers and magazines—often employs a voice that causes the writer to recede from the surface of the page and become a "fly on the wall" or a "lucid pool of water" in the belief that the reader can somehow see the action without the help of intervening perspectives. Lillian Ross rejected the fly analogy as it related to her work. "A reporter doing a story can't pretend to be invisible, let alone a fly; he or she is seen and heard and responded to by the people he or she is writing about; a reporter is always chemically involved in a story," she said.[36]

Voice and style can be difficult to define, but they are something we recognize. It seems more physical than literary. The presence of the narrator in the story gives us someone to travel with, someone whose thoughts we can hear, someone to act as a guide in a strange world.

Everyone I label as a literary journalist in this book has an identifiable style and voice. The list includes John Reed, John Dos Passos, Edmund Wilson, and Ernest Hemingway; advancing through George Orwell, A. J. Liebling, Lillian Ross, Joseph Mitchell; certainly the New Journalists such as Tom Wolfe, Hunter S. Thompson, Joan Didion, Norman Mailer, and Michael Herr; and including today's writers such as John McPhee, Tracy Kidder, Ted

Conover, Michael Paterniti, Susan Orlean, and Adrian Nicole LeBlanc. As I type their names, I can hear their voices. It's like reading a menu in a restaurant and recalling the tastes in your memory.

The story of American literary journalism seems like that of Moses and his wanderings in the desert, except this genre has taken longer to emerge.

After a promising start in the nineteenth century, literary journalists encountered opposition from a "facts consciousness" and the movement toward objective journalism early in the twentieth century. The opportunity to travel in Europe and Russia after World War I gave writers like Reed, Hemingway, and Dos Passos a chance to blend travel and reporting into a new genre. The Depression of the thirties stirred writers to voice their opinions, but most standard journalism continued to avoid that seemingly radical notion. Literary journalism survived a long dry spell during the forties and fifties at the oasis of *The New Yorker* magazine. A peak was achieved in the New Journalism era from 1960 until about 1974, and then once again the form declined in the face of direct criticism. Now the narrative and artistic disciplines of literary journalism have revived in the works of two succeeding generations of writers. The genre commands attention from the best writers and publishers. It has been an up-and-down journey punctuated with startling innovation.

Literary journalism has developed its styles and standards in a long evolution over several centuries—an evolution in which the most dramatic changes came in response to disruptive cultural forces such as revolution, economic depression, war, and liberation—and has its basis in the origins of nonfiction prose.

Its earliest practitioners, including Daniel Defoe, were among the early novelists as well. Some early travel writing, such as Samuel Johnson's tour of the Hebrides Islands in 1773, *A Journey to the Western Islands of Scotland,* contained all the elements of literary journalism. In the 1800s, however, literary journalism seemingly vanished into a world of small local publications.

Our story begins in the nineteenth century when newspaper writers and the earliest columnists produced narrative pieces that often had the style and voice of literary journalism. In Chapter 2, I suggest that a common form of newspaper writing in the 1800s linked it to modern literary journalism and created a species of writing that could evolve into the next century. Newspaper reporters and humorists created more of the modern voice for literary journalism in the 1800s than did the mannerly magazine writers.

The stars of Chapter 3 were among a large group of writers and ordinary citizens caught up in the aftermath of World War I. Hemingway started out as an ambulance driver and later became a newspaper reporter in Europe. Dos Passos grew up in what he called a "hotel childhood" in Europe that made him an experienced traveler. Reed, impassioned by the struggles of poor people and revolutionaries in the early twentieth century, followed his muse to Europe and Russia and eventually died of typhus in Moscow after covering the Russian Revolution. Their literary journalism shares historical roots with the earliest forms of prose in English—travel writing—and they also shared in the despair and excitement as a new generation encountered the worst of the modern world firsthand in a European war.

The rise of impersonal objectivity as a news style, most pronounced after World War I, pushed literary journalism into the desert. Many of the most promising writers turned from the newspaper and the nonfiction report to fiction, including Hemingway,

John Steinbeck, and Dos Passos. Chapter 4 examines the Great Depression literary journalism, which was published most frequently in the radical and alternative media, where it could hide, so to speak, from the dominant journalistic forces. Edmund Wilson, Louis Adamic, and many others published their work in small-circulation political journals such as *The Nation* and *The New Republic*. The American newspaper press took little notice of the Great Depression until late 1932 or early 1933, as James Boylan has observed. By then breadlines had formed and banks had closed. Chapter 4 focuses on the reporters who wrote about the Depression while it was still in its early stages and those who later produced innovative work. They traveled and talked to the unemployed and the down-and-out. These literary journalists included Wilson, Dos Passos, and the filmmaker Pare Lorentz. Even Agee's great work, *Let Us Now Praise Famous Men*—simultaneously the least popular and yet most significant of the new text-and-photos books that grew up in the Depression era—was ignored at the time.

Then a small group of literary journalists found the essential elements of the genre—support, time, and space—at *The New Yorker* beginning in the late thirties. Chapter 5 recounts how, for the first time, a group of writers with a coherent vision of literary journalism were joined at the same publication and had the support of editors Harold Ross and William Shawn. John Hersey, A. J. Liebling, Joseph Mitchell, Rebecca West, Lillian Ross, and several other former newspaper feature writers produced innovative literary journalism from the mid-thirties onward. Hersey's *Hiroshima* was the capstone of World War II reporting. The tradition was maintained by succeeding generations of *New Yorker* writers including John McPhee, Mark Singer, and Susan Orlean. Chapter 5 describes the contribution *The New Yorker* made toward keeping literary journalism alive in the desert-like journalistic landscape of the forties and fifties.

Although *The New Yorker* kept a firewall between itself and the New Journalism of the sixties, it nevertheless published some of the most noted pieces of New Journalism of the decade, including Truman Capote's *In Cold Blood.* Chapter 6 deals with the community of writers who expanded literary journalism outward from *The New Yorker* to include a much larger group of mostly young writers at the time. The New Journalism found new publishing venues in a troubled time during the sixties, just as Depression-era writers sought out the marginal and alternative publications in the thirties. The New Journalism was a gift to *New York* magazine, *Ramparts, Esquire,* and *Rolling Stone.* Starting with Norman Mailer at the Democratic National Convention in 1960 and continuing with the work of Capote, Tom Wolfe, Gay Talese, Gloria Steinem, Hunter S. Thompson, Michael Herr, and Joan Didion, the New Journalism mirrored the strange times of the sixties and early seventies. The New Journalism era was a breakout decade for literary journalism in the twentieth century. Since so much has been written about the New Journalists, including John Pauly's upcoming book *The New Journalism,* this chapter focuses more on the connections of the form to war and cultural upheaval, on the controversies over accuracy that unfortunately tainted the movement, and on its impact on the writers themselves. Its decline in the mid-seventies can be attributed to criticism from the journalistic establishment more than to a loss of readers. Nevertheless, literary journalism went into a slide as the tensions and turmoil of the sixties ebbed away.

After New Journalism declined, a decade passed before new generations of literary journalists brought readable, engaging, purposeful, and truthful narrative journalism back to public favor.

Writers such as Tracy Kidder and Madeleine Blais won Pulitzer Prizes in the early eighties for their literary journalism. Since then, another generation has taken the form in new directions. These younger writers include Ted Conover, author of *Coyotes* and *Newjack;* Adrian Nicole LeBlanc, author of *Random Family;* Doug Whynott, author of four books about ordinary people; and Michael Paterniti. Chapter 7 focuses on the connections across generational barriers that allow us to see how the form has matured and endured in the past hundred years from writers early in the twentieth century to those who are adapting today to new environments and allowing continual evolution of the form.

Written definitions of literary journalism are, at best, abstractions. At some point in those definitions, I always want to see an example and have the writer say, "Here, read this. It's literary journalism." Without some examples, I feel like a dinner guest with an empty plate. In this book, I hope to minimize that annoyance with five examples of the literary journalism from the periods under discussion. The first, which follows this chapter, starts us off with a contemporary, rather than a historical, taste of literary journalism: Michael Paterniti's "The Long Fall of One-Eleven Heavy" (2000). It is discussed at the end of Chapter 7. The other four examples include, in chronological order, John Dos Passos's "Red Caucasus" (1922), Edmund Wilson's "The Jumping-Off Place" (1932), Joseph Mitchell's "The Old House at Home" (1940), and another contemporary piece, "Family Journeys," by Adrian Nicole LeBlanc, an excerpt from her book *Random Family* (2003).

"THE LONG FALL OF ONE-ELEVEN HEAVY"

◈

MICHAEL PATERNITI

IT WAS SUMMER; IT WAS WINTER. The village disappeared behind skeins of fog. Fishermen came and went in boats named Reverence, Granite Prince, Souwester. The ocean, which was green and wild, carried the boats out past Jackrock Bank toward Pearl Island and the open sea. In the village, on the last shelf of rock, stood a lighthouse, whitewashed and octagonal with a red turret. Its green light beamed over the green sea, and sometimes, in the thickest fog or heaviest storm, that was all the fishermen had of land, this green eye dimly flashing in the night, all they had of home and how to get there—that was the question. There were nights when that was the only question.

This northerly village, this place here of sixty people, the houses and fences and clotheslines, was set among solid rocks breaching from the earth. It was as if a pod of whales had surfaced just as the ocean turned to land and then a village was built on their granite backs. By the weathered fishing shacks were anchors rusted like claws and broken traps and hills of coiled line. Come spring, wildflowers appeared by the clapboard church. The priest said mass. A woman drew back a curtain. A man hanged himself by the bridge. Travelers passing through agreed it was the prettiest earthly spot, snapping pictures as if gripped by palsy, nearly slipping off the rocks into the frigid waves.

Late summer, a man and woman were making love in the eaves of a garishly painted house that looked out on the lighthouse—green light revolving, revolving—when a feeling suddenly passed into them, a feeling unrelated to their lovemaking, in direct physical opposition to it: an electrical charge so strong they could taste it, feel it, the hair standing on their arms, just as it does before lightning strikes. And the fishermen felt it, too, as they went to sea and returned, long ago resigned to the fact that you can do nothing to stop the ocean or the sky from what it will do. Now they too

From Esquire magazine, July 2000.

felt the shove and lock of some invisible metallic bit in their mouths. The feeling of being surrounded by towering waves.

Yes, something terrible was moving this way. There was a low ceiling of clouds, an intense, creeping darkness, that electrical taste. By the light-house, if you had been standing beneath the revolving green light on that early-September night, in that plague of clouds, you would have heard the horrible grinding sound of some wounded winged creature, listened to it trail out to sea as it came screeching down from the heavens, down through molecule and current, until everything went silent.

That is, the waves still crashed up against the granite rock, the green light creaked in its revolutions, a cat yowled somewhere near the church, but beyond, out at sea, there was silence. Seconds passed, disintegrating time . . . and then, suddenly, an explosion of seismic strength rocked the houses of Peggy's Cove. One fisherman thought it was a bomb; another was cer-tain the End had arrived. The lovers clasped tightly—their bodies turning as frigid as the ocean.

That's how it began.

IT BEGAN BEFORE THAT, TOO, in other cities of the world, with plans hatched at dinner tables or during long-distance calls, plans for time to-gether and saving the world, for corralling AIDS and feeding the famine-stricken and family reunions. What these people held in common at first— these diplomats and scientists and students, these lovers and parents and children—was an elemental feeling, that buzz of excitement derived from holding a ticket to some foreign place. And what distinguished that ticket from billions of other tickets was the simple designation of a number: SR111. New York to Geneva, following the Atlantic coast up along Nova Scotia, then out over Greenland and Iceland and England, and then down finally into Switzerland, on the best airline in the world. Seven hours if the tailwinds were brisk. There in time for breakfast on the lake.

In one row would be a family with two grown kids, a computer-genius son and an attorney daughter, setting out on their hiking holiday to the Bernese Oberland. In another would be a woman whose boyfriend was planning to propose to her when she arrived in Geneva. Sitting here would be a world-famous scientist, with his world-famous scientist wife. And there would be the boxer's son, a man who had grown to look like his leg-endary father, the same thick brow and hard chin, the same mournful eyes, on a business trip to promote his father's tomato sauce.

Like lovers who haven't yet met or one-day neighbors living now in different countries, tracing their route to one another, each of them moved toward the others without knowing it, in these cities and towns, grasping airline tickets. Some, like the Swiss tennis pro, would miss the flight, and others, without tickets, would be bumped from other flights onto this one at the last minute, feeling lucky to have made it, feeling chosen.

In the hours before the flight, a young blond woman with blue, almost Persian eyes said goodbye to her boyfriend in the streets of Manhattan and slipped into a cab. A fifty-six-year-old man had just paid a surprise visit to see his brother's boat, a refurbished sloop, on the Sound, just as his two brothers and his elderly mother came in from a glorious day on the water, all that glitter and wind, and now he was headed back to Africa, to the parched veldts and skeletal victims, to the disease and hunger, back to all this worrying for the world.

Somewhere else, a man packed—his passport, his socks—then went to the refrigerator to pour himself a glass of milk. His three kids roughhoused in the other room. His wife complained that she didn't want him to fly, didn't want him to leave on this business trip. On the refrigerator was a postcard, sent randomly by friends, of a faraway fishing village—the houses and fences and clotheslines, the ocean and the lighthouse and the green light revolving, revolving. He had looked at that postcard every day since it had been taped there. A beautiful spot. Something about it. Could a place like that really exist?

All of these people, it was as if they were all turning to gold, all marked with an invisible X on their foreheads, as of course we are, too, the place and time yet to be determined. Yes, we are burning down; time is disintegrating. There were 229 people who owned cars and houses, slept in beds, had bought clothes and gifts for this trip, some with price tags still on them—and then they were gone.

Do you remember the last time you felt the wind? Or touched your lips to the head of your child? Can you remember the words she said as she last went, a ticket in hand?

EVERY TWO MINUTES AN AIRLINER moves up the Atlantic coast, tracing ribboned contrails, moving through kingdoms in the air, demarcated by boundaries, what are called corridors and highways by the people who control the sky. In these corridors travel all the planes of the world, jetliners pushing the speed of sound at the highest altitudes, prop planes puttering at the lowest, and a phylum in between of Cessnas and commuters and corporate jets—all of them passing over the crooked-armed peninsulas and jagged coastlines and, somewhere, too, this northern village as it appears and disappears behind skeins of fog.

The pilot—a thin-faced, handsome Swiss man with penetrating brown eyes and a thick mustache—was known among his colleagues as a consummate pilot. He'd recently completed a promotional video for his airline. In it, he—the energetic man named Urs—kisses his perfectly beautiful wife goodbye at their home before driving off, then he is standing on the tarmac, smiling, gazing up at his plane, and then in the cockpit, in full command, flipping toggles, running checks, in command, toggles, lights, check, command.

So now here they were, in their corridor, talking, Urs and his copilot, Stephan. About their kids; both had three. About the evening's onboard dinner. It was an hour into the flight, the plane soaring on autopilot, the engine a quiet drone beneath the noise in the main cabin, the last lights of New England shimmering out the west side of the aircraft, and suddenly there was a tickling smell, rising from somewhere into the cockpit, an ominous wreathing of—really, how could it be?—smoke. Toggles, lights, check, but the smoke kept coming. The pilot ran through his emergency checklists, switching various electrical systems on and off to isolate the problem. But the smoke kept coming. He was breathing rapidly, and the copilot, who wasn't, said, We have a problem.

Back in the cabin, the passengers in 30B and 16D were sipping wine and soda, penning postcards at thirty-three thousand feet. In first class, some donned airline slippers and supped on hors d'oeuvres while gambling on the computer screens in front of them. Slots, blackjack, keno. Others reclined and felt the air move beneath them—a Saudi prince, the world-famous scientist, the UN field director, the boxer's son, the woman with Persian eyes—an awesome feeling of power, here among the stars, plowing for Europe, halfway between the polar cap and the moon, gambling and guzzling and gourmanding. No one knew that even now, the pilot was on the radio, using the secret language of the sky to declare an emergency:

Pan, pan, pan, said Urs. We have smoke in the cockpit, request deviate, immediate return to a convenient place. I guess Boston. (Toggles, lights, check, breathe.)

Would you prefer to go into Halifax? said air-traffic control, a calm voice from a northern place called Moncton, a man watching a green hexagon crawl across a large, round screen, this very flight moving across the screen, a single clean green light.

Affirmative for one-eleven heavy, said the pilot. We have the oxygen mask on. Go ahead with the weather—

Could I have the number of souls on board . . . for emergency services? chimed in Halifax control.

Roger, said the pilot, but then he never answered the question, working frantically down his checklist, circling back over the ocean to release tons of diesel to lighten the craft for an emergency landing, the plane dropping to nineteen thousand feet, then twelve thousand, and ten thousand. An alarm sounded, the autopilot shut down. Lights fritzed on and off in both the cockpit and the cabin, flight attendants rushed through the aisles, one of the three engines quit in what was now becoming a huge electrical meltdown.

Urs radioed something in German, *emergency checklist air conditioning smoke.* Then in English, Sorry . . . Maintaining at ten thousand feet, his voice urgent, the words blurring. The smoke was thick, the heat increasing, the checklists, the bloody checklists . . . leading nowhere, leading—We are declaring emergency now at, ah, time, ah, zero-one-two-four. . . . We have to land immediate—

The instrument panel—bright digital displays—went black. Both pilot and copilot were now breathing frantically.

Then nothing.

Radio contact ceased. Temperatures in the cockpit were rising precipitously; aluminum fixtures began to melt. It's possible that one of the pilots, or both, simply caught fire. At air-traffic control in Moncton, the green hexagon flickered off the screen. There was silence. They knew what was coming: the huge fuck, the something terrible. God save them. One controller began trembling, another wept.

It was falling.

Six minutes later, SR111 plunged into the dark sea.

THE MEDICAL EXAMINER WOKE to a ringing phone, the worst way to wake. Ten-something on the clock, or was it eleven? The phone ringing, in the house where he lived alone, or rather with his two retrievers, but alone, too, without wife or woman. He lived near the village with the lighthouse, had moved here less than three years ago from out west, had spent much of his life rolling around, weird things following him, demons and disasters. Had a train wreck once, in Great Britain, early in his career, a Sunday night, university students coming back to London after a weekend at home. Train left the tracks at speed. He'd never seen anything like that in his life—sixty dead, decapitations, severed arms and legs. These kids, hours before whole and happy, now disassembled. Time disintegrating in the small fires of the wreckage. After the second night, while everyone kept their stiff upper lips, he sobbed uncontrollably. He scared himself—not so much because he was sobbing, but because he couldn't stop.

There'd been a tornado in Edmonton—it couldn't possibly have been, but, yes, a tornado, twenty-three dead. And then another train wreck in western Canada, in the hinterlands fifty miles east of Jasper. Twenty-five dead in a ravine. He'd nearly been drummed out of the job for his handling of that one. The media swarmed to photograph mangled bodies, and the medical examiner, heady from all the attention and a bit offended by it, knowing he shouldn't, stuffed some towels and linens on a litter, draped them with a sheet, and rolled the whole thing out for the flashing cameras. Your dead body, gentlemen.

Later, when they found out—oh, they hated him for that. Called for his head.

This had been a frustrating day, though, driving up to New Glasgow, waiting to take the stand to testify in the case of a teenage killer, waiting, waiting, four, five, six hours, time passing, revolving, nothing to do in that town except pitter here and there, waiting. Got off the stand around six, home by nine, deeply annoyed, too late to cook, got into the frozen food, then to bed, reading the paper, drifting, reading, drifting. And now the phone was ringing, a woman from the office: a jet was down. Without thinking, he said, It's a mistake. Call me back if anything comes of it. Set the phone in its cradle, and a minute later it rang again.

There's a problem here, she said.

I'll get on my way, he said, and hung up. He automatically put a suitcase on the bed, an overnight bag, and then it dawned on him: There'd been no talk about numbers yet, the possible dead. There could be hundreds, he knew that, yes, he did know that now, didn't he? He walked back and forth between his cupboard and his bed, flustered, disbelieving, *hundreds,* and then the adrenaline started to move, with hypodermic efficiency. Hundreds of bodies—and each one of them would touch his hands. And he would have to touch them, identify them, confer what remained of them to some resting place. He would have to bear witness to the horrible thing up close, what it did up close, examine it, notate, dissect, and, all the while, feel what it did, feel it in each jagged bone.

Flustered, disbelieving, it took him forty minutes to pack his bag with a couple pairs of khakis, some underwear, shirts, a pair of comfortable shoes, some shaving gear, should have taken five minutes.

He was a sensitive, empathetic man—at least he thought so (did his ex-wife? did his two faraway daughters?)—with a sharp if morbid sense of humor, a kind of loner in this northern place, Nova Scotia, where clans had carved out their lives over centuries and generations, where someone's great-great-grandfather had once fished someone else's great-great-grandfather from a storm at sea. He was an outsider, had always been, which qualified him for what was now coming, lurching toward him at the speed it would take him to drive in that thick night, in the warm rain that now fell like pieces of sky, from his home to his office.

No, he didn't know then, as he left his retrievers, Dan and Deputy, behind, as he closed the door on his house, everything freezing in time as he did, magazines fanned on a table, milk in the refrigerator, didn't know that summer would pass and fall would arrive, that the leaves would vanish from the trees before he returned.

But now all he did was drive, doing the math: There were twelve in the office and six in the morgue. The local hospitals might be able to cough up thirty more, but that didn't even begin to cover it. Where the hell were they going to find enough body bags?

MORE PHONES RANG, MORE PEOPLE woke. The coast guard, the Mounties, ministers, presidents. The navy, the airline, the media, everyone scrambling to figure out what was going on; without realizing it, everyone was now caught in the spreading fire. In the village, boats left for sea. The fishermen rolled from their beds, threw on rain gear, buddied up, and started out, unquestioning, reflexively. (You couldn't keep the sea and sky from what it would do.) Many of the fishermen thought they were going in search of survivors, were convinced of it, owing to the legacy of shipwrecks in these parts, which often meant someone was out there somewhere in all that inky black, in a yellow raft, waiting for help, cold, shivering, alive, waiting, waiting, waiting for *them*.

The television reporter stood on the shore, with a growing cabal of other reporters, fellow parasites. He stood apart, shifting from foot to foot, antsy, squinting out at the ocean. Shit, where? Others worked their cell phones, frantically scrounging for the story, but still nobody knew anything. Someone living in a trailer home nearby claimed to have seen a huge flash on the horizon; another said the plane had come so close to the village that you could see inside, cabin lights flickering on and off, people lit, then black, see those last moments playing out from the ground.

These waters were his, that's what the reporter thought. He'd sailed these coves and inlets all summer long, sailed past the lighthouse so many times it seemed a natural outcropping of the landscape. He was a solid, good-looking man who spoke quickly, moved at a clip, all of forty-two, with just-thinning hair. He'd worked twenty years on the nautical beat, covering the navy and ship sinkings and whatever else came along. He never forgot to register a name, and then never forgot it, kept a card catalog in his head that connected everyone to everyone else. One of his great strengths. And when he saw what looked like falling stars in the distance, parachute flares, he knew that was where the plane was. He turned to the cameraman.

We need to be under those, he said, pointing to the falling stars.

Before he left the office, he'd stashed extra cell-phone batteries in his pocket. You never knew, or maybe you already did. And now, in this night, in the seamless dark (there was no marking land but for the lighthouse, green light revolving), he was on his way in a hired boat with a cameraman. The wind blew, heavy swells, ten-foot waves, on his way, to see what? And why? He was as bad as the others, wasn't he? A fucking parasite. There were a lot of people on that plane, he knew that. At the UN, they called it the diplomatic shuttle: dinner meeting in Manhattan, breakfast meeting in Geneva. And now here they were, lost off the coast of this forgotten place.

It took an hour in those seas. The parachute flares and spotlights were blinding at first, the smell of diesel overwhelming. Sea King helicopters whirred overhead, flashing white beams; boats drifted through the wreckage, aimlessly, the water a bottomless black. They couldn't see anything, just heard it on the VHF radio, fishermen talking to one another: I got something over here. I think she's alive. Then thirty seconds passed. I need a body bag. And then other voices, this morbid call and response:

We got another one.

Over here, too.

Need a body bag, now!

Jesus, we got a foot in the water.

We have an arm.

We need a body bag! Who's got body bags?

Then the reporter saw a half-inflated life raft. Alive—someone was alive! But when they came upon it, it was empty, had inflated on impact. There were shoes fanning everywhere around them, hundreds and hundreds of shoes, in procession, riding the water's windrows—some with the laces still tied up. And underwear and ripped shirts, Bibles and stuffed animals. Money floating on the surface of the ocean now. Dollars and marks, rupees and francs and drachmas. You'd haul up a purse and expect to find a wallet, a driver's license, lipstick, anything, and it would be empty.

The plane had hit the water at more than four hundred miles per hour, nose first, two engines still firing, very unusual, extremely rare; the jet was two hundred feet long, and the tail rammed straight into the nose, everything exploding into more than one million pieces. Later, someone would be in charge of counting pieces at the military base, in a hangar where bits of the plane would fill thousands of crates and cardboard boxes. At impact, the bodies on board had been what the medical examiner would call degloved, simply shorn from the bones. You couldn't pick them up in your hands. You had to scoop them in nets.

No one has survived this crash, the television reporter told the world. From what we are seeing, there are no survivors.

But, said an anchorperson, the coast guard is calling this a search and rescue.

There are no survivors.

Until dawn, he was the only reporter under the parachute flares, a bizarre, surreal time, no believer in God, but you could feel something, 229 of them in this place. There were body parts and shoes—he'd dream about them for a long time. He was beamed into television sets around the world. No survivors. He told the pilot's wife that her husband was dead. He told the famous boxer that his son was dead. He told the father of the woman with Persian eyes that his daughter was dead.

When he finally came to shore the next day, when he stood near the lighthouse, green light revolving, doing more live feeds, carefully choosing his words for the world, running on adrenaline, he noticed a large man glaring at him. The man was a very big man, with a pockmarked face and greased-back hair, scary looking, glaring. And the reporter thought, He's going to kick my ass for being a parasite, for feeding off all these bodies.

When the reporter finished, the oversized man started for him and the reporter could do nothing but ready himself for the blow. But it never came. Something else did.

I want to thank you, he said. You told me my fiancée was dead. I got a phone call last night, in New York, and I was told there might be survivors and I thought, Well, if anybody survived this it was her, because we're gonna get married—and everyone was saying there are survivors, and you told me she was dead. You told me the truth. I needed to hear that.

Needed to hear that? This man needed to hear that? Yesterday the reporter had been covering some minor promotion ceremony at the military base; today he had told the world they could say goodbye to these 229 human beings, the ones with X's on their foreheads, the ones turning to gold, once wearing shoes, ghosts now, goodbye. And then the big man was gone, too, before the reporter could offer thanks back, or rather condolences, before he could think to ask the living man's name.

IT WAS EARLY MORNING IN GENEVA, and the father of the woman with the blue Persian eyes—a slight, erudite man with fine hair turning from orange to gray, turning at that very moment even—sat before a television, watching the reporter, in disbelief. He woke his wife and asked, Did she phone last night? And his wife said, She'll be phoning soon to have you fetch her in Zurich. And he said, She won't; the plane has crashed.

His wife roused herself, still half tangled in sleep, and stared at the reporter, listening, trying to grasp words that made no sense. It's all right, she said. There's nothing to worry about. We'll wait for her call.

The phone rang. It was her boyfriend in New York. What plane did she take? he asked. And the father said, But you tell me? No, he said, because we parted company at four in the afternoon, and she didn't know which plane she was on. And can you please tell me that she was on the Zurich flight?

No, the father said. And then he called the airline and insisted they tell him whether his daughter had been on the Zurich flight. We cannot, a voice said. But you must. You must. . . . There was silence, then a rustling of papers. We have to tell you, the voice said, she is not on the list.

Thank you, said the father.

Then he told his wife, and she said, Until they phone us with the news, we have to believe. And the man said, But darling, they're not going to phone with news like that. They'd come to the door—

And before he'd finished his sentence, the doorbell rang.

Grief is schizophrenic. You find yourself of two minds, the one that governs your days up until the moment of grief—the one that opens easily to memories of the girl at six, twelve, eighteen—and the one that seeks to destroy everything afterward. The man was fifty-eight and he'd given his daughter every advantage he could afford; the circumstances of his life—his work for a luxury-car company and then a fine-watch company—had given her the riding lessons and top-notch education and summer home in France. But then she'd given so much of herself, too. She'd been a championship swimmer and show jumper. She had a great knack for simplifying things, for having fun, for enjoying the moment so fully that those around her wanted to live inside those moments with her. She was contagious and beautiful and twenty-four, with those amazing eyes. She was about to come home and take a job.

After she was gone, the husband and wife made a promise to each other: They would stop their imaginations at that place where their daughter had boarded the plane, their minds would not wander past that particular rope. As usual, he broke the promise, unable to divert his mind from picturing his daughter at the end—it's possible she, like all of them, was unconscious at impact from the crushing g-forces inside the aircraft. Or that she suffered horribly, screaming, the flash of an entire life playing before her eyes. Whom did she sit next to in those moments? What was said?

The man couldn't help but imagine the pilots, too, their fate connected to a recurring dream he'd had for many years of himself as a pilot, trying to land a jet on a motor launch and not knowing what the hell he was doing. Though his wife stopped her mind on the gangplank as her daughter stepped into the jet, he followed his girl into the sea.

Nothing made sense, time was disintegrating, everything was a confusion, chaos. Walking through town, he'd see the river and have to keep himself from slipping into it. He'd go to the station and hold back from throwing himself before a train: how good it would feel, a matter of time now, not whether but *when*—today? Tomorrow? What would it feel like?

Since he couldn't sleep, he drank a bottle of Scotch daily, then couldn't remember anything. He followed the news accounts, halfheartedly reading words like *investigation, black box, recovery effort, debris field*. There had been a Picasso on board the plane and millions in rubies and diamonds. One day a postcard arrived from his daughter, detailing her stay in New York. Authorities called, wanting to send some of her effects (others now slept with ripped shirts and favorite sweaters, passports and stuffed animals), but the thought horrified him. What was worse, what the man could never have foreseen after thirty years of marriage, after having done so much to put a life together, was how quickly it became undone. He'd spent his life stitching up a beautiful life—the watch on his wrist a mysterious blue, cost the same as a small house. Now he didn't want to be with anybody, just alone, and his wife, his best friend—his wife had stopped at the gangplank. How could she? How could she not follow their beloved daughter into the ocean? Silly words comforted her while they enraged him; having family nearby was a source of strength for her, torment for him. This response or that response of hers seemed so . . . wrong. And in his mind he was asking: What's the point of this life? And she said, We must forget.

There was one thing that made him feel better. He flew alone to the northern village a few days after the crash, thinking he'd have to identify his daughter, drove down along the coast road to the lighthouse. (The media was now encamped here, among the houses and rocks and clotheslines, long-range lenses trained on anybody shedding a tear, beaming the image to the world.) He came to this village, and he felt something, some part of him rising, too. He knew he was going mad—and yet he could feel these waves churning inside him, his daughter there, too. When he returned to Geneva, he simply went back to devising ways to kill himself.

THE FULL SEVERITY OF THE CRASH dawned on the medical examiner only the morning after, when he rode a Sea King out to the debris field. The fishermen and others in Zodiacs kept shuttling body parts to a huge command ship, the captain on the radio to these men talking in calm tones. (Many would later say it was that voice, that reassuring voice, that pulled them through that night.) The media had already begun a body count, based on the body bags coming ashore, and yet there were no bodies out here whatsoever, not one intact body in those bags, which were running out fast. But for one, they couldn't identify a single soul visually.

Back at the military base, the medical examiner set up in Hangar B, refrigerated trucks called reefers parked outside to hold the remains. There were huge fans and scented candles to mask the smell, the whole place lit and flickering like a church. Like the strangest church. On one wall hung a huge diagram of the plane, a seating chart, and as the remains of a passenger were identified by dental records or DNA, by a distinctive tattoo or a wedding ring, a blue dot was placed on the passenger's seat. The medical examiner would eventually be in charge of four hundred people here—a cadre of pathologists and DNA experts, morticians, media liaisons, and staff. But when he came back to the hangar after having been at sea that first time, he thought, What if I go now, bugger off right now? But where? Back to his dogs? No, what he realized as the parts began to fill the hangar and the reefers, as the stench became overpowering, was that he was too afraid to leave. With each passing day inside the hangar, there was nowhere to vanish but inside these people, these bodies.

One day he was waiting to go on the stand in dead-end New Glasgow, killing time, and the next this complete Armageddon. There were three hundred family members gathered now at a hotel, and the medical examiner was asked to address them. Others spoke first—officials, the president of the airline, offering their deepest sorrow to these people—and then he stood up nervously, cleared his throat, perhaps recalling that day years before when he'd made a body out of rolled-up towels for the media, how simple and, well, hilarious that had been. But how do you tell grieving family members the average body is now in one hundred pieces, one hundred little stars? (A fisherman saw a human heart on the surface of the water.) You will never see your loved ones again, he said. Those were the first words out of his mouth, and the crowd let out a massive exhalation, as if hit in the stomach. One man began sobbing uncontrollably and was led from the room. Not only are they dead, *you will never see them again.*

He'd said it. However painful, he knew this much: If you look away, if you self-justify or obfuscate, then you're stuck with the lie. You may make it through the moment, but in a day, a week, a year, it will bring you down, like cheetahs on a gazelle. Yes, he told them. If anything, they could see their own fear in his eyes, feel their quaver in his voice, their tears welling in his eyes. No stiff upper lip here. Fuck the macho and whatever it was that made you a man. (There was a heart on the surface of the water.) He vowed he would not betray these people, there'd be no fake body under a sheet. He'd try to talk to each of them, answer their concerns and desires, treat each body as if he himself were the next of kin: the father, the son, the lover, the brother.

Inside the hangar, days and nights of horrific work, checking dental records, X rays, fingerprints. And on several occasions the medical examiner took fingers from which they could not get accurate prints, decomposed fingers, made an incision, and stuck his own finger inside, went inside these bodies, *became* them, so that he could lay an accurate mark of them on paper, return them to their rightful place. He knew each passenger by name and blood type. He found himself intensely identifying with some, one in particular, a newspaper executive, a man named John Mortimer—couldn't shake him and his wife from his mind. He put himself in that seat next to John Mortimer's wife, tried to imagine the dreadful plummet, the smash of atoms. He tried to do the math: A loving couple falls through the sky at four hundred miles per hour, with maybe six minutes until impact: What did they say? What could be done?

Day after day, more blue dots came to fill the seats of the imaginary plane. He was not a believer in God, but a priest had come to the hangar, and the medical examiner said, Do you feel it? And the priest said, The souls are hovering. And the medical examiner looked up and said, Yes. Yes they are.

Then that November day came when they were done. There would be more dredging, hundreds of pounds of remains to come, jagged bones in piles (the plane hitting so hard some were embedded with quarters and nickels), clean as a whistle from the currents of the sea, but they were basically done. There were only a few technicians left in the hangar and they were going to shut it down, and the medical examiner came in early, when no one was there.

He knew it was perverse, but he didn't want it to end. He was convinced that his entire life, one full of mistakes and masterstrokes, had been leading to this moment. He was exhausted, flirting with a breakdown. He knew that, could feel it, but he knew, too, that if he'd run, the cheetahs would have caught him, somewhere out there on the veldt they would have dragged him down. It was fall, the leaves off the trees. A season had passed. How many seasons had passed? Nothing made sense. He was going back to his life (his dogs, the daughter who thought he was grandstanding now, saw his public empathy as something he'd never once offered her), his best self traded back for his flawed self, and he stood for a long while in silence, time disintegrating. When he turned to walk away—even later when he retired and packed up and moved back west—most of him stayed right here.

THE PASSENGERS WERE blue dots now, and yet they were still alive. After that first night, even as time passed and the story fell from the news, the television reporter had been driven deeper into it; he learned the names, who connected to whom. He tracked the possible causes of the crash: a spark thrown from the wiring of the elaborate entertainment system, the flammability of the Mylar insulation. He was haunted by the prospect that if the pilot had landed immediately, hadn't gone by the book, dallying with checklists, just put the jet down, everyone might be alive.

But then he met the pilot's wife. He went to Zurich, flew in the cockpit of the same kind of jet that had crashed, with one of the dead pilot's best friends, an awesome feeling of power up in that kingdom of sky, plowing for Europe. He met the pilot's wife at her expensive home in a ritzy neighborhood with a lap pool and lots of sunlight inside. The woman was startlingly attractive, especially when she smiled, which wasn't often these days. In her former life, when she wanted to go to Manhattan or Hong

Kong or Tokyo, she didn't go first-class, she went in the cockpit. And when her husband spoke, a dozen people jumped. They'd met when she was a flight attendant, and now here she was describing how she and her three children were trying to carry on without their father, her husband, Urs.

She told a story about going to the crash site, on board a boat that took the families there, about how hard it had been for everyone, how the kids were down, very down, and coming back, over the side, in the water, there were suddenly dolphins running in the ocean, an amazing vision, like electrical currents, these dolphins up from the deep and slipping alongside them. Not too long after, she decided that she was going back to work as a flight attendant, for the same airline. Her first flight was the New York–Geneva route, on the same type of aircraft as the one her husband had ridden into the sea.

There were others, too, people so moved by the graciousness of those in this northern place that they returned or even bought property to be closer. One man sailed his sloop here, in honor of the brother who'd taught him to sail in the first place, the brother trying to save the world. The boxer, now an old man of seventy-eight but once a world champion, came despite himself and said he felt lighter when he left, after looking out from the lighthouse at the spot where his son's life ended. It somehow made him feel lighter. Others came and saw the hangar where the remains had been, the hangar where the million pieces of plane were still boxed and numbered, seats over here, armrests over there. The three jet engines were there, too, big, hulking things with mangled rotors.

How did these people do it? How did they go on? How could they? One woman whom the reporter had interviewed in New York had a box of stuff that had once been her daughter's: a French-English dictionary, a cup, a pair of binoculars, some glasses, a locket that she, the mother, had given her. She spent hours touching these things. And then another woman, who lost her husband, heard that they had found parts of his hand, had tested its DNA, and she asked that the remains be sent directly to her, though usually the remains were sent to funeral homes or hospitals. The reporter knew a counselor who spent four hours on the phone with the wife who had her husband's hand, and she finally sent the police because the woman was trying to put it back together. I can get the thumb, she said, but I can't get the next part.

The reporter didn't have the luxury of a breakdown, what with three kids. He still had the nightmares—shoes and body parts. He saw a therapist a few times, and she told the reporter to put the dream in a box, take the image of that black, bottomless sea and the debris field with its body parts and shoes, the smell of diesel drenching everything, and place it all in a box, take the box and put it high on a shelf. He did that, and he got past it. Yes, in an imaginary closet somewhere in his head, in an imaginary box, was everything that had actually, really, horrifically happened, and now sometimes, on a very good day, after some beers, maybe watching hockey or roughhousing with the kids, he could imagine for a moment that it hadn't.

ONE DAY, THE MAN from Geneva boarded a plane and came back to the village, left his wife behind, riffled through his closet of finely tailored suits and ridiculous leather dress shoes and packed some jerseys and books and left, for good, the only remnant of his former life that wristwatch with the stunning blue face, the same color as the sea here on certain windswept days, the color of his daughter's eyes.

The man left his wife, yes, but to save her from him. It sounded odd, but it was true. They'd made a promise and he'd broken it. He kept following his daughter into the ocean.

The last time he came to the village in this northern place, he saw a roadside restaurant and convenience store for sale nearby, and now, knowing nothing about restaurants or convenience stores, he bought it. It was a barnlike building with living quarters on the second floor, in some disrepair, but if grief was schizophrenic, then maybe here he could find a balancing point for his life before he lost his daughter and his life after. He had never conceived of the possibility that anything he did could be undone, let alone that he himself would become undone. But he'd become undone.

So he set to work, seven days a week, up at five-thirty, readying the coffee, cleaning the grill, playing opera on the stereo, checking the weather in the cove that let onto the ocean, a stunning place, and his daughter in this place. He'd open the doors at seven, and at seven-thirty a man named Leroy came to clean. They said he'd been half a man, a backward boy, before he'd been given this job, mopping floors and cleaning toilets at the restaurant. Now he was coming into his own. When the man asked him to do something, he smiled and saluted and said, Okay, copy ya!

The man redid the walls, opened up the dining space, began to build a large deck. He'd once traveled to the Middle East to sell hundreds of thousands of dollars' worth of watches at a time, and now he cooked Surf 'n' Turf burgers ($5.52) and Bacon & Egg Double Deckers ($2.99) just to hear someone, anyone, say, I think I've been sufficiently sufficed. Thank you kindly. He joked and laughed with the fishermen and the construction crews and the older men, too, who came just to sit and drink coffee. He stood in the middle of his restaurant in a rugby jersey, wearing a white apron, near a photograph of his daughter, and told a story about her.

She was sent to convent school when she was six years old, her hair cut incredibly short, not like it was at the end, long and streaked blond. There was an open school day, a parents' day, and they organized games for the kids. In one of the games you could fish for goldfish with a net, and his daughter came to him and said, Oh, can you imagine! All my life, my whole life, I've wanted a goldfish! I can't remember when I *haven't* wanted a goldfish! And the man looked at his daughter, who was beaming at him, her eyes lit all the blues of the world, and he laughed, her whole life and she was just six years old, sweet and precocious and it really was too funny. Well, a quarter of her life was over by then, doesn't seem—but it was, it was funny.

No, he hadn't left his wife. He talked to her every day, his best friend. But Geneva was her home and this was his now, this village. His beard had gone more gray over the winter here. Who could ever imagine where life would carry you, humbled and hopeful, lost and found and lost again as a storm blew in from sea? There would be a day when he and his wife would be together again. They would reach an understanding, and they would perhaps travel down to Morocco, to Marrakech, a place they'd loved for its colors and light, for its people, together again, released, absolved, together.

It would be a strange, wonderful resolution, thought the man, imagining it. They would make themselves clean. But now, there were hungry men at a table, and so this man with the spectacular wristwatch tied on his apron, went to the grill. This man, though he was hungry, too, he fed the others first.

IT WAS SUMMER; it was winter. The village disappeared behind skeins of fog. Fishermen came and went in their boats, boats that had been at the crash site all those seasons ago, under that dark ceiling of night clouds, in those swells of black, bottomless water. One of the men fished a baby from the sea, kneeling on deck, lit by the parachute tracers, holding fast to what was left of the child, time disintegrating. Those who braved the night said that something happened out there, something horrible, and then—and this is the odd part—something beautiful. In the strange, eerie silence, everything drenched in diesel, you could feel it, almost taste it, something rising up from this spot, up through the ocean, through the men who stood out there in boats, among the shoes, something rose through them, like electricity.

At the edge of the rocks stood the lighthouse, green light revolving, revolving. Sometimes, in the heaviest storm, that was all the fishermen had of land, this green eye dimly flashing in the night, all they had of home, and how to get there, that was the question. And there were other questions that lingered, too, when they dared to consider them. Even at noon on the brightest days of the year, especially on the brightest days of the year, when the wind whipped the laundry on the line, the questions lingered. Yes, what had happened here? And why did the clothes on the line look as if they were filled by bodies, though there were no bodies in sight anymore?

TWO

SKETCHES AND INNOVATION

Ah, it was a deep, deep satire, and most ingeniously contrived.
—Mark Twain

Tracing the history of literary journalism backward from the twentieth century into the 1800s, I find that it vanishes into a maze of local publications. The landscape for American literary journalism resembled that seen by settlers expanding their nation across the Great Plains—few landmarks stood out. Magazines were small-circulation literary publications. Most newspapers were rural weeklies that filled their pages with local news, items picked up from exchanges with other newspapers, sentimental poetry, flowery patriotic speeches from politicians, a sketch, maybe a prank or hoax, and want ads. Urban newspapers were often expensive and appealed to the business class, except for a limited number of Penny Press publications. Some newspapers circulated outside the local area, but only a few achieved large circulations until late in the nineteenth century. Political journalism dominated. Magazines had not yet found the national brand-name product advertising that sustains them now. Today's foundation for literary journalism in magazines and books had not developed.

Looking for literary journalism in the nineteenth century seems daunting, but it was incubating and would emerge in the large-circulation urban newspapers at the end of the century.

The core of nineteenth-century literary journalism can be found in a simple, widespread prose device used in the newspapers—the sketch. Like recipes for making soap, the sketch was widely appreciated in the nineteenth century but virtually forgotten today. It permitted newspaper reporters to be writers, playing with voice and perspective and challenging readers to evaluate the text.

In this chapter, I will represent the nineteenth-century transition from sketch writing to realist literary journalism in urban newspapers and national magazines using the stories of several writers—Mark Twain, Opie Read, Jack London, George Ade, and Finley Peter Dunne. Their lives and work are entwined, and Read, Ade, and Dunne—who were exploring emerging social types and communities in the city—knew each other in Chicago. The primary examples come from there, but similar explorations of literary journalism could be found among reporters in other cities such as New York and San Francisco that had equivalent newspaper clubs and bohemian literary styles.

Some clear-cut examples of sketches and literary journalism can be found in the nineteenth century. Washington Irving's *The Sketch Book of Geoffrey Crayon* in 1819–1820 contained the fictional sketches "Rip Van Winkle" and "The Legend of Sleepy Hollow" and is counted among the earliest literary works making use of the term. As a reporter, Charles Dickens shook off the boredom of covering political speeches by writing sketches of ordinary life and manners using the pseudonym "Boz" in 1833. They appeared in newspapers and magazines and were collected for his book *Sketches by Boz* in 1836, when he was twenty-four years old. Dickens later apologized for the crude and hasty character of his sketches, but a casual quality was representative of the form. Francis Parkman serialized *The Oregon Trail* in twenty-one installments in *Knickerbocker's Magazine* during 1847–1849. Parkman's account was a kind of participatory journalism as history. The Civil War produced some literary accounts by Whitelaw Reid and others that were outside of combat reporting. John F. Finerty, a reporter for the *Chicago Times,* accompanied General George Crook's troops in the war against the Sioux in 1876. His participation in the campaign, including dramatic and deadly battles, resonates with the techniques of literary journalism not only in his restrained use of voice but also in his immersion in the subject matter.[1] Eugene Schuyler's accounts of his travels, called *Turkistan: Notes of a Journey in Russian Turkistan, Kokand, Bukhara and Kuldja,* written in the 1870s, could be considered a variety of literary journalism. Late in the century, Stephen Crane published sketches of New York City, and Richard Harding Davis prepared sketches of Philadelphia when he worked for a newspaper. Of course there were more examples of narrative literary journalism, but they tend to be scattered among authors in different decades.

The best American example of mid-nineteenth-century literary journalism has to be the newspaper work of Mark Twain, who mastered the sketch. His later travel book *Innocents Abroad* (1869) was originally published as a series of journalistic reports in the *Daily Alta California,* the *New York Herald,* and the *New York Tribune* and later revised and expanded as a book.[2] His memoir of experiences in the

West, *Roughing It* (1872), although somewhat fictional, was also an example of nineteenth-century literary journalism. Twain experimented in the newspaper with point of view, voice, vernacular language, and narrative techniques that remain part of literary journalism today. Fortunately, the fictional qualities of his sketches have fallen away in modern literary journalism, but his experimental perspectives have endured.

The sketch, a form of literary journalism that was widely used and known to most journalists of the time, shared characteristics with modern literary journalism. In short, as a form it was the heart of nineteenth-century literary journalism. The sketch was such a common, ordinary form for journalism of the age that it almost escapes our notice.[3]

The term *sketch* appeared frequently in the vocabulary of nineteenth-century journalists, but today we have some difficulty understanding the term. In 1961, the *Oxford English Dictionary* accurately defined *sketch* as "a brief account, description, or narrative giving the main or important facts, incidents, etc., and not going into the details." It can be considered like an artist's sketch—not fully developed, or simply impressionistic—as opposed to, say, an oil painting. But newspaper sketches were not studies for later, more fully developed treatments; they were complete as published. Sketches were not burdened with important events or a heavily factual context. The newspaper sketch ranged effortlessly from pure fiction to pure reporting and used an easy and familiar prose style. Newspaper writers could give as many examples of a *sketch,* produced for a particular situation, as a skier can give different conditions for the word *snow.* My dictionary today unhelpfully defines a sketch as "a brief essay or literary composition." No definitions appear in *A Dictionary of Modern Critical Terms*[4] or in H. W. Fowler's *A Dictionary of Modern English Usage.*[5]

An editor of Mark Twain's collected works, Edgar Marquess Branch, gave an indication of the range of the nineteenth-century sketch when he wrote:

> The great preponderance of [Twain's] short items, however, are sketches—and these range from ambitious magazine articles several thousand words long to short, hundred-word trifles tossed off by the newspaperman during a working day. The sketches include comic letters to the editor, hoaxes, exaggerated accounts of the author's personal activities, burlesques of many kinds, comic or satirical feuds with fellow journalists, ingeniously contrived self-advertisements, commentary in a light and personal vein, descriptive reporting, reminiscences of past pleasures and adventures, and so on—but neither this nor any other list can easily be exhaustive. Sketches have been extracted from all kinds of sources, and we have occasionally isolated them from mundane material (such as lists and routine news) without any literary interest.[6]

Branch's term "descriptive reporting" comes closest to today's literary journalism, but the term *sketch* covered a lot of ground, including especially the humorous sketch. Franklin J. Meine, a scholar of American humor and storytelling, said the range of subject matter in southern humor from the 1830s to the 1860s included sketches of local customs such as courtships and weddings; law circuits and political life; hunting stories; oddities in character; travel, including the rustic in the big city; frontier medical stories; gambling; varieties of religious experience, including the circuit riding preacher; and fights.[7] Ralph Waldo Emerson, Ivan Turgenev, Stephen Crane, Abraham Cahan, George Ade, and Theodore Dreiser wrote sketches, and so did writers on many weekly and daily newspapers. Turgenev's *Sketches from a Hunter's*

Album, published in 1852, contains famous hunting memoirs that may have led to Turgenev's arrest—because the Russian bureaucrats were shocked by the author's revolutionary portrayal of serfs as human beings. These classics, some of them international, such as Turgenev's and Dickens's, have made a lasting impression on literary journalists. In 2004, contemporary literary journalist Michael Paterniti told me, "The other day I was reading Turgenev, the beginning of a sketch, and thinking, 'Wow. The distinctions being made in this first page between the peasants who live in *this* part of the country and the peasants who live in *that* part of the country, and the animals they go out and shoot and why they do it, and how they hold themselves as they do it.' The detail is so fine, so intricate, so amazing. This writing belongs only to itself. There's a dialectic there that is so completely unique."[8]

Some nineteenth-century reporters created newspaper sketches as tall tales or playful hoaxes that, if they appeared today, would be so disguised that we would not recognize them. In the nineteenth century, however, even fictional sketches stirred little criticism in the newspaper. In the era before the rise of objectivity, sketches were used to create features out of some small story, or to report a little thing that the writer came across, heard, or observed. They were factual or fictional, funny or straight, informative or descriptive. Writers rarely used a sketch when anything substantial was at hand. On a slow news day, however, a reporter could crank out a sketch and entertain readers.

The sketch provided writers with something we often miss today: an opportunity to write about ordinary life. The sketch did not require great events or disasters. Small, private events would do. It could be improved upon, in case real life didn't provide enough material. It could be funny. Sketches appeared in just about every newspaper and were sometimes carefully crafted pieces of literature. The sketch provided exactly the form that a newspaper literary journalist needed. It was short, done in a day, personal, free from restrictions, and grew from immersion in ordinary life. Today we sometimes see sketch writing in special departments—the "About New York" columns by Dan Barry, for example, that the *New York Times* described as "taking readers along a remarkable journey through the sounds and the smells, the sages and cranks, the pain and hidden beauty of the five boroughs."[9] These stories meet the conditions and limitations set on columns, except they may be written by reporters who have no other place to report what they actually see as they ramble about town.

When Samuel Clemens, who had not yet become Mark Twain, took a job at the *Virginia Daily Territorial Enterprise* in Virginia City, Nevada, in 1862, he had already worked at newspapers in Missouri and had written articles about his brief career as a riverboat pilot. His personality fit with the irreverent newspaper, where he stayed until May 1864. At the *Enterprise,* Clemens sometimes took liberties with a column—especially when the editor was out of town—and it was here that he first adopted the name Mark Twain. One of his first pieces was a sketch called "Petrified Man" that appeared on October 4, 1862.[10] The one-paragraph sketch made subtle fun of the formal and orthodox language of the news. Twain later said that newspapers all over the world picked it up, and most of them believed it. The stale newspaper voice sold the hoax. Twain reported that a petrified man had been found with all his limbs perfectly intact. He had been sitting for perhaps a hundred years with water dripping from a limestone deposit above and had been cemented to the rock face:

> The body was in a sitting posture, and leaning against a huge mass of croppings; the attitude was pensive, the right thumb resting

against the side of the nose; the left thumb partially supported the chin, the fore-finger pressing the inner corner of the left eye and drawing it partly open; the right eye was closed, and the fingers of the right hand spread apart.[11]

Although the average reader, bored silly by the mundane prose, might not think to do it, all you need do to determine that this is a hoax is to assume the physical position Twain described for "the defunct."

He published several short sketches reporting on "opportunities missed" as news. Here's one such sketch from 1862:

Free Fight.—A beautiful and ably conducted free fight came off in C street yesterday afternoon, but as nobody was killed or mortally wounded in a manner sufficiently fatal to cause death, no particular interest attaches to the matter, and we shall not publish the details. We pine for murder—these fist fights are of no consequence to anybody.[12]

Several of Twain's sketches, particularly "Journalism in Tennessee," made fun of newsroom practices. These sketches, like the one above, can be read as self-examinations that were critical of the news business. By examining newspaper work, even in a funny way, Twain encouraged readers to consider the writers who stood behind newspaper prose. His habit of self-examination predated by a hundred years the practice by New Journalists in the 1960s of revealing their presence in the text. Twain did no less in virtually all of his sketches, whether fictional or not.

Twain's sketches and humorous pieces—and several downright hoaxes—challenged readers to get into the habit of being skeptical of *all* texts and to exercise judgment about the voice of the newspaper narrator. Today, newspapers want to convince us that their reports can be trusted, but Twain apparently thought news-paper reporters were no more perfect than any other variety of human.

His most famous newspaper sketch was a minor disaster.

In late October 1863, Twain published a column-length piece in the *Enterprise* headlined "A Bloody Massacre near Carson." It began with a technique originally used by Daniel Defoe, that of reporting an event brought to the narrator by another person. Thus "Abram Curry" came to Virginia City from Carson City, Nevada, and reported that Philip Hopkins, who had been living with his wife and nine children "just at the edge of the great pine forest which lies between Empire City and Dutch Nick's," had ridden into town on horseback "with his throat cut from ear to ear, and bearing in his hand a reeking scalp from which the warm, smoking blood was still dripping, and fell in a dying condition in front of the Magnolia saloon." The scalp, citizens could attest, be-longed to Hopkins's wife. At the house they found the wife and children had been beaten to death. Toward the end of the piece, Twain explained that Hopkins had tipped over the edge of sanity as a result of investing in the Spring Valley Water Company of San Francisco on the advice of the *San Francisco Bulletin*. Shortly after his investment, Spring Valley had cooked a dividend—that is, bor-rowed money to pay a dividend, which increased the value of the stock and permitted the executives to "sell out at a comfortable figure, and then scramble from under the tumbling concern"[13]—after which the stock price plummeted.[14]

Not surprisingly, newspapers all over the West reprinted the bloody massacre story. The next day, however, Twain ran a little item in the *Enterprise* titled "I Take It All Back," explaining that the story was fiction, and brought down a storm of criticism. In 1870, Twain said that the piece was intended as a satire on the financial advice of San Francisco newspapers. One trick was to get the offending San Francisco papers to reprint it themselves, thus engaging in unintentional self-criticism. He assumed that his knowledgeable local readers would recognize the hints and be rewarded and entertained for their skepticism.

> Ah, it was a deep, deep satire, and most ingeniously contrived. But I made the horrible details so carefully and conscientiously interesting that the public devoured *them* greedily, and wholly overlooked the following distinctly stated facts, to wit: The murderer was perfectly well known to every creature in the land as a *bachelor,* and consequently he could not murder his wife and nine children; he murdered them "in his splendid dressed-stone mansion just in the edge of the great pine forest between Empire City and Dutch Nick's," when even the very pickled oysters that came on our tables knew that there was not a "dressed-stone mansion" in all Nevada Territory; also that, so far from there being a "great pine forest between Empire City and Dutch Nick's," there wasn't a solitary tree within fifteen miles of either place; and, finally, it was patent and notorious that Empire City and Dutch Nick's were one and the same place, and contained only six houses anyhow, and consequently there could be no forest *between* them; and on top of all these absurdities I stated that this diabolical murderer, after inflicting a wound upon himself that the reader ought to have seen would kill an elephant in the twinkling of an eye, jumped on his horse and rode *four miles,* waving his wife's reeking scalp in the air, and thus performing entered Carson City with tremendous *éclat,* and dropped dead in front of the chief saloon, the envy and admiration of all beholders.[15]

Mesmerized by the bloody details of the opening, few readers recognized the financial jab at the end. "Most of the citizens dropped gently into it at breakfast, and they never finished their meal," Twain recalled.[16] Outside papers could not detect the contradictions in the piece. His satisfaction reached a peak when the *San Francisco Bulletin* reprinted the sketch, thus criticizing its own financial advice.

Twain's adopted pseudonym linked him to the humorous storytellers who performed throughout the Midwest and South in this era, including Augustus Baldwin Longstreet, Johnson Jones Hooper, Joseph Glover Baldwin, and Joel Chandler Harris. In the late nineteenth century, a number of writers made a living preparing funny pieces for performance and for the newspapers. They used comic pseudonyms such as M. Quad (a term from the printing trade for a large blank space), Squibob, John Phoenix, Bret Harte, Mike Fink (who embodied the life of the riverboat men on the Mississippi), Artemus Ward (a New Englander who looked like the rural Yankee character we call Uncle Sam), and of course Mark Twain. The humorists who performed in the South also included some northerners, such as Josh Billings, a native of Massachusetts who wrote backwoodsy, misspelled tales in the 1860s; Petroleum V. Nasby, a New Yorker whose real name was David Ross Locke and who was also a newspaperman; and Artemus Ward, who lived in Maine, New Hampshire, and Ohio and who was a friend and inspiration to Twain. All used the backwoods American, the rural villager, and the hayseed as their subjects.[17]

Twain's hoaxes and many of his sketches, of course, were fiction. Newspapers all over the country carried sketches, but they were normally nonfiction. One sketch might tell about riding across town on public transportation, complete with some little drama about, say, a woman getting on the carriage with a big package.[18] Nothing important, but it was about real life in town.

Sketch writers learned to let their narrators tell the story in a voice natural to the character. That gave the reader more to do. Stories sounded real, but readers had to figure out what the narrator was talking about and simultaneously evaluate the personality and veracity of the narrator. They had to judge the information based on what they knew from past experience with the storyteller, or from what they could surmise from the character type. This was precisely the point—and especially true in Twain's case. The technique flourished among the humorists of the South and New England, the Chicago reporters of the 1890s, and newspaper sketch writers such as Opie Read.

Opie Read is a good example of the pure newspaper sketch writer, and later novelist, of the late nineteenth century. He entered the news business in Kentucky as a printer in the 1870s, shortly after Twain left Nevada for California. Times were tough. Read bounced from one newspaper to another in Kentucky, Tennessee, and Arkansas as a tramp printer and tramp journalist. He set type, covered local news, and wrote sketches, a couple of which were published in the *New York Sunday Mercury.* At a less accomplished level, his early career was similar to Twain's at small, backcountry newspapers. Read's travels took him on foot through the South and eventually to Little Rock, Arkansas. His travels were his "university of experience"—educational in both cultural and financial terms. Most of his sketches and the novels that followed dealt with this period of his life. "The nearest approach to the peripatetic philosopher was the American tramp printer," Read said. "He was acquainted with the habits and thoughts of every community."[19]

Read followed American traditions of rural storytelling and humor in his sketches, as did Twain. Read played on the distinctions between yokels and gentlemen, reproduced the dialect of African Americans and backwoodsmen, and used characters and dialogue, rather than exposition, to advance his tales. Dialect, vernacular language, and authentic patterns of speech were valued by Twain and Read, and by 1890s' journalists in Chicago, who were attempting to capture the street types of the city, and in Finley Peter Dunne's case the immigrant speech patterns.

Read worked at the *Louisville Courier-Journal,* where editor Henry Watterson liked his sketches. In 1878, he became city editor at the *Evening Democrat* in Little Rock, Arkansas. He chafed under the owner's demands for "news and no sketches" and concluded that his boss was "about as literary as a laundry list."[20] This was likely Read's first glimpse of the rising star of objectivity. Read spent several months during 1878 in Memphis covering the outbreak of yellow fever for James Gordon Bennett Jr.'s *New York Herald.* His news reporting was more literary than journalistic. By winter, he returned to Little Rock as city editor of the *Daily Arkansas Gazette,* the state's leading newspaper. Read wrote two or three unsigned but highly recognizable sketches a week, similar to the ones he would later write for his *Arkansaw Traveler.*

When former president and Civil War general Ulysses S. Grant visited Little Rock, Read found nothing of great importance in his speech or in an interview conducted at Grant's hotel. Instead of a straight news story, Read wrote a sketch called "Jerry at the Banquet," about an old Negro who expressed a great deal about being close to a famous man. In the midst of the banquet honoring Grant, as Read constructed the tale, the old river skiffman entered and announced that although his name was not on the program, he had been given apologies and would now respond to the toast. Old Jerry said he was running for governor—no doubt quite a joke in the Jim Crow South—and he said to the audience:

As I look up at dat man an he sets dar, I moralizes ter dis effeck: "An' is dis de man what has shuck de worl' wid de tread ob his feet?" His recon'ition doan cum frum de fack dat he doan talk much, but ef it did, wouldn't dar be a mighty demand fur de inmates of de deaf an' dumb 'sylems? Dar mus' be suthen else 'bout dis man, an' a part of his greatness rests in de fack dat de people can't fine out what hit is. In one respeck a great man is like a ghost. De closer you git ter him de less you is skeered. Gen'lemen doan tink dat becase I uses a nigger's blunt flosofy dat I is jealous ob dis man, case I aint. Dar is some difference twixt us. He is in his special car makin' his third trip ter de white 'ouse, while fur de fust time I's paddlin' my skiff toward de state house.[21]

After this sketch ran, Read asked his boss for a raise. His editor, Colonel Dick Johnson, replied in blunt fashion, typical of the times: "Yes, the sketches are all right in their way, but take this one for instance. It's simply a conversation between a nigger and a white man. Nothing remarkable about it. I've heard niggers talk that way all my life. I think you'd better stick to your job and pay a little more attention to news."[22] Read's sketches of African Americans did not play well with whites in Ohio, where he worked for a while, and his sketches of hicks and backwoodsmen raised hackles in Arkansas. He needed a new audience.

As a tramp printer who had seen many newspapers spring up at the start of a political campaign and close their doors the day after the election, Read knew how to start his own publication. In doing so, he escaped from the bigotries and facts consciousness of editors.

In 1882, Read founded the *Arkansaw Traveler,* where he had the freedom to print all the sketches he wanted. The *Traveler* was a humorous publication with a brilliant marketing scheme behind it. It sold to passengers on the railroads—the 1880s' version of today's Internet audience. Train travel created a large audience with nothing to do and money to spend. The *Arkansaw Traveler* offered diverting stories, literature, and several columns of advertising for things such as musical instruments, guns, patent medicines, opium cures, and Pennyroyal Pills. Read wrote about ten columns of material each week and supplemented his own work with stories from newspaper exchanges with Detroit, New York, London, and Edinburgh. Among the writers who appeared in the *Traveler,* with or without permission, were Charles Dickens, Bill Nye, Eugene Field, and Josh Billings.

When Read and his wife moved to Chicago in 1887, they had made it to the Big Time. The *Traveler* was popular enough to support an urban lifestyle. A large, lovable fellow who came to resemble a Kentucky colonel, Read stylistically did not belong in the vibrant new city. His fellow sketch writers and journalistic storytellers in Chicago were moving in a new direction that involved realism in literature and the examination of social problems in society. Read stepped off the train and into the midst of a transformation in journalism.

It was a moment when literary journalism had an opportunity to emerge from the domain of rural storytellers and sketch writers and into the mass-circulation mainstream of American newspapers.

Big, frightening, and promising, Chicago offered conflicting human stories. The city was bursting with growth, commerce, and optimism in the midst of a massive flow of immigrants and the resulting class conflicts. It struggled to reconcile older traditions with emerging new political forces. Reporters in the decade of the 1890s found new symbolic identities in their work, sought mechanisms to retain a voice in news stories, and focused attention on the social life of the new urban "types." They created a home for literary journalism and a voice that eventually crept into modern magazines as well.

In journalism, we can justify saying the modern era began with the rise of mass-circulation magazines and urban newspapers in the 1890s that significantly expanded the audience and the market for news. Newspaper editors started to control some of the practices of their reporters. In Chicago, New York, and Boston in the 1890s, it was not uncommon for reports to be unverified or even fabricated in one aspect or another, and editors for obvious reasons tried to stop the practice. Editors took two approaches to this problem. Some became increasingly "facts conscious"—wanting reporters to bring back information packaged in an almost scientific fashion. Others appreciated the storytelling background of journalism and encouraged narrative in their reports. The new trends pushed standardized and impersonal news at some papers, while at others sensationalism started to flourish. Neither approach served the interests of a developing literary journalism, which in the modern era would be based on factual reporting, characters, and ordinary life, but not on overdramatized sensationalism.[23]

Facts consciousness changed the nature of the occupation and conflicted with ideas about writing held by many reporters. They had gone into journalism to tell stories with a personal perspective and literary flair, but their editors were discouraging the sketch and eliminating these literary qualities. Modern mass-circulation newspapers were factories for gathering news and delivering it to the public, and within that world the reporter was a laborer. The rising professionalism within journalism helped standardize the product and rationalize the factory. Allan Forman, the editor of *Journalist,* "praised the disappearance of 'bohemians' whose slip-shod work, fabled inebriety, and literary pretensions were being replaced . . . by loyal, reliable, and efficient family men who saw journalism as a career."[24] Many reporters worked for large newspapers with a staff of a thousand, and they were only one category of worker-bee. If they harbored literary aspirations, it grew harder and harder to find a role for them within the world of the newspaper. There were a few exceptions, such as the experience of Lincoln Steffens as city editor of the *New York Commercial Advertiser* from 1897 to 1902.[25] But at most publications, the rapid industrial pace of the market pushed aside reflection and the leisurely production of sketches.

The sketch as a standard news story did not survive the facts trend at the beginning of the twentieth century. Newspapers increasingly avoided personal reporting and sketches; editors wanted readers to believe that the newspaper *was* the narrator and that the newspaper was a somber (and sober), ever-trustworthy citizen. That news style was much less entertaining than the literary approach that had been developed by Twain and Read, and it credited the reader with little ability to make distinctions or to understand nuance. The facts consciousness drove many reporters, including Frank Norris and Theodore Dreiser in the 1890s and Ernest Hemingway and John Dos Passos after World War I, to journalism's illegitimate sister, fiction.

Editors from nonsensational newspapers who had a greater appreciation for the sketch fenced off that kind of story into the "column," which became a playground for Eugene Field, George Ade, and Finley Peter Dunne in Chicago.

No longer personal observers and interpreters of events as their nineteenth-century counterparts had been, the urban reporters on the mass-circulation newspapers of the early twentieth century faced an industrial task. In this age, reporters lived on working-class wages, even if they were better educated than the workers of the time. Their assignments came to resemble factory work in that they covered standard beats and could write using routine formulas. Becoming a staff reporter at a newspaper, Ronald Weber has said, "meant exchanging precious independence for the routines of an employee and fitting words into ready-made forms that could be hard if not impossible to escape in future work. A salaried journalist was a writer, but a writer in captivity."[26] News work became specialized. Writers were pushed to abandon the older, more personal or literary form of journalism. They were squeezed between demands from editors for unopinionated copy and a desire to present their own views of life.[27]

A limited group of reporters in Chicago, many of whom were members of the legendary Whitechapel Club in the 1890s, fought back by creating an attitude and style that framed their identity. In part, this identity included a cynicism that helped them deal with emotions generated by the poverty, death, and urban struggle that were everyday stories on the streets. In part, it was a literary identification with the new style of realism. And in part, it was a reaction to the forces that sought to strip storytelling out of the news. Their resulting work framed the origins of literary journalism in the twentieth century.

George Ade, born in 1866, grew up in northern Indiana and attended Purdue University—college then being an unusual thing for a journalist. He then spent a couple of years as an apprentice writer of country journalism and advertising copy. In 1890, he arrived in Chicago and began working for $12 a week at the *Chicago Morning News,* the morning edition of the *Chicago Daily News,* the largest-circulation paper of ten major publications in the city. It later became the *News Record.* The city captivated the hick from Kentland, Indiana. He wrote to a friend in barely concealed joy that "the streets are so full of cable cars, hansoms, drays, express wagons, chippies, policemen, and other public nuisances that a man doesn't know when he starts downtown in the morning whether he will get back at night or land up in the morgue."[28] Ade was innocent of city life. By the same stage in life, Opie Read had reported the plague in Memphis and had been a tramp printer for years. But Ade impressed editors and rapidly advanced from cub reporter to covering the cops. He roomed with newspaper illustrator John T. McCutcheon, also a Purdue graduate, who had encouraged Ade to enter journalism; they lived in quarters next door to the notorious Levee vice district. Vagrants slept in the hallway, and there were shootings in the alleyway at night. Ade and McCutcheon remained aloof from such social worlds except as spectators. Ade, however, could not remain so aloof from the growing cynicism among reporters as he covered a steamship explosion, injustices done to labor organizers, murders in the streets, political corruption, the immorality of the Levee district, and the poverty of the riverfront and stock yards. Ade found a symbolic handle on these social arenas by organizing them as discrete cultures or communities within the city, much as the extraordinary sociologists at the University of Chicago would do later. Ade eventually joined the Whitechapel Club, became a realist, and developed into the first and one of the greatest chroniclers of the urban types of his age.

Ade was lifted from the ranks of reporter to the status of literary star through his daily column of sketches called "All Roads Lead to the World's Fair." He covered the Chicago World's Fair, also known as the Columbian Exposition, for a year starting in October 1892. John McCutcheon and William Schmedtgen, head of the art department at the *News Record,* provided illustrations for Ade's narrative columns. The lead paragraphs were carefully crafted, and Ade used personality sketches as a vehicle to describe the fair.

For example, instead of an adjectival tribute to the beauties of the Arkansas exhibit, he told readers about Mary Tivett. Miss Tivett was painting a six-foot high mural that circled the inside of the building. Readers could picture the inside of the room through the eyes of a human actor. McCutcheon's illustrations concentrated on details rather than on the landscape overview and are probably the best visual record we have of the World's Fair.

The World's Fair in 1893 symbolically proclaimed Chicago's position as a major American city, at last beating out St. Louis. At a time when Louis Sullivan (Frank Lloyd Wright's mentor) was producing some of America's greatest architecture in downtown Chicago—indigenous American architecture—the World's Fair committee built its "White City" on classic Greek lines. This was commercial Chicago's way of saying that even an inland city whose wealth came from butchering livestock could be as graceful and beautiful as they imagined ancient Greece.

It was hogwash, of course.

The "White City" was a symbol for the committee's aspirations, but not for the immigrant city or the black city or the city of broad shoulders.

The reporters knew it was hogwash. And so did Louis Sullivan, whose contribution to the World's Fair was a multicolored Transportation Building so out of sorts with the "White City by the Lake" theme that the fair organizers set it off by itself.

This conflict—between what select city fathers wanted Chicago to be and what it really was—contributed to a particular style of reporting. Reporters covered the White City, the world of wealthy meatpackers, commodity traders, and real estate developers, but reporters were also painfully and personally aware of the different conditions of life for the worker, the immigrant, and the ordinary people of the city. Many residents had been drawn to Chicago, like the reporters themselves, by images of success and growth. Reporters often lived in the middle, writing of wealth and social spectacle in one story and of grinding poverty in the next. They did not make much money at it, an average of about $25 a week in Chicago in the late 1890s, about the same as plumbers. They tried to interpret the dramas of city life, as best they could, in a world where the forces of the White City owned the newspapers.

Reporters could not print all they knew about the city. Their fairly radical ideas about commerce (some of the younger ones would just as soon shoot the tycoons as look at them) could not go into a family newspaper. They created new ways of dealing with the incongruities of rich and poor, democrats and plutocrats. Many adopted what Larzer Ziff called the twin defenses of cynicism and sentimentalism, which hardened them to the crime and tragedy they reported, yet allowed them to sympathize with the innocent victims of a harsh world.[29] Cynicism let them write crime stories and sentimentalism let them do human interest.

After the fair closed, Ade continued writing articles and sketches. His editor, Charles H. Dennis, recalled, "His copy went to the copy desk in the city room, where, in the massacre necessary to bring everything down to volume that would fit the restricted space allotted to local news, Ade's articles suffered grievous mutilation."[30] Dennis ended this offense by giving Ade and McCutcheon the two vertical columns of space on the editorial page formerly occupied by the "All Roads" column on the World's Fair. Ade started his column in November 1893, and it endured for seven years, soon to be known as "Stories of the Streets and of the Town." His column on the editorial page joined another open-ended, nonpolitical column written by Eugene

Field, called "Sharps and Flats." Ade had been given permission to publish sketches, but only if they fit the allotted space.

Ade brought his attitude from the World's Fair to the street life of Chicago. Most readers had not visited the junkshops on Clark Street, Shanty Town, the docks, or German Town. Could these places be introduced and described exactly as he had described the exhibits at the fair? Maybe not. Shanty Town was a culture made of real people, whereas the fair had been a controlled construction. Ade developed new techniques that would later be picked up by sociologists and ethnographers. He interpreted the strange new attitudes that were shaping the feelings of city dwellers as the twentieth century swept over them.

Ade's first "Stories" column began with this packed single paragraph in the realistic style:

> On that part of lower Clark street, where the houses have shriveled away until they are never more than twenty feet high, where the sidewalks are moldy and decayed, where flimsy lace curtains hang in the windows, and where no man looks you in the eye, a coal wagon was seen yesterday. It was overloaded, and a chunk weighing thirty pounds or more fell off when the wheel struck a deep rut. A little Italian lounging before the entrance to a basement saw the block of coal fall and he ran for it. But it had broken into several pieces. He captured the largest piece. A colored driver whose army coat was fastened about him by a piece of hemp twine, took two of the smaller pieces and then a woman with a basket trotted down a stairway and gathered up what was left even to the crumbs. In certain parts of the city coal will be coal this winter.[31]

Three days later, Ade published "A Young Man in Upper Life," a notable fictional short story of the vacuity, anonymity, and emptiness of city life. Later he wrote about market gardeners bringing their produce to sell in the Haymarket district, and about roominghouse residents who would move to slightly improved quarters whenever they received a small pay raise as a way of expressing their new social status. Worse than the outward display of materialism was the inward feeling of aloneness and restriction within the city. His fictional character types included Pink Marsh, an African American who worked in a barbershop, and a woman office worker named Min Sargent, who was among the incoming wave of female urban workers. His community portraits included workers, members of the uneasy new middle class, representatives of ethnic and religious groups, farmers, shopkeepers, aspiring housewives, and those social climbers who measured their worth by the location of a house or the elevation of an office in a high-rise. Ade's tone was sad. Life in the city's streets and offices was fragmented, shallow, and transient.

Circulation grew dramatically, to nearly two hundred thousand a day, at the *Chicago Record,* where Ade's column ran. "A historian of today," wrote Ade's biographer, "reading the 'Stories of the Streets and of the Town,' glimpses a golden age of journalism. McCutcheon did illustrations of striking excellence and Ade wrote not merely clever newspaper stuff but *literature!*"[32]

It can be difficult to separate fact from fiction in Ade's "Stories of the Streets," but we should remember that they were tales of everyday life, a legacy of the sketch writers of the mid-nineteenth century. As Ade's cynicism deepened, he later published (and syndicated) a wonderful series called "Fables in Slang." After telling a little sketch that employed entertaining capitalization to emphasize his satiric intent and to slow down the reader's march through the story, Ade concluded with a moral that was ironic or cynical and always entertaining.

In "The Fable of the Caddy Who Hurt His Head While Thinking," Ade's caddy was watching a couple of wealthy golfers dressed in the fashions of the day. The young caddy reflected that they were inferior to his father, who worked in a lumberyard. "His Father was too Serious a Man to get out in Mardi Gras Clothes and hammer a Ball from one Red Flag to another." The caddy kept thinking and thinking:

> The Caddy wondered why it was that his Father, a really Great Man, had to shove Lumber all day and could seldom get one Dollar to rub against another, while these superficial Johnnies who played Golf all the Time had Money to Throw at the Birds. The more he Thought the more his Head ached.
>
> Moral: Don't try to Account for Anything.[33]

Ade and Finley Peter Dunne both dealt with modern urban character types—people who represented aspects of community culture as it was expressed in the emerging cityscape of the twentieth century. Several other important literary journalists in the 1890s developed work based on both realism and the academic discipline of sociology, which along with politics was journalism's closest companion during the twentieth century.

Jack London grew up in San Francisco, where he was a street kid from the age of fourteen. He knew runaway sailors and opium smugglers, loafed in saloons, and with a young girl robbed oyster beds. In 1894, at the age of eighteen, London went on the road as a tramp during a national economic depression. He kept diaries and notes, which he later turned into a book called *The Road*. He returned home interested in sociology and studied for one semester at the University of California at Berkeley before lighting out for the Gold Rush in the Klondike. His writing in nonfiction was most notable in *The Road* and in *People of the Abyss,* about the East End slums of London, England.

Although he was a barely educated young man when he wrote it, London attempted some analyses in *The Road* that would later characterize sociology and literary journalism. For instance, he discussed the caste system among tramps and interpreted their lingo. His approach suggests a participatory journalism that was revived in the New Journalism of the 1960s. London expressed outrage at injustices and at how the system works and attempted an economic analysis of why there were tramps.[34]

Hutchins Hapgood used the distinctive sociological concept of "type" for his literary journalism on the Jewish ghetto, *The Spirit of the Ghetto* (1902), and three books focused on interviews with radicals, *The Spirit of Labor* (1907), *An Anarchist Woman* (1909), and *Types from City Streets* (1910). Lincoln Steffens, as editor of the *New York Commercial Advertiser* starting in 1897, pursued similar "types." Steffens once assigned Hapgood to write a feature on an urban intersection and the people who lived there.

A few years after Ade and Dunne created their columns portraying cultural communities in Chicago, a new collaboration of scholars grew in the same region. Known as the Chicago School of Sociology, it included such seminal figures as Charles Horton Cooley, John Dewey, W. I. Thomas, Robert Park, and George Herbert Mead. They saw individualism and community as connected through symbolic processes. In Chicago, they had a working laboratory of social change where the settlement movement and Jane Addams's Hull-House were available for observation. The residents of Hull-House provided services such as day care, an employment bureau, and art and music classes for the immigrant neighborhood on Chicago's West Side and advocated for laws against child labor and in favor of compulsory education. Much of the Chicago School work focused on particular groups, such as the Polish peasant, but today we generally read Thomas or Park for clues to their methodology and theoretical orientation. One of the more accessible statements of Thomas's methodology is found in the "Methodological Note" in *The Polish Peasant in Europe and America* (1918–1920), most of which was apparently written at the insistence of coauthor Florian Znaniecki. Thomas here tells us what to look for in society:

> Sociology, as theory of social organization, is thus a special science of culture like economics or philology, and is in so far opposed to social psychology as the general science of the subjective side of culture. But at the same time it has this in common with social psychology: that the values which it studies draw all their reality, all their power to influence human life, from the social attitudes which are expressed or supposedly expressed in them; if the individual in his behavior is so largely determined by the rules prevailing in his social group, it is certainly due neither to the rationality of these rules nor to the physical consequences which their following or breaking may have, but to his consciousness that these rules represent attitudes of his group.

The negotiation of meaning between the individual consciousness and the group led Chicago School sociologists to study cultural groups in the city much as Ade and Dunne did. Robert Park, who had been a Muckraking journalist, produced insightful studies of the newspaper and other modern social institutions. The newspaper, he wrote, had become the modern equivalent of custom and tradition and had replaced the gossip, speech, and face-to-face interaction common to the peasant village. He grew pessimistic about modern society based on such shallow interactions as compared with older forms of culture. These transformations were exactly what literary journalists such as Ade and Dunne had been portraying in the 1890s before the qualitative forms of sociology emerged in the publications of the Chicago School.

Ade and Dunne portrayed individuals in Chicago seeking to find their way in a swirling and confusing modern world, a subject that also appealed to the early sociologists. "Types" were urban shorthand for Ade, a way to introduce the players in the game of urban living. He pulled the names of types from urban slang—the "Caddy" or the "Tycoon" or "the Roomer"—the same vernacular language as the words with capital letters in his "Fables in Slang." Each type embodied a distinct symbolic world within the city. The successful presentation of character types provided prestige for a writer in the 1890s because realists admired the idea. Realists were drawn to write about the "actual," especially the lives of the working class, immigrant, and underclass as seen on the streets, as compared to "idealized" or imagined perspectives. The concept of "types" drew from both sociology and the literary conversation about realism.

Sometimes Ade sounds almost like an 1890s' version of Tom Wolfe, as when he said that if you were wrecked two thousand miles offshore and were approached by a man on the beach "with two cigars in one upper vest pocket, while from the other upper pocket protruded three sharpened pencils and the white bone handle of a tooth-brush; if you didn't know the name of the island or the name of the young man, you could at least be certain of one thing—viz.: that the young man was a telegraph operator." Ade asked, "What person, unless he chooses to consider it undignified to do so, has not studied these trade-marks as shown in the apparel of the men who crowd by him in the street?"[35] Rather than dealing in social abstractions, Ade and Dunne used realistic particularity in their stories. Outside forces such as economic depression or

war played a lesser role in their work than did the individual creation of symbolic meaning and community affiliation, although
class regularly lurked behind the scenes in their stories.

"Types" were related to realism because they were considered
scientific and could be identified by external representations.
There was no clear-cut understanding of what realism meant in
journalism, although a conversation about it developed in the late
nineteenth century. Emile Zola, the French novelist, connected
realism to scientific methods and facts, to observable characters,
and to real places. But realists also wanted to penetrate the soul's
secrets. The complicated principles of realism fell easily into place
in the journalistic world. "In order to mirror the common life,"
wrote Christopher Wilson, "an author had to rely upon skills of
observation, a knowledge of manners and customs, and an adept-
ness at mimicking speech."[36] Writers such as Dunne, Twain, and
Ade achieved all three, especially the ability to mimic speech, but
so could Opie Read, who was considered by his journalistic
friends as a romantic. As editors pushed for more facts from reporters, writers such as Ade adopted realism as a method that
would allow them to continue reporting the world in literary
terms without contradicting the principles of a scientific-factual
outlook. Ade said his ambition in the 1890s "was to be known as
a realist with a compact style and a clean Anglo-Saxon vocabulary
and the courage to observe human virtues and frailties as they
showed on the lens."[37] His analogy of "the lens" suggests the photographic quality that realists envied. The realist novelist and essayist William Dean Howells said that in reading Ade's portrayals of
life "you experience something of the bliss of looking at your own
photograph."[38] Definitions of newspaper realism are often self-
fulfilling. If the portrait matched someone's definition of reality,
then it was realistic. Michael Schudson said "the term 'realism,' in

the 1890s, was more a boast and an advertisement than a descriptive label." According to Schudson, these writers believed that the laws of natural and social science could measure reality: "This *was* new. The world was disenchanted as never before, and the realists, embracing disenchantment to distinguish themselves from their literary fathers, were delighted."[39]

Another great Chicago newspaper writer who illustrated the new realistic and sociological styles among urban literary journalists was Finley Peter Dunne, who along with Ade and Opie Read was a member of the Whitechapel Club in Chicago. The Whitechapel Club was a more extreme version of a number of similar reporters' hangouts in other cities.[40] The club began as a small group of reporters meeting in the back room of Charley Kern's saloon on Newsboy's Alley (later Whitechapel Alley), probably in 1887. Members decorated the club headquarters, which featured a full bar, in their peculiar fashion. One of the original members proclaimed that the group would henceforth be known as the Whitechapel Club upon hearing the news of another murder by the notorious "Jack the Ripper" in the Whitechapel District of London, and the name stuck. Many members were police reporters who brought souvenirs of killings, suicides, robberies, and executions into the club, a form of symbolic vaccination. Tobacco was set out for members to use in cups that were the tops of human skulls, and eerie light came from colored glass set in the eye sockets of skulls that were used as gaslights. A twelve-foot snakeskin, pieces of rope that had been used to hang murderers, bullets that had slain famous criminals, and a coffin-shaped bar studded with nails imprinted with the number of each member served as decorations. Each new member drank his initiation toast from the cranium of a famous prostitute. The club's first president, Charlie

Seymour, had reported on the Indian wars from the West. He contributed bloodied Indian blankets and ghost shirts from the battle of Wounded Knee; unfortunately, the wearers of the items had believed they would protect them against the soldiers' bullets. George Ade became a member in 1892. To aspiring young reporters, the Whitechapel Club was a forbidden and sacred zone, a realist's club.

In 1891, the Whitechapel ran a candidate for mayor—much like the Norman Mailer–Jimmy Breslin ticket in New York City in 1967—on the platform of "No Gas! No Water!! No Police!!!" They said lighting the streets with gas was objectionable since it might intimidate those whose chosen employment required them to be abroad in the dark hours. The water of Lake Michigan was judged far less wholesome than the liquids available on tap. And the police were objectionable because they tended to harass those who abstained from drinking water, worked at night, or chose to remove from circulation by lethal methods anyone who was a source of annoyance to them.

They got 350 votes.

Members drew the organizational structure of the Whitechapel Club from "Camp 20" of the Clan-na-Gael, a fund-raising organization in support of the Irish independence movement. Extreme secrecy surrounded the selection of new members. Much of this ritualistic protocol may have come from Dunne, a man of Irish descent who harbored hostile feelings toward the English and probably knew all about the Clan-na-Gael from his police reporting. Reporters gathered over drinks and talked about each other's work. Most of them worked night police and cultivated the hard-bitten, hard-drinking, cynical style of modern urban reporters. It was a literary society at heart, although some socialist, anarchist, and revolutionary political sentiments were heard, too. Realism was the only respectable style, in the sense that it cut straight to the sordid truth that was assumed to be hiding beneath the surface. Members who tried to write in a romantic fashion had their work eviscerated by the Whitechapel sharpshooters: Dunne, Charlie Seymour, Ben King, Charlie Perkins, and Charley Almy. Dunne had an Irish sense of humor that could cut a man off at the knees. Among the visitors entertained at the club were the literary and public figures Chauncey Depew, Rudyard Kipling, James Whitcomb Riley, Richard Harding Davis, and Theodore Roosevelt.

Dunne grew up in Chicago, started working for the newspapers at age sixteen, and by twenty-one was a city editor. Blessed with an Irish literary imagination, he eventually started writing a column about a composite character, bar owner, and bartender named Mr. Dooley. Dunne's raw radicalism could be filtered and purified through Mr. Dooley, who expressed opinions in an eventempered way. His columns became fabulously successful as Mr. Dooley insightfully commented on the quirkiness of Chicago ward politics, and later on national politics, including U.S. intervention in wars in the Philippines and China. His earliest columns on local customs grew from his personal knowledge and firsthand reporting of the city, and the later ones connected with a national audience through syndication.

In one story, Mr. Dooley was talking with his regular customer, Mr. Hennessy, about the Chinese situation. Dooley said, in his heavy Irish brogue, "It bates th' wurruld. An' what's it comin' to? You an' me looks at a Chinyman as though he wasn't good f'r annything but washin' shirts, an' not very good at that. 'Tis wan if th's spoorts iv th' youth iv our gr-reat cities to rowl an impty beer keg down th' steps iv a Chinee laundhry, an' if e'er a Chinyman come out to resint it they'd take him be th' pigtail an' do th' joynt swing with him. But th' Chinyman at home's a diff'rent la-ad.

He's with his frinds an' they're manny iv thim an' he's rowlin' th' beer kegs himsilf an' Westhren Civilization is down in th' laundhry wondhrin' whin th' police'll come along."

Eventually Hennessey tires of Dooley's line of reasoning. "End ye'er blather," said Mr. Hennessy. "They won't be anny Chinymen left whin Imp'ror Willum gets through."

"Mebbe not," said Mr. Dooley. "He's a sthrong man. But th' Chinymen have been on earth a long time, an' I don't see how we can push so manny iv thim off iv it. Annyhow, 'tis a good thing f'r us they ain't Christyans an' haven't larned properly to sight a gun."[41]

Acquiring a column was for Ade and Dunne the equivalent of Opie Read starting his own newspaper. Inside the column lines, Ade and Dunne had a degree of literary freedom not available outside the lines. Later, Ade's "Fables in Slang" and Dunne's "Mr. Dooley" columns were syndicated in the new national newspaper market and republished in book collection after collection, entertaining readers for decades, and they remain in print today.

This new market for writing influenced quite a few literary journalism efforts. W. E. B. DuBois, who can be considered a literary journalist and essayist, published several articles in *The Atlantic Monthly, The World's Work, Dial, The New World,* and the *Annals* of the American Academy of Political and Social Science. His scattered articles were then combined and lengthened to form a book, *The Souls of Black Folk* (1903) and sold again in the marketplace. Just as Twain's *Innocents Abroad* became divorced from its original context—originally a series of newspaper articles—so too was DuBois's work transformed from its journalistic origins as a series of separate magazine pieces into a classic work of racial justice. In 1903, DuBois was still using Victorian patterns of speech, addressing his "Gentle Reader," for example, which was common in the magazines of his age but not in the newspapers. Besides, as an African American, DuBois had good reason to imitate a Victorian tone in the hope that white readers would hear the story of life beyond the Color Line.

Financial independence followed for those who could gain wider audiences. Ade became a successful Broadway playwright, bought four square miles of Indiana farmland, and retired. Dunne moved East and basked in his fame and fortune. Literary excellence raised Ade and Dunne to a different social level. It also empowered them to achieve goals that many of their compatriots in the Whitechapel Club could never pursue. Part of the cynicism of the age grew from the fact that newspaper owners could control the content of their newspapers, except for the words written by their valuable literary columnists.

Dunne's and Ade's columns spoke the language of the realistic and cynical urban reporters who had gone into the business because of their literary ambitions. "The myth that was to survive well into the next century and lure such as Ernest Hemingway," wrote Larzer Ziff, "had its foundation in men who insisted on talking to one another about the hypocrisy of the social system even while they were being paid to explain it away, whose faith in the big scoop was not entirely alien to a faith in the power of prose, and who read everything they could lay their hands on and fanned one another's literary aspirations as they sat about the city room on a rainy night."[42] This urban identity for reporters survived through the twentieth century in the mythology of *The Front Page,* a play by Chicago newspapermen Ben Hecht and Charlie MacArthur that was made into films three times, and in Hecht's news features such as the ones reprinted in *1001 Afternoons in Chicago* (1922). Tom Wolfe drew on that mythology in writing his essay "The New Journalism" in 1973. Wolfe said, "Chicago, 1928, that was the general idea . . . Drunken reporters out on the ledge of the *News* peeing into the Chicago River at dawn . . . Nights down at the saloon listening to 'Back of the Yards' being sung by a baritone who was only a lonely blind bulldyke with lumps of milk glass for eyes . . . Nights down at the detective bureau—it was always nighttime in my daydreams of the newspaper life. Reporters didn't work during the day. I wanted the whole movie, nothing left out."[43]

Opie Read had a close relationship with the top reporters in Chicago. Several times he paid them for freelance pieces published in the *Arkansaw Traveler.* Read came into close contact with Ade, Dunne, and other accomplished Chicago reporters in the Whitechapel Club, which was the mother lode of the mythical newspaper style that Wolfe envied. Other members included Frederick Adams, Charles Almy, Hugh E. Kehoe, Ben King, Charles Perkins, Wallace Rice, and Charles Seymour, many of whom would aspire to write great prose but would die young. Brand Whitlock, a friend of Opie Read's from the *Cleveland Leader* and later a political reformer, was also a member.

Read had an important literary difference with this crowd. He was always a romantic. Read argued that the purpose of journalism was not to create photographs—as he put it, "photographic exposures of contemporary existence"—as the Whitechapel reporters did, but paintings.[44] He had his own publication that protected him from editors' harangues about a tighter, more factual style. He rejected the urban cynicism of his companions, who were known to visit with condemned men the night before a hanging and take their money in card games, operating on the sensible theory that the criminal wouldn't have his mind on the game.

Read once commented on such practices: "There is no work of standard ethics defining the polite usages and good breeding for reporters, but it is generally conceded that these restless nerve centres of the press should cease asking questions of the doomed man shortly before, or at least immediately after the death trigger is touched. . . . Neither is it thought to be in good form for a reporter, just previous to the conventional 'dull thud,' to advise the title role performer to take certain remedies for a cold or any other indisposition from which he may be suffering."[45]

In his sketches and novels, Read joined characters together through romantic notions of trust and brotherhood, whereas in the realistic writing of Ade and Dunne the bonds between people were a product of their station in life, their surroundings, their ethnicity, or their environment.

These differences led to an amazing and embarrassing episode. Read was ribbed out of the Whitechapel Club. Dunne probably had something to do with it because he had an artist's skill at flaying unrealistic conceptions. Read never mentioned it in his memoirs, but his biographer described the incident at the Whitechapel Club this way:

> After the first pricks of ambition had been satisfied and Opie had gained a considerable reputation as a popular novelist, he seemed to resent the constant and cynical criticism of these ruthless intellectuals. He probably felt that his public knew better what it wanted than this self-regarding clique of city "ninnies." It is recalled that the "huge, kindly, sentimental Opie Read, the club's greatest master of the humorous anecdote, hearing the evisceration of one of his ragged novels, walked out and never came back."[46]

Realism, "the record of life, the real, the true," as one scholar defined it, never appealed to Read.[47] He was clever enough to point out in several places that the "real" and the "true" can be socially defined concepts and applied equally to his romantic literary portraits. In practice, however, romanticism and realism were opposing camps. "Imagination is beset with the failure of design," Read lamented.[48] More than his sensitivity to criticism, his literary style alienated him from his fellow storytellers at the Whitechapel Club. Realism was coming in and romanticism was going out, which can be demonstrated in this case by the simple fact that the reputations of Dunne and Ade remain intact today, but almost no one remembers Opie Read.

The realistic literary style at urban newspapers in such places as Chicago, New York, San Francisco, and Boston emerged in advance of a change in the narrative voice of popular magazines.

The innovative newspaper voices, as seen in syndicated columns by Ade and Dunne, in later books that collected their works, and in the "story" press of the big cities, influenced narrative voice in the magazines as the new century dawned.

The history of voice in journalistic prose has attracted some attention, mostly at the point of cultural changes. Hugh Kenner published an article in the *New York Times Book Review* on the concept of the "plain style" that arrived with journalism, replacing a more formal prose style.[49] The transformation to vernacular prose accompanied the earliest rise of journalism in England. Voice moved from the essayist's desk into the streets in such publications as Addison and Steele's *Spectator* and Defoe's *Review,* which were foundation stones of literary journalism.[50] The plain style lacks rhetorical flourishes and complicated structures. As Kenner said, it persuades us that plain speech is without guile, though writers may work hard to achieve the guileless stance. "Couched in plain prose, even the incredible can hope for belief," said Kenner. He added, "Gradually newspapers gravitated toward the plain style, the style of all styles that was patently trustworthy. . . . A man who doesn't make his language ornate cannot be deceiving us; so runs the hidden premise."[51] While seeming commonplace, the plain style is carefully crafted. Roger Angell once said of his stepfather E. B. White that "writing almost killed you, and the hard part was making it look easy."[52] Voice, style, and tone help define the subtle relationship of the author to the reader. They immediately define our separate roles. Is the writer speaking from a position of authority, as nineteenth-century essayists often did? Or is the writer stumbling along a confusing pathway with the reader and seeking enlightenment, as writers from Defoe to Twain learned to do? Voice answers these questions for the reader.

Circulations increased in the magazine industry during the 1880s after postage rates and purchase prices went down, and particularly between 1893 and 1899. In the 1880s, a hundred thousand was a large national circulation, and by the early twentieth century some magazines approached circulations of one million, supported by a national advertising market for standard brands. *McCall's* magazine circulated two hundred thousand copies a month in 1900 and more than a million in 1910.[53]

The changing narrative voices in magazines lagged behind the growing circulations. During the 1890s, it was urban newspapers that first achieved mass circulations and that introduced new voices such as those pioneered by Ade and Dunne. By the early 1900s, the magazine world followed suit and adopted different attitudes among narrators, voices that can be traced back to the columnists and literary journalists of the newspapers. "The old leaders still looked across the sea and to the past," wrote Ted

Peterson of the magazine world. "The newcomers looked at America and to the present—or future."[54]

In the late nineteenth century, magazine style had not yet abandoned the elaborate rhetorical flourish. The following are samples of the old essayist style and voice from 1885 to 1889. Circulations had already started to rise at this time. Both were the lead paragraphs in the articles.

"A Story of Assisted Fate," Frank R. Stockton
The Atlantic, 1885

In a general way I am not a superstitious man, but I have a few ideas, or notions, in regard to fatality and kindred subjects of which I have never been able entirely to dispossess my mind; nor can I say that I have ever tried very much to do so, for I hold that a certain amount of irrationalism in the nature of a man is a thing to be desired. By its aid he clambers over the wall which limits the action of his intellect, and if he be but sure that he can get back again no harm may come of it, while he is the better for many pleasant excursions.

"The Invalid's World," A. B. Ward
Scribner's Magazine, January 1889, Volume 5, Issue 1

When I consider what the education of a doctor entails, what endless study and investigation, what patient labor; when I reflect upon the continual risks that he must take, the continual self-control that he must have, balanced by continual compassion; when I remember how he is ever contending in a face-to-face and hand-to-hand encounter with disease and death; I think that he should be an industrious and thoughtful, a brave and noble gentleman.

Stockton was a writer, journalist, and children's book author most active earlier in the century, and Ward's work appeared in several magazines of the era. Both examples have a voice and a first-person narrator. But each uses an idealized rhetorical prose style that makes the author seem like a stiff.

Now here are two examples of the new voice in early twentieth-century magazines:

"Tuppenny Travels in London," Kate Douglas Wiggin
The Atlantic, 1900

We think we get a kind of vague apprehension of what London means from the top of a bus better than anywhere else. We often set out on a fine morning, Salemina and I, and travel twenty miles in the day, though we have to double our twopenny fee several times to accomplish that distance.

We never know whither we are going, and indeed it is not a matter of great moment (I mean to a woman) where everything is new and strange, and where the driver, if one is fortunate enough to be on a front seat, tells one everything of interest along the way, and instructs one regarding a different route back into town.

"John the Yeggman," James Forbes
The Outlook, August 12, 1911
[A yeggman is a bank robber]

Such an outfit of tools, while not extraordinary, is exceptional. The careful yegg carries the "soup" in a rubber bottle. But, curiously, the more homicidal, notwithstanding the great danger to himself and his companions, is very apt to "tote" the explosive in a glass bottle in which it is readily detonated either by heat or by a sudden jar. All yeggdom is familiar with the death of "Baltimore Blue," of the infamous "Goat Hinch" band, who, while alighting from a freight train, was blown to pieces by the "soup" in his possession. Only a few months ago in a yegg camp on the outskirts of Seattle the careless brewing of nitroglycerine resulted in an explosion which killed three of the thieves and injured a round dozen more.

Wiggin was a children's book author and educator and Forbes was a Canadian playwright. Both passages show a casual voice that permits the reader to identify with the narrator. In the first, the author sounds like she is talking to a friend. Questions arise between the lines, especially when she mentions that not knowing where you're going is not important to a woman. The second uses crime slang—something Ade avoided in "Fables in Slang" because it was not common knowledge—to create a voice.

Certainly a number of more personal articles were published earlier. These are just a couple of examples, but they are fairly representative of magazine prose at the beginning of the mass-circulation period in the 1880s and the ensuing decades. Some might argue that a new, larger audience of middle-class readers accounts for the differences in voice. The audience had changed, but that fact doesn't explain a transformation in language, style, and voice. The readers did not write in with advice on how to reach them more effectively.

In the period between 1890 and 1910, new voices and styles were just starting to appear in the magazines, but the change had already happened at the newspapers. Writers such as Ade and Dunne in Chicago, Hutchins Hapgood and Abraham Cahan at the *Commercial Advertiser* in New York, and Stephen Crane, Richard Harding Davis, and several others had connected with a mass audience through their newspaper columns and journalism. The feature writers who worked for what Michael Schudson called the "story press" of the 1890s also pioneered a fresh, more personal, and literary style.[55] The distinction between the "information" press and the "story" press, according to David Eason, "is so entrenched in American culture that emphasizing the *story* in the term 'news story' is often a strategy for discrediting a report. Reporters, however, have no special method for determining the truth of a situation nor a special language for reporting their findings. They make sense out of events by telling stories about them."[56] New magazine writers could easily have read the columnists and the feature writers. Columns were syndicated in the late 1890s' market, and the mass-circulation newspapers reached huge urban audiences that included other writers. In a few cases, the columnists and feature writers *became* magazine writers. The connections appear evident, but direct evidence remains to be found. It's practically impossible to specify the "begats," that is, to say so-and-so's writing *begat* someone else's writing. It's just as hard to establish such connections with the New Journalism of the 1960s, but the style was so widely circulated that everyone was aware of it. Sometimes we can pin down a stylistic transformation, as at *The New Yorker* in the late 1930s, when the magazine hired a stream of feature writers from the newspapers, including A. J. Liebling and Joseph Mitchell, who transformed the publication's prose style. With the prose styles of the late nineteenth century, we can at least compare the magazines with the newspapers.

Here are some examples of column and feature-story prose from the urban newspapers of the 1890s—a time when magazines had not yet adopted a new voice. The first is from one of Ade's earliest columns, and the next two are from *The World,* one of New York's great story papers of the age. Note the different assumed relationship between the writer and the reader in these newspaper stories, with the writer at the same intellectual level as the reader and sharing unspoken assumptions about the way the world works. We can also see the use of scene in the narrative, something that later moved into magazine prose and was a distinguishing element in literary journalism.

From "All Roads Lead to the World's Fair," George Ade
Chicago News Record, January 12, 1893

No fancies lingered in the thoughts of the men at work. Their work and conversation had too much of practical problems in them. Some of the toilers were profane enough to have warmed up a reasonable area with sulfurous ejaculations. Down in the long tunnel that is to be turned into a mine under Chief Skiff's building, hardy laborers dug away at refractory frosted earth and thanked the fate that had put them under shelter. Up on the main floor of the building freight handlers were storing silver, tin and copper ores from New South Wales, stopping occasionally to relax stiffened fingers by the one stove that shone out in the big hall like a stump-fire on an iceberg.

"Frank Ellison Free:
Sing Sing's Doors Open and He Returns to New York"
The World, January 6, 1897, pp. 1–2

Just as the Sing Sing Prison clock marked 8.30 A.M. yesterday Warden Sage stepped briskly out of his office. There was a bit of a smile on his lips. Half a dozen blue-coated keepers loitered about the corridor, as many more curious villagers hung around in the roadway outside. The Warden walked to the head of the stairs leading to the pit, as the prisoners dub it.

"Sergeant," he said, quietly, "all ready for Ellison!"

The keepers craned their necks, the country folk crowded closer. There was a stir at the foot of the stairs leading down into the prison proper, and then the noisy clang of an opening gate. Upstairs walked a man nearly six feet tall, of stalwart presence and determined features. It was Frank Ellison, man about town, coming back to freedom.

> "A Day's Moves on the Checkerboard of Life
> in America's Metropolis"
> *The World,* January 5, 1898, p. 2

The house stood at No. 419 West Fifty-fourth street. It was an old wooden house and small, very small. It looked as if it had lost all its friends and suffered many hard knocks. Its windows gaped, its doors groaned and scraped the floor. Mrs. Burns owned it, but she lives in Yonkers.

In front of the old house thirty-eight small boys were feeding a sickly bonfire with scraps of damp wood. Mrs. Mary O'Neill, caretaker of the house, pitied the little chaps.

"You are good boys, so you are," said she, "and you may go into the house and take the straw you'll find and feed it to your fire."

Mrs. O'Neill was combining philanthropy with thrift, for she thought rightly that her back would never ache carrying out the rubbish the boys took. She made her error in not staying to watch them. The thirty-eight boys increased to ninety-eight. The street echoed with shrill cries of "Get your license!"

In the vocabulary of small boys talk those words mean, "Get something to feed our bonfire, so that you may enjoy our license to stand near it." The boys flew in and out of the little, old house. The last straw gone, they began ripping off loose boards.

In magazines of the early 1900s, we find a stance and a voice similar to that found in these newspaper columns and feature stories. Narrative, the use of scenes, characterization, and perspective increasingly made their way into magazine prose. Storytelling replaced the exposition of essayists. Point of view and symbolic perspectives were underlying foundations. The changes certainly were not universal, but styles were converging and reaching out to broader audiences. This new voice and style also lent itself to the development of an extended narrative form in the magazines that contributed to later developments in Muckraking and literary journalism.

From the sketches of Mark Twain and Opie Read to the stories of George Ade and Finley Peter Dunne to the social consciousness of Jack London and Hutchins Hapgood, literary journalism had grown into its new century.

THREE

A GENERATION GOES TRAVELING

I'd entertained visions of a real road trip, one that would begin with the simple exchange of a set of keys, maybe a phone number to call in case of mechanical problems, basically a rental-car kind of hello and good-bye. And then I would light out into the great unknown in search of the real face of China, some mysterious place behind the headlines that would reveal the evil plot that seeks to undo us—a vision, too, that would show us the future. It would require a bodyguard.
—Michael Paterniti (2006)

Of the three writers who most influenced literary journalism during and shortly after World War I, two were graduates of Harvard University and one graduated only from high school. They grew up in the great age of Muckraking journalism in the United States with its detailed analyses of policy, poverty, and injustice, and they all identified with the popular radicalism of their age. Although their nonfiction writing sometimes dove into labor issues and politics, their best literary journalism illustrates the form's close connection to travel writing.

One of the three—the high school graduate—would be

awarded the Pulitzer Prize and the Nobel Prize in Literature. All three worked in both nonfiction and fiction, and the substance of their writing generally grew from their travels. They were John Reed, John Dos Passos, and Ernest Hemingway.

In the early twentieth century, these three writers and a cohort of others traveled extensively in Europe to cover World War I and its aftermath, the Russian Revolution, and the Spanish Civil War; and Reed also covered a revolution in Mexico. They advanced the literature of war reporting as literary journalism by using the techniques and perspectives of travel writers. Travel writing and literary journalism again merged as the two forms had at the beginning in the 1700s and in Mark Twain's work, but this time it was in a dangerous and depressing environment. A desire to leave home and to visit the war-torn and emerging regions can be found at the same time in the fiction of Evelyn Waugh, Graham Greene, and D. H. Lawrence. Similar impulses to travel sent Hemingway, Dos Passos, and Reed on their journeys of discovery. More recently, a number of important writers have used travel writing to produce literary journalism, including Paul Theroux, V. S. Naipaul (*Among the Believers: An Islamic Journey,* and books about South America, India, and *A Turn in the South* about the United States), Edward Hoagland, Peter Matthiessen (*The Snow Leopard*), Jonathan Raban, Calvin Trillin of *The New Yorker,* David Quammen, Bill Bryson, Ian Frazier, John McPhee, and Barry Lopez.

Literary journalism and travel writing connect naturally in that both usually have a personal narrator, develop strong characters, and transform small events into symbolically larger meanings. In the cases of Reed, Dos Passos, and Hemingway, their courageous writing gave a glimpse of shattered post–World War I landscapes that, in most cases, their readers would never see and would never want to see.

• • •

Before the United States entered World War I in April 1917, a professor at Harvard University taught writing to a remarkable group of students, including two of these literary journalists. Some of his students would profoundly influence the development of literary journalism in the twentieth century, while others would become publishers and even win the Nobel Prize in Literature.

Charles Townsend Copeland, or "Copey" to his students, taught English 12 at Harvard. He has been called one of the greatest teachers ever and a person who changed more lives than any American of his era.[1] Copeland never admitted more than thirty students a year to English 12. Instruction included private tutorials in his office, where evaluations could often be harsh. While some students were granted the freedom to write about anything they wanted, others faced a weekly routine of a short story, then an essay, then a book review, and they were required to submit a brief translation every week. Often students hated him and discovered only later that his challenges had benefited them.

The long list of students who passed through Copeland's class includes—more or less in chronological order—Van Wyck Brooks, Maxwell Perkins, Conrad Aiken, Waldo Peirce, Heywood Broun, T. S. Eliot (who later won the Nobel Prize for his poetry), John Reed, Frederick L. Allen, Walter Lippmann, Robert Benchley, George Seldes, Gilbert Seldes, John Dos Passos, Malcolm Cowley, Bernard DeVoto, and Granville Hicks, among many others.[2] Several of Copeland's former students became publishers or editors, and quite a number found success in journalism. Walter Lippmann, an early friend of Reed's, was considered one of the greatest political journalists of the twentieth century.

Not everyone appreciated Copeland. T. S. Eliot said he never "hit it off" with Copeland during his junior-year studies in

1908–1909. "I don't really think, to be quite candid, that the course was very profitable to me," he said. Dos Passos said he shared an attitude of "armed neutrality" with Copeland. Bernard DeVoto recalled in the *Harvard Crimson* that his tutorial sessions with Copeland never revealed the instructor's true feelings. "I left with murder in my heart," DeVoto said. "But there was more than murder: there was a seething resolution to write, before I murdered him, just one set of twenty pages which would show the beggar that he was wrong. . . . Some years later I realized that this was the purpose behind those embellished groans—that, at his first glimpse of me, Copey had divined the best way to make me write."[3]

Copeland had worked as a reporter for the *Boston Advertiser* and the *Boston Post* before coming to Harvard. Van Wyck Brooks recalled that Copeland encouraged his students to go out and see life. This was not exactly advocacy of travel writing, but he did encourage his students to get away from the essayist's desk and confront the world. In his autobiography, Brooks noted that the young men of his era, "without knowing one another or even discussing their tastes," often ended up examining the squalor of the lower classes. His friend Max Perkins spent a summer "district visiting" at a settlement house "before he decided to go to New York like the Richard Harding Davis young man who took the first train from Yale to become a reporter. Copey, no doubt, the old newspaperman, had worked on Max's imagination." Brooks said Copeland's class readings revealed his taste for realism and the use of facts. "He included selections from Heywood Broun, Richard Harding Davis, Alexander Woollcott, O. Henry and R. C. Benchley,—entirely omitting Emerson, as he omitted Howells,—and his idols were the great journalist writers, especially Defoe."[4]

The human complications of the twentieth century were revealed in the first two decades of the century. A generation of American writers came of age as the country emerged from an economic depression in the 1890s, reformed during the era of Muckraking, watched a revolutionary war in Mexico, and then fought the nation's first modern war. World War I included protracted trench warfare, human wave attacks, poison gas, the new inventions of the machine gun, the flame-thrower, and the tank, and the slaughter of soldiers in unimagined numbers. The Great War, as it was called, permitted a generation of writers to leave home and travel in the exotic and storied lands of Europe. They responded to the opportunity with some of their best work. "May you live in interesting times" may be a Chinese insult, but for journalists it is a prayer for success.

Changes in literary style often accompany periods of social stress or political struggle. The arrival of immigrants in the urban areas during the 1890s, World War I, the Great Depression of the 1930s, and the Vietnam War all coincided with innovations in literary journalism. The writers involved in the transformations had different backgrounds as children and young adults—Jack London was a street kid, and John Reed, another westerner, was a Harvard graduate; John Dos Passos grew up as an experienced European traveler and earned a Harvard degree, while Ernest Hemingway, the son of a physician, only graduated from Oak Park High School. Reed, Dos Passos, and Hemingway came from privileged backgrounds, but nothing held them together as writers until they became expatriates in Paris. These young writers were often touched more by an expatriate sensibility than by the wanderlust that had moved hobos such as Jack London. They shared a complex love of travel, literature, and adventure.

Copeland's advice to go out and see life seemed to motivate the entire group, and not just those who passed through his classes. Hemingway worked as an apprentice newspaper reporter in Kansas City for a few months before he left for Europe to serve as an ambulance driver during World War I. After the war, he returned to Europe as a writer for the *Toronto Star*. Reed and Dos Passos sought out the experiences of war and European conflict, placing their travels and personal narratives at the core of the era's dramatic conflicts.

One of Copeland's favorite and most famous students, John Reed, went out, saw life in the wars and revolutions of the early twentieth century, and died in Moscow at age thirty-three.

Reed grew up in a wealthy family in Portland, Oregon. As a child he read Mark Twain and journalist Bill Nye. His father, Charles Jerome Reed, was a businessman who served as a U.S. marshal during Theodore Roosevelt's presidency. The elder Reed had an association with Lincoln Steffens and together they broke the Oregon Land Fraud Ring, which alienated Reed from his business associates.[5]

In 1906, John Reed entered Harvard, where he became an eager student, an athlete, and a radical. Copeland watched Reed rise to national prominence after graduation. Reed reported for the magazines on life among Pancho Villa's revolutionaries in Mexico and delivered eyewitness accounts of the war in Europe and of the Bolshevik revolution in Russia. When Reed returned to Boston, he often made appearances in Copeland's classes. Reed maintained his close relationship with Copeland until their politics diverged; Reed himself suggested that it would be safer for Copeland if they ended their correspondence.

As a young, ambitious reporter, Reed traveled to extraordinary places and used his growing talent to compete with Richard Harding Davis and Stephen Crane. His literary skills matured in long magazine pieces on the Mexican revolution and on the evangelist Billy Sunday, and in the gruesome experience of reporting from the Eastern Front during World War I. In 1916 he married Louise Bryant, a journalist and feminist. Their love affair and collaboration was the subject of a Warren Beatty and Diane Keaton movie, *Reds,* in 1981. In the period between 1914 and 1917, Reed achieved stardom writing for *The Metropolitan,* a fashionable New York monthly magazine with a circulation of a million copies. Other writers for the magazine included Rudyard Kipling, H. G. Wells, Walter Lippmann, Joseph Conrad, D. H. Lawrence, Richard Harding Davis, Ring Lardner, and Theodore Roosevelt.[6] Reed also wrote for *The Masses,* a small and genuinely radical journal in Greenwich Village. His conflict over the styles and politics of the two magazines would eventually resolve in favor of revolution and end his career with the large-circulation national magazines.

Reed combined literary journalism, war reporting, and travel writing in *Insurgent Mexico,* which contains his first-person coverage of Pancho Villa's revolutionary forces during the 1913 Mexican revolution. Reed dedicated *Insurgent Mexico* to Copeland, saying, in part, "And as I wrote these impressions of Mexico I couldn't help but think that I never would have seen what I did see had it not been for your teaching me. I can only add my word to what so many who are writing already have told you: That to listen to you is to learn how to see the hidden beauty of the visible world; that to be your friend is to try to be intellectually honest."[7] This book began Reed's mature career as a literary journalist.

While at Harvard Reed had pursued poetry and short story writing. The techniques learned there helped him create literary journalism. "Rather than applying the lessons learned in his journalism to the production of novels," wrote Daniel Lehman, "Reed used his poetic voice and the sketches he created and marketed as fictional tales to develop the descriptive power and sense of dialogue that he was to use successfully in his nonfiction." His book on Mexico rearranged the chronology of his experiences to place his chapter called "Meester's Flight" at the dramatic climax of the first section of the book, about three-quarters of the way through the section. He also changed the name of one of his informants, a war profiteer named MacDonald, or "Mac" in Reed's notebooks, who introduced him to Villa's army. In the book, Mac became an officer named Antonio Montoya. This practice would not work today and was probably done at the time to rid the manuscript of a shady gunrunning character. Although Mac opened doors, he was not consistent with Reed's growing anticapitalistic spirit. The rest of the manuscript coincides with the notes that Reed took at the time.[8]

Reed treated his war coverage in Mexico, and later in World War I, almost as travel writing. In travel writing, the narrator takes our hand to guide us through a strange land. The author's voice plays a natural role in scenes that permit readers to imaginatively live the experience. The travel writer adopts a strategic personality, according to contemporary writer Jonathan Raban. "There are a whole lot of other times—and I know this from my own periods of block at the typewriter—that I can think of tons of things to say," Raban said, "but they are not within the rhetoric of the book, so they won't fit."[9] Tracy Kidder once told me that a writer's choice of point of view determines everything that follows in a story. What gets said has to fit the narrator like a well-worn pair of jeans. In Reed's case, he adopted a personality in *Insurgent Mexico* and stuck with it. Reed's travel reports helped shape an understanding of world events by describing what was happening at that time and place. In such cases, travel writing often shades into literary journalism. Examples can be found in Hemingway's early reporting, in Dos Passos's travel books after the war, and in Reed's writing from Mexico, the Eastern Front, and Russia.

Narrators in travel writing adopt perspectives that turn them into companions for readers as we move through a set of experiences. Adopting the perspective of *tourists,* trailing around behind a guide on a package tour, often makes us feel illegitimate and out of place. Mark Twain used this fact of travel to his advantage in *Innocents Abroad* (1869), where his point concerned the social position of Americans. Today, the stance of *tourist* lacks authority for most writers. Travelers are able to adopt different identities. Describing oneself as a *reporter* gives a reason to be there and an excuse for asking probing questions. Being a *travel writer* is even better because it is less threatening and invites strangers to tell stories about a place. The most authentic but uncomfortable identity for travelers is as a *participant.* Joining the activities of your subjects may give momentary access to their feelings. But if your trip to a Caribbean island is suddenly beset by a hurricane, your connections to your previous life and identities can be destroyed. You participate at the same level as everyone else. Your money, your education, and your self-confidence won't rescue you from cholera, typhoid fever, or hunger and won't make the sun rise any sooner during a long, sleepless, wind-swept, and rainy night.

"The only aspect of our travels that is guaranteed to hold an audience is disaster," said Martha Gellhorn. "Horror journeys," she said, cause us to react the same way: "frayed and bitter at the time,

proud afterwards. Nothing is better for self-esteem than survival."
Homer Bigart, a *New York Times* war correspondent from World
War II to Vietnam, once told fellow war reporter Neil Sheehan
that one way to stay alive in a war zone was, "Never play tourist."
He might have added that one does not want to play participant
either. The participant's authenticity in war reporting has attracted
many writers, such as Michael Herr during the Vietnam War, but
often with unfortunate results, as was the case with John Reed
during the Russian Revolution.[10]

Patrick Holland and Graham Huggan, in their book *Tourists with
Typewriters,* list a range of travel narrative types with as much variety as literary journalism. "Travel narratives run from picaresque
adventure to philosophical treatise, political commentary, ecological parable, and spiritual quest. They borrow freely from history,
geography, anthropology, and social science, often demonstrating
great erudition, but without seeing fit to respect the rules that gov-
ern conventional scholarship," they wrote. They argue that travel
has become a form from which culture itself can be analyzed.[11]

Holland and Huggan also suggest that some travel writers, like
autobiographers, face a struggle between fact and fiction. Many in-
vest their narratives with solid reporting and would chafe at any
suggestion that they make things up. Nevertheless, a story must be
chosen from all the possible stories that a traveler might have in
mind.

"Yet actual journeys aren't like stories at all," said Jonathan
Raban, pointing to the problem in choosing a storyline:

> At the time, they seem to be mere strings of haps and mishaps,
> without point or pattern. You get stuck. You meet someone you
> like. You get a rude going-over in a bar. You get lost. You get
> lonely. You get interested in architecture. You get diarrhoea.

You get invited to a party. You get frightened. A stretch of country takes you by surprise. You get homesick. You are, by rapid turns, engrossed, bored, alert, dull, happy, miserable, well and ill. Every day tends to seem out of connection with every other day, until living from moment to moment turns into a habit and travelling itself into a form of ordinary life. You can't remember when it wasn't like this. There is a great deal of liberating pleasure to be had from being abroad in the world, continuously on the move, like one of Baudelaire's lost balloons, but a journey, at least as long as it is actually taking place, is the exact opposite of a story. It is a shapeless, unsifted, endlessly shifting accumulation of experience.[12]

If the story sifted from experience qualifies as literary journalism, it must be accurate, and the story needs a central character with an identity—be it tourist, travel writer, or participant.

While covering the Mexican revolution, Reed the reporter suffered a transformation from reporter into involuntary participant. He traveled with Villa's revolutionaries and created detailed portraits of the ordinary troops. One morning a soldier stepped into Reed's room and announced that about a thousand *colorados,* or government troops, were approaching. Reed recorded the hasty preparations of the revolutionaries, who mounted their horses and carried their rifles into battle. Without much warning, a company of *colorados* emerged from an arroyo, "hundreds of little black figures riding everywhere through the chaparral," Reed wrote. The revolutionaries launched into wild retreat as bullets whizzed past and crashed into the walls. "Come on Meester!" shouted one of Reed's friends. "Let's go!" Reed ran into the desert, tossing away his cumbersome camera and overcoat.

I ran. I wondered what time it was. I wasn't very frightened. Everything still was so unreal, like a page out of Richard Harding Davis. It just seemed to me that if I didn't get away I wouldn't be doing my job well. I kept thinking to myself: "Well, this is certainly an experience. I'm going to have something to write about."[13]

Two riders appeared behind as Reed and a young Indian boy were running together. Bullets were fired. The boy was hit before he changed course into the chaparral. The riders followed and killed him, giving Reed a moment to escape. Reed tripped and rolled down a hill, landing in a little arroyo, where he hid from the two riders. Half an hour later, still hearing shots fired behind him, Meester Reed ran away over a hill. Later that morning, he met a man who had killed a *colorado* and who directed Reed toward the safety of a *hacienda,* some four hours away.

Travel writing had gotten out of hand. Reed was transformed from reporter and observer with a Harvard education into revolutionary participant, at least as far as the government troops were concerned—and since they were firing real bullets, only their concerns counted. It made a wonderful pinnacle chapter—he placed the chase about 80 percent of the way through his opening narrative on "Desert War"—but no sensible writer gets into these circumstances intentionally. As Ted Conover has explained, you don't take the ferryboat that you know will capsize just to get a good story. Nor did Reed. Instead, he put himself in a position where *something* could happen—where he could watch, talk to the participants, experience their lives, and write vivid prose about it. Conover often follows similar strategies today, riding the rails with hobos, picking oranges in Arizona with illegal Mexican immigrants, and becoming a prison guard at Sing Sing.

Writing for *The Metropolitan* and for *The Masses,* Reed became a national superstar. Editor Carl Hovey said Reed's "writing was like the sweep of a sudden wind come to shake the closed windows of the literary scene out of their frames."[14] He recognized that war is boring and brutal and very rarely has the drama that writers covet. In that respect, his coverage of a war zone resembled Joan Didion's point of view more than that of standard war reporting. He spent time talking with ordinary people, and he made Pancho Villa seem human on the page. Like Crane, Reed did not seek to glorify warfare. He resisted the demands of editors for more violent coverage. Instead, Reed and Crane wanted to talk about the spirituality of the people they covered, about the conditions under which they lived, and about their motivation and endurance. The dramatic climax of "Meester's Flight" in *Insurgent Mexico,* however, came at the moment when Reed became a participant. This was, of course, the very drama his editors wanted.

Reed was a well-educated American in a foreign land among poor farmers turned warriors—people his readers considered inferior. He made an effort to put his readers there and to introduce characters in ways that encouraged empathy with them and with Pancho Villa. Like a good travel writer, Reed met new people in strange places and discovered their personal habits and customs. He described the feelings that those people had in a time of revolution. He conveyed everyday talk and the feel of ordinary life among the soldiers. In April 1914, Reed sent copies of his *Metropolitan* articles on Mexico to Copeland with a note that said, "If there's anything of good in them, it is due entirely to you and English 12. I feel that perhaps they are the first piece of reporting I have done. If they're bad, it's your fault, too." Copeland replied— no doubt referring to "Meester's Flight":—"It is all good, and more than good. As you know, I like to have writing march, and so I took my chief personal pleasure from the beginning of the skirmish to the end."[15]

World War I began in 1914 with cascading events. The assassination of Austrian Archduke Francis Ferdinand and his wife in Sarajevo in June led Austria to declare war on Serbia in July, followed by Germany on Russia, France, and Belgium in August. Britain responded by declaring war on Germany.

In the three years before the United States entered the war, Charles Copeland at Harvard acted as an unofficial recruiter for the ambulance service and for the Canadian, British, and French armed forces then engaged in battle. In 1916, having finished English 12 and graduated from Harvard, Dos Passos joined the ambulance service. Despite stories of the sinking of the *Lusitania* in 1915 and the conquest of Belgium, Dos Passos said, "So far as I can remember, as so often has happened in my life, I was on the fence." Eventually, he fell off the fence toward the side of pacifism: "I can't speak for the others, but Wilson's switch to a war policy gave me my first great disillusionment with statesmen and politicians. By the way, I still think that if we had kept out of that war and insisted on a negotiated peace—T. R.'s [Teddy Roosevelt's] attitude toward the Russo-Japanese war—the twentieth would have been a far easier century to live in for the tribes of men." Around eleven thousand Harvard students and graduates enlisted in the war, and 373 of them died.[16]

When Dos Passos became a driver for the Norton-Harjes Volunteer Ambulance in 1917, the war had been under way for years. In the years before the United States became engaged in World War I, driving an ambulance provided a way to experience war without joining a foreign armed force—according to Dos Passos, it was "a de luxe way of seeing the warfare of those days."[17]

Hemingway was also there, although he was three years younger than Dos Passos and only a high school graduate. In 1917, Hemingway was eagerly trying to learn the ways of the world. Only about 4 percent of eighteen- to twenty-four-year-old Americans attended college then, a figure that would grow by a factor of ten by the 1970s.[18] In Hemingway's era, the college graduate was a social oddity, although his school magazine reported that he planned to attend the University of Illinois and major in journalism.[19] Instead, he took a cub-reporting job at the *Kansas City Star.* A few months later he volunteered as a Red Cross ambulance driver and sailed for Europe.

Dos Passos and Hemingway met in May 1918 in Italy, where they both served as ambulance drivers. Hemingway could later recall the meeting, but Dos Passos had little recollection of it, or maybe he just could not remember the name. Later wounded while running from a trench mortar explosion and hit by a machine-gun bullet, Hemingway recovered in an Italian hospital and crafted a story of his own war heroism. A mature eighteen when he joined the ambulance service, Hemingway looked far older than his years. Back in his hometown of Oak Park, Illinois, a photo of him a year later shows a tall man with the dashingly stylish affectations of a mustache, a flashy Italian cloak, and military boots. He appears to be about thirty. Hemingway and Dos Passos next met in 1922 in Paris, the expatriate capital of the postwar world, and became close friends, at least from 1924 to 1937.[20]

During the war, Copeland's students from Harvard sent letters that eventually filled six bound volumes in his library. Reed wrote from Bucharest on August 8, 1915, to say that he detested Rumania.

> It is a comic opera country; officers in salmon-pink and baby-blue uniforms stolen out of "Rupert of Hentzau" sit at the cafés sipping ices and eating tartlets all day, or drive up and down the Calea Victoriei in cabs, winking at the throngs of women who parade there. They have bloated white faces. There is a dinky Hohenzollern king here, a dinky throne and court, a dinky aristocracy of fake Byzantine Emperor's spawn. Everybody is crooked. Everyone is disobliging,—shopkeepers prefer to rob you than to make a legitimate sale,—I mean that they will refuse to sell at a handsome profit when you refuse to be robbed. It is the most expensive place to live in the world. It reeks with millionaires, grown rich by hogging the oil-wells, or by the absentee ownership of vast lands, where the peasants sweat out their lives for a franc a day. Whenever they can, the rich here go to Paris or the Riviera to spend their money.[21]

Another one of Copeland's students, Waldo Peirce, who was Reed's friend in college, wrote in May 1916 about his winter at Haute Alsace, where one could crawl out to the lines for a look at the surrounding forest.

> First come the maimed trees, then the skeletons of those dead with their boots on, then a bare stump or two, a few ankle bones, then nothing. Before the war all was forest, and a damned thick one at that; then all our goodly timber grown to its prime, lulled into a false security, sun basking *en beau temps,* buffeting and jostling their neighbors in the wind. Crash, one fine day—out of a clear sky they all get unmercifully shat on—the nubbin, the old ridge, the spur, the razor back, whatever you call it, loses its pelt,

after its pelt its hide, after that its whole scorched anatomy is drubbed, hammered, ploughed, furrowed, ripped, scoured, torn, shattered (consult dictionary of synonyms) and beplastered with every caliber of obus that whines—for they whine, the bastards, they whine to tell you of their coming, and give the flesh a moment to goose itself in, and a damned pagan, like some of us, to find a religion.[22]

Peirce used the trees as symbols for the soldiers, but Reed on the Eastern Front saw the real thing.

For his *Metropolitan* war coverage and later for his book *The War on the Eastern Front,* Reed traveled in the war zone starting in August 1914, during which time he accompanied French, German, and Austrian troops to their battlefields on the front in such places as Hungarian Croatia, Austrian Bosnia, Montenegro, Herzegovinia, and Slovenia. In 1915, a genial young Austrian captain escorted him to the arena of the Battle Above the Clouds, which lasted for fifty-four days while the Austrians and Serbs attacked each other from trenches. Each side lost about ten thousand soldiers, and after the Austrians captured the battlefield they abandoned it. From a high vantage point, Reed described the deserted ground strewn with "brass cartridge-shells, trace-leathers, bits of Serbian uniforms, and the wheels of shattered cannon limbers." Reed, too, saw the shredded forests that Waldo Peirce described. More than metaphor lurked here:

On one side of this open space were the Serbian trenches, on the other side the Austrian. Barely twenty yards separated the two. Here and there both trenches merged into immense pits, forty feet around and fifty feet deep, where the enemy had undermined and dynamited them. The ground between was humped into irregular piles of earth. Looking closer, we saw a ghastly thing: From these little mounds protruded pieces of uniform, skulls with draggled hair, upon which shreds of flesh still hung; white bones with rotting hands at the end, bloody bones sticking from boots such as the soldiers wear. An awful smell hung over the place. Bands of half-wild dogs slunk at the edge of the forest, and far away we could see two tearing at something that lay half-covered on the ground. Without a word the captain pulled out his revolver and shot. One dog staggered and fell thrashing, then lay still—the other fled howling into the trees; and instantly from the depths of the wood all around came a wolfish, eerie howling in answer, dying away along the edge of the battlefield for miles.

We walked on the dead, so thick were they—sometimes our feet sank through into pits of rotting flesh, crunching bones. Little holes opened suddenly, leading deep down and swarming with gray magnots [*sic*]. Most of the bodies were covered only with a film of earth, partly washed away by the rain—many were not buried at all. Piles of Austrians lay as they had fallen in desperate charge, heaped along the ground in attitudes of terrible action. Serbians were among them. In one place the half-eaten skeletons of an Austrian and a Serbian were entangd, [*sic*] their arms and legs wrapped about each other in a deathgrip that could not even now be loosened. *Behind* the front line of Austrian trenches was a barbed wire barricade, significant of the spirit of the men pinned in that death trap—for they were mostly Serbians from the Austrian Slav provinces, driven at the point of a revolver to fight their brothers.[23]

His article "At the Serbian Front" appeared in *The Metropolitan* in October 1915, and in 1916 in *The War in Eastern Europe*. The 1918 edition of that book, published by Charles Scribner's Sons, omits the chapter called "The Valley of Corpses" containing the above passage. By that time, the United States had entered the war, and Reed's genial Austrian captain had become an official enemy, if he survived.

Despite the drama contained in the battlefield scene, Reed saw little of real warfare. Instead, he wrote a travel narrative of Eastern Europe and Russia. Reed said the most important thing was to know "how the different peoples live; their environment, tradition, and the revealing things they do and say."[24]

Reed's disaffection with war estranged him from *The Metropolitan*. He journeyed with Louise Bryant to Russia, where they became friends with V. I. Lenin and witnessed the revolution of November 1917. His most famous book, *Ten Days That Shook the World,* reported Lenin's victorious uprising and was scheduled for serial publication in *The Masses.* Back in the United States, two laws—the Espionage Act of 1917 and the Sedition Act of 1918— were used to deport radicals, communists, socialists, and labor organizers, and, as always happens with sedition laws, to suppress opinions that in this case did not support the entry of the United States into World War I. Reed was indicted for opposing the war. So was *The Masses,* which was put out of business. The government took his papers and notes from Russia. By 1920, after recovering his papers and completing *Ten Days,* Reed was back in Moscow attending meetings. He became feverish and delirious, and at the age of thirty-three he died of typhus. He is the only American buried inside the wall of the Kremlin as a hero of the Russian people.

Dos Passos, Hemingway, and Reed belonged to the vaguely defined culture of expatriates in Europe following the Great War. Donald Pizer, in his book on the expatriates in Paris, described it this way: "Reduced to its most fundamental level, the expatriate or self-exile state of mind is compounded out of the interrelated conditions of the rejection of a homeland and the desire for and acceptance of an alternative place. The world one has been bred in is perceived to suffer from intolerable inadequacies and limitations; another world seems to be free of these failings and to offer a more fruitful way of life."[25] American writers often found socialism a viable political perspective, at least for a period of time. Socialism and artistic freedom did not fare well in the States during wartime repression. A more open, tolerant, and sophisticated Paris became the center of their world.

The German forces had been stopped twenty-five miles from Paris in 1914, and the stagnation of trench warfare on the Western Front spared the city from devastation. If any city could be considered the cultural capital of the world after World War I, it would be Paris. During the twenties, a literary and artistic renaissance took place in the salons, where American expatriates mixed with Cubist painters, poets, novelists, and revolutionaries. It attracted the best and the brightest of that generation. Newspaper work provided a modest income for a few journalists, who were the leading edge of the larger American colony in Paris that "numbered perhaps (it was always a hazy matter) six thousand when Hemingway arrived, thirty thousand and rising by the middle of the decade, sixty thousand in all of France," according to Ronald Weber's *News of Paris.*[26] Many felt the States were hopelessly mired in Babbitism, crude commerce, and repressive conformity, while Paris offered the contrast of art, music, culture, and romance. Writers such as Hemingway could escape from Kansas City or Toronto and sit in a café writing a short story that would be filled with the power of realism, adventure, and rebellion. Paris inspired creativity and let writers imagine they were freed from their backgrounds and upbringing.

The carefully crafted literary journalism of this era came from those who traveled and saw the emerging modern world in its raw forms. Before the end of the war, Reed had traveled to the Eastern Front and Russia. After the war, Dos Passos and Hemingway traveled separately in Spain and the Middle East. Dos Passos went to Damascus and Baghdad. Both wrote about their travels. The expatriates who used Paris as a home base were frequently recent graduates of Harvard or Princeton, although Hemingway was an exception. By his early twenties, Hemingway was a leading figure in the Paris group. He had found a home for his literary impulses. So had Dos Passos, although he was older than Hemingway and came from a completely different background.[27]

Dos Passos differed from most expatriates. Hemingway, for example, was a newcomer to Europe and wrote many pieces for the Toronto newspaper about the wonders of traveling in Europe. Dos Passos, however, had grown up there. Between his birth in 1896 and his marriage in 1930, Dos Passos spent nearly fourteen years outside the United States. As a child, he lived and traveled in Europe with his mother in what he described as a "hotel childhood." Bred as much in Europe as in America, and speaking French before he learned English, he fit uneasily among the disaffected expatriates. If he had a sense of intolerable inadequacies in America, those feelings were probably acquired from his classmates at Choate and Harvard and from friends such as Hemingway who had not grown up in Europe. Yet, Dos Passos loved Paris, and he lived among some of the most famous of expatriates.

Pizer suggested that lingering shell shock from the war produced the expatriate mood, quoting Ezra Pound on soldiers who:

> walked eye-deep in hell
> believing in old-men's lies, then unbelieving
> came home, home to a lie,
> home to many deceits, home to old lies.[28]

Pizer argued that the mix of a Harvard group infatuated with socialism, the vision of the Russian Revolution, and revulsion for the Great War engendered in Dos Passos an expatriate's attraction for Paris. That may be, but it is hard to imagine that Dos Passos felt dissatisfaction with America any more fully than he felt the pull of a European childhood.

Instead, Dos Passos seemed a natural-born traveler and a polymorphous writer. At this time in his life, he actively wrote novels, journalism, and poems—much as he would have done for Copeland's class at Harvard—and he made watercolor drawings that illustrated his book *Orient Express*. As Shelley Fisher Fishkin said, "Dos Passos wrote straightforward factual reportage, autobiographical reminiscences, cultural history, literary criticism, and allegorical fictional narratives." In the fourteen years after his Harvard graduation in 1916, he published sixty pieces of nonfiction reportage in *The Nation,* the *New York Tribune, New Masses,* the *Daily Worker, The New Republic,* and journals such as *Bookman* and *Dial*.[29] Hemingway was similarly attached to journalism but craved recognition as a writer of short stories and fiction. Literary historians tend to dismiss Hemingway's journalism as mere preparation for writing fiction. Charles A. Fenton, for example, said that "the principal instrument of [Hemingway's] literary apprenticeship was journalism."[30] Both Dos Passos and Hemingway sought the public eye and favor at a time when there was relatively little praise or status for journalism. After Hemingway returned to Toronto, his aspirations started to bear fruit with the publication of his short stories, and he found the routine assignments of the newspaper a waste of time. Burdened with pride and conflicts with an editor, Hemingway left the newspaper, but he continued to publish journalism throughout his life.

Dos Passos wrote letters from Europe to his friends, constantly mentioning the state of his published works that for the most part were unsuccessful. He expressed his feelings in letters to former classmates as he journeyed across the Arab world in 1921. During his travels across the Syrian desert to Damascus, he reported his diminishing finances and described the trip to Teheran from Constantinople: "by boat to Batum, then by a buggy Bolo express, very jolly, full of tea and Kavaritch and Ruskin conversation—to Tiflis. Thence on various box cars through Armenia where everyone was dying of cholera and typhus and starvation, and Adjerbaidjan to the Persian border. Then in an insane four-horse cab known as a phaeton across deserts and mountains and the fresh trails of nomad raiders, in the company of a Persian doctor who was a great judge of melons, to Teheran, where I recline in somewhat exhausted state at this funny little French hotel."[31]

At that moment, Dos Passos had two novels being considered by New York publishing houses, one of which, *One Man's Initiation: 1917,* would sell sixty-three copies in its first six months. The other would be rejected.[32] The successful travel writing and journalism that grew out of his desert journey in 1922 would later become *Orient Express* (1927). During this trip, Dos Passos expressed his ambivalence about journalism in several letters. "Incidentally," he wrote to Rumsey Marvin, "I'm no more a journalist than I am a guinea pig and the sooner I go home and get to work writing and stop playing Richard Harding Davis the better."[33] Strange sights and sounds were no consolation. In October 1921, he wrote from Baghdad, "Nowhere have I seen East and West, so-called, mingle to worse advantage than in this dismal spot. Still it may all be mere humors—shake the malarial quinine bottle! Now my great problem is how to get out of this God damn place."[34] He objected to the kind of travel that separated him from the local residents. In another letter from Baghdad, he wrote, "If one's got to travel one should have the courage of one's convictions, take a staff and a begging bowl and a jar of hashish like a proper dervish and a fig for the city bred world. But this half-ass Cook's Miss Humphrey Ward manner of wandering is too low for words. If one hasn't any more imagination one should stay at home and learn accounting. Journalism is the stinkingest of compromises. One comes into contact with nobody but personages, chambermaids and drummers."[35] This business of interviewing the high-placed and at other times meeting only the chambermaids and fellow residents of the world's hotels—"a low form of existence," he called it—suggests that Dos Passos wanted to write instead about ordinary people as he traveled. "Journalism is the business of fussing with bigbugs—and above anything on earth I detest bigbugs," he said.[36] Literary journalism also generally dispenses with bigbugs.

Hemingway disparaged journalism in similar terms yet he continued to write long-form narrative journalism. Some of his best newspaper reporting took place in Thrace, which included portions of Bulgaria, Greece, and Turkey, and in Afghanistan when he was working for the *Toronto Star.* His terse style and cynical tone matched the endless streams of refugees who trudged past his hotel. Reporting on a twenty-mile line of staggering refugees from Adrianople, Hemingway wrote: "It is a silent procession. Nobody even grunts. It is all they can do to keep moving. Their brilliant peasant costumes are soaked and draggled. Chickens dangle by their feet from the carts. . . . A husband spreads a blanket over a woman in labor in one of the carts to keep off the driving rain. She is the only person making a sound. Her little daughter looks at her in horror and begins to cry. And the procession keeps moving."[37] In his newspaper dispatches, one can see the beginnings of his tone, which in this case resembles Dos Passos on the "twilight of things." During his lifetime, Hemingway published four nonfiction books: *Death in the Afternoon* in 1932 about Spanish bullfighting; *The Dangerous Summer* in 1960 about a bullfighting controversy; *Green Hills of Africa* centering on his experiences on an African safari; and *A Moveable Feast* about his friends and experiences in Europe. His largest book—not that counting pages means much for a man who specialized in a spare style—is the collection of his *Toronto Star* dispatches edited by William White. The news stories in *Dateline: Toronto* were written during 1920–1924 in the aftermath of World War I.

Dos Passos continued to write magazine journalism for many years as he covered politics and the Depression in the United States. Some of his work, particularly "Detroit, City of Leisure," met the standards of literary journalism. Many reports were later reconfigured to create his masterwork, a trilogy of novels called *U.S.A.* that includes *The 42nd Parallel* (1930), *Nineteen Nineteen* (1932), and *The Big Money* (1933). The three books worked the edge of the fiction-nonfiction border, weaving together fictional and historical characters, nonfiction biographies, and autobiographical sketches in stream-of-consciousness prose. In his "Newsreel" vignettes in *U.S.A.,* Dos Passos created a montage of newspaper headlines, clichés, propaganda, and popular culture, slightly out of context, that lets us examine such everyday expression in a fresh way. The Newsreels tied his novels to real time by assembling the phrases that were echoing through everyone's head at the time. Dos Passos researched these in the Chicago Public

Library; each one is painstakingly exact for a given year. They provide a realistic context for his narrative. Our current media contribute similar language snippets—headlines, images from television and Internet video, jokes from standup comedians, little radio reports, song lyrics, advertising images, all blended together to give a feel for a *period of time.* It's almost like travel writing, but more about time than place. The images and sounds echo in our thoughts, and Dos Passos was able to translate them into prose. It's part of the *felt* quality of time. Fishkin said, "*U.S.A.* is a book whose unique strength stems from its firm footing in the world of fact and its brilliant restructuring of that world to extricate the reader from preconditioned patterns of perception."[38] Not since Daniel Defoe's *Journal of the Plague Year* had the forms been so distinctively and creatively merged as in Dos Passos's fictional trilogy.

Of the several forms that nonfiction writing takes—the essay, the history, biography and autobiography, the scientific report, and the news report—one that arrives early and retains its shape over time is the travel report.

The earliest forms of eighteenth-century prose writing in English are said to be closely connected to travel writing in such forms as ships' captains' logs. Daniel Defoe wrote about his tour of the British Isles in 1724, and Dr. Samuel Johnson wrote about his trip to Scotland and the Hebrides Islands in 1775. Europeans coming to America in the seventeenth and eighteenth centuries wrote reports that established the style—the confident upper-class English traveler visiting a country peopled by primitive, backward, or quaint inhabitants. But travel writing is much more than taking notes on a foreign land. Jonathan Raban, an English travel writer and literary journalist, said, "To the idea that the 'travel book' simply writes itself, or is a more or less decorated version of the ship's log: *hooey!*"[39]

Mark Twain reversed the pattern of the educated and well-heeled tourist writing about primitives with *Innocents Abroad*. Right after the American Civil War he took a package tour and dribbled cigar ash and sarcasm all over the famous European and Middle Eastern cultural arenas. His reports were serialized in San Francisco and New York newspapers. According to Raban, Twain gave American travel writers their attitude and stance with respect to the rest of the world. "Writing it, he hammered out a style of plainspoken moral skepticism," Raban said, "intimate in tone, funny, deflating and superbly flexible. This is the book in which Twain found his voice—a voice which America at large immediately recognized as her own."[40]

In the twentieth century, travel writing and literature are intricately bound together. We think of life as a journey, as a story with a beginning and ending during which we meet strange people and have adventures. Journeys suggest stories. As a historical antecedent of literary journalism, travel writing brings personal voice along with a narrator or guide. It tends to provide portraits of ordinary life. It delivers dramatic scenes that a writer can collect in a butterfly net while dashing through the country. These fluttering small experiences take on a symbolic or a representative value for the reader. While selective, travel writing can have meaning. It has an open-ended style that encourages literary innovation.

Like autobiography, a travel report also depends on our selective memories of details recalled after the fact. Raban has said that keeping a journal rarely helps his travel writing, except for stray facts and dates. The memory eventually produces the narrative. "Memory . . . is always telling stories to itself, filing experience in narrative form. It feeds irrelevancies to the shredder, enlarges on crucial details, makes links and patterns, finds symbols, constructs plots. In memory, the journey takes shape and grows; in the notebook it merely languishes, with the notes themselves like a pile of cigarette butts confronted the morning after a party."[41]

Raban's comments were echoed by Martha Gellhorn when she said, in her travel memoir, that "the trouble is that experience is useless without memory."[42] In my own conversations with contemporary literary journalist Tracy Kidder, he said that at the end of his research and interviewing for a book he often has a stack of eighty or more notebooks filled with details. He writes a first draft without opening the notebooks, relying instead on the story that has been shaping itself in his head. Later he goes back and finds the exact quotes, corrects the details, and confirms his memories. Memory, however, provides the story.

Travel writing can be about the place visited or about the times experienced while one lives among strangers away from home. Raban said, "In fact the literary journey is more likely to be about time than place."[43] In Dos Passos's "Red Caucasus," for example, it's understood that the world he witnessed was formed by the events of the moment. This is not the ordinary culture of *the place* but rather *the times* as a product of recent world events. Journalism can be descriptive, but a focus on the feelings that inhabit a particular time in a particular place and what they mean to someone are the hallmarks of literary journalism—and anthropology for that matter.

Raban argued that critics and scholars have largely ignored travel writing. Since Raban made that argument in 1981, a number of books have dealt with the literature of travel, including Larzer Ziff's *Return Passages: Great American Travel Writing 1780–1910* (2000). Houghton Mifflin has started a Best American Travel

Writing series with volumes edited by Paul Theroux, Bill Bryson, Ian Frazier, and Jamaica Kincaid. But on the whole, the form has been as thinly appreciated as literary journalism. Raban said of travel writing—and we could substitute literary journalism for travel in this passage:

> At present the form stands in a similarly dubious position to that once occupied by landscape painting. As recently as 1800, landscapes were commonly thought of as a species of painterly journalism. Real art meant pictures of allegorical or biblical subjects. A landscape was a mere record or report. As such, it couldn't be judged for its imaginative vision, its capacity to create or embody a world of complex meanings; instead it was measured on the rack of its "accuracy," its dumb fidelity to the geography on which it was based. Of course this was nonsense, as Turner gloriously proved, and as the mainstream of 19th-century French painting went on to vindicate. In literature, though, the distinction between realistic fiction and the imaginative recreation of a real journey through life has been maintained with pedantic assiduity. The novel, however autobiographical, is *writing;* the book of travel, however patterned, plotted, symbolized, is just *writing-up.* It is a damnable and silly piece of class discrimination.[44]

Dos Passos and Hemingway traveled to the Basque country of Spain in the 1920s and became close friends in Spain and France starting in 1924. In 1921, Dos Passos and e. e. cummings sailed from New York to Lisbon. They traveled together in Spain and France, including hiking in the Pyrenees—a trip that provided material for Dos Passos's *Rosinante to the Road Again* (1922). Hemingway went to Pamplona, where the running of the bulls appealed to his sensibilities, and the following year Dos Passos joined him. Wherever Hemingway went, he developed crowds of friends for continuous drinking, fishing, visits to bullfights, laughter, reminiscences, and stories. His third wife, Martha Gellhorn, said this behavior was a system of research for Hemingway. "Aside from being his form of amusement," Gellhorn said, "he learned about a place and people through the eyes and experiences of those who lived there."[45] In the twenties, the Basque world of northern Spain and southern France was so self-sufficient and isolated that it could maintain a completely separate language, a remnant of what may have been Europe's first language. Dos Passos wrote portraits of ordinary life, and Hemingway found a warm, friendly, open, and energizing people. By 1924, Hemingway and his first wife, Hadley Richardson, had adopted Spain as home. "In no other place did he feel, physically, so contented, as if he so much belonged," wrote critical biographer Peter Griffin.[46]

In 1929, Dos Passos married Katy Smith, who had been a childhood friend of Hemingway's from Michigan. Dos Passos was introduced to Katy at Hemingway's home in Key West, Florida. Many trips followed as Katy and John bounced from Provincetown, Massachusetts, to England, France, Cuba, and Spain, often visiting with Hemingway and the Fitzgeralds. Hemingway felt F. Scott Fitzgerald was competition for him in the world of writing, but everyone else surrounding Hemingway had to be inferior. He considered Dos Passos "Class A," maybe even "Double A," but not in his league as a writer.[47] By 1937, however, Dos Passos had published his great trilogy of novels, U.S.A., and this presented more of a challenge to Hemingway's status. U.S.A. received excellent reviews, including one on the front page of the *New York Times Book Review,* and Dos Passos appeared on the cover of *Time* magazine, thus threatening Hemingway's position as king of the hill. The trilogy stands as one of the great literary efforts of the twentieth century. After William Faulkner ranked Dos Passos ahead of Hemingway on a list of best contemporary writers, Hemingway told Faulkner that Dos Passos was "a 2nd rate writer."[48] Competitors were subject to attack.

The Spanish Civil War horrified them both. In 1937, Dos Passos, the experienced European traveler, said in "Madrid under Siege" that as he awoke to an artillery barrage—in a hotel where shells actually hit the building—he "couldn't help thinking of other Madrids I'd known, twenty years ago, eighteen years ago, four years ago."[49] The civil war was prelude to World War II; it provided practice for the Luftewaffe in saturation bombing a Basque town, Guernica, and for the Communists in practicing lies about their pact with Hitler. The civil war killed much of what Hemingway and Dos Passos loved in Spain, and it ultimately ended their friendship. They started work on a film about Spain, but after 1937 saw little of each other. There had been personal conflicts earlier, some centered around Hemingway's infidelities and his rudeness toward Katy Dos Passos. During the Spanish Civil War, Hemingway was winding down his second marriage and courting Martha Gellhorn, who would become his third wife. But the politics in Spain tore apart his friendship with Dos Passos.

In the civil war, several leftist factions squabbled and assassinated among themselves while opposing Franco's fascists, who were aligned with Hitler's Germany. Another great literary journalist of that age, George Orwell—he and Dos Passos met in Barcelona in 1937—had joined the anti-Franco forces and was nearly killed in the struggle. In *Homage to Catalonia,* Orwell wrote about the civil war and the same factional fights, which he considered a betrayal of the workers by the Spanish Communist Party. In 1937, armed men—probably Stalinists—took Dos Passos's close friend and hiking companion, José Robles, one of the left-wing leaders of the Republican government, from his apartment in Valencia and killed him in an unknown location; no record of the arrest was made. In the deceitful, treacherous environment of Spain, both Dos Passos and Hemingway were lied to about Robles's death. Hemingway repeated to friends the Stalinist-planted lie that Robles had become a fascist spy and suggested that Dos Passos was on Robles's side. The death of Robles estranged Dos Passos from Hemingway, whose interests in fishing and bullfighting had suddenly been replaced by politics. Hemingway would tolerate no criticism of the Communist forces in Spain. Hemingway told Dos Passos he was either "with them or against them." Dos Passos referred to Hemingway as among the "romantic American Communist sympathizers." Hemingway did not agree with Dos Passos on Robles's death and afterward libeled him on several occasions. Their differences boiled over into anger and hatred. History has confirmed Dos Passos's view of the many killings by the Stalinist Communists, such as that of Robles—although the body was never found.[50] Dos Passos was guilty of the sin of reporting accurately on the leftist conflicts within Spain. During the 1950s, his political journey drifted toward the right.

Today, the Catalan and Euskal languages are both alive and spoken every day despite Franco's long campaign to stamp them out. The Basque country shows signs of prosperity, at least in the tourist towns, which are clean, restored, often modern, and bustling with urbane commerce, as has often been the case in this long-industrialized section of Spain. Hemingway and Dos Passos would not like Basque cities now, but maybe back in the woods they would find the same characters running taverns, harvesting cork, making wine, farming, or just sitting in the plazas. The Basques remain as welcoming as they were when Hemingway and Dos Passos were traveling friends.

◈

JOHN DOS PASSOS

1. The Twilight of Things

Behind a cracked windowpane mended with tapes of paper, Things sit in forlorn conclave. In the center is the swagbellied shine of a big samovar, dented a little, the whistle on top askew, dust in the mouldings of the handles. Under it, scattered over a bit of mothchewed black velvet two silver Georgian sword-scabbards, some silver cups chased with a spinning sinewy pattern, a cracked carafe full of mould, some watches, two of them Swiss in tarnished huntingcases, one an Ingersoll, quite new, with an illuminated dial, several thick antique repeaters, a pair of Dresden candlesticks, some lace, a pile of cubes of cheap soap, spools of thread, packets of pins. Back in the shop a yellowfaced old man droops over a counter on which are a few bolts of printed calicos. Along the walls are an elaborate Turkish tabouret inlaid with mother-of-pearl, a mahogany dressing table without its mirror, and some iron washstands. The wrinkles have gathered into a deep cleft between the old man's brows; his eyes have the furtive snarl of a dog disturbed on a garbage pile. He looks out through narrowed pupils at the sunny littered street, where leanfaced men sit with their heads in their hands along the irregular curb, and an occasional drovshky goes by pulled by bony racks of horses, where soldiers loaf in doorways.

The old man is the last guardian of Things. Here possessions, portable objects, personal effects, Things, that have been the goal and prize of life, the great center of all effort, to be sweated for and striven for and cheated for by all generations, have somehow lost their import and crumbled away and been trampled underfoot. The people who limp hungrily along the rough-paved streets never look in the windows of the speculators' shops, never stop to look enviously at the objects that perhaps they once owned. They seem to have forgotten Things.

From John Dos Passos, *Orient Express,* written in 1922.

Only an occasional foreigner off a steamer in the harbor goes into the old man's shop, to haggle for this trinket or that, to buy jewels to resell in Europe, or in back rooms behind locked doors to paw over furs or rugs that can be smuggled out of the country only after endless chaffering and small bribery. The boat the night before we got to Batum was full of talk of this and that which might be picked up for nothing, pour un rien, per piccolo prezzo. People scrubbed up their wits, overhauled their ways and means, like fishermen their tackle the night before the opening of the trout season.

As one glances into the houses strolling through the tree-shaded streets of Batum one sees mostly high empty rooms, here and there a bed or a table, some cooking utensils, a scrap of mosquito-netting or a lace curtain across an open window. All the intricate paraphernalia, all the small shiny and fuzzy and tasseled objects that padded the walls of existence have melted away. Perhaps most of them went in the war under the grinding wheels of so many invading and occupying armies, the Russians, the Germans, the British, the Turks, the Georgian Social-Democrats and lastly the Red Army. After these years of constant snatching and pillage, of frequent terrified trundling of cherished objects into hiding-places, seems to have come apathy. People lie all day on the pebbly beach in front of the town, with their rags stripped off them, baking in the sun, now and then dipping into the long green swells that roll off the Black Sea, or sit chatting in groups under the palms of the curious higgledy-piggledy Elysium of the Boulevard along the waterfront. With half-starvation has come a quiet effortlessness probably sweeter than one might expect, something like the delicious sleep they say drugs men who are freezing to death.

And the poor remnants of what people persist in calling civilization lie huddled and tarnished and dusty in the windows of second-hand dealers, Things useful and useless, well made and clumsily made, and little by little they are wafted away west in return for dollars and lire and English pounds and Turkish pounds that lie in the hoards with which the dealers, the men with the eyes of dogs frightened on a garbage pile, await the second coming of their Lord.

2. The Knight of the Pantherskin

There is a bright sliver of the moon in the sky. On the horizon of a sea sheening green and bright lilac like the breast of a pigeon a huge sun swells red to bursting. Palmfronds and broad leaves of planes sway against a darkening zenith. In the space of dust outside of their barracks Georgian soldiers are gathered lazily into a circle. They wear ragged greyish uniforms, some with round fur caps, some with the pointed felt helmets of the Red Army. Many of them are barefoot. Blows off them a sweaty discouraged underfed smell. One man, seated, starts thumping with his palms a double shuffle on a small kettledrum held between his legs. The rest beat time by clapping until one man breaks out into a frail melody. He stops at the end of a couple of phrases, and a young fellow, blond, rather sprucely dressed with a clean white fur cap on the back of his head, starts dancing. The rest keep time with their hands and sing Tra-la-la, Tra-la-la to the tune in a crooning undertone. The dance is elegant, mincing, with turkeylike strut-tings and swift hunting gestures, something in it of the elaborate slightly farded romance of eastern chivalry. One can imagine silver swords and spangled wallets and gaudy silk belts with encrusted buckles. Perhaps it is a memory that makes the men's eyes gleam so as they beat time, a memory of fine horses and long inlaid guns and toasts drunk endlessly out of drink-ing horns, and of other more rousing songs sung in the mountains at night of the doughty doings of the Knight of the Pantherskin.

3. Proletcult

On the walls some crude squares of painting in black and white, a man with a pick, a man with a shovel, a man with a gun. The shadows are so exaggerated they look like gingerbread men. Certainly the man who painted them had not done many figures before in his life. The theater is a long tin shed that used to be a cabaret show of some sort, the audience mostly workmen and soldiers in white tunics open at the neck, and women in white muslin dresses. Many of the men and all the children are barefoot and few of the women wear stockings. When the curtain goes up romping and chattering stop immediately; everyone is afraid of missing a word of what is said on the stage. It's a foolish enough play, an Early-Victorian sob-story, about a blind girl and a good brother and a wicked brother, and a bad marquis and a frequently fainting marquise, but the young people who play it—none of them ever acted before the Red Army entered Batum three months ago—put such conviction into it that one can't quite hold aloof from the very audible emotion of the audience dur-ing the ticklish moments of the dagger-fight between the frail good brother and the wicked and hearty elder brother who has carried off the little blind girl against her will. And when at last all wrongs are righted, and the final curtain falls on felicity, one can't help but feel that the lives of these people who crowd out through the dilapidated ex-beergarden in front of the theater have somehow been compensated for the bareness of the hungry livingrooms and barracks they go home to. In the stamping and the abandon with which the two heroes fought was perhaps an atom of some untrammelled expression, of some gaudy bloodcurdling ritual which might perhaps replace in people's hopes and lives the ruined dynasty of Things.

4. Bees

The secretary of the commission for schools recently set up in Batum was a blackhaired man, hawknosed, holloweyed, with a three-day growth of beard. Undernourishment and overwork had made his eyes a little bloodshot and given them a curious intense stare. He had a sheaf of papers in front of him among which he scribbled an occasional hasty word, as if pressed for time. He spoke French with difficulty, digging it up word by word from some longforgotten layer of his mind. He talked about the new school-system the Bolsheviki were introducing in the new republic of Adjaria, of which Batum was the capital, explained how already children's summer colonies had been started in several villages, how every effort was being made to get equipment ready to open the primary and secondary schools at the end of September.

—All education is to be by work, nothing without actual touch; he spread his hands, that were angular tortured painful hands, wide, and closed them with a gesture of laying hold onto some slippery reality. The words he used, too, were concrete, dug out of the soil.—From the very first, work. . . . In summer in the fields, the children must cultivate gardens, raise rabbits, bees, chickens, learn how to take care of cattle. They must go into the forests and learn about trees. Everything they must learn by touch. Then in the winter they must study their native languages and Esperanto. . . . Here there will be schools for Armenians, Greeks, Muslims, Georgians, Russians . . . and the rudiments of sociology, arithmetic, woodworking, cooking. For in our republic every man must be able to attend to his wants himself. That will be the primary education. You see, nothing by theory, everything by practice. Then the secondary education will be more specialized, preparation for trades and occupations. Then those who finish the high schools can go to the universities to do independent work in the directions they have chosen. You see, merit will be according to work, not by theories or examinations. And all through there will be instruction in music and gymnastics and the theater; the arts must be open to anyone who wants to work in them. But most important will be nature; the young children must be all the time in the fields and forests, among the orchards where there are bees. . . . It is in the little children that all our hope lies . . . among orchards where there are bees.

5. *Bedbug Express*

Ce n'est pas serios, the tall Swede had said when he and I and an extremely evil-looking Levantine with gimlet-pointed whiskers had not been allowed to go down the gangplank at Batum. Ce n'est pas serios, he had said, indicating the rotting harbor and the long roofs of the grey and black town set in dense pyrites-green trees and the blue and purple mountains in the distance and the Red Guards loafing on the wharf and the hammer and sickle of the Soviet Republic painted on the wharfhouse. The last I saw of him he was still standing at the end of the gangplank, the points of his standup collar making pink dents in his thick chin, shaking his head and muttering, Ce n'est pas serios.

I thought of him when, accompanied by a swaggering interpreter and by a cheerful man very worried about typhus from the N.E.R. [Near East Relief], I stood in front of the Tiflis express waving a sheaf of little papers in my hand, passes in Georgian and in Russian, transport orders, sleeping car tickets, a pass from the Cheka and one from the Commissar for Foreign Affairs of the Republic of Adjaria. The Tiflis express consisted of an engine, three huge unpainted sleepers and a very gaudy suncracked caboose. One car was reserved for civil officials, one for the military and one for the general public. So far it was extremely serious, but the trouble was that long before the train had drawn into the station it had been stormed by upwards of seven thousand people, soldiers in white tunics, peasant women with bundles, men with long moustaches and astrakhan caps, speculators with peddlers' packs and honest proletarians with loaves of bread, so that clots of people all sweating and laughing and shoving and wriggling obliterated the cars, like flies on a lump of sugar. There were people on every speck of the roof, people hanging in clusters from all the doors, people on the coal in the coalcar, people on the engine; from every window protruded legs of people trying to wriggle in. Those already on board tried to barricade themselves in the compartments and with surprising gentleness tried to push the newcomers out of the windows again. Meanwhile the eastbound American ran up and down the platform dragging his hippopotamus suitcase, streaking sweat from every pore and trying to find a chink to hide himself in. At last recourse had to be had to authority. Authority gave him a great boost by the seat of the pants that shot him and his suitcase in by a window into a compartment full of very tall men in very large boots, six of the seven soldiers who occupied his seat were thrown out, all hands got settled and furbished up their foreign languages and sat quietly sweating waiting for the train to leave.

Eventually after considerable circulation of rumors that we were not going to leave that day, that the track was torn up, that a green army had captured Tiflis, that traffic was stopped on account of the cholera, we started off without the formality of a whistle. The train wound slowly through the rich jade and emerald jungle of the Black Sea coast towards tall mountains to the northeast that took on inconceivable peacock colors as the day declined. In the compartment we nibbled black bread and I tried to juggle French and German into a conversation. Someone was complaining of the lack of manufactured articles, paint and women's stockings and medicine and spare parts for automobiles and soap and flatirons and toothbrushes. Someone else was saying that none of those things were necessary: The mountains will give us wool, the fields will give us food, the forests will give us houses; let every man bake his own and spin his own and build his own; that way we will be happy and independent of the world. If only they would not compromise with industrialism. But in Moscow they think, if only we get enough foreign machinery the revolution will be saved; we should be self-sufficient like the bees.

Strange how often they speak to you of bees. The order and sweetness of a hive seem to have made a great impression on the Russians of this age. Again and again in Tiflis people talked of bees with a sort of wistful affection, as if the cool pungence of bees were a tonic to them in the midst of the soggy bleeding chaos of civil war and revolution.

By this time it was night. The train was joggling its desultory way through mountain passes under a sky solidly massed with stars like a field of daisies. In the crowded compartment, where people had taken off their boots and laid their heads on each other's shoulders to sleep, hordes of bedbugs had come out of the stripped seats and bunks, marching in columns of three or four, well disciplined and eager. I had already put a newspaper down and sprinkled insect powder in the corner of the upper berth in which I was hemmed by a solid mass of sleepers. The bedbugs took the insect powder like snuff and found it very stimulating, but it got into my nose and burned, got into my eyes and blinded me, got into my throat and choked me, until the only thing for it was to climb into the baggage rack, which fortunately is very large and strong in the Brobdignagian Russian trains. There I hung, eaten only by the more acrobatic of the bugs, the rail cutting into my back, the insect powder poisoning every breath, trying to make myself believe that a roving life was the life for me. Above my head I could hear the people on the roof stirring about.

At about midnight the train stopped for a long while at a station. Tea was handed round, made in great samovars like watertanks; their fires were the only light; you could feel that there was a river below in the valley, a smell of dry walls and human filth came up from some town or other. Huge rounded shoulders of hills cut into the stars. Enlivened by the scalding tea, we all crawled into our holes again, the bunches of people holding on at the doors reformed, and the train was off. This time I went very decently to sleep listening to the stirring of the people on the roof above my head, to the sonorous rumble of the broadgauge wheels and to a concertina that wheezed out a torn bit of song now and then in another car.

In the morning we look out at a silver looping river far below in a huge valley between swelling lioncolored hills. The train casts a strange shadow in the morning light, all its angles obliterated by joggling, dangling figures of soldiers; on the roofs are the shadows of old women with baskets, of men standing up and stretching themselves, of children with caps too big for them. On a siding we pass the long train of the second tank division of the Red Army; a newpainted engine, then endless boxcars, blond young soldiers lolling in the doors. Few of them look more than eighteen; they are barefoot and scantily dressed in canvas trousers and tunics; they look happy and at their ease, dangling their legs from the roofs and steps of boxcars and sleepers. You can't tell which are the officers. Out of the big clubcar decorated with signs and posters that looks as if it might have been a diner in its day, boys lean to wave at the passing train. Then come flatcars with equipment, then a long row of tanks splotched and striped with lizard green.—A gift of the British, says the man beside me. The British gave them to Denikin, and Denikin left them to us.

Our train, the windows full of travelgrimed faces and the seats full of vermin, gathers speed and tilts round a bend. The sight of the green tanks has made everybody feel better. The man beside me, who used to be a banker in Batum and hopes to be again, exclaims fervently: All these words, Bolshevik, Socialist, Menshevik, have no meaning any more. . . . Conscious of it or not, we are only Russians.

6. The Relievers

Members of the N.E.R. sign a pledge not to drink fermented or distilled liquors. A private car full of members of the N.E.R. is in Tiflis trying to decide whether starving people or people with full bellies are more likely to become communists. In Tiflis twenty people a day die of cholera, forty people a day die of typhus, not counting those who die where nobody finds them. At the N.E.R. headquarters we all sleep on canvas cots and gargle with listerine to avoid infection and to take the vodka off our breaths. Headquarters swarms with miserable barons and countesses who naturally sigh for the old régime and color the attitude of even the honest men among the relievers. What American can stand up against a title, much less against a refugee title in distress? Why, she might be the Princess Anastasia in disguise! The Russian government understands all that but wisely argues that a live White child is better than a dead Red child; so it gives the relievers a free hand to decide what sheep shall live and what goats shall die.

But the real energy of the relievers goes into the relief of Things. To a casual eye Tiflis is bare of Things, nothing in the shopwindows, houses empty as the tents of arabs, but towards the N.E.R. there is a constant streaming of diamonds, emeralds, rubies, silver-encrusted daggers, rugs, Georgian, Anatolian, rugs from Persia and Turkestan, watches, filigree work, silver mesh bags, furs, amber, the Mustapha Sirdar papers, cameras, fountain pens. My dear, the bargains! For a suitcase full of roubles you can outfit yourself for life. I guess the folks back home'll be surprised when I tell 'em what I paid for that sunburst I bought the wife.

And, carrying the things, greyfaced people, old men and women terribly afraid of the Cheka of brigands of the cholera, of their shadows, débris of a wrecked world, selling for a few days' food, Things that had been the mainstay of their lives up to 1917; swaggering young men who had picked the winning team and were making a good thing of it; professional speculators, men who were usually but not always Greeks, Armenians, or Jews, men with sharp eyes and buzzard beaks, dressed in shabby overcoats, humpbacked with respect and politeness, rubbing their hands that never let go a banknote however depreciated the currency was, men who will be the founders of great banking houses in the future, philanthropists and the founders of international families. The bargains, the bargains!

And the pride and virtue of the members of the N.E.R. who had signed a pledge not to drink alcoholic or fermented liquors, who are relieving the sufferings of humanity at the risk of their lives, who are exposing themselves to the contamination of Bolshevism, communism, free love, nationalized women, anarchy and God knows what—their virtuous pride in the dollar king of the exchange as they paw over the bargains; rugs stolen out of the mosques, lamps out of churches; pearls off the neck of a slaughtered grand duchess; the fur coat of some poor old woman who sits hungry in her bare room looking out through a chink in the shutters at this terrible young people's world, a world jagged and passionate and crude that she can never understand, an old woman looking out through the shutters with the eyes of a cat that has been run over by an automobile.

7. Funicular

The inevitable Belgian Company still runs the funicular. You pay your fare to a little Polish girl neat as a mouse in a white dress. On her legs a faint ruddiness of sunburn takes the place of stockings. She complains of the lack of talcum powder and stockings and wonders what she's going to do when her shoes wear out. The car creaks jerkily up the hill. Above the shelter of the town a huge continual wind is blowing.

Back from a walk over the hills, I sit at a table outside a little shanty, drinking a bottle of wine of Kakhetia no. 66. Old Tiflis, dustcolored with an occasional patch of blue or white on a house, is loosely sprinkled in the funnel out of which the copper-wire river pours into the plain. Out of the defile rises a column of steam from the sulphur springs. Farther down, the enormous grey buildings of the Russian town straggle over the plain. From the valley bulge row after row of vast stratified hills, ochre and olivecolor, that get blue into the distance until they break into the tall range of the Caucasus barring the north. The huge continual streaming wind out of Asia, a wind so hard you can almost see it streaked like marble, a wind of unimaginable expanses, whines in the mouth of my glass and tears to tatters the insane jig that comes out of the mechanical piano behind me. I have to hold the bottle between my knees to keep it from blowing over.

We used to dream of a wind out of Asia that would blow our cities clean of the Things that are our gods, the knick-knacks and the scraps of engraved paper and the vases and the curtain rods, the fussy junk possession of which divides poor man from rich man, the shoddy manufactured goods that are all our civilization prizes, that we wear our hands and brains out working for; so that from being an erect naked biped, man has become a sort of hermit crab that can't live without a dense conglomerate shell of dinnercoats and limousines and percolators and cigarstore coupons and eggbeaters and sewing machines, so that the denser his shell, the feebler his self-sufficience, the more he is regarded a great man and a millionaire. That wind has blown Russia clean, so that the Things held divine a few years ago are mouldering rubbish in odd corners; thousands of lives have been given and taken (from where I sit I can make out the square buildings of the Cheka, crammed at this minute with poor devils caught in the cogs) a generation levelled like gravel under a steamroller to break the tyranny of Things, goods, necessities, industrial civilization. Just now it's the lull after the fight. The gods and devils are taking their revenge on the victors with cholera and famine. Will the result be the same old piling up of miseries again, or a faith and a lot of words like Islam or Christianity, or will it be something impossible, new, unthought of, a life bare and vigorous without being savage, a life naked and godless where goods and institutions will be broken to fit men, instead of men being ground down fine and sifted in the service of Things?

Harder, harder blows the wind out of Asia; it has upset the table, taken the chair out from under me. Bottle in one hand, glass in the other, I brace myself against the scaring wind.

8. International

The eastbound American had dinner of caviar and tomatoes and Grusinski shashlik and watermelon washed down with the noble wine of Kakhetia in the pleasant gone-to-seed Jardin des Petits Champs, where nobody thinks of cholera or typhus or the famine along the Volga. Afterwards strolling through unlit streets, you met no old people, only crowds of young men in tunics and dark canvas trousers, some of them barefoot, young girls in trim neatly cut white dresses without stockings or hats, strolling happily in threes and fours and groups, filling the broad empty asphalt streets.

The night was warm and a dry wind drove the dust. The Grusinski garden, that used to be the Noblemen's Club, was crowded with the new softly laughing youngsters. A band was playing Light Cavalry. A few colored electric bulbs hung among the waving trees. There was nothing particular to do. In spite of famine and cholera and typhus everybody seemed nonchalant and effortlessly gay. A certain amount of wine was being sold, illegally, I think, at a table in a corner, but nobody but the Americans seemed to have any roubles to buy it with. Gradually the crowd was trickling into a theater that had great signs in Russian and in Georgian over the door. The eastbound American found himself in a narrow corridor being addressed as Amerikanski Poait and before he knew what was happening he found himself being settled in a seat in a curiously shaped room; as he was reaching for someone who spoke a known language one wall of the room rose and he found that he was on a stage facing an enormous auditorium packed with people. In the front row were broad grins on the faces of certain companions he had been with earlier in the evening. Then somebody behind his chair whispered in French into his ear that it was an international proletarian poetry festival and that he was expected to recite something. At that news the E. A. almost fainted.

The proceedings were splendid. Not more than ten people present ever understood any one thing. Poems were recited, chanted and sung in Armenian, Georgian, Turkish, Persian, Russian, German and God knows what else. Everything was received with the greatest enthusiasm. The E. A. managed to stammer out as his own a nursery rhyme by William Blake, the only thing he could remember, which revolutionary outburst was received with cheers. The E. A. retired in confusion and in a muck of sweat, feeling that probably he had mistaken his vocation. Certainly *Oh Sunflower weary of time* can never have been recited under stranger conditions. After a long poem in Russian by a thin young soldier with a conical head shaved bald that made everybody roar with laughter until the building shook, the meeting broke up amid the greatest international merriment and singing and everybody started streaming home through the pitchblack streets, young men in white tunics, bareheaded girls in white dresses, strolling about without restraint in this empty world like children playing in an abandoned house, gradually swallowed up by the huge black barracklike buildings.

On the way up the hill we passed the Cheka. The pavements round it were brilliantly lit. There was barbed wire in the windows. Sentries walked back and forth. As we walked past, trying to close our nostrils to the jail smell, the idyll crashed about our ears.

Up at the N.E.R. there was considerable excitement. One of the relievers was with difficulty being got into his cot. Others were talking about typhus and cholera. One man was walking round showing everyone a handful of heavy silver soupspoons.—Five cents apiece in American money, what do you think of that?—Are you sure they're not plated?—Genuine English sterling silver marked with the lion; can't get anything better'n that.—Because Major Vokes bought a necklace in Batum and it turned out to be paste.

I lay curled up on my cot listening to all this from the next room; the uneasy smell of the summer night came in through the open window with a sliver of moonlight. The street outside was empty and dark, but frailly from far away came the sound of a concertina. The jiggly splintered tune of a concertina was limping its way through the black half desert stone city, slipping in at the windows of barracks, frightening the middleaged people who sat among the last of their Things trembling behind closed shutters, maddening the poor devils imprisoned in the basement of the Cheka, caught under the wheels of the juggernaut of revolution, as people are caught under the wheels in every movement forward or back of the steamroller of human action. The jail is the cornerstone of liberty, thought the E. A. as he fell asleep.

FOUR

THE DISCOVERY OF THE
DEPRESSION

Go out around the country and look this thing over. I don't want sta-
tistics from you. I don't want the social-worker angle. I just want your
own reactions, as an ordinary citizen. . . . Tell me what you see and hear.
All of it. Don't ever pull your punches.
　—Harry Hopkins

John Dos Passos in 1932 published "Detroit, City of Leisure" in
The New Republic.[1] He reported an encounter with a newspaperman in Detroit who knew of "a story that keeps coming in that
we don't dare touch." The newspaperman told about a crowd of
the unemployed entering a chain grocery store and openly taking
food they needed to survive. The clerk calls the manager, who says
to do nothing about it. The newspaperman agreed that this event
should not be reported because others would get the same idea.

　Looking back today at the era of the Great Depression in America from 1929 until the arrival of World War II in 1941, we take
for granted that such a devastating period of financial crisis and unemployment was the leading news topic of the age. At the start of
the Depression, however, the economic condition of the country

was not widely understood or much noticed in standard newspaper journalism. Hoping that it would not last, publications avoided negative financial news when possible, as did the reporter Dos Passos met in Detroit.

Long before newspapers recovered from this attitude, Dos Passos and several other writers who held progressive or radical political perspectives were able to travel around the country and report on conditions for the magazines. "This was the period of the Great Depression," Dos Passos recalled in his memoir. "It didn't affect me very much personally. Katy owned the Provincetown house where we made our headquarters, and I scraped up what money I could for trips. I used to tell people I had been just as broke before the stockmarket crash as after it. My books could hardly have sold less anyway. It was what I saw of other people's lives that brought home the failure of New Era capitalism."[2]

A few literary journalists, such as Dos Passos and Edmund Wilson, who was an associate editor at *The New Republic,* were writing for progressive political magazines where they could report on the emerging Great Depression. The literary journalism of the Depression, according to James Boylan, "becomes important only in a time so out of joint that conventional journalism defaults. So it was with the depression and depression reportage."[3] As the economic crisis deepened, and as the newspapers eventually faced up to the situation, innovative new forms of literary reportage, most importantly the text-and-picture book and the documentary film, vividly expressed what was happening in the Dust Bowl and other hard-hit areas of America. Writers such as Dos Passos, Wilson, John Steinbeck, and James Agee created significant literary portraits of the Depression, sometimes in fiction and occasionally in the form of literary journalism.

• • •

Oddly enough, the literary journalists, such as Dos Passos, who often needed weeks or months to complete their reporting, actually scooped the newspaper writers in revealing the Depression to readers.

The Great Depression, which began in America around 1929, was not much noticed, or was ignored, in the newspapers until 1932 or 1933.[4] This was a major failing, but a depression can be hard to identify. There had been recessions before, in 1908 and 1921, and the country quickly recovered. Looking back at it now, we wonder how the newspapers could have missed the Great Depression, but sometimes the evidence was contradictory. The stock-market crash of 1929 is often considered the start of the Depression, but it was an ambiguous event. Within five months, the market had recovered to within a few points of its high. The American stock market suffered a similar crash in October 1987. Was that the sign of a depression? The *Wall Street Journal* recently commented: "When the Dow Jones Industrial Average plunged nearly 23% on Oct. 19, 1987, many observers saw it as a watershed event. It wasn't. Instead, the 1987 crash turned out to be a mere blip in an extraordinary two-decade run that carried the Dow Industrials from 776.92 in mid-1982 to 11722.98 in early 2000. That, of course, was when stocks crashed again. This time, however, it really was a financial watershed."[5] Even that confidently stated "financial watershed" in 2000 could be called a blip, since the Dow average climbed the hill again and reached new record heights above 14,000 by 2007. Trends were not much more evident in the early thirties, even with banks failing by the dozen. Simply put, it seems a whole lot clearer when you're looking in the rear-view mirror.

Even when unambiguous evidence of economic decline—soup lines, massive unemployment, bank closings—could be seen on the streets in the early thirties, newspapers from the *New York Times* to small-town dailies often avoided mention of hard times. Boylan wrote that editors thought the mention of such things contributed to the decline. They maintained silence whenever possible for fear of creating a panic and making things worse. Depressions had always been called "panics," so this was a reasonable position. Editors called for "newspaper leadership," which meant they should exert a steadying influence by not talking about the troubles.[6]

The first serious newspaper coverage of the downturn came sometime around the latter part of 1932. By that time, there was great erosion of confidence and trust among the middle class. President Franklin D. Roosevelt took office in March 1933 with the economy virtually at a standstill, but things got much worse: the suicide rate rose, more people left the country than entered it, a million unemployed wandered the country, thirty-eight states closed their banks, and both the New York Stock Exchange and the Chicago Board of Trade closed their doors.[7] As Boylan discovered, newspaper editors failed to report the "'cold bay fog' of fear" creeping into the middle classes. Editors assumed the business community was the most important social group, and they were hostile to labor unions and radicals, who were making the most noise about the Depression. Boylan said the task "fell to a small band of litterateurs turned journalists to produce reporting that helped define the crisis more sharply in the American mind. In doing so, they created a style of journalism that drew on such predecessors as the sociological style of the Muckrakers and anticipated many of the characteristics of the New Journalism of the 1960s."[8]

Boylan called this style "literary reportage," and among its authors he included Dos Passos, labor writer Mary Heaton Vorse, Louis Adamic, Sherwood Anderson, and to some extent George

Soule, Malcolm Cowley, Bruce Bliven, and Edmund Wilson. Writing as early as 1929 for magazines such as *The New Republic, Harper's, Scribner's, The Atlantic,* and *The Nation,* these writers helped expose the reality of the Depression to the American public.

Government at the time did not have the elaborate statistical information that feeds policy decisions today. In the fall of 1933, according to John Bauman and Thomas Coode in their book *In the Eye of the Great Depression,* the government went on an aggressive but private reporting campaign. Harry Hopkins, recently appointed director of the Federal Emergency Relief Administration, sent sixteen reporters to inquire into conditions and the mood of America. They investigated welfare efforts, talked to ordinary citizens, visited relief agencies, and wrote about what they had seen and heard. Lorena Hickok, a journalist and a close friend of Eleanor Roosevelt's, spearheaded this project. Hickok had worked at the *Milwaukee Sentinel,* the *Minneapolis Tribune,* and the Associated Press. Hopkins asked Hickok and her corps of reporters

> to go out around the country and look this thing over. I don't want statistics from you. I don't want the social-worker angle. I just want your own reactions, as an ordinary citizen. Go talk with preachers and teachers, businessmen, workers, farmers. Go talk with the unemployed, those who are on relief and those who aren't; and when you talk with them don't ever forget that but for the grace of God, you, I, and any of our friends might be in their shoes. Tell me what you see and hear. All of it. Don't ever pull your punches.[9]

Such an assignment should always produce good reporting. Freed from formal rules, Hickok's group produced some classic reportage. The reporters went to the South, to West Virginia and

Kentucky, and into the mines of Colorado and New Mexico. They lived among the migrant workers in California, toured the idle industries of Pennsylvania, visited with farmers on the Great Plains, and camped with the armies of unemployed in the cities. Their reports were sent to Hopkins and influenced key government policies such as the Social Security Act and the Works Progress Administration (WPA), but they only rarely reached the public.

The best writer in this government crew was Martha Gellhorn, one of five women among Hickok's sixteen reporters. Gellhorn, who had come from a wealthy background and gone to Bryn Mawr College, covered the textile beat in New England and the Carolinas. She had written a novel and worked for a newspaper in Albany, New York. Gellhorn "evoked in her reports the pallor and gloom of the Great Depression," said Bauman and Coode. Unlike many of the other government reporters, Gellhorn published her reporting from the mill towns in *The Trouble I've Seen* (1936). Soon she was in Europe writing about the Spanish Civil War and the rise of Hitler. After she met Ernest Hemingway in 1936 in Key West, they kindled a love affair while covering the Spanish Civil War in 1937. Their marriage, his third and her second, lasted from 1940 until 1945, when Gellhorn left him. In between, they traveled and covered wars—Cuba, China, Finland, Barcelona, and the invasion beaches of Normandy. After the war, she continued writing journalism and fiction and earned a reputation as a distinguished writer.[10]

Hickok's reporters fanned out across the nation. Robert Collyer Washburn covered Connecticut cities and Boston. Louisa Wilson and Lincoln Colcord covered the automobile industry in Detroit, Grand Rapids, Cleveland, and Akron. Colcord came from a wealthy, seagoing background in Maine, worked for a

Philadelphia newspaper as a Washington correspondent, became a progressive, and wrote for *The Nation*. The letters these reporters sent to Hickok helped the administration and formed what Bauman and Coode called "a unique and fascinating literary tapestry of life in Depression America"; but only a few rays of sunlight struck that tapestry through the window of publication.[11]

Some literary journalists distinguished themselves by covering the Depression in the early years before the newspapers began to report on it regularly. What made their reportage different? Were they more sensitive to the times? Did they know more than others did? Or were they simply willing to say more?

The answers are complex, according to Boylan.

First, most of them were radicals who either wanted to change the American system or felt the Depression was a sign of collapse of the capitalist system. Their reporting tended to be about the impoverished, the unemployed, and the underprivileged—exactly the groups that the newspapers wanted to avoid. Second, their style of writing was more artistic, personal, and opinionated than newspaper journalism permitted. Third, these journalists found places to publish outside the newspaper press, often in journals such as *The New Republic, The Nation, Harper's, Scribner's,* and *The Atlantic.*[12]

Edmund Wilson, for example, who is best known as a critic and as one of the most prolific writers of his generation, contributed reportage to several magazines including *The New Republic* and *The New Yorker*. In 1929, Wilson was thirty-four years old. He was discovering Marxism, like many in his generation, and became increasingly devoted to journalism during the Depression era. He covered a Communist demonstration in New York in 1931,[13] did a portrait of the automobile industry and its kingpin Henry Ford, and went to the coal country of Kentucky to write about racism and poverty. Later he traveled in the West, writing about the construction of Boulder Dam and then trekking onward to Los Angeles and San Diego. This was about two years before consistent newspaper coverage of the Depression began.

In San Diego, Wilson wrote "The Jumping-Off Place" (1931), which is reprinted in this volume. The piece is filled with statistics and facts about death, all common enough in the news. His article is comparable to his notes from San Diego, which were reprinted in his book *The Thirties*.[14] Wilson recorded the facts and descriptions of the suicides and of the Coronado Beach Hotel in his notes, but the notes have none of the spark that he put into the article through careful structuring and the creative organization of details. In the context of the Depression, a time in which there were many down-and-out people who were prone to suicide, he added an end-of-the-continent symbolism. The country had run out of opportunity; there was nowhere to go except the end of the continent, the end of the capitalistic empire, and the end of life. No place to go but to the sea. Facing westward to the broad Pacific Rim later became part of the bright, promising mythology of California, but for the migrants fleeing the despair of the Depression, it proved less promising than they had dreamed it would be. Boylan mentioned this indirect quality in Depression-era literary reportage.[15] A newspaper story about a massive layoff at a local factory might produce an obvious conclusion. Reportage had an indirect, symbolic element. Wilson, in "The Jumping-Off Place," for example, was talking about more than a local statistic.

The personal voice found in reportage links it to literary journalism. Writers such as Wilson had a great advantage over their readers in the Depression. Writers could travel, and in their travels they associated not only with government officials but also with the kinds of people most travelers avoided, including the depressed, the suicidal, the unemployed, and the embittered. The personal experiences of the writers—their voices on the page guiding readers through an ominous world—became a powerful and persuasive tool for explaining what was happening in the country.

New forms of literary journalism started to appear at around this time that involved photography and film. Photography as a popular medium took a leap forward when *Life* magazine began publication in 1936 with a cover photo by Margaret Bourke-White. At the start, *Life* could not print enough copies to meet the demand. Its large-format black-and-white photographs brought the world into the living rooms of a huge audience in an age before television. At the same time, successful and artistic photographers—some out of work because of the Depression—found themselves doing social documentary and journalism under government sponsorship.

The type of book that combined documentary photographs and journalistic text was not new, but it came of age in the Depression. Jacob Riis had documented in text and photography the lives of immigrants and poor workers in New York in his 1890 book *How the Other Half Lives.* The later combination of journalistic description and photography in text-and-picture books found success with the public during the Depression and, as Alan Trachtenberg put it, "led the way toward a new cultural mode, the choreographed rapport of word and text."[16] Lewis Hine's artistic images of working people were published in *Men at Work* in 1932, a year when the number of men at work was declining dramatically. A several-year spurt of talent followed in this new journalistic genre. In 1937, Margaret Bourke-White and Erskine Caldwell published a bestselling text-and-picture book titled *You Have Seen Their Faces.* The magazines, including *Fortune* and *Life,* did photo essays accompanied by text on the lives of workers and ordinary people. A selection of photos accompanied a long poem by Archibald MacLeish called *Land of the Free—USA* in 1938. Dorothea Lange and Paul Taylor published *An American Exodus: A Record of Human Erosion* in 1939. Under the direction of Roy Stryker, the federal Farm Security Administration started a photography project that produced hundreds of thousands of high-quality photographs by famous artists, and selections were later used in text-and-picture books such as Nicholas Lemann's *Out of the Forties* (1983).[17]

Margaret Bourke-White was one of the highest-paid women in America. She had a background in advertising photography and was the only staff member at *Fortune* and *Life* whose photos got a by-line. She was in her late twenties when she and Caldwell spent the summer of 1936 and early 1937 in nine southern states documenting the lives of sharecroppers and the poor. Caldwell, author of the popular novels *Tobacco Road* and *God's Little Acre,* said he wanted to "show that the fiction I was writing was authentically based on contemporary life in the South."[18] *You Have Seen Their Faces* was his idea. During their months of research in the South, they fell in love, and they were later married for three years. The book was a commercial success, but it was controversial for over-dramatizing and manipulating the individuals photographed for the book.

The government also sponsored films that were important in the documentary expression of the Depression. Two of the most impressive films are Pare Lorentz's *The Plow That Broke the Prairie* (1936) and *The River* (1937). Lorentz, born in 1905, went to college and became a film critic for *Vanity Fair,* the *New York Evening*

Journal, and other publications. He briefly had a syndicated column for Hearst called *Washington Sideshow,* but he wrote something favorable about the New Deal and was promptly fired. Out of a job, Lorentz lucked upon Rexford Guy Tugwell, director of the New Deal Resettlement Administration. Tugwell asked Lorentz if he could make a film about the Dust Bowl for $6,000, and Lorentz said yes. He had never made a film. His film would eventually cost $20,000. Lorentz was paid $18 a day for his work, but he got stuck paying most of the costs. He enlisted cameramen Ralph Steiner, Paul Strand, and Leo Hurwitz, all artists of some renown, and Virgil Thomson did the music. Lorentz edited the film himself and got it distributed to a few theaters. It opened in 1936 and was a smash, of sorts, eventually showing in some three thousand theaters without the benefit of Hollywood distribution.

In 1936, Tugwell—now with a different government agency—convinced Lorentz to do a film about the Mississippi River. This time Lorentz was promised $50,000 and paid $30 a day for his work. Again he assembled a quality production crew, and they began filming from Minnesota southward, eventually focusing on agricultural hardship in the South. Paramount distributed *The River* beginning late in 1937. Accompanied by the sound of downbeat orchestral music and images of sharecroppers around a kitchen table, the closing passage of Lorentz's prose-poem narration read:

> . . . a generation facing a life of dirt and poverty,
> Disease and drudgery;
> Growing up without proper food, medical care, or schooling,
> "Ill-clad, ill-housed, and ill-fed"—
> And in the greatest river valley in the world.

Both artistic productions stand legitimately within the traditions of thirties' documentary work and of literary journalism. In many respects, they were also propagandistic. Both films were labeled "A U.S. Documentary Film" and sponsored by agencies of the U.S. Department of Agriculture, but the art of propaganda was raised to a new level here. Earlier in the Depression, the political angle of literary journalism written by Dos Passos or Wilson had been critical in tone. Something awful was happening and these writers wanted to persuade their readers that it existed. They were right, of course, but their documentary work carried a negative message. Later in the Depression era, as in the case of Lorentz's films, the political message of documentary was pro–New Deal and pro–Tennessee Valley Authority. Instead of a critical edge, these documentaries applauded the work of the government, especially its efforts to provide electrical power in the South. It was affirmative propaganda.

During an economic depression, artists often see their careers collapse because no one has discretionary income to spend on their products. WPA state guidebook writing projects and government films such as those by Lorentz brought together extraordinary collaborations of creative artists in the service of journalism, even if it did have a built-in political message at the end. Lorentz produced films that were appeals for ecological awareness, erosion control, and benefits for the poor. But the Tennessee Valley Authority dams were not entirely beneficial. Most dams are ecological disasters, although that was not fully understood at the time. Government sponsorship during the Depression easily converted journalism into a form of persuasive cheerleading.

One of the greatest fictional works of the twentieth century, John

Steinbeck's *The Grapes of Wrath,* began as a text-and-picture non-fiction project.

Steinbeck was writing reportage alongside his fiction. In 1937 and 1938, he reported from California with two purposes, according to William Howarth: "to garner publicity for federal efforts at flood relief, and to gather material for a text-and-picture book about California's farm migrants."[19] Steinbeck collaborated with Horace Bristol, a *Life* photographer who traveled for several weekends with Steinbeck in the agricultural regions of California and took some two thousand photographs. Bristol negotiated a lucrative offer from Time, Inc., for their book. Steinbeck talked with Pare Lorentz about making a documentary film as well. His efforts in nonfiction, both here and when he later reported on bombing runs into Europe during World War II, were less creative and inspiring than his fiction. Ultimately, Steinbeck turned away from Bristol, Lorentz, and literary journalism. He cloistered himself with his fictional masterpiece. The characters, images, and events in *The Grapes of Wrath,* especially the last chapter, where Rose-of-Sharon miscarries, closely mirrored what Steinbeck and Bristol saw near Visalia, California, in early 1938.

At that time, the benefits of writing fiction outweighed the appeals of reportage, documentary, or literary journalism. As Steinbeck contemplated a large writing project, fiction won the competition with literary journalism. Fiction promised higher status and respect for the author. The intimate details of ordinary lives could be made up rather than reported, and the characters could be shaped for symbolic purposes. Although the text-and-picture books were earning a lot of money in the thirties, fiction was a more profitable and respected genre.

Four alternative nonfiction forms other than the text-and-pictures genre might be considered as available to a writer such as Steinbeck during the Great Depression.

One option was a travel book. The promising work done by Margaret Bourke-White and Erskine Caldwell was almost a travel book with photos. If it also had a sensationalist tone to it—exploitive in some people's opinion—that helped sales. Steinbeck produced a travel book in 1962 called *Travels with Charley: In Search of America,* but it did not resemble his novels. It fell into the "I Have Seen America" genre that was also used by Bill Moyers in *Listening to America* (1971), Calvin Trillin in *U.S. Journal* (1971), and Charles Kuralt in his *On the Road* series that began broadcasting in 1967.

Another option could have been a sociological report, typically used during the Depression to create a social portrait of a particular town, as in, for example, Robert S. and Helen M. Lynd's studies of Muncie, Indiana, and Newburyport, Massachusetts. The best examples of this genre were either case studies or participant-observation studies. Participant observation had been pioneered by the sociology department at the University of Chicago and was widely used in descriptions of hobos, street-corner societies, and gangs. An example is Nels Anderson's *The Hobo: The Sociology of the Homeless Man* (1923), which was prepared as a participant-observation study when Anderson was a graduate student at Chicago. Anderson's book has been an inspiration to a number of literary journalists, including Tracy Kidder and Ted Conover, because it was written by a former hobo who had become a sociology grad student, rather than the other way around. But academic formalism was not Steinbeck's style.

A third option, standard journalism, attracted Steinbeck for a time as a means of publicizing the plight of migrant workers. He wrote several news pieces, including one for the *Monterey Trader* in

1938.[20] Standard journalism had previously hushed up the Depression, was less open to political interpretation, and by necessity needed short treatment.

Finally, he could have expressed his ideas in an essay. Aside from being the wrong form for certain sensitivities, the essay faced a problem in that age that it also faces in our own. A reader who sits down to an essay is often predisposed to read about analysis today. In the 1930s, the essay seemed to have the same problem. It was likely to be political—and written by some Marxist theorist who could bore you to death. Realism was more powerful: the focused, detailed, dramatic presentation of everyday life, either in fiction or nonfiction.

Steinbeck narrowly escaped writing his book as a photo essay with Horace Bristol. The other options available would have been a loss for American literature. If Dos Passos had written his three-novel series *U.S.A.* as nonfiction, one assumes that also might have been a loss. Dos Passos included a great deal of memoir and nonfiction in the *U.S.A.* trilogy, and many of his characters were based on real people, but it stands as fiction. Both writers had difficulty deciding between genres. In desperate, strained times such as the Depression or the Vietnam War era, nonfiction becomes increasingly attractive. Many writers of fiction, such as Caldwell, Dreiser, and Hemingway, found nonfiction a powerful form of writing during the Great Depression and afterward. It may be that during the Depression the literary power started to shift from the novel to nonfiction. The models that could make literary journalism a powerful and artistic form of expression were just emerging.

The most impressive experiment in literary journalism during the Depression came in the form of a participatory text-and-picture book.

The nonfiction book *Let Us Now Praise Famous Men* by James Agee and Walker Evans is today considered a classic of thirties' documentary reporting and photography. Its reputation has grown in the intervening years, while such bestsellers as *You Have Seen Their Faces* have faded into the background. When I first heard about *Let Us Now Praise Famous Men* in 1968, it was described to me as a "cult classic," which was a professor's trick to get me to read it. It proved nearly unreadable. For one thing, Agee spends many pages copying from a family Bible and describing in great detail everything his subjects owned, right down to the grain in the wood, an inventory of several thousand words.[21] Like a self-reflexive New Journalist of the sixties, Agee revealed his own strategies as a writer to the reader:

> Let me say, then, how I would wish this account might be constructed.
>
> I might suggest, its structure should be globular: or should be eighteen or twenty intersected spheres, the interlockings of bubbles on the face of a stream; one of these globes is each of you.
>
> The heart, nerve, center of each of these, is an individual human life.[22]

It was astonishingly ambitious and inspiring. *Let Us Now Praise Famous Men* had a persistence of feeling that has lingered with me ever since, even though I could not stand parts of it and skipped some sections. One measure of a book's greatness is how long you can recall its voice, characters, and scenes after you put it back on the shelf. I can clearly remember my first encounter with Agee sitting alone in a sharecropper's spare cabin. He despaired of ever capturing the elusive humanity, dignity, and suffering that he saw and felt. His lonely sense of insignificance struck me then, and still does, as a metaphor for the seemingly hopeless tasks that all reporters face.

The book had a checkered history. In June 1936, Agee and Evans left New York to prepare an article on tenant cotton farmers in Alabama. Agee was a staff writer at *Fortune,* an expensive magazine founded for businessmen. Evans had been working in the South for several months taking carefully composed and effective photographs for the government project run by Roy Stryker, who later criticized Evans because he was insufficiently "political"—that is, propagandistic—in his work.[23] Agee insisted that Evans be the photographer, and Stryker released him from his government assignments with the stipulation that his photos become government property. The other option for a photographer at *Fortune* would have been Bourke-White, who had illustrated an earlier Agee article about drought, but Agee did not care for her melodramatic photos from the South.[24]

Agee, a Harvard-educated native of Tennessee, was a poet who found a position at *Fortune* magazine immediately after college. Dwight Macdonald, who worked at the magazine, put in a good word with Henry Luce, the owner of *Fortune* and *Time.* At first, Agee sat around the office and moped. From his nearby office, Archibald MacLeish encouraged Agee to get out and find topics to engage his spirit. Agee started writing standard magazine pieces, learning as he went along. His topics included the manufacture of glass and gunpowder, the restored old colonial town of Williamsburg, butlers, the drought in the South, and the landscape along American roads. None was particularly important, but Agee was finding his voice and discovering techniques to sneak commentary past the editors. Eventually he took on more challenging assignments, such as writing about the Tennessee Valley Authority, which was building dams and providing electricity to the rural and impoverished South.[25]

In 1936, the editors at *Fortune* wanted a fourth article for their "Life and Circumstances" series on average workers and families; the previous three articles had covered a paint spray operator, an unemployed man on relief, and a telephone company employee.[26] Everyone was talking about sharecroppers, a term that symbolized the agricultural underclass during the Depression. Agee and Evans took the assignment and disappeared into Hale County, Alabama, in the summer of 1936. They lived with three sharecropper families during July and August, twice the period they had been allotted.[27] Agee turned in an article that ran ten times the standard length of "Life and Circumstances" articles; according to Evans, it was "pretty thunderous." It was "pessimistic, unconstructive, impractical, indignant, lyrical, and always personal," according to Dwight Macdonald.[28] Noticeably absent was the condescension that *Fortune* had always assumed in these matters for the benefit of its prosperous audience. The article has since been lost. It took a year, but *Fortune* finally rejected the piece.

During the wait, Agee wrote the following about the editors who sent him to Alabama to write about sharecroppers:

> It seems to me curious, not to say obscene and thoroughly terrifying, that it could occur to an association of human beings drawn together through need and chance and for profit into a company, an organ of journalism, to pry intimately into the lives of an undefended and appallingly damaged group of human beings, an ignorant and helpless rural family, for the purpose of parading the nakedness, disadvantage and humiliation of these lives before another group of human beings, in the name of science, of "honest journalism" (whatever that paradox may mean),

of humanity, of social fearlessness, for money and for a reputation for crusading and for unbias which, when skillfully enough qualified, is exchangeable at any bank for money (and in politics, for votes, job patronage, abelincolnism, etc. [Money]) and that these people could be capable of mediating this prospect without the slightest doubt of their qualification to do an "honest" piece of work, and with a conscience better than clear, and in the virtual certitude of almost unanimous public approval.[29]

Harper and Brothers agreed to publish a revised version of the manuscript as a book, which Agee completed in 1939. Harper expected something with a text by Agee and photos by Evans on the model of *You Have Seen Their Faces.* Instead they got a true original, a book that undermined the values of the era and insulted and shocked people. Harper wanted changes in the manuscript. When Agee and Evans refused, the editors rejected the book. Three other publishers turned down expanded treatments. On a fluke—actually through the personal influence of the wife of a Harper editor—Houghton Mifflin agreed to publish it after Agee deleted a few words that were illegal in Massachusetts. It was published in 1941, when the country was already sliding toward war and the symbolic power of sharecroppers had waned. The book, *Let Us Now Praise Famous Men,* was a flop, even though most reviewers liked it and some even recognized its innovations.

Agee's deeply personal text went well beyond the standards of taste of the time, which was the one reason so many publishers refused it.

Evans's photographs, presented without captions at the start of the book, were strikingly respectful of the tenant farmers; the resulting portraits were quite different from Bourke-White's. He avoided Bourke-White's use of odd camera angles to highlight photographs or lens filters to emphasize the weathered lines in a face. He posed family members and made sure everyone was comfortable before taking their pictures. He took candid shots mainly of children, who were impatient with the posed portraits. He did not photograph the flies crawling all over their food, as Bourke-White had done. He photographed a baby asleep on the floor with a flour sack over its head to keep the flies off, but the reasoning is not exactly clear because he never put a caption on a picture. He felt the camera should show what it found. Many of his images are unpeopled interiors of the clean but spare sharecroppers' cabins. His subjects are not degraded by his photography or overdramatized. He never wrung emotion from the viewer.

Evans had a perfect partner in Agee. Ronald Weber said this about Agee's struggles:

> Part of the deep tension of the book stems from Agee's straining against his awareness of the impossibility of the task he has set himself. He, in effect, paints himself into a technical corner and then struggles mightily against the barrier. "If I could do it," he says in a famous passage, "I'd do no writing at all here. It would be photographs; the rest would be fragments of cloth, bits of cotton, lumps of earth, records of speech, pieces of wood and iron, phials of odors, plates of food and excrement." He asks the reader to "so far as possible forget that this is a book." But of course it is a book, it is writing, and so "I'll do what little I can in writing." The work will be done not through the familiar forms of art or journalism but through what he calls "open terms." Yet it will tell only a relative truth, the truth of language and not of life.[30]

Let Us Now Praise Famous Men did not dramatize its subjects as "sharecroppers." These farmers did not do the things one might expect. There are no big conflicts with landlords; we barely even see them farming. The book is more about their personal lives. It did not exploit them as representative types—that is, a sharecropper as representative of all sharecroppers. In much journalism in the thirties, an unemployed steelworker or someone on relief was presented as a representative of a class of people. Using representative types can be a form of persuasive or propagandistic writing where the reader is asked to believe that all of the people in a class suffer the same fate. But maybe not everyone had the same experience.

The very concept of the "sharecropper" was inflammatory at the time and symbolic of anyone who was a victim of the Depression, although few knew what a sharecropper really was. Bourke-White's photos have been criticized for being too dramatic, emotional, and exploitive. Among her harshest critics was Walker Evans, who said *You Have Seen Their Faces* was

> a double outrage: propaganda for one thing, and profit-making out of both propaganda and the plight of the tenant farmers. It was morally shocking to Agee and me. Particularly so since it was publicly received as *the* nice thing to do, the *right* thing to do. Whereas we thought it was an evil and immoral thing to do. Not only to cheapen them, but to profit by them, to exploit them— who had already been so exploited. Not only that but to exploit them without even *knowing* that that was what you were doing. . . . You notice that Agee is saying ad nauseam almost throughout the book [*Let Us Now Praise Famous Men*]: "For God's sake, we must *not* exploit these people, and how awful it is if we are. And we *are* working for this goddam profit-making corporation that's paying us, and we feel terrible about it." You didn't find that in Bourke-White anywhere. Nor even awareness of the fact that she should have felt this.[31]

Bourke-White's *You Have Seen Their Faces* was an immense bestseller. Even when she was taking time off from her lucrative endeavors and trying to document an underprivileged class, Bourke-White grew richer at it. Agee and Evans published their book—which was researched the same summer—four years later and sold only a few hundred copies. Sharecroppers were less of an issue after the arrival of World War II.

The conflicting perspectives in Bourke-White's and Evans's photographs grew out of the passions of the age and the debate about sharecroppers. These writers and photographers allowed themselves to feel passionately about their subjects. Using immersion techniques pioneered by sociologists and literary journalists, Agee and Evans had moved in with the poor families they covered. Bourke-White and Caldwell had similarly close connections as they toured through the South. Literary journalism differed from standard journalism in precisely this way: it was acceptable to be passionate and to have a point of view. Point of view comes automatically and without fanfare in photographs. In viewing photos, we are looking through the photographer's viewfinder. Comparing Evans with Bourke-White became an artistic analysis based on a form of journalism that permitted the expression of perspective.

Although *Let Us Now Praise Famous Men* was a case study, it did not try to imply anything about anyone else. Each person was unique rather than a symbol of a class of people. It was not political propaganda, nor even reformist. Agee felt nothing would ever be done to improve these people's lives, and history has largely borne him out on that. In 1990, Dale Maharidge and *Washington Post* photographer Michael Williamson won the Pulitzer Prize for General Non-Fiction for their book, *And Their Children After Them*. Maharidge and Williamson found the descendants of the

Burroughs, Tingle, and Fields families (Agee changed the names to Gudger, Ricketts, and Woods) that Agee and Evans had met. With a couple of exceptions, their descendants were still suffering under the burden of rural poverty.

Agee first tried to write in the subjects' own voice. Here's a snippet from his "How were we caught?" segment:

> How did we get caught? Why is it things always seem to go against us? Why is it there can't ever be any pleasure in living? I'm so tired it don't seem like I ever could get rest enough. I'm as tired when I get up in the morning as I am when I lay down at night. Sometimes it seems like there wouldn't never be no end to it, nor even a let-up. One year it'll look like things was going to be pretty good; but you get a little bit of money saved, something always happens.[32]

Eventually he gave up that experiment and went back to his own voice. Agee showed the subjects, with considerable delicacy, as people who had emotions and concerns. Agee let his own narrator have a full range of emotions, including thinking he'd like to sleep with a couple of the women. His simple acknowledgment of the sexuality of everyday life was embarrassingly personal and out of step with the nonfiction standards of the time. More importantly, Agee the narrator wasn't sure: he didn't have solutions, didn't know what should be done. He wasn't even sure what he had witnessed. Agee felt the lives of sharecroppers were incomprehensible—"incommunicable," as William Stott put it: "But though the language of reality cannot be mastered, Agee (unlike Sherwood Anderson, for example) found this no reason not to struggle toward its 'inachievable words.' His direct reportage suggests what documentary writers might do if they really took the life of their subjects without preconception, on its own terms, with the eye of a stranger who is yet, as Agee found himself to be, a close relation."[33] Agee struggled to convey realistically what he had seen and felt, and he despaired at the impossibility of the task.

Before he wrote *Let Us Now Praise Famous Men,* Agee had been a standard magazine writer at *Fortune,* and not particularly innovative—especially when writing about the Tennessee Valley Authority. After the summer of 1936 when he and Evans were in the South, however, something came unglued. He reached the limit of his tolerance, or maybe things became clear to him. He wrote one more article of note in the following year. In September 1937, his article "Havana Cruise" appeared as a rebellion against the standard reporting style of *Fortune.* The article was unlike his previous work and burdened with social criticism of the tourist industry and its victims, the striving middle-class tourists seeking luxury, romance, and possibly redemption on a cruise ship. But that was as far as he could go.[34] He was twenty-seven years old. Agee left *Fortune* and never came back. He did some writing for *Time,* but mainly he wrote film criticism and a novel, which made him famous.

Agee and Evans' book had been published and flopped in 1941. In 1943, part of the stock was remaindered.[35] In 1960, at the dawn of the New Journalism era in America, Houghton Mifflin reissued it with additional photographs by Evans. It had a modest success, but Agee was well known by then for his film criticism and had won a Pulitzer Prize for *A Death in the Family* before his own death in 1955, and Evans had become a famous photographer. Houghton Mifflin reissued *Let Us Now Praise Famous Men* in 1966 and it became successful—that was at the heady start of the New Journalism period, when Agee's kind of personal reporting became greatly admired—and the book has been continuously in print ever since.

Let Us Now Praise Famous Men is legitimately a classic of literary journalism of the late Depression years and should not be diminished with a term like "cult classic." It contains nothing on the order of Dos Passos in his *U.S.A.* book *1919*, say, but Agee was working in nonfiction and could not make up characters. *Let Us Now Praise Famous Men* failed financially, and it was not influential in the forties as a literary experiment. Agee dealt with the same social problem as Steinbeck, but he could not create a nonfiction *Grapes of Wrath* out of the sharecroppers' lives. Unlike Steinbeck, Agee stuck with nonfiction. Few nonfiction models existed for what John Dos Passos or John Steinbeck or James Agee wanted to say in the thirties. Agee had characters, ordinary lives, access, and masses of lyrical detail. If he had written in a *Fortune* magazine style, his story would have never breathed life. Instead he invented techniques, tried being personal, tried listing inventories, tried using Faulknerian rhythms, tried this and tried that. Agee had to invent the wheel.

Later, writers and readers recognized *Let Us Now Praise Famous Men* as a tremendously daring and experimental classic of literary journalism, but it can also be considered the most monumental and impressive failure of the twentieth century.

Some of the problems that made literary journalism difficult during the Depression had already started to change during the thirties. Writers had been relatively isolated from other writers who might share their vision, as was Agee in working at *Fortune.* The kind of strong editorial leadership and financial support at the magazines that could encourage long-form artistic journalism was slow to develop. In the next chapter, we will see how both problems were corrected at one magazine that created an oasis for literary journalism in the ensuing years.

"THE JUMPING-OFF PLACE"

◈

EDMUND WILSON

The Coronado Beach Hotel was built by the California millionaire John Spreckels and opened in 1887. Spreckels had made his money in Hawaiian sugar, and in 1887 the United States signed a treaty with the Hawaiian king—a treaty which guaranteed to the Americans the exclusive use of the harbor at Honolulu.

In the same year, the first vestibule train was put on the tracks by George Pullman, and the revolt of the Apaches under the formidable Geronimo, the last attempt of the Indians to assert their independence, had been put down by the government and the Apaches penned up in a reservation; the American Federation of Labor had just been founded, Kansas and Nebraska were parching with a drought, and Henry George had just run for mayor of New York and had been beaten only with difficulty by a coalition against him of the other parties; Grover Cleveland was in the middle of his first term of office and threw the capitalists into consternation by denouncing the protective tariff, and an Interstate Commerce Act designed to curb the rapacity of the railroads was in process of being put through by the small businessmen and farmers; inquiries into the practices of the trusts were being got under way in Congress, while the Standard Oil Company, entering the drilling and pumping field, was already well embarked on the final stage of its progress; and Edward Bellamy had a huge and unexpected success with his socialist novel, *Looking Backward,* which prefigures an industrial utopia.

The Coronado Beach Hotel must represent the ultimate triumph of the dreams of the architects of the eighties. It is the most magnificent specimen extant of the American seaside hotel as it flourished on both coasts in that era; and it still has its real beauty as well as its immense magnificence. Snowy white and ornate as a wedding cake, clean, polished and trim as a

Appeared originally in *The New Republic,* December 23, 1931.

ship, it is a monument by no means unworthy to dominate this last blue concave dent in the shoreline of the United States before it gives way to Mexico.

The bottom layer of an enormous rotunda is slit all around with long windows that remind one of those old-fashioned spinning toys that made strips of silhouettes seem to move, and surmounted, somewhat muffled, almost smothered by a sort of tremendous bonnet. This bonnet involves a red roof, a second layer of smaller windows and an elaborate broad red cone that resembles an inverted peg-top and itself includes two little rows of blinking dormer windows and an observation tower with a white railing around it, capped in turn by a red cone of its own, from which, on a tall white flagpole, flies an American flag. Behind this amusing rotunda extends the main body of the great hotel: a delirium, a lovely delirium, of superb red conical cupolas, of red roofs with white-lace crenellations, of a fine clothlike texture of shingles, of little steep flights of stairs that run up the outside of the building and little outside galleries with pillars that drip like wedding-cake icing, and of a wealth of felicitous dormers, irregular and protrusive, that seem organic like the budding of a sea-hydra. In the pavement of the principal entrance have been inlaid brass compass-points, and brass edges mark the broad white stairs which, between turned banister-rungs, lead up to the white doors of bedrooms embellished with bright brass knobs.

The whole building surrounds a large quadrangle, admirably planted and gardened. The grass is kept vivid and tender by slowly revolving sprays, and against it blooms a well-conceived harmony of the magenta and vermilion and crimson of begonia and salvia and coxcomb, bouquet-like bushes of rose-red hibiscus and immense clumps of purple bougainvillea that climbs on the stems of palms, tall-grown and carefully trimmed, in mounds of green fern or myrtle. The trees are all labeled with Latin names, as in a botanical garden. In the middle stands a low polygonal summerhouse, vine-embowered and covered with bark, inside which a boy is chalking up on a blackboard the latest stock-market quotations, while interested male guests sit and watch them in silence.

This courtyard has real dignity and brilliance. With its five tiers of white-railinged porches like decks, its long steep flights of steps like companion-ways, its red ladders and brass-tipped fire hose kept on hand on red-wheeled carts around corners, the slight endearing list of its warped floors and the thin wooden pillars that rise, at the bottom, from flagstones flush with the ground, it manages to suggest both an ocean liner and the portico of a colonial mansion. As you look out from one of the higher galleries at the tops of the exotic tame palms and at the little red ventilators spinning in the sun, you feel that you can still enjoy here a taste of the last luscious moment just before the power of American money, swollen with sudden growth, had turned its back altogether on the more human comforts and ornaments of the old non-mechanical world.

In the lobby, you walk as on turf across carpeting of the thickest and softest. There are wicker chairs; soft plush couches; panels of greenish-bluish tapestries on which ladies with round pulpy faces take their pleasance in Elysian boskage; sheets of stock-market quotations on hooks at the head of the stairs going down to the barbershop; and a masterpiece of interior decorating, elaborate and not easily named, but combining a set of mirrors covered with yellow curlicues, yellow-varnished rows of banister-rungs and an ambitious stained-glass window representing red poinsettias.

In the spacious, round and many-windowed dining room, where yellow-shaded candles light white tables, old respectable ladies and gentlemen eat interminable American-plan meals. After dinner, they sit on couches and talk quietly or quietly play cards in the card room.

You can wander through long suites of apartments—passing from time to time through darkish in-between chambers, made unlivable by closed-up grates, glossy mahogany mantels and sometimes a pair of twin vases cold as funeral urns.

Eventually reaching the rotunda, you come upon a swarming convention of the California Federation of Business and Professional Women's Clubs. (The General Federation of Women's Clubs was organized about two years after the opening of the Coronado Beach Hotel.) The business and professional women are fussing on the outskirts of the ballroom: "I've just seen Mildred, and she hasn't done anything about the corsages yet! Do you think we ought to give them to all the officers or just to the incoming ones?" And in a conclave under hanging electric lamps in the shape of enormous coronets, they are solemnly reading aloud and debating, one by one, the amendments proposed to their innumerable by-laws.

From time to time the chambers of the vast hotel resound to a chorus of feminine voices, deliberate, school-girlish, insipid. They have composed an anthem of their own, to the tune of *John Brown's Body,* in connection with a fund they are trying to raise:

Twenty thousand dollars by nineteen thirty-four!
Twenty thousand dollars by nineteen thirty-four!

Twenty thousand dollars by nineteen thirty-four!
  Our fund is marching on!
Glory, Glory, Hallelujah!
Glory, Glory, Hallelujah!
Glory, Glory, Hallelujah!
  Our fund is marching on!

These business and professional women are not altogether sure about what they are going to do with this money after they have succeeded in raising it; but they have arranged for a speaking contest at which a speaker from each district will be given three minutes to offer suggestions on "How can the income of $20,000 be used to the greatest advantage of the Federation?"

The new hotel at Agua Caliente across the border, where people go to see the Mexican races, has taken a good deal of the trade away from the Coronado Beach Hotel; but people still come from all over the country to San Diego across the bay.

The Americans still tend to move westward, and many drift southward toward the sun. San Diego is situated in the extreme southwestern corner of the United States; and since our real westward expansion has come to a standstill, it has become a kind of jumping-off place. On the West coast today, the suicide rate is twice that of the Middle-Atlantic coast, and the suicide rate of San Diego has become since 1911 the highest in the United States. Between January, 1911, and January, 1927, over five hundred people have killed themselves here. The population in 1930 was only about 148,000, having doubled since 1920.

For one thing, a great many sick people come to live in San Diego. The rate of illness in San Diego is 24 per cent of the population, whereas for the population of the United States the sick rate is only 6 per cent. The climate of Southern California, so widely advertised by Chambers of Commerce and Southern California Clubs, but probably rather unhealthy with its tepid enervating days and its nights that get suddenly chill, brings invalids to San Diego by the thousand. If they have money to move about and have failed to improve in the other health centers, the doctors, as a last resort, send them to San Diego, and it is not uncommon for patients to die just after being unloaded from the train. In the case of "ideational" diseases like asthma—diseases which are partly psychological—the sufferers have a tendency to keep moving away from places, under the illusion that they are leaving the disease behind. And when they have moved to San Diego, they find they are finally cornered, there is nowhere farther to go. According to the psychoanalysts, the idea of the setting sun suggests the idea of death. At any rate, of the five-hundred-odd suicides during the period of fifteen years mentioned above, 70 per cent were put down to "despondency and depression over chronic ill health."

But there are also the individuals who do not fit in in the conventional communities from which they come and who have heard that life in San Diego is freer and more relaxed. There at last their psychological bents or their peculiar sexual tastes will be recognized, allowed some latitude. It is certain that many such people find here what they are seeking; but if they fail to, if they feel themselves too different from other people and are unable to accept life on the same terms, they may get discouraged and decide to resign. And then there are the people who are fleeing from something in their pasts they are ashamed of or something which would disgrace them in the eyes of their friends in the places where they previously lived. San Diego is not quite big enough so that the members of the middle-class groups do not all know one another and follow one another's doings with the most attentive interest. If your scandal overtakes you and breaks, your whole circle will hear about it; and if you are sensitive, you may prefer death. And then there are settlers in San Diego who are actually wanted by the law. This September the city is being searched for a gangster escaped from New York, who, in a beer-war, turned a machine-gun on some children. California has been a hideaway for gangsters in trouble elsewhere ever since Al Capone came here. And there are also the people with slender means who have been told that San Diego is cheap, but who find that it is less cheap than they thought; and the girls (married young in this part of the world) deserted by husbands or lovers; and the sailors and naval officers who have had enough of the service.

Since the depression, the rate has increased. In 1926, there were fifty-seven suicides in San Diego. During nine months of 1930, there were seventy-one; and between the beginning of January and the end of July of 1931, there have already been thirty-six. Three of these latter are set down in the coroner's record as due to "no work or money"; two to "no work"; one to "ill health, family troubles and no work"; two to "despondency over financial worries"; one to "financial worry and illness"; one to "health and failure to collect"; and one to "rent due him from tenants." The doctors say that some of the old people who were sent out to San Diego by their relatives but whose income has been recently cut off, have been killing themselves from pride rather than go to the poorhouse.

These coroner's records in San Diego are melancholy reading, indeed. You seem to see the last futile effervescence of the burst of the American adventure. Here our people, so long told to "go West" to escape from ill health and poverty, maladjustment and industrial oppression, are discovering that, having come West, their problems and diseases remain and that the ocean bars further flight. Among the sandcolored hotels and power plants, the naval outfitters and waterside cafés, the old spread-roofed California houses with their fine grain of gray or yellow clapboards—they come to the end of their resources in the empty California sun. In San Diego, brokers and bankers, architects and citrus ranchers, farmers, housewives, building contractors, salesmen of groceries and real estate, proprietors of poolrooms and music stores, marines and supply-corps lieutenants, machinists, auto mechanics, oil-well drillers, molders, tailors, carpenters, cooks and barbers, soft-drink merchants, teamsters, stage-drivers, longshoremen, laborers—mostly Anglo-Saxon whites, though with a certain number of Danes, Swedes and Germans and a sprinkling of Chinese, Japanese, Mexicans, Negroes, Indians and Filipinos—ill, retired or down on their luck—they stuff up the cracks of their doors and quietly turn on the gas; they go into their back sheds or back kitchens and eat ant-paste or swallow Lysol; they drive their cars into dark alleys, get into the back seat and shoot themselves; they hang themselves in hotel bedrooms, take overdoses of sulphonal or barbital; they slip off to the municipal golf-links and there stab themselves with carving-knives; or they throw themselves into the bay, blue and placid, where gray battleships and cruisers guard the limits of their broad-belting nation—already reaching out in the eighties for the sugar plantations of Honolulu.

FIVE

THE BOMB

To tell you the truth, after a while I got an idea that if I had any skill,
it grew out of this fact that I'm not easily bored. I can talk to anybody.
   —Joseph Mitchell

In early discussions of the New Journalism, which arrived in the
blazingly nonconformist decade of the 1960s, not much was said
about the 1940s and 1950s, which by comparison seemed
straitjacketed.

Tom Wolfe said the only literary competition in the 1950s involved "The Novel." In that era, he added, "There was no such
thing as a *literary* journalist working for popular magazines or
newspapers."[1] Wolfe's wonderful essay from 1973 on the origins
of the New Journalism only reluctantly credited *New Yorker* writers in an appendix, possibly for reasons personal to Wolfe that I
will cite in the next chapter. From Wolfe's perspective and viewed
from the decades of the sixties and seventies, the forties and fifties
seemed like a vast desert that literary journalists had to cross in
order to reach the promised land of the New Journalism.

Under the subheading "Not Half-Bad Candidates," Wolfe

reviewed some predecessors of the New Journalism. He included the "reportage" of the 1930s and "several of John Hersey's articles in the early 1940's, such as a sketch called 'Joe Is Home Now' (*Life,* July 3, 1944)." Joe was a composite character created from forty-three returning soldiers Hersey had interviewed. While that was mentioned in *Life,* it was not always mentioned when the article was republished. "Here we start getting into the direct ancestry of the present-day New Journalism," Wolfe wrote. He also included Hersey's *Hiroshima,* calling it "very novelistic" and noting that it took up "a whole issue of *The New Yorker* in 1946" and had had "great influence on other *New Yorker* writers, such as Truman Capote and Lillian Ross." Finally, he listed "Capote's profile of Marlon Brando and his account of an American cultural-exchange troupe's trip to Russia; A. J. Liebling's profile of an old *National Enquirer* columnist called 'Colonel Stingo' [*Note:* another composite character]; Lillian Ross's famous evisceration of Ernest Hemingway ('How Do You Like It Now, Gentlemen?') [and] . . . various writers for *True,* notably Al Stump, author of an extraordinary chronicle of the last days of Ty Cobb."[2] Twice in his essay Wolfe cited *True* as a source of the New Journalism. Using *True* supported his thesis that nonfiction was not acknowledged by the literary community of the time and was considered a working-class form. Everette E. Dennis and William L. Rivers, in their book *Other Voices: The New Journalism in America* (1974), cited only A. J. Liebling as an ancestor, and primarily for his press criticism. Others, for example Michael L. Johnson in *The New Journalism* (1971), equated earlier journalism with the establishment press. Such writers failed to see that literary journalism had long existed in pockets outside of the establishment press, as did the New Journalism itself in the sixties.

Yet, as Wolfe and readers of *The New Yorker* knew, the tradition of literary journalism at that magazine ran much deeper than at any other American publication. Starting in the late thirties, a group of writers with a coherent vision of literary journalism gathered at *The New Yorker* and had the support of editors Harold Ross and William Shawn. John Hersey, A. J. Liebling, Joseph Mitchell, Lillian Ross, Meyer Berger, and many other writers produced stunning articles and books from the mid-1930s onward, and their tradition has been carried forward by succeeding generations of *New Yorker* writers, including John McPhee, Mark Singer, Susan Orlean, Calvin Trillin, and Nick Lemann.

Mitchell and Liebling experimented with self-expression in their literary journalism in subtle ways that were never matched during the New Journalism era. During a series of interviews that began in 1988, Mitchell told me that when he worked for the newspapers, his fellow feature writers were always reading *The New Yorker,* and he saw the possibilities in working there. "That's the magazine that changed everything," Mitchell said. "For one thing, the detail was important but it seemed to lead to something."[3] Not only was *The New Yorker* an oasis for literary journalism, it also published work similar to what would be done by the New Journalists some twenty years later. McPhee, a *New Yorker* literary journalist during the New Journalism era and for thirty years afterward, once told me, "When the New Journalists came ashore, Joe Mitchell was there on the beach to greet them."

American culture in the forties and fifties did not lend itself easily to the spirit of literary journalism. World War II was a hard-news event filled with death and disaster on a massive scale. The news style (if not the substance) of objectivity triumphed, particularly in the fifties, pushing aside feature writers and literary journalists at many publications. The James Dean rebelliousness represented by motorcycles and the imminent rise of rock 'n' roll started in the fifties, but it would have its fullest flowering in the following decade. Wolfe correctly pointed to a new cultural sensibility in the New Journalism of the sixties that had not been there before. Conformity—symbolized by the rise of suburbia, the standard ranch home, and the repressive politics of Senator Joseph McCarthy and the Cold War—created problems for the experimental ethos of literary journalism.

In this desert of conformity, literary journalism found an oasis at *The New Yorker* magazine, beginning, most prominently, in 1939. New York was the most liberated city in America, and *The New Yorker* sheltered a handful of literary journalists for decades.

Harold Ross and his wife, Jane Grant, a *New York Times* reporter, founded *The New Yorker* in 1925 as a magazine dedicated to humor, criticism, short fiction, and reportage. *The New Yorker* also promised to cover contemporary events, the arts, books, and fiction.

In 1925, there were no city or regional magazines like *Boston, Chicago,* or *Texas Monthly.* Ross was a decent writer and reporter who had helped start *Stars and Stripes* during World War I and had published some volumes of wartime humor. He and Grant had many friends among the New York literati. Their social group—known as the Algonquin Round Table because they met for lunch at the Algonquin Hotel—included Alexander Woollcott, Heywood Broun, Robert Benchley, Franklin P. Adams, Dorothy Parker, George F. Kaufman, Marc Connelly, Ring Lardner, Robert Sherwood, and Edna Ferber. They were cosmopolitan, literary, bohemian, part of Greenwich Village culture at the time, and rather proud of it.[4] Ross's background in publishing humor, and clever one-liners from the Algonquin Round Table, helped frame the original *New Yorker* as a humor magazine. Molly Ivins in a 2005 column said, "One of my favorite examples of wit came during a game played by the Round Table set at the Algonquin Hotel in New York in the 1920s. They threw a word at you, and you had to use it immediately in a funny sentence. Dorothy Parker got 'horticulture' and promptly said, 'You can lead a whore to culture, but you can't make her think.'" A man once rubbed Marc Connelly's bald head and said, "That feels like my wife's behind." Connelly rubbed his own head and replied, "Why, so it does!"[5]

Quirky, innovative, and with a sure sense of taste, Ross and Grant invested their $20,000 savings in the new magazine, and Raoul Fleischmann invested $25,000 from his family's yeast and baking fortunes. Several more infusions of cash cost Fleischmann $195,000 in the first year. In 2005 dollars, Fleischmann's investment would be more than $2 million when compared to the Consumer Price Index.[6] Ross saw an opening in the publishing marketplace because most humor magazines sought national advertising but lost the local ads from department stores, theaters, and restaurants. *The New Yorker,* with its circulation approximately split between New York and the rest of the world beyond the Hudson River, attracted both national and local ads. The publishing formula worked, but the content of the magazine quickly moved away from humor toward broader arts and cultural materials. Edited for New York sophisticates, it traded on the reputation of the Algonquin Round Table, in effect putting their social sophistication on the newsstand for sale.

Its early success in the thirties owed only a little to literary journalism, but a great deal to a talented staff. Morris Markey wrote "Reporter at Large" pieces from 1925 until the early thirties and "kept the flame of literary journalism alive (rather dim, perhaps, at times, but still burning)," wrote Les Sillars. "Markey didn't only display his emotions in his stories, he displayed himself, habitually structuring them around the act of reporting. This near-revolutionary unveiling of the traditionally invisible reporter pre-figured the 'new journalists' of forty years hence." Markey was not especially popular, and according to Sillars, his unveilings revealed "elitist condescension" that may not have played well with his colleagues.[7]

Others established *The New Yorker* "voice." Katharine Angell edited the fiction department, while E. B. White, author of the classic children's stories *Charlotte's Web* and *Stuart Little,* developed the voice that would be called "*The New Yorker* style" in his "Notes and Comment" essays. Janet Flanner wrote her "Paris Letter." Lois Long covered New York fashions. James Thurber con-tributed short pieces and humorous drawings—originally penned on the plaster wall near his desk—that cemented both his reputa-tion and the magazine's.

Ross needed an organized and brilliant managing editor. He was shy around women, had difficulty firing people, and insisted on close editorial contact with writers, which, among several other characteristics, could leave him buried in details. He hired several important editors, including Stanley Walker, in his search for a ge-nius (the staff said he was looking for a "Jesus") who could under-stand his quirks and the staff's.[8] In 1933, he hired William Shawn, who not only made sense of Ross's editorial system but also made a difference in the future of literary journalism. In 1939, Shawn became managing editor. After Ross's death in 1951, Shawn suc-ceeded him and served for another thirty-five years. Shawn came to power when three of the foundation stones of *The New Yorker* were crumbling. Thurber's eyesight was failing and he steadily withdrew. Katharine Angell and E. B. White, who had married, moved to Maine in 1938, temporarily depriving the magazine of their guidance and contributions.[9] In the coming years, many of the magazine's best writers left for military service. Shawn and Ross sent many of the remaining writers out to report on World War II, including John Lardner, Philip Hamburger, E. J. Kahn Jr., Janet Flanner, Mollie Panter-Downes, Rebecca West, St. Clair McKelway, and Joel Sayre, and many of them produced literary journalism. Most important were A. J. Liebling reporting from France and John Hersey reporting first from Europe and later from China and Hiroshima, Japan.

Mitchell suggested to me that Shawn, editor Gardner Botsford, and managing editor Stanley Walker in the thirties hired feature writers from the New York newspapers who made enduring contributions to literary journalism. He included a generation of writers such as Meyer Berger, A. J. Liebling, Lillian Ross, Richard O. Boyer, St. Clair McKelway,[10] Alva Johnston, and Joel Sayre. Others present at the same time included John McNulty, Geoffrey Hellman, Philip Hamburger, John Lardner, Brendan Gill, Berton Roueché, and John Bainbridge. "I still think *The New Yorker*'s reporting before we got on it was pretty shoddy," Liebling once wrote, referring to himself, Mitchell, Jack Alexander, Boyer, and Berger.[11]

Conditions were lush and welcoming for literary journalism in the *New Yorker* habitat. Even the big New York newspapers limited their best feature writers in the time they could spend reporting and in the length of presentation. Newspapers did not pay well for features, according to Mitchell. Moving to *The New Yorker* gave writers more time to work, more space (in print, if not in their offices), superb editing, more money, greater autonomy, and in the cases of at least Mitchell, Liebling, and Lillian Ross opportunities to pursue their literary goals in nonfiction. Ross invested a larger-than-normal percentage of the budget in editorial department salaries. In return, he got some of the best writing in America.

Another Ross tradition was close editorial involvement in the pieces of writing that went into the magazine. Ross read every piece, scribbled comments and queries such as "Who he?" all over manuscripts, questioned just about everything, and in an effort to get all the facts right created a first-rate fact-checking department. The "Profile," or the journalistic biography, which was pioneered at *The New Yorker,* increased in size and complexity in this era. Nonfiction or "fact" pieces grew to considerable length, such as the five-part Profile of William Randolph Hearst in 1927. Some readers—including Joseph Pulitzer Jr.; Lawrence Winship, editor of the *Boston Globe;* and even Katharine White—began to complain about lengthy stories as Profiles were broken up and published in successive weeks. In 1940, the Profile was expanded from biographies of people to portraits of institutions in Geoffrey Hellman's twenty-thousand-word article on the Metropolitan Museum of Art.[12] The "Reporter at Large" features—generally prepared by writers who had a topic they could develop at length—became a dominant style of reporting. Humor and fiction occupied less and less of the magazine, although, like today, there were always cartoons and short humor pieces. Under Shawn, nonfiction began to rule.

Until the late 1950s, magazine writing had not fully exploited storytelling; one student of the era found little use of scenes, dramatization, or first-person narrative outside of *The New Yorker.*[13] No American magazine offered the consistent freedom and encouragement found at *The New Yorker.* The payoff came rapidly from writers such as Mitchell, Liebling, Hersey, Berger, and Ross, among others. Mitchell described magazines of the thirties such as *McCall's, Cosmopolitan,* and *Hearst's International* as "a digested form of newspaper journalism" and "absolutely perishable." Mitchell's literary journalism, as well as that of his friend Liebling, probed deeper into the borderlands of literature than did many of the highly publicized experiments of the New Journalism. "With *The New Yorker,* you were trying to write something that could be read again," Mitchell said.

I first met Joseph Mitchell in 1988. He had been with *The New Yorker* for fifty years. Although he was eighty-one years old and rumored to be a ghostly presence in the corridors of the magazine, he carried the grace of a much younger man. Mitchell's last *New Yorker* article appeared in 1964. He had regularly worked in his office since then, feeding speculation that this very private man had been writing some magnificent addition to the books he had published between 1938 and 1965. Curiosity had been fed by Mitchell's own last work, *Joe Gould's Secret.* For decades—and unintentionally—Mitchell had stirred the rumor mill by turning down requests for interviews. Mark Singer, a *New Yorker* writer whom I had known for several years, carried my request for a chat, and Mitchell agreed to meet with me. I had previously published an anthology of literary journalism, and although I did not know it at the time, Mitchell was preparing to publish his collected works, which appeared four years later. So many of his friends had died. Maybe, he said, much as we hate to think about it, the time had come to talk. We spent many hours together. Finding out what he had been doing for the past twenty-five years—tending to family business, working to establish the Fulton Fish Market as a cultural heritage zone, dealing with his own health problems, and writing pieces that he said were not yet ready for publication—was the least of my objectives. There were deeper mysteries in his writing.

Mitchell was a slim, bright-eyed, energetic man who puzzled over things and took pains to get them right. He dressed as he wrote, in a stylish and precise, yet comfortable, manner. As I think back on our several meetings, I remember Mitchell's probing, friendly eyes. My attention was repeatedly drawn to his delicate fingers as he handled a glass in Sloppy Louie's restaurant in the Fulton Fish Market or carefully sought a passage in a book. He mused about the ambiguous term "golden bass" on the menu at the mahogany-paneled Century Club until he decided it was in fact striped sea bass. He never intruded on a conversation, preferring to hear others talk. Courtesy may have been his most distinctive trait, along with an incredible memory. During one meeting, he told me a story about a New York anarchist, Carlo Tresca, from the thirties. He couldn't remember the name of the restaurant where they met once. Losing that detail at age eighty-one annoyed him. He called the *New Yorker* fact-checking department to see if anyone could retrieve for him the name of a restaurant that had probably been out of business for forty years.

Mitchell grew up in the cotton and tobacco region near Fairmont, North Carolina, where his ancestors had lived since before the Revolutionary War. After four years at the University of North Carolina, he became a reporter for the *New York Herald Tribune*. He worked as a feature writer at the *Herald Tribune* and *World-Telegram* until 1938, except, as he wrote, "for a period in 1931 when I got sick of the whole business and went to sea."[14] As was the case with Liebling, Mitchell apparently recognized the deficiencies of standard journalism while he was a newspaper writer. Liberated by conditions at *The New Yorker,* he wrote dozens of Profiles. His subjects were waterfront workers, people on the Bowery, Mohawk Indians working on high structural steel, and characters from the Fulton Fish Market in lower Manhattan near the Brooklyn Bridge.

Mitchell wrote in a way that "manages to get the marks of

writing off his writing," Calvin Trillin of *The New Yorker* told
me. "His writing has a 'magic slate' feel. You can't see him struggling with it. In narrative writing, getting yourself out of the way
is a wonderful thing. He often has a lot about himself in it, but
you can't see him being clever or striving or struggling. It reads as
if it just happens. He's a simple presence, like Joe DiMaggio."
The literary critic Stanley Edgar Hyman placed Mitchell in the
tradition of William Faulkner, Saul Bellow, and James Joyce.
Hyman said Mitchell "is a reporter only in the sense that Defoe
is a reporter."[15]

Like Defoe's *A Journal of the Plague Year,* Mitchell's book *Old Mr.
Flood* (1948) contained a composite character who was created at
the suggestion of Harold Ross, according to Mitchell. "Mr. Hugh
G. Flood," a 93-year-old retired house-wrecking contractor who
lived in a waterfront hotel and pursued his remaining ambition of
eating fish every day (and practically nothing else) and thereby living to be 115, was the composite character. "Mr. Flood is not one
man," Mitchell said. "Combined in him are aspects of several old
men who work or hang out in Fulton Fish Market, or who did in
the past. I wanted these stories to be truthful rather than factual,
but they are solidly based on facts."[16] John Hersey created a similar composite character in one of his World War II pieces, as did
A. J. Liebling in his "Colonel Stingo" book. Tom Wolfe later
cited Hersey's "Joe Is Home Now" composite and Liebling's
"Colonel Stingo" as "Not Half-Bad Candidates" in literary history
for the New Journalism, possibly without knowing they were
composites. At the time they were written, composites were part
of the journalistic landscape, but in the era of New Journalism
standards changed and writers were criticized especially for unacknowledged composites. When Mitchell later reprinted his Mr.
Flood pieces, they were labeled as fiction. A few other pieces

about "Black Ankle County" in North Carolina were also short fiction, identified as such from the beginning, as were four short stories from his book *McSorley's Wonderful Saloon*.

In our interviews, Mitchell was direct and clear: everything said by the characters in all of his nonfiction articles had been spoken by them and all the details were accurate. Mentioning the "Mr. Flood" stories in this context distorts Mitchell's extraordinary record. He justifiably stands in the top tier of twentieth-century literary journalists based on the work contained in *McSorley's Wonderful Saloon* (1943), *The Bottom of the Harbor* (1960), and *Joe Gould's Secret* (1965)—all reprinted in *Up in the Old Hotel* in 1992—in addition to *My Ears Are Bent* (1938), which contained his newspaper features, and *Apologies to the Iroquois with a Study of the Mohawks in High Steel* (1960), copublished with Edmund Wilson. Contemporary literary journalist Alec Wilkinson said, "Joseph Mitchell is the great artist/reporter of our century. The bulk of his writing is unshakably factual, but I feel when I read it the way I do when I look at a landscape or a still life by Giorgio Morandi, or a statue or portrait by Giacometti—that is, that I have absorbed an image of the way the world appears to a gifted, penetrating, and highly intelligent sensibility, and that I understand more of the world because of it."[17]

Mitchell's approach to journalism included the use of symbolic backgrounds and a technique he attributed to T. S. Eliot. "One thing you have to do, if you're going to write this sort of thing," he said, "is realize that people have buried their pain and have transformed experience enough to allow them to endure it and bear it. If you stay with them long enough, you let them reveal the past to themselves, thereby revealing it to you. Then they will dare to bring out the truth of something even if it makes them look bad." The people in Mitchell's literary journalism are more rounded characters than the people we meet in standard journalism who are flattened by the routine facts of age, occupation, appearance, and achievements. Mitchell took readers into a character's inner life. "You're trying to report, at the beginning without knowing it, the unconscious as well as the consciousness of a man or woman," Mitchell said. He wanted to report symbolic backgrounds in his journalism, producing an experience that we are capable of understanding more clearly than we can in everyday life.

Writing about moments that reveal inner life demanded an approach different from the frontal assault of standard journalism. "T. S. Eliot called it the 'objective correlative,'" Mitchell said. "It's where you write about one thing and you're actually writing about another. Or where you make one thing represent another." He recalled, as an example, a passage in D. H. Lawrence's *Sea and Sardinia* in which a man is roasting a young goat at a large, open fireplace. The scene presents a primitively spitted goat being roasted by an Italian peasant, greasy from the work he is doing, against the flickering shadows cast by the open flames and the bluish glow of burning fat, Mitchell said. "Suddenly you begin to realize that Lawrence is showing you how it was in the caves. He doesn't anywhere imply that, but you can't miss it. In other words, first you write the background for something to happen, and then it happens against this background. It has to be in the round. You have to have the person against the background. That gives a story meaning and significance, rather than plot."

Much of Mitchell's nonfiction seems to hold a persistently ugly outside world at arm's length. He found quiet places in the city, cemeteries, lonely docks, fishing boats, and bars peopled by old men. With the city—and the presence of the past—humming as a backdrop, peace inhabited those places. "Whatever quality is in my newspaper or magazine writing," Mitchell said, "has come

from the desire to put in a background, which is constantly changing, people who are constantly changing, but an *attitude* toward life
and death that doesn't change."

Stanley Edgar Hyman detailed some of the directly symbolic elements in Mitchell's *The Bottom of the Harbor:*

> Dusty hotel rooms shut up for decades and now reluctantly ex-
> plored are infantile experience; the wrecks on the bottom of the
> harbor, teeming with marine life, are festering failures and guilts;
> the rats that come boldly out of their holes in the dark before
> dawn are Id wishes; Mr. Poole's dream of the draining of New
> York harbor by earthquake is a paradigm of psychoanalysis; Mr.
> Hunter's grave is at once tomb and womb and marriage bed.[18]

At a party, Mitchell once met and questioned the literary critic
and scholar Kenneth Burke. "I was trying to find out, did there
exist in the fish market or in some saloons some kind of enigmatic
presence? I said, 'Do you think it's possible? Hovering around in
the fish market, is there something I can capture that would be
more than a distillation or compendium of facts?' He said, 'You
should be a poet.' And I said, 'Can't I be some other way?' I was
almost pleading with him." Instead of poetry, Mitchell tried lyricism in his fact writing. His work shows the power that comes
from the most commonplace words, small words used in just the
right way.

In *Joe Gould's Secret* and *The Bottom of the Harbor,* Mitchell explored an avenue for self-expression not often found in journalism.
How does a writer inject himself into the narrative without upsetting readers who are accustomed to impersonal newspaper prose?
How does he keep himself off the page, as Trillin observed, and
still have something to say? Some writers, such as James Agee,
threw themselves and their psyches into the foreground. Writers,

it seemed, could become a dominant part of the narrative, or else stand apart from it and erase their personalities and motivations. Both choices were uncomfortable for literary journalists. Liebling portrayed himself as a secondary character along the margins of the storyline, especially in his early work. In 1952, Liebling, writing about Colonel John R. Stingo ("The Honest Rainmaker"), "discovered a way to infuse himself into another man's nature in such a manner that he created an ostensibly real portrait that was in one sense fictional, in another, a retouched composite of two flesh-and-blood men," his biographer Raymond Sokolov wrote. In Liebling's case, Sokolov said, "his reportage turned into an indirect form of autobiography. His articles became character studies of himself, a writer at work in the demimonde."[19] Mitchell had already pioneered that ground. "I think Liebling's Colonel Stingo is my Mr. Flood, to tell you the truth," Mitchell said.

Few nonfiction writers before the New Journalism experimented so aggressively in self-expression as did Liebling and Mitchell. Those who did included Agee in *Let Us Now Praise Famous Men;* Hemingway in his nonfiction reports on Spain and Africa; George Orwell in *Homage to Catalonia, Down and Out in Paris and London,* and *The Road to Wigan Pier;* and John Dos Passos in *Orient Express.* Mitchell is present in his work as much as Norman Mailer and Joan Didion were in theirs as New Journalists, but modernist writers such as Didion and Mailer self-consciously played a role that the reader must interpret. Mitchell's presence remains in the background. He set motives and purposes behind a veil of symbolism while his personality merged into that of another character. In several respects, this was territory not explored by the New Journalists; few others have moved to this borderland.

"You hope the reader won't be aware," Mitchell told me. "If I read something and I think, 'Oh, God, here comes the myth,' I'm tired of it already. But if it's inherent and inescapable, then the reader will go along. You want to take the reader to the last sentence. I don't want to take him there just by *fact*. I want to take the reader there by going through an experience that I had that was revealing. There's something I like about that word 'reveal.'"

Mitchell's *Joe Gould's Secret* was a two-part profile for *The New Yorker* with the parts separated by twenty-two years. In Greenwich Village in 1932, Mitchell first saw Joe Gould, a short, gaunt, garrulous bohemian with a disheveled beard and a wild look. On the Bowery, Gould wore castoff clothes, and he cadged drinks by noisily demonstrating how he conversed with seagulls. Mitchell wrote that Gould was the son of a New England doctor and a graduate of Harvard's class of 1911. His ancestors had been in the New World since the 1630s. The first Profile, in 1942, was titled "Professor Sea Gull."[20]

Gould constantly scribbled in nickel composition books, writing the "Oral History of Our Time," which had grown over the years to fill hundreds of notebooks with millions of words. As reported by Mitchell and by writers for several other publications, "The Oral History" contained ordinary conversations, biographies of bums, sailor's tales, hospital experiences, harangues from speakers in Union Square and Columbus Circle, dirty stories, graffiti found in washrooms, gossip, accounts of Greenwich Village parties, and arguments about topics of the day such as free love, birth control, psychoanalysis, Christian Science, alcoholism, and art. Gould's inspiration came from William Butler Yeats, who once commented, "The history of a nation is not in parliaments and battlefields, but in what the people say to each other on fair days and high days, and in how they farm, and quarrel, and go on pilgrimage." Gould explained to Mitchell:

All at once, the idea for the Oral History occurred to me: I would spend the rest of my life going about the city listening to people—eavesdropping, if necessary—and writing down whatever I heard them say that sounded revealing to me, no matter how boring or idiotic or vulgar or obscene it might sound to others. I could see the whole thing in my mind—long-winded conversations and short and snappy conversations, brilliant conversations and foolish conversations, curses, catch phrases, coarse remarks, snatches of quarrels, the mutterings of drunks and crazy people, the entreaties of beggars and bums, the propositions of prostitutes, the spiels of pitchmen and peddlers, the sermons of street preachers, shouts in the night, wild rumors, cries from the heart.[21]

The idea behind the "Oral History" resonated with Mitchell. His own Profiles for *The New Yorker* had focused on ordinary people, especially on the Bowery and in the fish market—people who lived life fully but in ordinary ways. Describing the articles in *The Bottom of the Harbor*, Noel Perrin said that "each tells its story so much in the words of its characters that it feels like a kind of apotheosis of oral history."[22]

As a story, "Professor Sea Gull" had a problem: Mitchell never got a chance to read the "Oral History," which had been reported as containing nine million words and filling so many notebooks that they could be stacked higher than Gould himself. A man who lived in flophouses and temporary quarters, Gould had stashed his notebooks in friends' basements and attics. The opportunity never arrived for Mitchell to read them.

In the second part of the profile, his 1964 book *Joe Gould's Secret,* Mitchell reported his efforts to find the "Oral History," read some portion of it, and possibly get it published. (Warning: If you haven't read the book and do not want to know the secret, skip to the next break below (on page 186), to the paragraph beginning with "Of the several other *New Yorker* writers . . .")

His search led to a few notebooks filled with repetitive and obsessive memories of Gould's father, who had once made a psychologically damaging remark about his son's chances in life. After considerable searching, Mitchell discovered Joe Gould's secret: the "Oral History" did not exist. Gould's convincing patter had seemed unassailable to Mitchell and several other reporters. After confronting Gould and accusing him of making it all up, Mitchell immediately regretted it:

> I returned to my office and sat down and propped my elbows on my desk and put my head in my hands. I have always deeply disliked seeing anyone shown up or found out or caught in a lie or caught red-handed doing anything, and now, with time to think things over, I began to feel ashamed of myself for the way I had lost my temper and pounced on Gould.[23]

Charitably, Mitchell decided the "Oral History" existed in Gould's head and might one day be written down on paper.

> It was easy for me to see how this could be, for it reminded me of a novel that I had once intended to write. I was twenty-four years old at the time and had just come under the spell of Joyce's "Ulysses." My novel was to be "about" New York City. It was also to be about a day and a night in the life of a young reporter in New York City. . . . But the truth is, I never actually wrote a word of it. . . . When I thought of the cataracts of books, the Niagaras of books, the rushing rivers of books, the oceans of books, the tons and truckloads and trainloads of books that were pouring off the presses of the world at that moment, only a very few of

which would be worth picking up and looking at, let alone reading, I began to feel that it was admirable that he *hadn't* written it.[24]

Later on, Mitchell wrote, he received a letter from a friend of Gould's. "I have always felt that the city's unconscious may be trying to speak to us through Joe Gould," the letter said. "And that the people who have gone underground in the city may be trying to speak to us through him. And that the city's living dead may be trying to speak to us through him. People who never belonged anyplace from the beginning. People sitting in those terrible dark barrooms."[25]

Stanley Edgar Hyman's essay "The Art of Joseph Mitchell" presented this interpretation of the book:

> In literary terms, *Joe Gould's Secret* is a Jamesian story of life's necessary illusion. . . . The book is written, however, not in intricate Jamesian prose, but in the bubbling, overflowing manner of James Joyce. . . . In deeper terms, Gould is a masking (and finally an unmasking) for Mitchell himself. In *Joe Gould's Secret* Mitchell seems freer than ever before to talk about himself, his resolutions and intentions, his methods of reporting and writing, even his life. . . . By the end of the book, when he discovers Gould's secret, Mitchell becomes, not Gould's bearer or Gould's victim, but Gould himself, and the unwritten Oral History merges with Mitchell's own unwritten novel, a New York *Ulysses* (which Blooms magnificently even in four-page synopsis). Then we realize that Gould has been Mitchell all along, a misfit in a community of traditional occupations, statuses, and roles, come to New York to express his special identity; finally we realize that the body of Mitchell's work is precisely that Oral History of Our Time that Gould himself could not write.[26]

I may have taken Hyman's thesis—that Gould was actually Mitchell—too literally, but it seemed to make sense of several clues that I had encountered. For a while, I imagined that Gould never existed, and I could see hints in the text and our interviews:

- Mitchell had dealt with a fictionalized character before, "Mr. Flood," although he was based on fact. Mitchell told me that one part of "Mr. Flood" was Joe Mitchell—the part of the character who only ate seafood. "All the things I said in there about eating fish, that's what I believe," Mitchell said. He called it a "seafoodetarian diet."

- Gould said things about the "Oral History" that sounded like the Joe Mitchell I had been interviewing. For example, Gould is quoted as saying, "Some talk has an obvious meaning and nothing more, . . . and some, often unbeknownst to the talker, has at least one other meaning and sometimes several other meanings lurking around inside its obvious meaning." In another passage, Gould said, "In autobiography and biography, as in history, I have discovered, there are occasions when the facts do not tell the truth."[27] Gould looked for the revealing remark in conversations, which was a hallmark of Mitchell's reporting technique. Mitchell would sit for many hours listening to someone like Mr. George H. Hunter on Staten Island, waiting for comments that cast light on a lifetime. "He was the sad old man you see in Balzac or Thomas Hardy," Mitchell said of Mr. Hunter, "the sad old figure in the corner someplace who wants to tell you what he learned going through life, but he never got the chance."

- Gould's father, a doctor, had driven him away from home with his high expectations. Mitchell's father had contributed to his move to New York City, although less harshly. He had wanted Mitchell to become a cotton trader, but Mitchell had discovered while standing next to his father on the cotton-trading platform that he was almost a dyslectic in arithmetic. He knew he could never handle cutthroat cotton trading, so when he learned to write in college he took the opportunity to leave. "I always felt like an exile," he told me. So had Gould.

- Some passages in *Joe Gould's Secret* read like revelations in a mystery. For example, one night a bohemian in Goody's bar said to Gould, "You don't seem to be yourself." Gould answered, "I'm *not* myself. I've never been myself."[28]
- Last, the parallels were entirely too close. What had Mitchell been doing the previous twenty-five years while wandering around *The New Yorker* offices—writing an oral history? Mitchell's secret might parallel Gould's. Had he been not-writing nonfiction pieces, or a novel, or his own oral history that would portray New York as James Joyce had portrayed Dublin? Had he avoided the Niagara of books while actually creating a mask?

Eventually, I opened the subject and asked Mitchell if his interests had mingled with Gould's to create this work.

"Oh, Lord, yes," Mitchell said, startling me. "We were in the same boat. We both came from small towns and didn't fit in, and both had an idea. He had the same feeling about people on the park bench talking. I was talking about myself here. He was talking about himself and I was talking about myself."

"With all the people in New York City," I asked, "why does Joe Gould become an interesting person to you?"

"Because he is me," Mitchell said. "God forgive me for my version of Flaubert's remark about Madame Bovary. I think all of us are divided up into lots of different aspects, you might say. To mix them up, you almost have to say, 'I am so-and-so,' just as I tried to do with Gould and all the different aspects of the people who had seen him."

Mitchell later elaborated. "Everything in the Gould book is documented, all those things in the *Dial* and all the records of his family. But I could have used this documentation in a different way. The creative aspect of it is the particularity of the facts that you choose, and the particularity of the conversations that you choose, and the fact that you stayed with the man long enough to get a panoply of conversations from which you can choose the ones that you decide are the most significant. The Gould I described, I think, is the absolutely true Gould. But another person could have written the story about Joe Gould far differently."

Double-checking saves many errors. I made a phone call to Harvard that confirmed that Gould had graduated in 1911 and his father from Harvard Medical School in 1888. Then, I realized that such documentary evidence did not answer any of the literary questions. I believe Gould really did exist, because I have seen pictures of him and several reporters testified to his existence. Still, Mitchell occupied a good portion of Gould's character as he appeared on paper. Gould was not a fictionalized character as were "Mr. Flood," Liebling's "Colonel Stingo," or Hersey's "Joe." Mitchell selected the facts that made sense. Whatever the nature of Gould's personality, the symbolism of this book is pure Mitchell. Gould had created his own identity, a mask that gave him safety and security, as do all our masks. Mitchell always sought the true stories behind those masks, the window on the personality opened by the revealing remark. He found the truth in Gould's story, but part of Mitchell's life got entangled with it and created a mystery.

In *Joe Gould's Secret,* Mitchell used both structure and symbolism purposefully. He says he knows what happened to the "Oral

History" fairly near the start, but we do not learn the truth until close to the end. He finally reveals the secret about three-quarters of the way through the piece of writing. At that point, Mitchell indulges in a personal digression about the novel he himself had envisioned writing—modeled after Joyce's *Ulysses,* his favorite book. The preacher in this novel would talk about symbols of resurrection: eggs. Eggs are always symbols, Mitchell told me—whether they are Easter egg hunts in the cemeteries of North Carolina where he grew up, the shad roe in "The Rivermen," or the eggs Gould eats in the diner. At the climax of the book, Mitchell reveals Joe Gould's secret and talks about resurrection symbols like shad roe. This was not accidental for Mitchell.

One of the crucial underdeveloped talents for critics of nonfiction is the ability to read it as a creative medium that permits an author's expression in subtle and symbolic ways. When we pick up a piece of fiction by someone like John Updike or Anne Tyler, we know there's a purpose behind it. The writing is an expressive medium for the author. We may be entertained by the story; we may be informed. But ultimately we're trying to find out what the author wants to say to us about something. Nonfiction gets treated differently. We typically think nonfiction is about something other than the author—the Chinese economy, fishing, new computer techniques, or what has become of government policy. When we read Mitchell, however, we have something that is simultaneously journalism and literary, something that informs us about a person or a culture and at the same time expresses the author's ideas and feelings. He develops his symbolic presence most clearly in "The Rivermen" and in *Joe Gould's Secret.* It's a little harder to see in the piece on McSorley's Wonderful Saloon, reprinted in this volume, and in "Mr. Hunter's Grave," but it's still there. All of Mitchell's attitudes about the city, about ordinary people, about life and death and the purposes of life, about families, and so forth are expressed in these pieces.

The symbolism matters to the extent that it deepens our knowledge of Mitchell's work and of modern literary journalism. There are mysteries in Mitchell's prose that I could have asked him to explain, although I knew he might decline to answer. He was open about the tasks that had kept him busy for the past thirty years, but he preferred to have the written works speak for themselves. The mystery, after all, gives the prose an embedded edge. Was Mitchell really Joe Gould? Was *Old Mr. Flood* an incomplete novel presented as a *New Yorker* nonfiction Profile? Were his shad fishermen and Fulton Fish Market types a Joycean vision of the city, or were they merely results of interviews with ordinary people? James Rogers wrote that Mitchell, after discovering Joyce's *Ulysses,* wanted "to write a comparable book that was equally encyclopedic about New York."[29] Or perhaps he hoped to build a background for the Fulton Fish Market in the same way that Herman Melville had constructed *Moby-Dick.* The texts delivered puzzling clues, and along that edge of uncertainty Mitchell's work soared toward greatness.

Of the several other *New Yorker* writers who were creating innovative literary journalism before and after the war, the most important model for others was A. J. Liebling, a native of the city.

Joe Liebling got a job on the *New York World* Sunday magazine in 1931. *The World* was failing at the time. Later that year, he started working as a reporter for the *World-Telegram,* owned by Roy Howard. Liebling hated him with a passion because Howard, along with his habit of wearing garishly off-color sport coats, had taken over *The World,* a great newspaper, and diminished it through a merger with the *Evening Telegram.*

Liebling was twenty-six years old when he went to the *World-Telegram*—where he and Joe Mitchell became close friends—and thirty when he left, completing a twelve-year newspaper career that had begun when he was eighteen. He didn't care for the features he wrote there because he had in mind a higher literary standard. True literary craft required a long apprenticeship, Liebling assumed, and he generally coasted, but he knew that he was capable of better work. He kept telling Mitchell that he wanted to work for *The New Yorker* because writers there had a chance for creative growth.

In 1935, Liebling got his chance at *The New Yorker,* and he ended up writing for the magazine until his death. Liebling specialized in writing about con men, character types who, he believed, had something in common with newspaper reporting. Raymond Sokolov, his biographer, wrote this about Liebling's feature-writing experience and impression of newspapers:

> News, [Liebling] implied, was not an objective phenomenon reported on by passive observers; it was simply what reporters and editors decided was news. Interviews were not random affairs, didn't just occur, but were arranged and staged by reporters and interviewees, both of whom almost always had something to gain by their association; quotes, then, were a form of dialogue, lines in an artificial conversation from which every other speech (the reporter's questions) had been suppressed. Finally, reportorial anonymity was a convention and nothing more; reporters were not cameras but people who participated in news events—sometimes even caused them for their own purposes—and later wrote about them in highly artificial accounts called news stories. To put it plainly, Liebling implied that journalism was a confidence game like all the other arts. News was a contrivance; reporters

were mountebanks. The facts in newspapers were a kind of
fiction.[30]

The passage constitutes a sophisticated view of objective journalism that was way ahead of the scholarship of its day—but Liebling
knew his subject firsthand.

Liebling wrote about the same sorts of ordinary people as
Mitchell—prizefighters, con men, detectives, small shop owners,
restaurateurs—who were often worthy of his bemused tone of
voice. Mitchell and Liebling shared a literary vision, and they became lifelong friends. They raised journalism about ordinary—if
quirky—people to a national art form.

Their bookshelves included works by Charles Dickens,
Stephen Crane, Robert Louis Stevenson, and Mark Twain. They
also shared eclectic literary tastes: George Borrow's books on the
gypsies in Spain, François Villon, Ben Hecht's *Erik Dorn,* François
Rabelais, Ivan Turgenev, Fyodor Dostoevsky, Sherwood Anderson, and Robert Graves. Mitchell was a special fan of James Joyce
and of Russian literature, and Liebling built his book on boxing,
The Sweet Science, around the original nineteenth-century boxing
book by Pierce Egan. "I don't think of influencing Joe, or Joe influencing me at all," Mitchell said. "But it liberated me to talk to
Joe about writing, and he gave me a great feeling. We walked a
good deal coming up to the *World-Telegram.* He lived in the Village and so did I, and our wives were good friends—his first wife.
We talked a lot about books but not so much about our own writing. That was a private thing."

David Remnick, the current editor of *The New Yorker,* said
Liebling and Mitchell transformed the magazine. In his introduction to a book of selected works by Liebling, Remnick wrote:

In voice and carriage, the two men complemented each other. They walked the city together and ate lunch together at the Red Devil and Villa Nova and drank at Bleeck's and Costello's, and, on weekends, they went to the Rockaway beaches together to wade in the ocean and listen to the crowds. Mitchell was a courtly North Carolinian; unlike Liebling, he came to the city from the outside in, though his sympathy for its characters was no less absolute. The temperaments of the two men, especially on the page, diverged. In person, Liebling could be unnervingly quiet, but in print he was an ebullient Falstaff to Mitchell's Feste, the melancholic clown in *Twelfth Night.* Liebling was ribaldly comic, prolific, a writer of big effects, while Mitchell could be as spare in his line as he was in his output.[31]

At *The New Yorker,* William Shawn handled Liebling's copy and his training from the beginning. From 1936 until he left for Europe in September 1939, Liebling wrote Profiles of street characters, popular entertainers, con men, and boxers. Liebling claimed he received the assignment to Europe on the eve of World War II because he spoke French, but he was already a proven writer and just the kind of person who would find a different approach to a spectacular war story. Liebling's adult experience in France had started with a gift from his father in 1926—a year in Paris at the peak of the expatriate era during which young Abbott learned to eat French food with gusto on a budget. During the war, he encamped in Paris, followed the retreat to the coast, and returned with the invasion of Normandy.

While other reporters wrote about combat in Europe, Liebling sought out the stories of ordinary soldiers and of the French civilians who had survived occupation by two armies. After the war he retraced his route from a Normandy beachhead, where as a wobbly and overweight reporter he had come ashore under fire on D-Day, through the farmhouses and restaurants he had visited on the road back to Paris. A sophisticated gourmand who spoke French, he was celebrated in those farmhouses with bottles of aged Calvados hauled up from the wells as soon as the German army departed. Liebling's earthy first-person war reporting far exceeded the literary standards of contemporary journalism. He was later best known as *The New Yorker*'s press critic and as the author of *Chicago: The Second City* and *The Earl of Louisiana*.

The New Yorker provided Mitchell, Liebling, Lillian Ross, and other former feature writers with things they had longed for—money, space, and time. A fifteen-hundred-word newspaper feature, fed time and money, can grow into a piece on McSorley's. But this grown-up literary journalism does not have the same voice, tone, or style as the typical newspaper feature. For one thing, when you move from fifteen hundred words to eight thousand words, you need more elaborate structures and a different pacing.

Lillian Ross (no relation to Harold Ross) made the most of such conditions at *The New Yorker* and created a stir with her articles on Hemingway, the making of a movie, and the unlikely arrival in New York City of a high school graduating class from Bean Blossom, Indiana. Ross wrote for decades for the magazine but kept personal details so secret that it has been difficult to find out even such simple information as her date of birth. In 1998, she published a memoir, *Here But Not Here: My Life with William Shawn and* The New Yorker, which explained a great deal, including that she had been Shawn's extramarital companion. She has been widely recognized as a leading writer of the century, not only by Tom Wolfe

when he listed her as a "Not Half-Bad Candidate" for literary status in his essay "The New Journalism," but also by publishers of
literary anthologies. Anthologies regularly reprint her piece called
"The Yellow Bus"—making an unusual exception and ignoring
its nonfiction status to include it among ranking examples of fiction. "The Yellow Bus" (1960) documents a class trip to New
York City by an unsophisticated group of high school seniors from
rural Indiana. Ross treated the students respectfully as ordinary
people while contrasting them with the New Yorkers they encountered. Some students withdrew in shock; others exhibited
courageous curiosity about the city, which in many ways was alien
to their upbringing. Ross reported the story so thoroughly that the
narrator sometimes seems to be in two places at once.

Ross's work in the fifties offers further evidence that the
"nonfiction novel" of the New Journalism era was not new
when it arrived. One of her most famous *New Yorker* pieces was
"Production Number 1512," published in five issues in 1952. Titled *Picture* in book form, it followed John Huston's filming of
the movie *The Red Badge of Courage*. While in Hollywood at
Huston's invitation, Ross said, she recognized the possibility of
writing "this new story using a novelistic form." In a letter to
Shawn in 1950, she wrote, "You see, if the story turns out to be
what I think it is, it's really almost a book, a kind of novel-like
book because of the way the characters may develop and the variety of relationships that exist among them. I don't know
whether this sort of thing has ever been done before, but I don't
see why I shouldn't try to do a fact piece in a novel form, or
maybe a novel in fact form."[32]

Ross said she was guided by a set of enduring journalistic principles. Her rather conservative list from 1964 represents the evolution of literary journalism as it stood in the fifties and would be modified a bit by New Journalists in the sixties, but the realists among them could subscribe to her ideas. Ross identified with "-who-what-when-where-why-and-how guidelines" in her journalism, yet she enjoyed "the challenge of pushing traditional structures" and finding new ways to tell a story. "Every now and then," she noted, "journalism has been found to be timeless; and its writers have been considered to be on a par with the best in literature."[33] In 1981, her list of principles included such items as writing clearly; writing about people, situations, and events that attracted her; writing only about people she liked and who wanted to be written about; trusting her own reactions; and avoiding "interpretation, analysis, passing judgment, telling readers what to think." She included careful advice to take responsibility in regard to one's subjects, who had opened their lives, formed a friendship with the writer, and deserved discretion and protection. She wanted to avoid drawing attention to herself, as did the realists among the New Journalists, but she said, "The soul and nature of any writer are invariably found in his writing."[34]

In 2002, Ross listed the *New Yorker* writers who had most influenced her work. She included Mitchell, Liebling, E. B. White, and contemporary writers such as Mark Singer, Roger Angell, Susan Orlean, Malcolm Gladwell, David Owen, Ian Frazier, John Seabrook, Calvin Trillin, and David Remnick. She focused particularly on Mitchell. After Ross published an article, she said, Mitchell would come into her office and express admiration. "'It's that thing, that thing that takes hold of your fingers? It's doin' it for you, isn't it?' And he would shake his head from side to side and laugh in wonder," Ross said. "What Joe Mitchell called 'that thing' is indefinable. Readers, I know, respond to it. The nicest compliments have come from readers who say: 'You make me feel that I am right there with you.'"[35]

• • •

Harold Ross and Raoul Fleischmann created the conditions that allowed literary journalism to flourish at *The New Yorker*. The magazine became profitable in 1928 and by 1935 achieved a circulation of more than 125,000, with strong advertising support even during the Depression.[36] Ross paid writers well. He used a complex system, and according to Mitchell, Shawn felt that some writers were exploited, but the tradition of paying well for writing and for artwork endured at the magazine.

John McPhee once told me that no one was ever "assigned" a story at *The New Yorker* in the era of Shawn. They wrote what they wanted. If McPhee went to the editor and said he wanted to write about an exotic car auction, Shawn—if persuaded—would reserve the topic for him. Even if McPhee didn't complete the piece of writing for fifteen years, no one else would publish a piece about an exotic car auction in the magazine. Under Shawn, all the writers at the magazine were essentially freelancers; they got paid according to what they published in the magazine. A staff writer such as Mitchell, who was notoriously slow, might go two or three years and never publish anything. During that time, the writer could draw on an account. In effect, writers took a salary, but it was an advance on their published works. Space in print was flexible. McPhee published every word of *Coming Into the Country* (1977) in *The New Yorker* at an estimated fifty cents per word, and it runs 417 pages in paperback. After publication in the magazine, it was then published as a book and became a bestseller. As usual at *The New Yorker*, all publication rights reverted to the author after the magazine went to press. Janet Malcolm filled practically the whole magazine with her book on Sylvia Plath, and then published the book, which was reviewed on the front page of the *New York Times Book Review*. Only the first serial rights went to *The New Yorker*.

More than money, time, and space, the magazine allowed literary freedom for writers. This was the challenge Liebling, Mitchell, and Lillian Ross had been waiting for, and they responded. Funny thing about giving writers lots of time, money, space, and freedom—you tend to get the best writing in the country in return.

One of the best *New Yorker* writers was rambling through China at the end of World War II. John Hersey, the son of American missionaries, was born in China in 1914 and had an insider's knowledge that he built into his postwar pieces for *Life* and *The New Yorker.*

The war ended in August 1945 after the United States dropped atomic bombs on Hiroshima and Nagasaki. In the late spring of 1946, Hersey arrived in Hiroshima. He had no particular instructions from *The New Yorker* about what or how to write. His story involved one of the most spectacularly destructive forces of the twentieth century. At that time, only the trench warfare during World War I (8.5 million soldiers killed), the flu epidemic of 1918 (between 20 million and 40 million dead), the Great Depression, and the dawning reality of the Holocaust in Europe (11 million dead) occupied the popular imagination in the same way the A-bomb would. While the loss of life at Hiroshima and Nagasaki (150,000 to 200,000 killed) did not rival those other disasters, The Bomb instantly joined the Top Ten List of Worst Horrors of the Twentieth Century. The *potential* for nuclear war has plagued us ever since, even though the weapon has not yet been used on humans again. The Bomb unleashed a true physical and psychological horror. Newspaper stories published shortly after the A-bomb was dropped carried a hint of guilt and concern. Even in the context of a long and bloody war, people wondered if this weapon was a good idea.[37]

Hersey could have reported on life in Hiroshima several months after the bombing, something that was terrifying enough on its own. The population of Hiroshima had returned to about 130,000 in the months after the atomic explosion and devastating fire. After interviewing many survivors of the bombing, he could have compiled a larger panorama of the effects of The Bomb by including more people. By 1946, the statistics of The Bomb were becoming better known, and most Americans had heard about the force of the explosion, the number of square miles destroyed, the amount of radiation, and so forth. All these things were of interest to the military and had been extensively studied, first by the Japanese and then by the Americans.

Instead, he chose to write the personal stories of six individuals who had survived the blast. The six people did not represent any points of view and were not selected for their diversity. Their proximity to "ground zero" (the center point of a nuclear blast zone, where nothing survives), their injuries, their occupations—none of that mattered. They were merely the ones who had been good interview subjects.[38]

Hersey planned his first draft as a three-part article. *The New Yorker* traditionally published book-length manuscripts in three or more parts during consecutive weeks. But when he returned to New York, plans changed. Shawn immediately decided to publish it in one issue. Hersey spent ten 16-hour days rewriting, producing a single article in four sections. Shawn and Harold Ross were editing the copy as it came out of Hersey's typewriter. It went into the magazine very quickly, on August 31, 1946, a little over a year after the bombing—the first and only time that the entire editorial space in *The New Yorker* was devoted to a single work. That edition stunned readers of the magazine, not only because of the violation of magazine tradition but also because of the content.

It remains the single most valuable issue of the magazine in antique stores and on eBay.

Hersey's readers understood what had happened in general terms even if the physics remained a mystery. A bomb capable of enormous destruction, equivalent to 12,500 tons of TNT—whatever that means—had been created and used against a civilian population. The truth of the situation was even worse. The American public did not know at that time that the United States had planned the nuclear destruction of Hiroshima and Nagasaki in detail; the U.S. objectives for the strategy are still being debated.[39] As Hersey mentioned, by July 1945 most of the large cities in Japan had been bombed or, like Tokyo, firebombed. Hiroshima, along with Kyoto, considered a holy city by the Japanese, had been spared. Hiroshima was left untouched so that the devastation of the atomic bomb could be measured as an experiment. The United States rushed its only two atomic bombs to the theater of war and hurriedly dropped them in August because the military feared that the war would end before the weapons could be used. Negotiations in August 1945 were already under way for the surrender of Japan through third-party intermediaries, and the U.S. military knew of the negotiations. Most of Japan's cities were in ruins. Its political structure was crumbling. It was prepared to surrender. But Hersey did not know all of this in 1945.

The Bomb had been enormously expensive and military funds were secretly diverted for that purpose. Later, some argued that the military felt it was necessary to justify such a secret expense by using the weapon in warfare.

Hersey was writing in a climate of ambivalent public opinion. On one hand, after four years of war his readers were accustomed to hearing about the killing of Japanese. After Pearl Harbor one

billboard exhorted: "KILL JAPS, KILL JAPS, KILL MORE JAPS."[40] But
on the other hand, Americans had a sense of guilt about the bomb-
ings and wondered whether using the atomic bomb could have
been wrong.

Hersey wisely avoided any political context whatsoever. His
main theme was that some people had survived. His characters had
been thrown into one of the most devastating situations imagina-
ble. In the coming years, writers who had not been there could
only imagine atomic warfare. Works of fiction from *On the Beach*
to *Terminator* proposed a post–nuclear war world—suggesting a violent, chaotic aftermath. But in the real postnuclear Hiroshima,
culture and civility did not disintegrate after the bombing. People
who were buried and abandoned in burning houses, Hersey
wrote, called out to passers-by, "*Tasukete kure!* Help, if you
please!"[41] Dire circumstances did not break their formal politeness.
Individuals—and society—survived.

Hersey had the skills of a novelist, as he later proved in books
such as *The Child Buyer* (1960). And beforehand, in 1944, he had
turned one of his wartime news stories into a novel called *A Bell
for Adano,* which won the Pulitzer Prize for fiction. In Japan,
Hersey faced an event so unnaturally spectacular that he had to be
careful. The force of The Bomb can easily overwhelm words.
Hersey adopted a restrained, understated tone from the beginning.
He could assume that people were concerned, worried, and ap-
palled, and that they would fill in the gaps he left in his vision of
the horror. It was already in their minds.

Hiroshima shares characteristics with other pieces of literary
journalism. It focuses on ordinary people and their personal experiences. The experiences are symbolic of many others, yet these
characters are presented as individuals. Whereas most standard reporting is based on statistics, celebrities, and generalities, Hersey

described the experiences of individuals in specific detail. He revealed culture in the attitudes and responses of people rather than writing about the event itself. The narrative moves forward in time without a narrator's all-knowing viewpoint, leaving the reader in the moment with the subjects.

Hersey concentrated on the details and resisted the temptation to comment. He kept the reader inside the world that his subjects inhabited whether buildings were shattering, trapped neighbors were burning, or people were helplessly awaiting the dawn. They did not know what had caused this disaster, and they often could not leave their immediate location—and neither can the reader. When we encounter the soldiers whose eyes have melted, or the people whose skin is peeling off in strips—moments when we might avert our eyes from a film—we cannot help but recognize that survival is the only issue in such circumstances.

This was one of those occasions where truth is stranger than fiction. Hersey had many true stories of great intensity and emotionalism, and he had access to the people who had experienced them firsthand. In that situation, nonfiction won its age-old battle with fiction. Historian Stanley Weintraub said, "*Hiroshima* may be the most unforgettable work of journalism of the 20th century."[42] For Steinbeck in the Great Depression, fiction prevailed, but nonfiction was genuinely a better medium for dealing with The Bomb. The power of Hersey's work came from the fact that it was true. *This actually happened.*

When *The New Yorker* published "Hiroshima" in 1946, it was an astounding success. The *New York Times* in an editorial the next day said every American ought to read it. Albert Einstein requested a thousand copies. The Book-of-the-Month Club gave free copies of the book to all its members. It was distributed worldwide by the end of 1946, with the exception of Japan, where the American military effectively banned it for several years. It has been reprinted in about sixty editions since then.

Hersey, Mitchell, Ross, and Liebling were writing only about ten years after John Steinbeck wrote *The Grapes of Wrath* (1939), but something had changed in the world of literature and journalism. *The New Yorker* had a lot to do with that change. The writers and editors at *The New Yorker* were working on a new vision of nonfiction that was not viable for Steinbeck. Just around the corner, the New Journalists of the 1960s, including Norman Mailer and Tom Wolfe, were preparing to come ashore on a beach where Hersey, Liebling, Ross, and Mitchell were wading in the ocean and sunning on the sand.

"THE OLD HOUSE AT HOME"

◈

JOSEPH MITCHELL

McSorley's occupies the ground floor of a red-brick tenement at 15 Seventh Street, just off Cooper Square, where the Bowery ends. It was opened in 1854 and is the oldest saloon in New York City. In eighty-eight years it has had four owners—an Irish immigrant, his son, a retired policeman, and his daughter—and all of them have been opposed to change. It is equipped with electricity, but the bar is stubbornly illuminated with a pair of gas lamps, which flicker fitfully and throw shadows on the low, cobwebby ceiling each time someone opens the street door. There is no cash register. Coins are dropped in soup bowls—one for nickels, one for dimes, one for quarters, and one for halves—and bills are kept in a rosewood cashbox. It is a drowsy place; the bartenders never make a needless move, the customers nurse their mugs of ale, and the three clocks on the walls have not been in agreement for many years. The clientele is motley. It includes mechanics from the many garages in the neighborhood, salesmen from the restaurant-supply houses on Cooper Square, truck-drivers from Wanamaker's, internes from Bellevue, students from Cooper Union, and clerks from the row of second-hand bookshops just north of Astor Place. The backbone of the clientele, however, is a rapidly thinning group of crusty old men, predominantly Irish, who have been drinking there since they were youths and now have a proprietary feeling about the place. Some of them have tiny pensions, and are alone in the world; they sleep in Bowery hotels and spend practically all their waking hours in McSorley's. A few of these veterans clearly remember John McSorley, the founder, who died in 1910 at the age of eighty-seven. They refer to him as Old John, and they like to sit in rickety armchairs around the big belly stove which heats the place, gnaw on the stems of their pipes, and talk about him.

Old John was quirky. He was normally affable but was subject to spells of unaccountable surliness during which he would refuse to answer when

Originally in *The New Yorker.*

spoken to. He went bald in early manhood and began wearing scraggly, patriarchal sideburns before he was forty. Many photographs of him are in existence, and it is obvious that he had a lot of unassumed dignity. He patterned his saloon after a public house he had known in his hometown in Ireland—Omagh, in County Tyrone—and originally called it the Old House at Home; around 1908 the signboard blew down, and when he ordered a new one he changed the name to McSorley's Old Ale House. That is still the official name; customers never have called it anything but McSorley's. Old John believed it impossible for men to drink with tranquillity in the presence of women; there is a fine back room in the saloon, but for many years a sign was nailed on the street door, saying, "NOTICE. NO BACK ROOM IN HERE FOR LADIES." In McSorley's entire history, in fact, the only woman customer ever willingly admitted was an addled old peddler called Mother Fresh-Roasted, who claimed her husband died from the bite of a lizard in Cuba during the Spanish-American War and who went from saloon to saloon on the lower East Side for a couple of generations hawking peanuts, which she carried in her apron. On warm days, Old John would sell her an ale, and her esteem for him was such that she embroidered him a little American flag and gave it to him one Fourth of July; he had it framed and placed it on the wall above his brass-bound ale pump, and it is still there. When other women came in, Old John would hurry forward, make a bow, and say, "Madam, I'm sorry, but we don't serve ladies." If a woman insisted, Old John would take her by the elbow, head her toward the door, and say, "Madam, please don't provoke me. Make haste and get yourself off the premises, or I'll be obliged to forget you're a lady." This technique, pretty much word for word, is still in use.

In his time, Old John catered to the Irish and German workingmen—carpenters, tanners, bricklayers, slaughter-house butchers, teamsters, and brewers—who populated the Seventh Street neighborhood, selling ale in pewter mugs at five cents a mug and putting out a free lunch inflexibly consisting of soda crackers, raw onions, and cheese; present-day customers are wont to complain that some of the cheese Old John laid out on opening night in 1854 is still there. Adjacent to the free lunch he kept a quart crock of tobacco and a rack of clay and corncob pipes—the purchase of an ale entitled a man to a smoke on the house; the rack still holds a few of the communal pipes. Old John was thrifty and was able to buy the tenement—it is five stories high and holds eight families—about ten years after he opened the saloon in it. He distrusted banks and always kept his money in a cast-iron safe; it still stands in the back room, but its doors are loose on their hinges and there is nothing in it but an accumulation of expired saloon licenses and several McSorley heirlooms, including Old John's straight razor. He lived with his family in a flat directly over the saloon and got up every morning at five and took a long walk before breakfast, no matter what the weather. He unlocked the saloon at seven, swept it out himself, and spread sawdust on the floor. Until he became too feeble to manage a racing sulky, he always kept a horse and a nanny goat in a stable around the corner on St. Mark's Place. He kept both animals in the same stall, believing, like many horse-lovers, that horses should have company at night. During the lull in the afternoon a stablehand would lead the horse around to a hitching block in front of the saloon, and Old John, wearing his bar apron, would stand on the curb and groom the animal. A customer who wanted service would tap on the window and Old John would drop his currycomb, step inside, draw an ale, and return at once to the horse. On Sundays he entered sulky races on uptown highways.

From the time he was twenty until he was fifty-five, Old John drank steadily, but throughout the last thirty-two years of his life he did not take a drop, saying, "I've had my share." Except for a few experimental months in 1905 or 1906, no spirits ever have been sold in McSorley's; Old John maintained that the man never lived who needed a stronger drink than a mug of ale warmed on the hob of a stove. He was a big eater. Customarily, just before locking up for the night, he would grill himself a three-pound T-bone, placing it on a coal shovel and holding it over a bed of oak coals in the back-room fireplace. He liked to fit a whole onion into the hollowed-out heel of a loaf of French bread and eat it as if it were an apple. He had an extraordinary appetite for onions, the stronger the better, and said that "Good ale, raw onions, and no ladies" was the motto of his saloon. About once a month during the winter he presided over an on-the-house beefsteak party in the back room, and late in life he was president of an organization of gluttons called the Honorable John McSorley Pickle, Beefsteak, Baseball Nine, and Chowder Club, which held hot-rock clambakes in a picnic grove on North Brother Island in the East River. On the walls are a number of photographs taken at outings of the club, and in most of them the members are squatting around kegs of ale; except for the president, they all have drunken, slack-mouthed grins and their eyes look dazed. Old John had a bull-frog bass and enjoyed harmonizing with a choir of drunks. His favorite songs were "Muldoon, the Solid Man," "Swim Out, You're Over Your Head," "Maggie Murphy's Home," and "Since the Soup House Moved Away." These songs were by Harrigan and Hart, who were then called "the Gilbert and Sullivan of the U.S.A." He had great respect for them and was pleased exceedingly when, in 1882, they made his saloon the scene of one of their slum comedies; it was called "McSorley's Inflation."

Although by no means a handshaker, Old John knew many prominent men. One of his closest friends was Peter Cooper, president of the North American Telegraph Company and founder of Cooper Union, which is a half-block west of the saloon. Mr. Cooper, in his declining years, spent so many afternoons in the back room philosophizing with the workingmen that he was given a chair of his own; it was equipped with an inflated rubber cushion. (The chair is still there; each April 4th for a number of years after Mr. Cooper's death, on April 4, 1883, it was draped with black cloth.) Also, like other steadfast customers, Mr. Cooper had a pewter mug on which his name had been engraved with an icepick. He gave the saloon a life-sized portrait of himself, which hangs over the mantel in the back room. It is an appropriate decoration, because, since the beginning of prohibition, McSorley's has been the official saloon of Cooper Union students. Sometimes a sentimental student will stand beneath the portrait and drink a toast to Mr. Cooper.

Old John had a remarkable passion for memorabilia. For years he saved the wishbones of Thanksgiving and Christmas turkeys and strung them on a rod connecting the pair of gas lamps over the bar; the dusty bones are invariably the first thing a new customer gets inquisitive about. Not long ago, a Johnny-come-lately annoyed one of the bartenders by remarking, "Maybe the old boy believed in voodoo." Old John decorated the partition between barroom and back room with banquet menus, autographs, starfish shells, theatre programs, political posters, and worn-down shoes taken off the hoofs of various race and brewery horses. Above the entrance to the back room he hung a shillelagh and a sign: "BE GOOD OR BEGONE." On one wall of the barroom he placed portraits of horses, steamboats, Tammany bosses, jockeys, actors, singers, and statesmen. Around 1902 he put up a heavy oak frame containing excellent portraits of Lincoln, Garfield, and McKinley, and to the frame he attached a brass title tag reading, "THEY ASSASSINATED THESE GOOD MEN THE SKULKING DOGS." On the same wall he hung framed front pages of old newspapers; one, from the London *Times* for June 22, 1815, has in its lower right-hand corner a single paragraph on the beginning of the battle of Waterloo, and another, from the New York *Herald* of April 15, 1865, has a one-column story on the shooting of Lincoln. He blanketed another wall with lithographs and steel engravings. One depicts Garfield's deathbed. Another is entitled "The Great Fight." It was between Tom Hyer and Yankee Sullivan, both bareknuckled, at Still Pond Heights, Maryland, in 1849. It was won by Hyer in sixteen rounds, and the prize was $10,000. The judges wore top hats. The title tag on another engraving reads, "Rescue of Colonel Thomas J. Kelly and Captain Timothy Deacy by Members of the Irish Revolutionary Brotherhood from the English Government at Manchester, England, September 18, 1867." A copy of the Emancipation Proclamation is on this wall; so, inevitably, is a facsimile of Lincoln's saloon license. An engraving of Washington and his generals hangs next to an engraving of a session of the Great Parliament of Ireland. Eventually Old John covered practically every square inch of wall space between wainscot and ceiling with pictures and souvenirs. They are still in good condition, although spiders have strung webs across many of them. New customers get up on chairs and spend hours studying them.

Although Old John did not consider himself retired until just a few years before he died, he gave up day-in-and-day-out duty back of the bar around 1890 and made his son, William, head bartender. Bill McSorley was the kind of person who minds his own business vigorously. He inherited every bit of his father's surliness and not much of his affability. The father was by no means a lush, but the son carried temperance to an extreme; he drank nothing but tap water and tea, and bragged about it. He did dip a little snuff. He was so solemn that before he was thirty several customers had settled into the habit of calling him Old Bill. He worshipped his father, but no one was aware of the profundity of his worship until Old John died. After the funeral, Bill locked the saloon, went upstairs to the family flat, pulled the shutters to, and did not come out for almost a week. Finally, on a Sunday morning, gaunt and silent, he came downstairs with a hammer and a screwdriver and spent the day painstakingly securing his father's pictures and souvenirs to the walls; they had been hung hit or miss on wires, and customers had a habit of taking them down. Subsequently he commissioned a Cooper Union art teacher to make a small painting of Old John from a photograph. Bill placed it on the wall back of the bar and thereafter kept a hooded electric light burning above it, a pious custom that is still observed.

Throughout his life Bill's principal concern was to keep McSorley's exactly as it had been in his father's time. When anything had to be changed or repaired, it appeared to pain him physically. For twenty years the bar had a deepening sag. A carpenter warned him repeatedly that it was about to collapse; finally, in 1933, he told the carpenter to go ahead and prop it up. While the work was in progress he sat at a table in the back room with his head in his hands and got so upset he could not eat for several days. In the same year the smoke- and cobweb-encrusted paint on the ceiling began to flake off and float to the floor. After customers complained that they were afraid the flakes they found in their ale might strangle them to death, he grudgingly had the ceiling repainted. In 1925 he had to switch to earthenware mugs; most of the pewter ones had been stolen by souvenir hunters. In the same year a coin-box telephone, which he would never answer himself, was installed in the back room. These were about the only major changes he ever allowed. Occasionally one of the pictures his father had hung would fall off the wall and the glass would break, and he would fill in the gap. His contributions include a set of portraits of the wives of Presidents through the first Mrs. Woodrow Wilson, a poster of Barney Oldfield in a red racing car, and a poem called "The Man Behind the Bar." He knew this poem by heart and particularly liked the last verse:

When St. Peter sees him coming he will leave the gates ajar,
For he knows he's had his hell on earth, has the man behind the bar.

As a businessman, Bill was anachronous; he hated banks, cash registers, bookkeeping, and salesmen. If the saloon became crowded, he would close up early, saying, "I'm getting too confounded much trade in here." Agents for the brewery from which he bought his ale often tried to get him to open a checking account; he stubbornly continued to pay his ale bills with currency, largely silver. He would count out the money four or five times and hand it to the driver in a paper bag. Bill was an able bartender. He understood ale; he knew how to draw it and how to keep it, and his bar pipes were always clean. In warm weather he made a practice of chilling the mugs in a tub of ice; even though a customer nursed an ale a long time, the chilled earthenware mug kept it cool. Except during prohibition, the rich, wax-colored ale sold in McSorley's always has come from the Fidelio Brewery on First Avenue; the brewery was founded two years before the saloon. In 1934, Bill sold this brewery the right to call its ale McSorley's Cream Stock and gave it permission to use Old John's picture on the label; around the picture is the legend "As brewed for McSorley's Old Ale House." During prohibition McSorley's ale was produced mysteriously in rows of barrels and washtubs in the cellar by a retired brewer named Barney Kelly, who would come down three times a week from his home in the Bronx. On these days the smell of malt and wet hops would be strong in the place. Kelly's product was raw and extraordinarily emphatic, and Bill made a practice of weakening it with near beer. In fact, throughout prohibition Bill referred to his ale as near beer, a euphemism which greatly amused the customers. One night a policeman who knew Bill stuck his head in the door and said, "I seen a old man up at the corner wrestling with a truck horse. I asked him what he'd been drinking and he said, 'Near beer in McSorley's.'" The prohibition ale cost fifteen cents, or two mugs for a quarter. Ale now costs a dime a mug.

Bill was big and thick-shouldered, but he did not look strong; he had a shambling walk and a haggard face and always appeared to be convalescing from something. He wore rusty-black suits and black bow ties; his shirts, however, were surprisingly fancy—they were silk, with candy stripes. He was nearsighted, the saloon was always dimly lit, and his most rigid conviction was that drink should not be sold to minors; consequently he would sometimes peer across the bar at a small-sized adult and say, "Won't sell you nothing, bud. Get along home, where you belong." Once he stared for a long time at a corner of the saloon and suddenly shouted, "Take your foot off that table!" Evidently he had been staring at a shadow; no one was sitting in the corner. Bill was tyrannical. Reading a newspaper, he would completely disregard a line of customers waiting to be served. If a man became impatient and demanded a drink, Bill would look up angrily and shout obscene remarks at him in a high, nasal voice. Such treatment did not annoy customers but made them snicker; they thought he was funny. In fact, despite Bill's bad disposition, many customers were fond of him. They had known him since they were young men together and had grown accustomed to his quirks. They even took a wry sort of pride in him, and when they said he was the gloomiest, or the stingiest, man in the Western Hemisphere there was boastfulness in their voices; the more eccentric he became, the more they respected him. Sometimes, for the benefit of a newcomer, one of these customers would show Bill off, shouting, "Hey, Bill, lend me fifty dollars!" or "Hey, Bill, there ain't no pockets in a shroud!" Such remarks usually provoked an outburst of gamy epithets. Then the customer would turn proudly to the newcomer and say, "See?" When prohibition came, Bill simply disregarded it. He ran wide open. He did not have a peephole door, nor did he pay protection, but McSorley's was never raided; the fact that it was patronized by a number of Tammany politicians and minor police officials probably gave it immunity.

Bill never had a fixed closing hour but locked up as soon as he began to feel sleepy, which was usually around ten o'clock. Just before closing he would summon everybody to the bar and buy a round. This had been his father's custom and he faithfully carried it on, even though it seemed to hurt him to do so. If the customers were slow about finishing the final drink, he would cough fretfully once or twice, then drum on the bar with both fists and say, "Now, see here, gents! I'm under no obligoddamnation to stand here all night while you hold on to them drinks." Whenever Bill completely lost his temper he would jump up and down and moan piteously. One night in the winter of 1924 a feminist from Greenwich Village put on trousers, a man's topcoat, and a cap, stuck a cigar in her mouth, and entered McSorley's. She bought an ale, drank it, removed her cap, and shook her long hair down on her shoulders. Then she called Bill a male chauvinist, yelled something about the equality of the sexes, and ran out. When Bill realized he had sold a drink to a woman, he let out a cross between a moan and a bellow and began to jump up and down. "She was a woman!" he yelled. "She was a goddamn woman!"

Bill was deaf, or pretended to be; even so, ordinary noises seemed to bother him unduly. The method he devised to keep the saloon tranquil was characteristic of him. He bought a fire-alarm gong similar to those used in schools and factories and screwed it to the seven-foot-tall icebox behind the bar. If someone started a song, or if the old men sitting around the stove began to yell at each other, he would shuffle over to the gong and give the rope a series of savage jerks. The gong is there yet and is customarily sounded at a quarter to midnight as a warning that closing time is imminent; the customers grab their ears when it goes off. Bill was consistent in his aversion to noise; he didn't even like the sound of his own voice. He was able to go for days without speaking, answering all questions with a snort or a grunt. A man who drank in McSorley's steadily for sixteen years once said that in that time Bill spoke exactly four intelligible words to him. They were "Curiosity killed the cat." The man had politely asked Bill to tell him the history of a pair of rusty convict shackles on the wall. He learned later that a customer who had fought in the Civil War had brought them back from a Confederate prison in Andersonville, Georgia, and had given them to Old John as a souvenir.

Bill would sometimes take an inexplicable liking to a customer. Around 1911 a number of painters began hanging out in McSorley's. Among them were John Sloan, George Luks, Glenn O. Coleman, and Stuart Davis. They were all good painters, they didn't put on airs, and the workingmen in the saloon accepted them as equals. One night, Hippolyte Havel, the anarchist, came in with the painters. Havel was a long-haired, myopic, gentle-mannered Czech whose speeches often got him in trouble with the police. Even Bill was curious about him. "What's that crazy-looking fellow do for a living?" he asked one of the painters. Playing safe, the painter said Havel was a politician, more or less. Havel liked the place and became a steady customer. Most nights after making a fiery speech in Union Square, he would hurry down to McSorley's. To the amazement of the old-timers, a strong friendship grew up between him and Bill, who was a Tammany Democrat and an utter reactionary; no one was ever able to figure out the basis of the friendship. Bill called the anarchist Hippo and would let him have credit up to two dollars; other customers were not allowed to charge so much as a nickel cigar. Bill had an extremely vague idea about Havel's politics. Charles Francis Murphy, the Tammany boss, occasionally dropped in, and once Bill told Havel he was going to speak a good word to the boss for him. "Maybe he'll put you in line for something," Bill said. The anarchist, who thought no man was as foul as a Tammany boss, smiled and thanked him. A police captain once took it upon himself to warn Bill against Havel. "You better keep your eyes on that long-haired nut," he said. "Why?" asked Bill. The question annoyed the police captain. "Hell fire, man," he said, "Havel's an anarchist! He's in favor of blowing up every bank in the country." "So am I," said Bill. Bill's friendship for Havel was extraordinary in every way. As a rule, he reserved his kindness for cats. He owned as many as eighteen at once and they had the run of the saloon. He fed them on bull livers put through a sausage grinder and they became enormous. When it came time to feed them, he would leave the bar, no matter how brisk business was, and bang on the bottom of a tin pan; the fat cats would come loping up, like leopards, from all corners of the saloon.

Bill had been married but was childless, and he used to say, "When I go, this place goes with me." In March, 1936, however, he changed his mind—why, no one knows—and, to the surprise of the veteran customers, sold both saloon and tenement to Daniel O'Connell, an old policeman, who, since 1900, had spent most of his leisure at a table in the back room. O'Connell retired from the Department two days before he purchased the saloon. He was the kind of man of whom people say, "If he can't speak a good word about you, he won't speak a bad one." He was almost as proud of the saloon's traditions as Bill and willingly promised he would make no changes; that was one of the conditions of the sale. Almost from the day Bill sold out, his health began to fail. He took a room in the house of a relative in Queens. Sometimes, in the afternoon, if the weather was good, he would shuffle into the bar, a sallow, disenchanted old man, and sit in the

Peter Cooper chair with his knotty hands limp in his lap. For hours he would sit and stare at the painting of Old John. The customers were sure he was getting ready to die, but when he came in they would say, "You looking chipper today, Billy boy," or something like that. He seemed grateful for such remarks. He rarely spoke, but once he turned to a man he had known for forty years and said, "Times have changed, McNally." "You said it, Bill," McNally replied. Then, as if afraid he had been sentimental, Bill coughed, spat, and said, irrelevantly, "The bread you get these days, it ain't fit to feed a dog." On the night of September 21, 1938, barely thirty-one months after he quit drawing ale, he died in his sleep. As close as his friends could figure it, his age was seventy-six.

The retired policeman made a gentle saloonkeeper. Unlike Bill, he would never throw a quarrelsome drunk into the street but would try to sober him up with coffee or soup. "If a man gets crazy on stuff I sold him, I can't kick him out," he said one day. "That would be evading my responsibility." He was proprietor for less than four years. He died in December, 1939, and left the property to a daughter, Mrs. Dorothy O'Connell Kirwan. A young woman with respect for tradition, Mrs. Kirwan has chosen to remain in the background. At first customers feared that she would renovate the place, but they now realize that this fear was groundless. "I know exactly how my father felt about McSorley's," Mrs. Kirwan said, "and so long as I am owner, no changes will be made. I won't even change the rule against women customers." She herself visits the saloon only on Sunday nights after hours. Even so, early in her ownership she made a mistake in judgment that brought about a crisis in McSorley's. She had a hard time getting over this mistake, but she now looks back on it as a blessing in disguise and regards the crisis as a kind of inevitable demarcation between McSorley's past under Old John and Old Bill and her father and McSorley's present under her. She enjoys telling about this.

"For some months after my father's death," she says, "I let things drift in McSorley's. I left everything in the hands of my father's two old bartenders, the day bartender and the night bartender, but the responsibility was too much for them and things gradually got out of hand, and I saw I had to find a manager—someone to look after the books and pay the bills and just generally take charge. And the more I thought about it the more I thought that the exact right person for the job was an uncle of mine named Joe Hnida. Well, I grew up in an Irish family that has lived in one of the old Irish neighborhoods on the west side of Greenwich Village for generations, in among the bohemians and the erratical personalities, and I thought I knew quite a lot about human behavior, but I soon found out that I didn't. Joe Hnida is a Czech, and he's an uncle of mine by marriage—he's my father's sister's husband. He worked for a limousine service that specializes in weddings and funerals; he was the supervisor of the drivers. Joe's a kind, decent, hardworking, trustworthy man, and I spoke to him and asked him if he would care to take over the management of McSorley's. He thought it over and decided he would. Well, Joe started out in McSorley's on a Monday morning and by the end of the week I was getting telephone calls from some of the real old-timers among the customers, all of them old friends of my father's, complaining about him. What I hadn't taken into account is that Joe is a man of few words, a very few—he just doesn't have any small talk. In addition, he's unusually self-sufficient. And also in addition, and I think he himself would agree, if he has any sense of humor at all it's a Czech sense of humor—it certainly isn't an Irish sense of humor. Anyway, it seemed that some of the old men who sit in those chairs along the wall in McSorley's all day long and do a lot of talking and arguing back and forth among themselves would try to start conversations with Joe and Joe just wouldn't participate. As one of them told me, 'He'll go so far as to say "Good morning" or "How do you do?" and he'll answer you yes or no, but that's about the full extent and sum total of what he has to say. He won't even comment on the weather.' 'If he's behind the bar,' another one told me, 'he'll draw an ale for a customer and take his money and give him his change, and that's the end of it. He just will not speak a single unnecessary word.' A few of the old men developed a liking for Joe, but they were ones who never had much to say themselves. And before long, little by little, most of the old men convinced themselves that Joe considered them to be just a bunch of old bores and windbags and they also convinced themselves that he looked down on them, and to get back at him they began to mock him behind his back and call him 'that stuck-up Czechoslovakian hearse-driver.' When the old men telephoned me I tried to explain Joe to them and stand up for him and smooth things over. 'After all,' I said, 'Bill McSorley didn't exactly knock himself out talking. According to my father, there were days you couldn't get a word out of him.' But that didn't do any good. Bill McSorley was different—he owned the place and he had earned the right to do as he pleased, and he might not necessarily care if you lived or died but he didn't give you the impression that he looked down on you. This new man comes in here out of nowhere and he won't even be polite. It went on and on like that. Weeks went by and months went by and things didn't get any better. And then one day the oldest of the bartenders, a man I completely trust, telephoned me and said that just about the worst that could happen had happened. 'It's completely ridiculous, Dot,' he said, 'but the old men have discovered that Joe doesn't like ale. He's done his best to hide this, but it somehow slipped out, and they began right away picking on him about it, whereupon he got his back up and told them that he not only doesn't like the taste of ale, he doesn't like the smell of it. In fact, he said that the smell of it sometimes gives him a headache. Well, as I said, it sounds ridiculous, but the old men are acting as if they have found out something about Joe that is shocking beyond belief. And I know them—they're not going to let this die down. And furthermore, to add to everything else, a number of them have suddenly become very sensitive and touchy—the situation in general has brought back to the surface differences between them that they thought they had buried and forgotten long ago, and they have stopped speaking to each other, only sometimes they can't exactly remember why they stopped speaking, and they go around avoiding each other and at the same time looking puzzled. It's a mess.' I saw I had to do something. It was up to me. Now, it so happens that my husband, Harry Kirwan, grew up in an old, old town in Ireland named Ballyragget, down in Kilkenny. Ballyragget is a market town that is noted for its old public houses. Harry's mother died when he was a child and he lived with his grandmother. And quite early in his schooldays he started working for an old public house called Staunton's. On his way to school, he would stop off and sweep the place out, and after school he would stop off for the rest of the afternoon and wash glasses and fill the coal box and run errands and generally make himself useful. Harry has a studious nature; he's always read a lot. He wanted very much to be a professor in Ireland, but he couldn't afford the education. So when he was around nineteen he came to the United States and got a job in a manufacturing chemist company in the Bronx, and by the time we got married—which as a matter of fact was less than a year before the death of my father—he had worked himself up to where he was head bookkeeper. And so, anyway, when Harry came home that night, I said to him, 'Sit down, Harry. I've got something very serious I have to discuss with you.' I filled him in on the situation in McSorley's, and then I said to him, 'Harry, I know how much you love your job, and I hate to ask this, but do you think you could possibly find it in your heart to give it up and take over the management of McSorley's?' 'Well, Dot,' he said, and I remember every word he said that night, 'first of all, I don't love my job, I pretend to, but I hate it. And second of all, Dot, why in the name of God did it take so long for this thought to occur to you? You've heard me talk a lot about Staunton's back in Ballyragget, and most of the customers in there were hard-to-get-along-with old men, and I got along with them. I not only got along with them, I enjoyed getting along with them. I enjoyed observing them and I enjoyed listening to them. They were like actors in a play, only the play was real. There were Falstaffs among them—that is, they were just windy old drunks from the back alleys of Ballyragget, but they were Falstaffs to me. And there were Ancient Pistols among them. And there was an old man with a broken-hearted-looking face who used to come in and sit in a chair in the corner with a Guinness at his elbow and stare straight ahead for hours at a time and occasionally mumble a few words to himself, and every time he came in I would say to myself, "King Lear." There were good old souls among those men, and there were leeches among them, leeches and lepers and Judases, and I imagine the cast of characters down in McSorley's is about the same. In other words, Dot,' he said, 'in answer to your question, yes, I'm willing to take a chance and go down to McSorley's and see if I can handle it.' The changeover didn't take long. Early next morning I went to Joe Hnida's apartment and had a heart-to-heart talk with him and begged him to forgive me for getting him into all of this, which he did, and he went back to the limousine service. And the very same day Harry gave notice up in the Bronx. And two Mondays later, he started in at McSorley's. I remember that day so well. I was worried half sick that I might've made another big mistake, so in the middle of the afternoon I telephoned McSorley's and asked to speak to Harry. 'Everything's O.K., Dot,' he said. 'I'm amazed at how much I'm enjoying this. I feel like I'm back home again—back home in Ballyragget, back home in Staunton's.' And when he got home that night and opened the door, the first thing he said was, 'I think I have finally found my right and proper place in the world.'"

Like Old John and Old Bill and like his father-in-law and his wife, Harry Kirwan is strongly opposed to change, and since he took over he has made only one change and that was a fiscal one and long overdue. He gave raises to the old bartenders, Eddie Mullins and Joe Martoccio, and he gave a raise to Mike Boiko, the cook, who is an old Ukrainian, and he gave a raise to Tommy Kelly, who broke down and cried when Harry told him about it. Tommy Kelly is perhaps the most important member of the staff of McSorley's, but his duties are so indefinite that the old men call him Kelly the Floorwalker. When business is brisk, he acts as the potboy—he carries mugs of ale from the bar to the tables, hooking his fingers through the handles of the mugs and carrying two in each hand. He is sometimes the fill-in bartender. He makes an occasional trip to the butcher or the grocery store for Mike. He answers the coin-box telephone. In the winter he keeps the fire going in the stove. When he shows up, around 8:30 A.M., he is just a sad-eyed little man with a hangover, but by noon lukewarm ale has given him a certain stateliness; by six he is in such a good humor that he stands near the door and shakes hands with incoming customers just as if he were the proprietor. Some strangers think he is the proprietor and speak to him as Mr. McSorley. Kelly says that he had a long succession of odd jobs before he wound up in McSorley's. "And when I say odd," he says, "I mean odd." Once, for a brief period, he took a job as night clerk and night watchman in a large funeral parlor in Brooklyn, quitting because a corpse spoke to him. "I sat up front in the office all night," he says, "and I used to keep a pocket-sized bottle of gin in my coat hanging up in the locker in the back room, and I would go back there every little while and take a sip—not a real swallow, just a sip, just enough to keep me going through the night—and to get back there I had to pass through the parlor, the room where the coffins and the corpses were kept, and on this particular night I had to go past an open coffin that had a corpse in it, a man all laid out and fixed up and ready for the funeral in the morning, and I must've already gone past him a half a dozen times, passing and repassing, and this time, as I was going past him, he spoke to me, and quite distinctly too. 'Take off your hat,' he said, 'and put out that cigar and pour out that gin and turn off that damn radio.'"

To a devoted McSorley customer, most other New York City saloons are tense and disquieting. It is possible to relax in McSorley's. For one thing, it is dark and gloomy, and repose comes easy in a gloomy place. Also, the barely audible heartbeatlike ticking of the old clocks is soothing. Also, there is a thick, musty smell that acts as a balm to jerky nerves; it is really a rich compound of the smells of pine sawdust, tap drippings, pipe tobacco, coal smoke, and onions. A Bellevue intern once remarked that for some mental states the smell in McSorley's would be a lot more beneficial than psychoanalysis or sedative pills or prayer.

At midday McSorley's is crowded. The afternoon is quiet. At six it fills up with men who work in the neighborhood. Most nights there are a few curiosity-seekers in the place. If they behave themselves and don't ask too many questions, they are tolerated. The majority of them have learned about the saloon through John Sloan's paintings. Between 1912 and 1930, Sloan did five paintings, filled with detail, of the saloon—"McSorley's Bar," which shows Bill presiding majestically over the tap and which hangs in the Detroit Institute of Arts; "McSorley's Back Room," a painting of an old workingman sitting at the window at dusk with his hands in his lap, his pewter mug on the table; "McSorley's at Home," which shows a group of argumentative old-timers around the stove; "McSorley's Cats," in which Bill is preparing to feed his drove of cats; and "McSorley's, Saturday Night," which was painted during prohibition and shows Bill passing out mugs to a crowd of rollicking customers. Every time one of these appears in an exhibition or in a newspaper or magazine, there is a rush of strangers to the saloon. "McSorley's Bar" was reproduced in Thomas Craven's "A Treasury of Art Masterpieces," which came out in 1939, and it caused hundreds to go and look the place over. There is no doubt that McSorley's has been painted more often than any other saloon in the country. Louis Bouché did a painting, "McSorley's," which is owned by the University of Nebraska. A painting, "Morning in McSorley's Bar," by a ship's purser named Ben Rosen won first prize in an exhibition of art by merchant seamen in February, 1943. Reginald Marsh has done several sketches of it. In 1939 there was a retrospective exhibition of Sloan's work in Wanamaker's art department, and a number of McSorley patrons attended it in a body. One asked a clerk for the price of "McSorley's Cats." "Three thousand dollars," he was told. He believed the clerk was kidding him and is still indignant. Kelly likes the Sloan paintings but prefers a golden, corpulent nude which Old John hung in the back room many years ago, right beside Peter Cooper's portrait. To a stranger, attracted to the saloon by a Sloan painting, Kelly will say, "Hey, Mac, if you want to see some real art, go look at the naked lady in the back room." The nude is stretched out on a couch and is playing with a parrot; the painting is a copy, probably done by a Cooper Union student, of Gustave Courbet's "La Femme au Perroquet." Kelly always translates this for strangers. "It's French," he says learnedly. "It means 'Duh Goil and duh Polly.'"

McSorley's bar is short, accommodating approximately ten elbows, and is shored up with iron pipes. It is to the right as you enter. To the left is a row of armchairs with their stiff backs against the wainscoting. The chairs are rickety; when a fat man is sitting in one, it squeaks like new shoes every time he takes a breath. The customers believe in sitting down; if there are vacant chairs, no one ever stands at the bar. Down the middle of the room is a row of battered tables. Their tops are always sticky with spilled ale. In the centre of the room stands the belly stove, which has an isinglass door and is exactly like the stoves in Elevated stations. All winter Kelly keeps it red hot. "Warmer you get, drunker you get," he says. Some customers prefer mulled ale. They keep their mugs on the hob until the ale gets as hot as coffee. A sluggish cat named Minnie sleeps in a scuttle beside the stove. The floor boards are warped, and here and there a hole has been patched with a flattened-out soup can. The back room looks out on a blind tenement court. In this room are three big, round dining-room tables. The kitchen is in one corner of the room; Mike keeps a folding boudoir screen around the gas range, and pots, pans, and paper bags of groceries are stored on the mantelpiece. While he peels potatoes, he sits with early customers at a table out front, holding a dishpan in his lap and talking as he peels. The fare in McSorley's is plain, cheap and well cooked. Mike's specialties are goulash, frankfurters, and sauerkraut, and hamburgers blanketed with fried onions. He scribbles his menu in chalk on a slate which hangs in the bar-room and consistently misspells four dishes out of five. There is no waiter. During the lunch hour, if Mike is too busy to wait on the customers, they grab plates and help themselves out of the pots on the range.

The saloon opens at eight. Mike gives the floor a lick and a promise and throws on clean sawdust. He replenishes the free-lunch platters with cheese and onions and fills a bowl with cold, hard-boiled eggs, five cents each. Kelly shows up. The ale truck makes its delivery. Then, in the middle of the morning, the old men begin shuffling in. Kelly calls them "the steadies." The majority are retired laborers and small businessmen. They prefer McSorley's to their homes. A few live in the neighborhood, but many come from a distance. One, a retired operator of a chain of Bowery flop-houses, comes in from Sheepshead Bay practically every day. On the day of his retirement, this man said, "If my savings hold out, I'll never draw an-other sober breath." He says he drinks in order to forget the misery he saw in his flophouses; he undoubtedly saw a lot of it, because he often drinks twenty-five mugs a day, and McSorley's ale is by no means weak. Kelly brings the old men their drinks. To save him a trip, they usually order two mugs at a time. Most of them are quiet and dignified; a few are eccentrics. Some years ago one had to leap out of the path of a speeding automobile on Third Avenue; he is still furious. He mutters to himself constantly. Once, asked what he was muttering about, he said, "Going to buy a shot-gun and stand on Third Avenue and shoot at automobiles." "Are you going to aim at the tires?" he was asked. "Why, hell no!" he said. "At the driv-ers. Figure I could kill four or five before they arrested me. Might kill more if I could reload fast enough."

Only a few of the old men have enough interest in the present to read newspapers. These patrons sit up front, to get the light that comes through the grimy street windows. When they grow tired of reading, they stare for hours into the street. There is always something worth looking at on Seventh Street. It is one of those East Side streets completely under the domination of kids. While playing stickball, they keep great packing-box fires going in the gutter; sometimes they roast mickies in the gutter fires. In McSorley's the free-lunch platters are kept at the end of the bar nearer the street door, and several times every afternoon kids sidle in, snatch handfuls of cheese and slices of onion, and dash out, slamming the door. This never fails to amuse the old men.

The stove overheats the place and some of the old men are able to sleep in their chairs for long periods. Occasionally one will snore, and Kelly will rouse him, saying, "You making enough racket to wake the dead." Once Kelly got interested in a sleeper and clocked him. Two hours and forty minutes after the man dozed off, Kelly became uneasy—"Maybe he died," he said—and shook him awake. "How long did I sleep?" the man asked. "Since the parade," Kelly said. The man rubbed his eyes and asked, "Which parade?" "The Paddy's Day parade, two weeks ago," Kelly said scornfully. "Jeez!" the man said. Then he yawned and went back to sleep. Kelly makes jokes about the constancy of the old men. "Hey, Eddie," he said one morning, "old man Ryan must be dead!" "Why?" Mullins asked. "Well," Kelly said, "he ain't been in all week." In summer they sit in the back room, which is as cool as a cellar. In winter they grab the chairs nearest the stove and sit in them, as motionless as barnacles, until around six, when they yawn, stretch, and start for home, insulated with ale against the dreadful loneliness of the old. "God be wit' yez," Kelly says as they go out the door.

SIX

TOURIST IN A STRANGE LAND: TOM WOLFE AND THE NEW JOURNALISTS

I whacked the back of the driver's seat with my fist. "This is impor-
tant, goddamnit! This is a true story!" The car swerved sickeningly,
then straightened out.
—Hunter S. Thompson

My first encounter with New Journalism came in the sixties when I borrowed Tom Wolfe's *The Electric Kool-Aid Acid Test* from a university library. I sat down on a nearby brick wall to read the first chapter. The unseen narrator's voice astonished me, as did his access to the inner lives of the Merry Pranksters. Wolfe's portrayal of young druggies who recognized undercover police by their shiny black shoes sounded about right at the time. Then I noticed, just above the top of the book, the shoes that were passing by, some of which were frighteningly shiny. This connection between the secret lives of counterculture figures, journalism, and the ordinary world seemed like something new indeed. I couldn't put the book down; Wolfe's voice captured me. At about the same time, friends were buzzing about Hunter S. Thompson's *Hell's Angels,* a portrait constructed through participant-observation of a group that held as much iconographic value for that generation as did surfboards and the Rolling Stones.

New Journalism came from writers at several publications who interpreted the changing social norms of the early sixties to mid-seventies using seemingly liberated styles. Some interpreted public events by exploring the perspectives of the characters in-volved—including the reporters themselves. Writers became characters in their own stories. They gave events context against the cultural and historical background. Some challenged the ability of a reporter to discover and comprehend what was really going on at events. To a remarkable extent, New Journalists used techniques not available to standard reporters. For example, Tom Wolfe would report on what someone was *thinking*.

Along with Tom Wolfe, who was credited with giving the form its name, Norman Mailer, and Truman Capote, the most celebrated New Journalists included Joan Didion, who often wrote from her native California, the geographical center of the decade; Hunter S. Thompson, writing for *Rolling Stone* magazine; former *New York Times* reporter Gay Talese; and Michael Herr re-porting from Vietnam for *Esquire*. Another dozen or so writers, in-cluding a number of women, were closely associated with this style. Didion, Sara Davidson, Gail Sheehy, and Gloria Steinem produced first-rate literary journalism. Some were drawn off to other pursuits, such as Steinem, who became a leading figure in the women's movement. Frances Fitzgerald, Susan Sheehan, and Jane Kramer could be on the list, but as *New Yorker* writers they did not identify with the term *New Journalism*. Jimmy Breslin, Timo-thy Crouse, John Sack, Marshall Frady, Richard Goldstein, George Plimpton, Ed Sanders (writing about the Charles Manson murders), and several others contributed important New Journal-ism pieces. When in 2003 *Esquire* magazine listed its all-time greatest articles during seventy years of publication, Talese's "Frank Sinatra Has a Cold" (1966) was number one, followed by New Journalism pieces written by Herr, Mailer, Sack, and Wolfe.

In the sixties, avid readers agreed that something more was needed if journalism were to adequately represent the new worlds of American cultural styles, sexual and gender roles, rock 'n' roll music, and the anti–Vietnam War sentiment that was sweeping the younger generation. The New Journalists had grown up in a postwar world that seems pretty dull, in retrospect. The late forties and fifties were highlighted by anxiety—fear of communists and The Bomb—and by a deeply rooted, stubborn, oppressive conformity, which Mailer would term the visible river of American life. In 1960, John F. Kennedy was elected president after eight years of Dwight Eisenhower. Kennedy was a young, refreshing, and invigorating personality. Then, suddenly, he was assassinated. The decade turned violent with the killings of Freedom Riders in the South and the assassination of leaders such as Malcolm X.

The civil rights movement became the dominant domestic issue, followed in the mid-sixties by the Vietnam War and the associated unrest, especially among the Baby Boom generation that was eligible for the draft. The assassinations in 1968 of Martin Luther King Jr. and Bobby Kennedy exacerbated these troubles. Not only were these deadly events spectacular, they also involved complicated cultural movements. Many good writers started to say openly that the standard routines of reporting, or even standard fiction, could not cope with the complexity of the modern world. They looked for new ways to interpret and represent events, and they found answers in the New Journalism. New Journalism gave an identity and a style to this group of literary journalists.

Complicated questions about accuracy plagued New Journalism throughout its heyday in the sixties and early seventies.

Capote's *In Cold Blood* (1965) was questioned in *The London Review of Books,* and accusations arose that Sheehy's "Redpants and Sugarman" (1971) article in *New York* magazine was a composite.[1] Alleged factual errors and team loyalty generated a controversy that reverberated among the literati over Tom Wolfe's "Tiny Mummies!" series in 1965 about *The New Yorker.* Sarah Harrison Smith, a former fact-checker for *The New Yorker* and the *New York Times Magazine,* in a recent book on the craft echoed those attitudes when she wrote: "One could argue that the New Journalists' looseness with facts changed reporting standards for some writers, making fabrication seem both more acceptable and more necessary. Traditional reportage began to look dull when compared with the excitement offered by 'fictionalized' nonfiction."[2] Much of this criticism was unfair—just insider baseball talk, an argument among the literati, a defense of William Shawn by *New Yorker* writers—and a bit of it was true, but it spread outward to color impressions of the New Journalism in general.

Questions about subjectivity in the New Journalism would tag along on this debate like ticks on a dog. New Journalists fought back against the attack from old journalism, which had its own problems with objectivity during the Cold War and the Vietnam War. Mailer, for example, at the opening of his Pulitzer Prize–winning *The Armies of the Night,* quoted a *Time* magazine story about his appearance in Washington. At the end of the quoted passage, Mailer pointedly remarked: "Now we may leave *Time* in order to find out what happened." Hunter S. Thompson once wrote, "The only thing I ever saw that came close to Objective Journalism was a closed-circuit TV setup that watched shoplifters in the General Store at Woody Creek, Colorado. I always admired that machine, but I noticed that nobody paid much attention to it."[3]

Accuracy in journalism remains a major issue today, but in a different form than during the late sixties. At least it does not carry the same cultural conflicts. When Jayson Blair of the *New York Times* fabricated stories in 2003, for example, it was upsetting and cost the editor's job, but no one tagged Blair a "New Journalist." As a result of the controversies over New Journalism, the standards that apply to real works of literary journalism have been drawn more tightly than ever before, especially regarding composite characters. Some of the controversies will be reviewed in this chapter, along with the philosophical stances adopted by New Journalists and their experiences reporting during the sixties and seventies. The New Journalism was much more important, influential, experimental, and valuable than the controversies would lead us to believe.

Tom Wolfe led the way, brilliantly, in pushing the contest between nonfiction and the novel into the public's consciousness. For the first time outside of the offices of *The New Yorker,* a group of writers, who self-identified as New Journalists, publicly discussed what some thought was a new form of literature, one that might actually supplant fiction as the dominant literary form. Wolfe felt he could do just as much in journalism as in fiction, and that was one claim made by the New Journalism. Wolfe did not have all the arguments, but he had his finger on a cultural force, as he so often did in his journalism.

The most-often cited early New Journalism pieces came from Norman Mailer writing in *Esquire* about the 1960 Democratic National Convention that nominated John F. Kennedy for president, and from Truman Capote writing a much less distinguished first-person piece for *The New Yorker* about a touring opera company performing *Porgy and Bess* in Russia in 1956. Mailer, Capote, and

Terry Southern were among the oldest of the New Journalists, having entered their early forties in the mid-1960s. (Most of their compatriots were in their twenties or early thirties at that time, which made New Journalism seem like a youth movement.) Mailer despairingly once said it was possible that he had "received more praise as a new journalist than ever as a novelist."[4]

Locating the origins of New Journalism with Mailer and Capote became traditional among historians and commentators, but it required ignoring similar reporting that happened earlier and not only at *The New Yorker.* Looking back on a spectacular decade from the perspective of 1972, *Esquire* editor Harold Hayes took note of the forerunners. He cited the earlier work of Lillian Ross, Joe Mitchell, and Alva Johnston at *The New Yorker.* He suggested that historians should look to the work of Edmund Wilson, James Agee, George Orwell, and articles in the *American Mercury, Vanity Fair,* and *Harper's* under editor Jack Fischer (who published James Baldwin), and in *The New Yorker* for the origins of the New Journalism. He did not like the use of the term *new.* Instead, he pointed to Dwight Macdonald, who had characterized himself as a "literary journalist." Hayes said that "literary journalism allows, indeed encourages, conceptual writing and there is nothing new about conceptual writing except when there occurs the ever-new miracle of a single writer's originality—that of a Mailer, a Talese, a Wolfe—responding to his own singular concepts, and no matter the point in time at which this wondrous intersection occurs." Tom Connery added to Hayes's list: "Yet it was the *Saturday Evening Post* that published Joan Didion's literary journalism in the early 1960s, and in the 1950s the *Post* had published other pieces that might qualify, including "Death on M24" by John Bartlow Martin and "They Give the Kids a Chance" by Morton W. Hunt, both published in 1952. Although John Hersey's work is commonly associated with *The New Yorker*, he wrote works of literary journalism for *Life* in the 1940s, and James Agee's "Havana Cruise" was published in *Fortune.*"⁵

The New Journalism era, however, seemed so coherent—writers knew they had colleagues working the same field, unlike Agee, who had felt isolated and alone at *Fortune.* If we look toward writers who were counted as New Journalists, then Mailer and Capote are as good a starting point as anyone else.

Mailer had written excellent and well-received novels following World War II. He lived in Greenwich Village and was a founder of *The Village Voice* newspaper. He had an ego the size of Manhattan, a personal history studded with some notoriously sexist episodes, and a sneering attitude that often caused readers to despise him personally while admiring his writing.

In "Superman Comes to the Supermarket" (*Esquire,* November 1960), Mailer covered the Democratic political convention. He focused not so much on what was happening as what he thought and felt about events. He reported on who made the speeches, the demonstrations, and the crowds, but events got submerged into his own interpretations of trends in American culture. Mailer saw two rivers of American culture flowing through the politics of 1960. He said, "Since the First World War Americans have been leading a double life, and our history has moved on two rivers, one visible, the other underground." The visible river he described as our conversion into mass man, wherein we became buried beneath subscriptions to *Reader's Digest,* appeals for Mental Health in Your Community, and television. The underground river was individualistic, heroic, the myth that "each of us was born to be free, to wander, to have adventure and to grow on the waves of the violent, the perfumed, and the unexpected."⁶ Mailer said these two cultures competed for America's attention in 1960, the visible river symbolically represented by the Republican presidential candidate, Richard Nixon, and the underground river by Democratic nominee John F. Kennedy, and as it would turn out, these two rivers were also represented by the old versus the New Journalism.

With the convention article, Mailer was one of the first examples of what would become a staple of the New Journalism: the writer who believes that what he has observed has no substance outside of something that has been filtered through his own psyche. He believed the political convention existed; but it held no meaning for him outside of what had passed through his brain. Shouldn't the reader examine the psyche that had filtered this experience, along with the experience itself? Isn't that relevant? he asked.

For example, in a passage about meeting Kennedy after the convention that nominated him for president, Mailer wrote:

> What struck me most about the interview was a passing remark whose importance was invisible on the scale of politics, but was altogether meaningful to my particular competence. As we sat down for the first time, Kennedy smiled nicely and said that he had read my books. One muttered one's pleasure. "Yes," he said, "I've read . . ." and then there was a short pause which did not last long enough to be embarrassing in which it was yet obvious no title came instantly to his mind, an omission one was not ready to mind altogether since a man in such a position must be obliged to carry a hundred thousand facts and names in his head, but the hesitation lasted no longer than three seconds or four, and then he said, "I've read *The Deer Park* and . . . the others," which startled me for it was the first time in a hundred similar situations, talking to someone whose knowledge of my work was casual,

that the sentence did not come out, "I've read *The Naked and the Dead* . . . and the others." If one is to take the worst and assume that Kennedy was briefed for this interview (which is most doubtful), it still speaks well for the striking instincts of his advisers.[7]

Mailer was flattered, as anyone would be. But his story about the interaction with Kennedy brought the author's character, his feelings, and the objectivity of the narrator up to the surface of the document. An objective-style reporter could have justified omitting this scene because only the external events would be important to his view, not the filtering mechanism of the journalist's own psyche. Mailer's insistence on bringing up the narrator's flaws and feelings seemed new in journalism.

Mailer had time to ponder his opinions, and he had knowledge of literary heritage to remind him "that the world is not supposed to be reassembled by panels of prefabricated words." He recalled his situation at the Democratic convention this way:

> I was a novelist. It was expected of me to see the world with my own eyes and own words. See it by the warp or stance of my character. Which if it could collect into some kind of integrity might be called a style. I was enlisted then on my side of an undeclared war between those modes of perception called journalism and fiction. When it came to accuracy, I was on the side of fiction. I thought fiction could bring us closer to the truth than journalism, which is not to say one should make up facts when writing a story about real people. I would endeavor to get my facts as scrupulously as a reporter. (At least!) The difference would be found elsewhere. Journalism assumes the truth of an event can be found by the use of principles which go back to

Descartes. (A political reporter has a fixed view of the world: you may plot it on axes which run right to left on the horizontal and down from honesty to corruption on the vertical.) Indeed, the real premise of journalism is that the best instrument for measuring history is a faceless, even a mindless, recorder. Whereas the writer of fiction is closer to that moving world of Einstein. There the velocity of the observer is as crucial to the measurement as any object observed. For fiction probably makes the secret assumption that we learn the truth through a comparison of the lies, since we are obliged to receive the majority of our experience at second hand through parents, friends, mates, lovers, enemies, and the journalists who report it to us. So our best chance of improving those private charts of our own most complicated lives, our unadmitted maps of reality, our very comprehension, if you will, of the way existence works—seems to profit most if we can have some little idea, at least, of the warp of the observer who passes on the experience. Fiction, as I use the word, is then that reality which does not cohere to anonymous axes of fact but is breathed in through the swarm of our male and female movements about one another, a novelistic assumption, for don't we perceive the truth of a novel as its events pass through the personality of the writer?[8]

Mailer's suggestions about the "warp of the observer" and style in journalism became the core of the New Journalism movement, which sought to return the voice and consciousness of the writer to journalism. His major journalistic achievement came with *The Armies of the Night,* written about a 1967 anti–Vietnam War demonstration at the Pentagon in Washington. Mailer was a celebrity at the event, a noted literary figure who was invited so he could lend legitimacy to the goings-on. He marched, intentionally crossed a line of federal marshals, and was arrested. He made his little sprint through the line early so he could be processed and return to New York in time for a dinner party with his wife. Instead, he spent a night in jail and was in court the next day. During the night, a few thousand hard-core demonstrators at the Pentagon sat peacefully in a circle, surrounded by federal marshals and troops. The demonstrators were obviously dangerous because they had threatened to use Eastern chants to levitate the Pentagon off the ground. They were systematically beaten with clubs by the marshals and troops and hauled away. Mailer, inconveniently in jail, had missed the big event.

Yet his book won the Pulitzer Prize. He presented reporting as a philosophical dilemma. Mailer decided he could report most accurately on his own actions, thoughts, and feelings, and he did so in a long first section called "History as a Novel." In the second section, he included the brutality of the night—the wedge of marshals battering their way through young men and women who offered no resistance. But Mailer wasn't there. He reconstructed the story from other accounts, as standard reporters had done for ages in covering crime and war. He called this account, which reads more like what we think of as standard journalism, "The Novel as History." Because he had not been there, because he pieced the text together out of other accounts and stories, was journalism therefore a novel? A battle was drawn. New Journalism had challenged the sacred totem of objectivity.[9]

Tom Wolfe produced some of the most stylistic, innovative, and accurate literary journalism of the era. While his work was not as psychologically complicated as that of Mailer or Didion, he created a distinctive style that can be recognized on the page within a couple of sentences. Who else would have written this?

Thirty-nine years old! A recluse! Bonafide! Doesn't go out, doesn't see the light of day, doesn't put his hide out in God's own unconditioned Chicago air for months on end; years. Right this minute, one supposes, he is somewhere there in the innards of those forty-eight rooms, under layers and layers of white wall-to-wall, crimson wall-to-wall, Count Basie–lounge leather, muffled, baffled, swaddled, shrouded, closed in, blacked out, shielded by curtains, drapes, wall-to-wall, blond wood, screens, cords, doors, buzzers, dials, Nubians—he's down in there, the living Hugh Hefner, 150 pounds, like the tender-tympany green heart of an artichoke.[10]

Wolfe played the literary community like a guitar, and in a manner that created some of the greatest controversy surrounding the New Journalism. He believed his journalism should gather up the status that the modern novel had abandoned when it left realism in favor of literary experimentation. In 1967, he wrote to his editor about his project that would become *The Electric Kool-Aid Acid Test:* "I am in the thick of the Kesey thing right now and am trying some things that have never been done, even by Joyce, and I think they will startle and delight. . . . I can do things no other writer can do or has ever done—and there is no earthly, forgivable reason why I shouldn't do them in this second book." The literary community of novelists, poets, and critics had been paddling Mailer's underground river for years, struggling against the conformity of American life. Then along came this upstart feature writer who had completed a Ph.D. in American studies at Yale and worked for a Springfield, Massachusetts, newspaper before coming to New York and eventually writing articles for a marginal Sunday newspaper magazine. His most outrageous claim was that New Journalism would supplant the novel as the leading literary form. No such thing has happened, but in the late fifties the trend was becoming apparent. "One thing is certain," Norman Podhoretz, editor of *Commentary* magazine, wrote in 1958: "that a large class of readers, with or without benefit of theories about the rise and fall of literary forms, has found itself responding more enthusiastically to what is lamely called 'nonfiction' (and especially to magazine articles and even book reviews) than to current fiction."[11]

Today, nonfiction tends to sell better than fiction, especially if all forms of nonfiction are included, such as history, travel, cooking, and self-help books. In 2005, for example, 1.5 million sales of *The Da Vinci Code* by Dan Brown, one of the blockbuster novels of the year, were easily outdistanced by 1.7 million sales for *1776* by historian David McCullough, whose book ranked fifth on the nonfiction sales list. Nevertheless, blockbuster novels with press runs of 2 million copies outnumber works of literary journalism. For the fiction community, Wolfe's claim that New Journalism could supplant the novel came as a traitorous attack from the shores of its own river. Even worse, Wolfe launched an assault on one of the gods of the journalism community, William Shawn, editor of *The New Yorker.*[12]

In April 1965, Wolfe published a two-part article in *New York* magazine, then the Sunday supplement of the *Herald Tribune.* The first of these, titled "Tiny Mummies! The True Story of the Ruler of 43d Street's Land of the Walking Dead!" attacked Shawn as the "embalmer" of a dead institution. Usually a reticent man, Shawn called the articles "false and libelous." In a letter to John Whitney, publisher of the *Herald Tribune,* Shawn said, "I know exactly what Wolfe's article is—a vicious, murderous attack on me and on the magazine I work for. It is a ruthless and reckless article; it is pure sensation-mongering. It is wholly without precedent in respectable American journalism—in one stroke, it puts the *Herald Tribune* right down in the gutter with the *Graphic,* the *Enquirer,* and *Confidential.*"[13] Given how Wolfe felt about *True* and other such working-class publications, he might have been flattered by Shawn's comparisons. Wolfe later described the *New York* magazine of that era as only slightly better than "sheets like the *National Enquirer* in its 'I Left My Babies in the Deep Freeze' period."[14] Murray Kempton, Nat Hentoff, Walter Lippmann, and Joseph Alsop expressed their displeasure. Lippmann, one of the greatest political journalists of the twentieth century, said of Wolfe's piece: "The author of it is an incompetent ass. . . . He tried to throw a bomb. All he could manage was a rotten egg. I despise such journalism."[15] Wolfe later described Lippmann and Alsop as "paralyzing snoremongers."[16] Several *New Yorker* writers rose in indignation to defend Shawn and attack New Journalism. Renata Adler and Gerald Jonas of *The New Yorker* said Wolfe's articles were "reportorial incompetence masquerading as a new art form."[17] Within a year *New Yorker* staff writer Dwight Macdonald called Wolfe's work "parajournalism" and "a bastard form."[18] Ved Mehta, then working for *The New Yorker* and now the head of Random House, pushed the criticism toward the New Journalism itself. He wrote Lippmann to say, "If it were just Wolfe himself, one might ignore him, but he seems to represent something that is happening to journalism everywhere."[19]

In historical perspective, Wolfe's "Tiny Mummies!" episode only matters in that it created a split between him and an institution that had nurtured literary journalism through the previous decades. In response, most *New Yorker* writers rejected any effort to label them as New Journalists, even when they had the credentials. Wolfe, on the other hand, never saw his work in *The New Yorker* and largely ignored the contributions of the magazine when he published his account of the New Journalism in 1973.

On the surface, Wolfe's "Tiny Mummies!" articles were not so bad as the vigorous response would have us believe. He profusely complimented Lillian Ross, something he could not bring himself to do when he wrote "The New Journalism" in 1973. Even if intended as parody, "Tiny Mummies!" reads like the work of a critic—targeting, for example, the magazine's habit of publishing long, convoluted sentences. Wolfe called such constructions "the whichy thicket." Toward the end, Wolfe wrote a treatise on the readers of *The New Yorker:* "Since the war, the suburbs of America's large cities have been filling up with educated women with large homes and solid hubbies and the taste to . . . *buy expensive things.*" Wolfe said this trend explained a certain bourgeois trend in *The New Yorker:* "After all, a girl is not really sitting out here in Larchmont waiting for Stanley Kowalski to come by in his ribbed undershirt and rip the Peck & Peck cashmere off her mary poppins."[20]

Any antifemale attitude aside, it was classic Tom Wolfe social criticism—pop sociology, his critics would say—very similar to his stylized critiques of modern art and architecture. Except that those pieces of cultural opinion had not been written yet. *Radical Chic & Mau-Mauing the Flak Catchers* was published in 1970; *The Painted Word* in 1975; and *From Bauhaus to Our House* in 1981. Those later cultural critiques were not New Journalism. In 1965, readers could only assume the "Tiny Mummies!" articles were part of Wolfe's journalistic repertoire, not an essay or a parody of cultural criticism.

The crew at *The New Yorker* was livid. Wolfe had reported—even citing Cook County Court records in Chicago—that

William Shawn had been on a list of intended victims prepared by the young killers Nathan Leopold and Richard Loeb, and as a result Shawn became "*retiring.*" Adler and Jonas said it was simply not true and that Chicago records did not support this story. At first, Wolfe defended the pieces. He said in a radio interview that the Leopold and Loeb story was "common dinner-table conversation," although he could not find anything conclusive to confirm it.[21] In 2000, Wolfe said his source was in the New York Public Library, but he did not name it. Wolfe's stance changed a bit in his 1973 essay, "The New Journalism." He said the pieces were "lighthearted . . . a very droll *sportif* performance, you understand." A defensive reaction, perhaps—but Wolfe correctly pointed out that his critique of *The New Yorker* was *not* New Journalism: "It used neither the reporting techniques nor the literary techniques; underneath a bit of red-flock *Police Gazette* rhetoric, it was a traditional critique, a needle, an attack, an 'essay' of the old school."[22] Wolfe jabbed at the entrenched literary community like a mounted picador in a bullfight, and no doubt Shawn and *The New Yorker* had become an established part of that community.

Wolfe's articles generated bitterness that remained on both sides. Years later, John Hersey and others had still not forgiven him. In 1980, Hersey published "The Legend on the License." Discussing Wolfe's "Tiny Mummies!" articles, Hersey said, "In them one finds in gross form the fundamental defect that has persisted ever since in Wolfe's writing, and that is to be found in the work of many of the 'new journalists,' and also indeed in that of many 'nonfiction novelists'—namely, the notion that mere facts don't matter." It was particularly ironic that Hersey, who had created a composite character (or, by the standards of the eighties, a fictional character) in his own World War II article, "Joe Is Home Now," would complain about Wolfe's "fiction-aping journalism."[23] With the exception of Capote (who was the target of Hersey's "nonfiction novelists" comment), *New Yorker* writers after the "Tiny Mummies!" episode refused association with Wolfe or the New Journalism.

This little literary war between Wolfe and *The New Yorker* contributed to an unjustified taint on New Journalism as a whole—that it was somehow inaccurate. Wolfe's reputation has improved more recently among some *New Yorker* writers, even those who were around in the mid-sixties. In 1982, when I first interviewed longtime *New Yorker* writer John McPhee, he complimented the accuracy of Wolfe's book *The Right Stuff* (1979). While working on his own book about an aircraft, McPhee said, he had talked with several authorities who told him that Wolfe was completely correct in his reporting.

In 1973 in "The New Journalism," Wolfe described how some reporters had paid homage to "The Novel." His article remains an oracle for scholars of the New Journalism. He suggested that the power of New Journalism "was derived mainly from just four devices." They were:

- "Scene-by-scene construction, telling the story by moving from scene to scene and resorting as little as possible to sheer historical narrative."
- Witnessing as many of these scenes as possible through extraordinary "saturation reporting," and "record[ing] the dialogue in full." Dialogue powerfully establishes character, Wolfe said.
- Use of third-person point of view, "the technique of presenting every scene to the reader through the eyes of a particular character, giving the reader the feeling of being

inside the character's mind and experiencing the emotional
reality of the scene as he experiences it."

- Recording details that might be symbolic "of people's status
life," meaning "the entire pattern of behavior and possessions
through which people express their position in the world or
what they think it is or what they hope it to be." Wolfe said
these details—including gestures, habits, manners, customs,
and styles—were "as close to the center of the power of
realism as any other device in literature."[24]

Wolfe's list of devices and techniques did not describe New Journalists such as Didion, Mailer, and Thompson, who did not use
third-person point of view very often. Scene-by-scene construction, however, characterized most New Journalists. Much standard journalism begins with the outcome of a set of events and
then works backward looking for an explanation. Literary journalism—based on character and evolving scenes—holds the reader in
a forward-moving web of time, often without knowledge of the
outcome. In that way, it produces an experience similar to fiction
rather than a report. Wolfe's list captured quite well the techniques
used by Capote in one of the earliest book-length pieces of literature produced by New Journalists.

In September and October 1965, Truman Capote published "In
Cold Blood" in *The New Yorker,* and it came out later in 1965 as a
book. Using scene-by-scene construction and dialogue from the
participants, Capote traced the pathway of two killers to the home
of the Herbert and Bonnie Clutter family in Holcomb, Kansas,
where on November 15, 1959, they killed Mr. and Mrs. Clutter
and two of their children, Nancy and Kenyon, with close-range
shotgun blasts. The dialogue reveals the enormous cultural differ-

ence between the stable, rock-solid, and modestly successful Clutter family and the psychologically abused and twisted lower-class killers. The motive was robbery, but the killers netted only forty or fifty dollars, a pair of binoculars, and a portable radio. Six weeks later they were arrested. Capote went to Kansas in 1959 after he read about the crime and spent the next six years interviewing residents. He spent hours with the killers as they waited on appeals of their death sentences. The two killers, Dick Hickock and Perry Smith, were hanged on April 14, 1965.

Capote wrote in third person, although he sometimes referred to himself, as, for example, "a journalist with whom he [Hickock] corresponded and who was periodically allowed to visit him."[25] He immersed himself in the story and noted the many small details of ownership and perspective that symbolized the lives of his characters. Contemporary literary journalist Madeleine Blais said Capote had reason to claim that he had invented something. "His use of cinematic devices," Blais said, "the way he enters a scene as late as possible and gets out of it as early as possible, the cross-cutting, and especially the agonizing slow motion when he finally gets around to describing the crime itself underscored the notion that this was a new, fresh approach."[26]

The *New York Times* reported that Capote earned $2 million in 1965 from the book, which eventually sold six hundred thousand copies in hardback, and had paperback, magazine, and film payments. That was a tremendous sum of money, equivalent to somewhere between $12 million and $31 million in 2005. It also put a work of literary journalism on a financial par with the blockbuster novel. By way of comparison, John Steinbeck's *The Grapes of Wrath* reportedly sold two million copies in the 1930s. *In Cold Blood* has stood the test of time and remains a great, dramatic read.[27]

Capote had written fiction, including *Breakfast at Tiffany's* (1958), which was also made into a movie starring Blake Edwards, Audrey Hepburn, and George Peppard, as well as memoir and nonfiction, including *The Muses Are Heard* (1956) about the Russian tour of the opera *Porgy and Bess.* Structured like a psychological thriller, *In Cold Blood* benefited from Capote's narrative skills developed in fiction writing.

The book rests on solid reporting that took years to complete. Capote and Holcomb, Kansas, were an unlikely combination. Capote described Holcomb as "out there"—a country defined by "hard blue skies and desert-clear air" where men dressed in "narrow frontier trousers, Stetsons, and high-heeled boots with pointed toes" and spoke "with a prairie twang."[28] Capote, in contrast, was described by Robert McCrum as "a very short Southern homosexual with an affected, high-pitched southern diction that some found quite off-putting." McCrum added, "And yet he had the perverse charm of the court jester," and quoted Lauren Bacall as saying, "When you meet him, . . . you can't believe that he's real. And then after a while, when you get to know him a little bit, you just want to put him in your pocket and take him home."[29] After the book was published Capote became a New York celebrity; he's still remembered for hosting one of the all-time great parties at the Plaza Hotel on November 28, 1966, a black-and-white masked ball with five hundred guests. Those who attended "Truman's ball" included Frank Sinatra, Norman Mailer, and Douglas Fairbanks Jr.; Katharine Graham, publisher of the *Washington Post,* was guest of honor. When Capote made regular appearances on *The Tonight Show* with Johnny Carson, his squeaky voice was broadcast across the nation. His longtime partner was Jack Dunphy, yet Capote showed up in Holcomb with southern novelist Harper Lee, the soon-to-be bestselling author of *To Kill a*

Mockingbird (1960), who participated in the reporting and helped establish connections with the characters in the book. *In Cold Blood* is dedicated to Dunphy and Lee. In an age when tolerance for such differences was rare, this flamboyant homosexual managed to interview all the relevant local residents and get the inside story from police officers, members of the Kansas Bureau of Investigation, and the killers themselves. The reporting grew from classic New Journalism immersion.

Shortly after publication, critics questioned the book's authenticity. Given Capote's narrative approach and the fact that details came from interviews that were not tape-recorded, readers needed to accept certain conventions common to the reconstruction of dramatic events. In a work of this type, some quotations will be incorrect; there is no way to make them perfect. Reconstruction of scenes always involves that convention, or that danger, depending on how you look at it. Six months after the book was published, however, Phillip K. Tompkins, in an unfriendly *Esquire* article, "In Cold Fact," cited other interviews and court records to challenge several factual points in Capote's book, including the auction of Nancy Clutter's horse Babe and other relatively minor but nevertheless fabricated incidents. Presumably the biggest fabrication in the book was the final scene between investigator Al Dewey and Susan Kidwell, who was Nancy Clutter's close friend, at the Clutter family gravesite.[30] Most damaging was Capote's admission, reported by Kenneth Tynan and others in 1966, that he took no notes during his interviews with the killers. After complimenting Capote's lengthy reporting, Tynan said, "In all this prodigious research, spread over five years, he neither took notes on the spot nor employed a tape recorder. Instead, he relied on his memory, which he had sedulously trained until it could retain 95 percent (or 92 percent or 97 percent: his interviewers differ) of total recall."

Capote said he wrote down his notes from memory immediately following each interview.[31]

Many criticisms were matters of interpretation. Did Capote identify with Perry Smith because they had similar childhoods? Did Capote's characterizations of the killers line up with someone else's interpretation—someone who might have met them only in the pages of *In Cold Blood*? Did the killers' interviews with Capote match up perfectly with the police interrogations? Should Capote, as Tynan suggested, have used some of his $2 million in earnings to hire first-rate psychological testimony and legal assistance to save the killers from the hangman?

Tynan picked on the issue of responsibility. One of his sources suggested that Capote had set himself up "as [the killers'] analyst and confessor; not, however, to bring them comfort but to gain their trust and obtain information." When it comes down to writing the story, Tynan asked, "does the work come first, or does life?"[32] Because most reporters never develop a deep relationship with their ordinary (or their criminal) subjects, a relationship where personal responsibility would enter the ethical debate, the question seemed relatively new in journalism. In the sixties, as more and more journalists engaged in saturation reporting with "ordinary"—meaning non-celebrity, non–notoriety seeking, and unsophisticated—subjects, responsibility would become an issue. Although I advocate for responsibility as one of the attributes of literary journalism, in this case I am on Capote's side, but I don't mean to be callous about it. The book was published *after* Hickock and Smith were executed. Beforehand, even if Capote had the inclination to intercede on their behalf, he didn't have the cash. Kansas law at the time made insanity defenses extremely difficult, and the killers' attorneys were thwarted when they pursued that defense. Perhaps Capote's appropriate role was to reveal these legal difficulties, and it was a responsibility for someone who was moved by the issue to challenge state laws. Capote was not "assigned" to the subject like other reporters, and he carried no obligation to provide any interpretation but his own. Nor was he obligated to provide any solutions for the issues raised in this case of murder and capital punishment. He went to Kansas to tell a story.

The experience of reporting on murders that were committed "out there" by two misguided punks may have been personally troubling for Capote. Blais mentioned that "Capote said somewhere that he felt writing the book, or more precisely, living with the details of that story so intimately for so long, catapulted him into ill health and led to the insomnia and substance abuse that dogged him during his final years. There is something creepy about the prettiness of the prose in contrast to the grotesquerie of the killings. In the end, the author may have driven himself nearly insane with the question: what purpose is served by making art out of something so vile?"[33]

Why did Capote take on this story rather than another for a five- or six-year term? There has been speculation about a homoerotic attraction to Smith. But as David Hayes has suggested, Capote was probably more obsessed with creating a work that he could claim was a nonfiction novel about low-profile characters and situations that were like those found in fiction. Even if there was a sympathetic response to one of the characters, does Capote's human connection to the victims or the killers require that he abandon the project in order to intervene? Responsibility to the subjects of a story would later become a question in Hunter S. Thompson's *Hell's Angels,* Sara Davidson's *Loose Change,* and other works of literary journalism. Janet Malcolm, a *New Yorker* writer who was defending herself in an issue of responsibility, said in

1989, "Every journalist who is not too stupid or too full of himself to notice what is going on knows that what he does is morally indefensible. He is a kind of confidence man, preying on people's vanity, ignorance, or loneliness, gaining their trust and betraying them without remorse." Joan Didion referred to the same sort of moral no-man's-land when she wrote in 1968: "My only advantage as a reporter is that I am so physically small, so temperamentally unobtrusive, and so neurotically inarticulate that people tend to forget that my presence runs counter to their best interests. And it always does. That is one last thing to remember: *writers are always selling somebody out*."[34]

The story itself was a topic of discussion. Did it adequately represent the event and the feelings of the participants? Not only did New Journalism bring artistry to the public's attention, it also questioned how writers represent reality in reports. "The form calls attention to language as mediation, not merely as a stylistic embellishment which connects writer and reader but in the primordial sense of that which stands between the writer and the event," said David Eason. Repeatedly during the New Journalism era, writers questioned their own ability to interpret and understand reality or to tell stories that would represent it. Their reports, Eason wrote, "can be read as practical exercises in working out those problems."[35]

In Cold Blood, the first blockbuster triumph of the New Journalism, had been challenged on factual accuracy and on issues such as Capote's responsibility to the subjects. The book gives great insight into the crimes, yet it stands tainted to some degree. At its best, *In Cold Blood* carried a model for reporting and writing that held more significance for the New Journalism than did some inaccuracies about the price paid for a horse named Babe. Indeed, if the *New Yorker* fact-checker who traveled to Holcomb, Kansas, with Capote had caught a couple of the problems, then some of this controversy would never have arisen, but those fact-checkers had great respect for Capote's record of accuracy. He had access that writers envy. He spent years on the topic. He wrote a nonfiction book with significant literary appeal that was, as Blais said, "more brazen, more unremitting, and on a larger scale" than previous works by Mitchell, Ross, Orwell, or Hersey. Capote gave in to his instincts as a fiction writer and fabricated a couple of scenes unnecessarily. Blais summarized the costs when she said, "Capote deserves a better legacy than the one he unwittingly left for himself. In the end, Capote gave into lesser impulses and produced a flawed document when there was no logical reason to do so, with no one to blame but himself. The fallout is not possible to calculate, except to say that Capote's failure to deliver the goods he claimed to be delivering has tarnished what should be embraced as a classic and fed into the dubious hands of lesser practitioners for whom accuracy was a detachable option to begin with."[36]

A gap was opening between New Journalists and the standard reporters and writers who worked for newspapers or magazines and who felt their work was factually accurate. Capote referred to the crowd of reporters who gathered for the arrival of the accused killers after their arrest as "professional spectators"—not participants in the literary marathon that engaged Capote but a crew that would go back home as soon as the courthouse doors closed behind the accused. Even Tynan, one of Capote's harshest critics, distinguished the author of *In Cold Blood* from the commoners: "And we are not discussing a third-rate crime reporter or professional ghoul; one does not waste space on condemning trash."[37]

Later interviews with Capote showed another aspect of his pride, or hubris, that separated him even from Tom Wolfe. Capote loved fiction. In an interview with George Plimpton,

Capote said, "It seemed to me that journalism, reportage, could be forced to yield a serious new art form: the 'nonfiction novel,' as I thought of it. Several admirable reporters—Rebecca West for one, and Joseph Mitchell and Lillian Ross—have shown the possibilities of narrative reportage; and Miss Ross, in her brilliant 'Picture,' achieved at least a nonfiction novella. Still, on the whole, journalism is the most underestimated, the least explored of literary mediums."[38] Asked by Plimpton his opinion of the New Journalism as practiced particularly at the *Herald Tribune,* Capote responded with a blast across Wolfe's deck: "If you mean James Breslin and Tom Wolfe, and that crowd, they have nothing to do with creative journalism—in the sense that I use the term—because neither of them, nor any of that school of reporting, have the proper fictional technical equipment. It's useless for a writer whose talent is essentially journalistic to attempt creative reportage, because it simply won't work." He created a distinction between good fiction writers who wrote journalism, such as himself, Mailer, Hersey, and Didion, and those who came strictly from the world of journalism, such as Wolfe, Talese, and other magazine writers. He felt his "nonfiction novel" could be as good as fiction, but he did not take the leap with Wolfe in declaring that New Journalism would supplant the novel.

Oddly, this argument about the value of writing fiction before attempting literary journalism has recently reversed. Terry Whalin, a fiction acquisitions editor at Howard Books, an imprint of Simon and Schuster, in 2006 said, "Some of these people who are trying hard (and unsuccessfully) to write fiction should probably move into the nonfiction arena. There is value in learning the craft of storytelling in the magazine world." His comments testify to the acceptance of narrative technique in standard magazine journalism since the New Journalism era.[39]

• • •

Capote's feeling that writers needed "proper fictional technical equipment" to write literary journalism—that novelists would be better at it than journalists—never caught on. Later, however, scholar David Eason proposed a more philosophical distinction among New Journalists that has weathered well over the years.

Eason grouped New Journalists into two philosophical camps.[40] Writers almost never talk about their work using the language of literary criticism, but this distinction seemed to make sense to many writers when I talked to them.

In the first camp, New Journalists were like ethnographers who provided an account of "what it is that's going on here." Wolfe, Talese, and Capote, among others, removed themselves from their writing and concentrated on their subjects' realities. They were realists.

The second group included writers such as Didion, Mailer, Herr, Thompson, and John Gregory Dunne. They saw life through their own filters, describing what it felt like to live in a world where shared public understandings about "the real world" and about culture and morals had fallen away. Without an external frame of reference, they focused more on their own realities and even questioned their own ability to grasp reality, as Didion would do in her famous opening to *The White Album:* "I was supposed to have a script, and had mislaid it."[41] For writers like Mailer, Didion, and Thompson, reality is something created; it exists only in the author's terms; it has all of the solidity of a movie script or a comic book. The authors in this second group were often a dominating presence in their works. Eason called them phenomenologist or modernist (or now, postmodernist) writers. The distinction holds for most New Journalists and for the generation of writers that followed them.

Today, however, such matters may be an artistic decision by a writer seeking the best point of view rather than something dictated by an overriding philosophical stance. In reading a recent work, *Mountains beyond Mountains,* by Tracy Kidder, normally a realist, I wondered if the distinction between the realist and the modernist writers has broken down.[42] Eason himself has lost interest in the distinction. He recently said it was the experimentation that made New Journalism interesting for him. "I think of it primarily as a series of literary experiments, less a thing than some ventures," Eason said. He feels Michael Herr's *Dispatches,* originally published as a series of magazine articles for *Esquire* and later as a book, was the greatest of the New Journalism books and also one of the best books ever about war. "But I think the most significant new journalists were the prolific ones, Wolfe (whom I didn't do enough with), Thompson, Didion, and Mailer, whose sense of experimentation pervaded several books for each of them."[43]

When it comes to historical experiments in literary journalism, we have already encountered many of them. Eason mentioned "those that explore the nature of representation like *Let Us Now Praise Famous Men, Armies of the Night, Fear and Loathing on the Campaign Trail,* [and] *The White Album.*" He added, "*Fear and Loathing* may not fit, but I think of it as postmodern, the *Daily Show* of its era."

Shelley Fisher Fishkin, an expert on Mark Twain and on the intersections of journalism and history with fiction, in a 1990 essay sought to include other writers outside "the usual suspects" in New Journalism. She ranked Tillie Olsen among the experimental journalists. Olsen, in her book *Silences* (1962, 1978), was concerned with the books that never were written and about those who could not tell their stories. In this experiment, she included portions of her own experience, which was "as foreign to the world of criticism . . . as was the concept of analyzing 'silences,'" wrote Fishkin. Another writer who experimented on the borderlands of culture and literature, according to Fishkin, was Gloria Anzaldúa in her 1987 book *Borderlands/La Frontera*. The New Journalists did not often portray minority or underclass dramas. Anzaldúa, writing a generation later, found the border between Mexico and the United States a land where the interactions among people with Mexican, Indian, and Anglo heritage, and her own cultural background, were available for analysis.[44]

Tom Wolfe's list of techniques described well the work of realists, but in the work of Michael Herr, Joan Didion, and Hunter S. Thompson other qualities were present. Writers such as Didion, Herr, and Thompson were sending back reports from the front lines; they ended up on the psychological barricades whether they were in Vietnam or not, and their breakdowns tended to happen in the pages of their journalism.

New Journalists had few restrictions; they were young, and it was an age of rebellion. It was also an age filled with spectacular events. The Vietnam War seemed to form a theatrical backdrop to the consciousness in all the later works in the genre. For Michael Herr, however, Vietnam was foreground.

Herr had practically begged *Esquire* editor Harold Hayes for an opportunity to write for the magazine since the day he had graduated from Syracuse in 1961 with a major in literature and minors in history and fiction writing. In 1967, Herr proposed six articles he could write from Vietnam, including items on the press, a piece about Saigon ("It is like some Apocalyptic City, where the final view is not a matter of politics, power or morality, but of sensibility"), and another on "The Aces, or The Veterans," meaning those who had put in a lot of time and had developed a personal style for valor. He did not feel that journalism functioned well in Vietnam. "If standard journalism really worked, if all the sophistication of our communications could really engage and purge, there would be no need for the kind of work I want to do now," Herr wrote in 1967.[45] In the last paragraph of an eight-page letter to Hayes, Herr commented, "This would be dangerous work."

In late 1967, Herr, twenty-seven years old, found himself in Vietnam to write periodic "columns" on the war for *Esquire.* The articles he had initially planned with Hayes were not working out. Herr told his editor that statistics and intelligence reports had been arranged to suit the military's notions of success. First, General William Westmoreland had seen the light at the end of the tunnel, then President Lyndon Johnson had seen the same glow, and now everyone was telling Herr, "They're on the ropes, you dig, we've scattered their command, recruitment is down, it's as good as over, all but the mopping up."[46] Herr felt otherwise. "This spring will be the worst of the war, the most savage, the bloodiest time of all, but no one here will admit it," he said on January 7, 1968.

His next letter to Hayes came a month later from the formerly beautiful city of Hue about a week after the start of the Tet Offensive, when the Viet Cong and North Vietnamese attacked major cities and captured the American embassy in Saigon. Herr asked Hayes to hold the articles he had sent for publication; everything had changed. The most experienced correspondents were "shattered by the offensive," and Herr had not expected it despite his prediction of a bloody spring. "I lost my non-combatant status in the Delta on the first day of the offensive, during an ambush, and I have passed through so many decimated towns and cities that they get all mixed up in my mind," he wrote. "Here in Hue

('They'll never hit Hue,' the Command was always fond of saying. 'They'll never hit Saigon, they'll never hit Dalat, they'll never hit Can Tho, etc. etc.') the destruction has been incredible, air strikes knocking out whole blocks of the one really lovely city in Vietnam, destroying the university, the walls around the Citidal [*sic*] and, probably tomorrow, the Citidal itself."

Herr had been with a Special Forces unit in Can Tho when the Tet Offensive started. He ended his letter with a note that he was "trying to get to Khe Sanh now, but it's difficult." After the Tet Offensive, Herr's vision for his Vietnam reporting was coming clear; he returned to a plan from nearly a year earlier and told Hayes he wanted *Esquire* to support him "ranging around the country, mixing with all sorts of company, occasionally going in and out of combat. Digging the war, you might say."[47] In May 1968, he signed off another letter by saying, "I'll either come back to New York or go back up to the A Shau Valley with the 1st Cav. It seems an odd choice."

Eventually, his "ranging about" and immersion in the war produced brilliant articles for *Esquire,* and later the best book written about the Vietnam War, *Dispatches.* One character in his *Esquire* articles warped back to his idea to write about "The Aces." Herr included a character called "the General" in an August 1968 *Esquire* piece about the war. An expert in insurgency and counterinsurgency, the General was at best a composite character; Herr left him out of *Dispatches.* But *Esquire* editor Harold Hayes signed off on the general's character. Marc Weingarten said, "*Esquire*'s policy on scene reconstructions and composites remained consistent during this period, when the magazine's best nonfiction writers were pushing their reportage into murky territory where creative interpretation mingled with straight documentation." Herr said later that he had the voices of soldiers in his head. "I don't think that it's any secret that there is talk in the book that's invented. But it is invented out of that voice that I heard so often and that made such penetration into my head." Weingarten also said that Herr "invented" the soldiers Day Tripper and Mayhew from the Khe Sanh story. In the context of Vietnam, Herr commented that "straight reporting" was "just as surreal and insane" as fiction.[48]

Herr hung with the soldiers who drank beer, smoked weed, and sweated out the incoming. He hopped helicopters into hot landing zones and into camps of protracted boredom, all the while listening to music. His list of copyright acknowledgments includes lyrics from "Magical Mystery Tour," "The Tighten Up," "Trouble Comin' Every Day" by Frank Zappa, "Lil' Red Riding Hood," ten words from "Shotgun," two lines from "Ring of Fire," eight words from "Black Is Black," and fifteen words from "We Gotta Get Out of This Place." Music in the sixties sometimes had completely different interpretations in Vietnam. In the States, a song by The Byrds called "Eight Miles High" was about drug tripping. In Vietnam, people could interpret it from the perspective of B-52 bombing runs. Herr always appealed to the senses. Alongside the rock 'n' roll soundtrack, he had painfully vivid descriptions of smells, particularly the smell of soldiers who had been in the jungle, wet all the time for days, their body odors mixing with the smells of blood, death, fear, and Old Spice aftershave. He let them be his guns, but he also brought their voices and feelings to the surface, as at the besieged firebase of Khe Sanh. He described a C-47 gunship at Khe Sanh carrying weapons "that could fire out 300 rounds per second, Gatling style, 'a round in every square inch in a football field in less than a minute,' as the handout said." With every fifth round a tracer, at night the gunships rained fire on the ground. Herr said some soldiers called it Puff the Magic Dragon, but the Marines called it Spooky:

If you watched from a close range, you couldn't believe that anyone would have the courage to deal with that night after night,
week after week, and you cultivated a respect for the Viet Cong
and the NVA [North Vietnamese Army] who had crouched
under it every night now for months. It was awesome, worse
than anything the Lord had ever put down on Egypt, and at
night, you'd hear the Marines talking, watching it, yelling, "Get
Some!" until they grew quiet and someone would say, "Spooky
understands." The nights were very beautiful.[49]

Dispatches is personal, with a first-person narrator who can
hardly believe what he sees, the language a rich and evocative vernacular. It concentrates on the experiences of ordinary people: soldiers, not civilians. It presents a world so complex that the author
doubts his own ability to understand it. In that sense, it is a postmodernist text. Or, as Herr put it: "I went there behind the crude
but serious belief that you had to be able to look at anything, serious because I acted on it and went, crude because I didn't know,
it took the war to teach it, that you were as responsible for everything you saw as you were for everything you did. The problem
was that you didn't always know what you were seeing until later,
maybe years later, that a lot of it never made it in at all, it just stayed
stored there in your eyes. Time and information, rock and roll, life
itself, the information isn't frozen, you are."[50]

After *Dispatches* was published, Herr wrote narration for the
movie *Apocalypse Now*—with its classic scenes of napalm in the trees,
playing Wagner from loudspeakers on attack helicopters, and surf-
ing on the waves after the battle. With Stanley Kubrick, he did the
screenplay for another excellent Vietnam movie, *Full Metal Jacket*.
He also wrote a book about rock 'n' roll and a historical novel about
Walter Winchell; but nothing engaged him like Vietnam.

The way Herr described himself in the beginning of *Dispatches*—"Day one, if anything could have penetrated that first innocence I might have taken the next plane out. Out absolutely."[51]—was not an overly dramatized fictionalization, but a realistic portrait of a guy going crazy. His journalistic colleagues Dana Stone and Sean Flynn died in Cambodia and their bodies were never found; Herr survived Tet; he contrasted the amazing blandness of public information officers with the eloquent and beautiful language of soldiers in combat. It added up for him like mercury in a swordfish, maybe even faster than it did for the soldiers themselves; correspondents had officer status and could fly around in hundreds of helicopters and absorb more of the war than a soldier would have.

"I was pretty crazy when I came back," Herr told an interviewer. "For a long time I was, in fact, *very* crazy." Herr returned from Vietnam in 1969 with plans to write his book. Then he ran into several problems, "not the least of which was the famous post-Vietnam syndrome," Herr later said. He had two-thirds of the book done when he returned, and yet it took him until 1977—a time in which he endured paralysis, "massive collapse," depression, and psychoanalysis—to finish it. Posttraumatic stress disorder among Vietnam veterans was not well treated, although many suffered from it, and as many as 20 percent of Iraq War veterans do as well. Few talked about war correspondents suffering from the same psychological disability.[52]

The magazine cover featured a photo of a dude with his face painted, wearing beads and a top hat with an "LSD" badge. An unlit cigarette protruded from his smiling lips. The cover headline read: "THE HIPPIE CULT. Who they are. What they want. Why they act that way."

This was a bit of a departure. The magazine was the venerable *Saturday Evening Post,* originally founded by Ben Franklin and famous for its Norman Rockwell covers depicting idyllic small-town scenes. It would later fail, as did most such large-circulation magazines like *Life* and *Look,* because its millions of readers lived in unfashionable Zip Codes that did not appeal to advertisers. While the *Saturday Evening Post* had featured Rockwell covers depicting the civil rights movement, this particular issue sitting on the coffee tables of Middle America in 1967 may have been a surprise to readers. The rest of the magazine featured an article on the Smothers brothers, reflections on the Detroit riots, and the editor's thoughts on kudzu.

Joan Didion had two articles in the issue. One, "The Howard Hughes Underground," she would later retitle as "7000 Romaine, Los Angeles 38," which was the address of the Howard Hughes "communications center" and not far from Didion's home. It was featured as the "Points West" column with her husband John Gregory Dunne.

In the first paragraph of her cover article, "Slouching towards Bethlehem" on the hippie generation (although the magazine could not decide whether to spell the term "hippie" or "hippy"), she wrote that America, at the moment,

> was a country of bankruptcy notices and public-auction announcements and commonplace reports of casual killings and misplaced children and abandoned homes and vandals who misspelled even the four-letter words they scrawled.

The magazine circulated in a country where things were not working out. Didion, a native Californian, went to the Haight-Ashbury center of the acid culture in San Francisco, "where the social hemorrhaging was showing up." Her reporting strategy was pure literary journalism: "I did not even know what I wanted to find out, and so I just stayed around awhile and made a few friends."[53]

The essays and journalism reprinted in her 1968 collection, *Slouching towards Bethlehem,* appeared in the *Post,* the *New York Times Magazine, Holiday,* and *The American Scholar.* Odd places for New Journalism, but her brooding writing was irresistible.

Didion explained something about her reporting in her 1966 essay "On Keeping a Notebook." The point of keeping notes, Didion said, was not to have "an accurate factual record." Instead, the notes told her afterward "*How it felt to me.*" The notebook was never about other people, even though they occupied its pages. Maybe that was self-centered, but Didion did not apologize for it. She realized, as E. B. White said, that the opus to be translated was herself. She was also neurotic, anxious, and filled with angst.[54]

In her reports from El Salvador, a land of prolonged violent revolution and repression in the eighties where thousands had died and even more had simply "disappeared," she talked about how it felt to be her in this place and time. She visited a notorious body dump, where she watched a woman learning how to drive a Toyota pickup truck—the kind of vehicle often used to secretly drop bodies off the cliff. After a visit to the morgue, where such bodies ended up, threatening uniformed agents of the military trapped her in a car. Sitting with her husband on the porch of a Mexican restaurant one night, she was unnerved by the sight of armed men on the street and the realization that the candle on their table cast the only pool of light on the street, making them an easy target. They resisted blowing it out. "Nothing came of this," she said, "but I did not forget the sensation of having been in a single instant demoralized, undone, humiliated by fear, which is what I meant when I said that I came to understand in El Salvador the mechanism of terror."[55]

Didion's narration often included personal perspectives. Memoir increasingly played a role in literary journalism from the seventies onward. Blais, who has written a memoir herself, called this form an equal opportunity employer that both men and women use. Examples include Didion, Frank Conroy, Annie Dillard, Gretel Ehrlich, Frances Fitzgerald, Ian Frazier, Francine du Plessix Gray, Ernest Hemingway, Itabari Njeri, Richard Rhodes, Gay Talese, John Edgar Wideman, and Geoffrey and Tobias Wolff. They are not writing simply to tell us about their lives. They are reporting on a time, a culture they once inhabited, and for them the window of memoir lets light into that world. Stories that might never be told in standard journalism gain access to an audience through memoir. "Just about everyone feels marginalized as a child," Blais said. "Memoir encourages the writer to look at all kinds of fringe experiences, whether they come from childhood, or being gay, or having a disease, or belonging to an ethnic minority, or being rich or being poor. As such it is a very humanizing genre, which may finally be what accounts for its popularity." Facing a world of hypocrisy, fraud, and shattered cultural connections, modernist writers found the solidity of personal experience a foundation for their literary journalism.

William Zinsser, who edited *Inventing the Truth: The Art and Craft of Memoir* and *They Went: The Art and Craft of Travel Writing,* has acknowledged that intention is everything in evaluating a memoir, where the author is the protagonist and "tour guide." As the joke goes, you can tell when the tour guide is lying because his lips are moving. The more reliable kind of memoir that Zinsser advocates, however, deals with fact and tells a true story that can open the ordinary life of an age for readers. "I think the truth is sacred and you have to stick to the facts," Zinsser told an audience in 2006. Recent examples of such "reported memoirs" include Blais, *Uphill Walkers* (2001), and Walt Harrington, *The Everlasting Stream: A True Story of Rabbits, Guns, Friendship, and Family* (2002). Harrington described the work that went into his interracial family memoir, the kind of reporting that readers never notice: "To say that the farm house sits below a nine-hundred-foot bluff, you'll swing by the country soil conservation office and get a copy of the farm's geological survey map. To mention that someone has Vivaldi roses in a vase on the sideboard, you'll spend an hour on the phone interviewing rose experts. You'll go back to the scene of the crime the next day and walk off distances. You'll check maps to determine north, south, east, and west. You'll dig out decades-old weather reports to be sure it actually rained on the day someone says it rained."[56]

The first-person presence of the writer that became so prevalent in the New Journalism—and which infuriated standard journalists of the time—plays a greater role today. Harrington, in the preface to a collection of personal journalism, said, "These writers didn't have to be in their stories. Yet the choice allowed them to add insights and touches and observations that only being personal could create. Their stories were not the *only* stories that could have been told from the material, but they were all made more vibrant by the journalist's presence."[57]

In 1979, Didion provided the best example of the conundrum faced by writers whose personal histories inform their journalism. In the introduction to her book *The White Album,* named after the famous Beatles album, she recounted how she felt, beginning in about 1966 during the early years of the New Journalism era and running through 1968, a time when she kept house, wrote articles, and was named a "woman of the year." Then she suffered "an attack of vertigo, nausea, and a feeling that she was going to pass out" and was evaluated at a psychiatric clinic as a person who "feels deeply that all human effort is foredoomed to failure, a conviction which seems to push her further into a dependent, passive withdrawal." It was a world of protests, race riots, police riots, cultural upheaval, Black Panthers dying in police raids, war, assassinations, missing people, body counts, and political controversy, a world where the center could not hold. "By way of comment," Didion said, "I offer only that an attack of vertigo and nausea does not now seem to me an inappropriate response to the summer of 1968."[58]

Capote, Herr, and Didion all suffered difficult personal and psychological reactions as a result of such intense involvement with the people and the cultures they were reporting on. As they researched their stories, they were not separate from the worlds they were researching; they were participants.

The New Journalism controversies over fact vs. fiction, first-person vs. third-person perspective, and memoir vs. journalism hardly applied to Hunter S. Thompson, author of *Hell's Angels* and *Fear and Loathing in Las Vegas.* Those two books are worlds apart. *Hell's Angels* grew from the years Thompson spent associating with members of the motorcycle gang in California during the early sixties. It shows every sign of being solidly factual. *Fear and Loathing in Las Vegas* contributed the most to creating a persona for Thompson as a drug-crazed counterculture freak, and it has only tenuous connections with objective reality. I laugh out loud every time I read certain passages in either book. Contemporary literary journalist Tracy Kidder once told me that while he normally wants to know whether he's reading fact or fiction, with Thompson he doesn't much care.

Thompson committed suicide in 2005 rather than face a struggle with terminal illness. Matching the real man with his persona as Raoul Duke in *Fear and Loathing in Las Vegas* or as Duke in the *Doonesbury* comic strip by Garry Trudeau led many people to misunderstand him. When I was told of his death, I asked if it had been a drug-induced shooting accident. Evaluations of his work were often distorted by that same knee-jerk reaction.

I met Thompson once in Boulder, Colorado. I was enlisted as a university professor to serve as moderator during his appearance before two thousand stoned and screaming fans who had paid admission to see the gonzo journalist in Macky Auditorium. He arrived late from the airport and told me to go ahead and introduce him, but that he would interrupt me and come onstage before I was finished. He warned that he often rambled and demanded that I slap him on the leg when he did so. Since I knew a little about his work, he remained backstage through my introduction until I called for him. He had short hair and a casual, yet hyper-tense style. His eyes flicked back and forth to take in everything at a glance.

Thompson never gave speeches; he answered questions, often with funny and meaningful stories of his personal experiences as a reporter. My job as volunteer moderator was to select audience members who would ask the questions. I was constantly on edge that a shirtless young man slowly waving his arms while standing in the first row of the balcony would tip forward and quietly fall onto the crowd below. Drinking some of Thompson's Chivas Regal and a beer—both required in his contract as part of the stage set-up—helped cut the tension.

Thompson had been covering the 1984 presidential primaries. His favorite candidate, Senator Gary Hart from Colorado, was struggling against Walter Mondale. Thompson wanted to talk about politics; the audience wanted him to talk about drugs. His insights and firsthand stories from the campaign trail fell harmlessly on an audience that may have been overserved.

Thompson was an abstract expressionist among the New Journalists, adapting Jackson Pollock's drip paintings to prose. Yet, like Picasso, when he wanted to he could also paint in a representational style. His abstract journalism required the reader to interpret the artist's mind in order to understand the subject matter. In Boulder, he urged the audience to get into politics and not just take his word for it. During his years at *Rolling Stone* magazine, he explained, people would send unidentified drugs in the mail, and Thompson would ingest them. "You can't trust my word about politics," Thompson told the crowd. "I tested drugs at *Rolling Stone* magazine for three years. Go find out for yourself." The audience cheered, but may have missed the point about political participation.

Writing after Thompson's death, *Rolling Stone* editor Rich Cohen said that since 1970, Thompson had "used drugs quite deliberately to create a new kind of reportorial voice—a voice that could be listened to but never trusted, because the reporter was hammered and seeing trails. By bringing narcotics into his prose, he introduced a hallucinatory element into nonfiction writing, his own kind of magic realism. He took the American realist tradition and ran it through a wood chipper."[59]

Striding across the stage in Boulder, Thompson seemed remarkably fit and able for a man who stayed up all night and ran on uppers and downers. At one point, Thompson decided that since the audience in Boulder had an attention span of fifteen seconds, he would limit his answers. A journalism student who had squeezed into the orchestra pit asked what advice he had for young journalists. "Run like rats on the tundra," he said, beating his time limit with room to spare.

We left the stage, picking up a few packages of substances that had been tossed our way. "You bastard!" he said to me backstage. "You never slapped me on the leg!" I never thought he rambled. Without even sniffing it, Thompson lit up a half-smoked joint that had been thrown onstage tucked inside a book of matches. This act convinced me that he probably did test drugs at *Rolling Stone.* Late in life he had major dependencies, according to those who knew him. "Well, he was an addict," Cohen wrote after the suicide. "No doubt about that. Addicted to cocaine and pills and alcohol. Addicted to being addicted, forever chasing the perfect state of chemical balance in which he could write."[60] But that druggie reputation distorted the core of his work. People who are stoned or drunk do not write well.

Thompson loved politics. In March 1968, he wrote a letter to Ted Sorenson, Senator Robert Kennedy's aide in Washington. Kennedy was running for the Democratic nomination for president in the primaries against President Lyndon Johnson and Minnesota Senator Eugene McCarthy, an anti–Vietnam War candidate. For all practical purposes McCarthy had defeated the sitting president in the New Hampshire primary—or close enough that Johnson could read the writing on the wall. The leading Republican candidate was once again Richard Nixon. Thompson told Sorenson that he wanted to work for Kennedy in the presidential race. He wasn't offering to ring doorbells in his hometown of Woody Creek, Colorado. He volunteered to "write something for you; that's the only thing I do better than most people, so I guess that's what I should offer."

He explained his reasoning to Sorenson. "With the lone exception of the 1960 presidential campaign, I've gone out of my way to avoid any personal involvement in politics . . . but I have the feeling that we're down to bedrock again, and if that's the case I guess I want a piece of the action," Thompson wrote. "Nixon is a monument to all the bad genes and broken chromosomes that have queered the reality of the 'American Dream.' Nixon is the Dorian Grey [*sic*] of our time, the twisted echo of Jay Gatsby—the candidate from almost–Los Angeles." His motive for volunteering? "I'm not looking for a career in politics or even a dam for Woody Creek. All I really want to do is get that evil pigfucker out of the White House and not let Nixon in . . . and the only real hope I see right now is your friend Robert."[61]

Sorenson passed the letter along to Kennedy's aide Pierre Salinger, but nothing came of it. The letter was dated March 28, 1968, just three days before President Johnson unexpectedly announced that he would not seek reelection. Kennedy fought a long spring of primary battles with McCarthy and Vice President Hubert Humphrey. Sirhan Sirhan, a Palestinian Arab, assassinated Robert Kennedy in Los Angeles on the night of the California primary, June 5, 1968. Humphrey won the Democratic nomination after a convention in Chicago marked by bloody demonstrations in the streets that were dubbed a "police riot," but Nixon won the election. Thompson's beast had regained power.

Thompson became an unlikely hero to a number of standard reporters who covered sports and politics, if for no other reason than that he symbolically described the core problem of reporting. In *Fear and Loathing in Las Vegas,* for example, he was hired to cover the Mint 400 motorcycle race in the desert. As soon as it started, two hundred racers disappeared into rolling clouds of dust. "None of us realized, at the time, that this was the last we would see of the 'Fabulous Mint 400,'" Thompson wrote. "It was like trying to keep track of a swimming meet in an Olympic-sized pool filled with talcum powder instead of water."[62] Telling the truth about the race was impossible and meaningless, so he went back to the bar and casino—"where I began to drink heavily, think heavily, and make many heavy notes."

In Boulder, after Thompson's appearance in Macky Auditorium, I left early, but the heavy drinking and sportage apparently continued at the Boulderado Hotel late into the night. By that evening in 1984, the New Journalism movement was long dead. Joe Nocera blamed Thompson for killing the New Journalism. It was true, as Nocera said, that Thompson had created a persona for himself in *Fear and Loathing* and afterward could not escape it. He had to "constantly be doing interesting or amusing things," and his efforts over time were not particularly interesting. Tom Wolfe during the sixties sometimes wore a white suit and spats, but later he abandoned the persona before becoming trapped by it. Nocera said, "The ideal of New Journalism—to find a form that explains, enlightens, and entertains all at once—has not died."[63] The narrative and immersion styles of New Journalism caught on, especially among a younger generation of reporters who created livelier newspaper reporting and who sometimes developed into literary journalists themselves. By the mid-seventies, however, time and the weight of controversy had smothered the New Journalism as a movement, although the ideal survived, as Nocera proved in his own writing. By the eighties, however, even Tom Wolfe, who had invented the term, parked "New Journalism" in the closet with his white suit, which he brought out only on ceremonial occasions.

◈

ADRIAN NICOLE LEBLANC

[Editorial Note: The extended network of people in Random Family *includes a large and often informally related group of members. Coco is the mother of Mercedes and Nautica, with Cesar, and of Nikki with another father. Cesar's mother, Lourdes, accompanies Coco on a visit to prison, where Cesar is serving time for killing an associate. Cesar's sister, Jessica, is also incarcerated—for a drug crime. Her three children, Brittany, Stephanie, and Serena, one of whose fathers was murdered, live with a friend.]*

Part 1

Back in the Bronx, in their frilly bedroom at Milagros's, the twin girls sat on their beds excitedly. The beds were rafts. The girls' thoughts floated, bound for Coney Island, where they were going to celebrate Serena's birthday at the beach. It was the first year all the girls had lived together and shared a bedroom without worrying that their big sister had to stay behind, or leave. Below them, on the linoleum floor, were their purple summer clogs from Payless, capsized shoe-boats, decorated with turquoise and yellow hippie flowers.

Brittany and Stephanie were six, still twiggy, with prominent brows on moony faces that tapered upward to wispy topknots, giving their heads the shape of tulip bulbs. Milagros had given them home-style bangs that accented the mournful expression of their heavy-lidded eyes. But the twins were actually lighthearted and agile, squealing as they chased one another. Serena shared none of their breeziness. She was only slightly bigger, but her bearing seemed much heavier. The morning of her eighth birthday, she slept late; Brittany and Stephanie wished she'd wake up. They sat on the side of their bed, watching her, their four skinny legs swinging impatiently.

Revised by Adrian Nicole LeBlanc from chapters 15, 17, and 20 of *Random Family: Love, Drugs, Trouble, and Coming of Age in the Bronx,* 2003.

Serena rolled over, her legs spread across the sheet's flat faces of Beauty and the Beast. Her long hair fell in tangles. She didn't usually sleep well. The street noises scared her. The music, the sirens, the hollering and shooting from the after-hours club on University, sounds on top of sounds. Serena blinked, then slowly pushed herself up. She rubbed her eyes.

Serena's half-brother Lucas, Trinket and Puma's two-year-old, made a brief appearance in the doorway. He was the child in Puma's arms the night he was gunned down. Serena glanced at Lucas dispassionately. Strapped to his stroller, he'd propelled himself forward by violent jerks. Milagros's fat arm swept him away.

"Happy birthday, Serena!" Stephanie said.

"Yeah, happy birthday!" Brittany added.

Serena swatted away their attention as she yawned. She inspected a stick-on tattoo heart on her arm. Milagros boomed, "BrittanyStephanieSerena! Come eat!" Serena dropped off the bed. "Come on," she instructed her sisters, leading them into the hall.

Milagros, a close friend of Jessica's, was always taking care of other peoples' children—like Kevin, the son of one of her incarcerated friends. When Jessica went to prison, Milagros did the same with Jessica's kids—Serena, Brittany and Stephanie.

"You didn't say happy birthday to Serena," Brittany reminded Trinket, who was clicking around the apartment hurriedly in her high heels, late for work. Trinket came to a dead stop, placed her hands on Serena's shoulders, and backed her into the bedroom. "Happy Birthday" wafted out. Serena emerged with a sly smile and, on her cheek, a lipstick kiss. Except for the beds, and a few chairs, Milagros had no furniture. The children squeezed into tiny plastic chairs at a pint-size table that they had already outgrown. Serena served her siblings the pancakes Milagros had prepared.

Elaine bustled in with her two spotless sons and recalcitrant husband, Angel, in tow. Angel had stopped using drugs, but Elaine hadn't forgiven him. Just that morning she had been reminded of the camera that could have taken Serena's birthday pictures if it hadn't been hawked for dope. Once, she had sold off all her furniture; luckily, Jessica had given them a bedroom set from one of George's apartments, following his arrest. Elaine had needed money so badly that year that she'd even milled some of George's drugs under his guidance from the MCC.

Angel parked the cooler in Milagros's kitchen and joined Kevin on the floor; Kevin, who was ten, was watching a bootleg video of the gang movie

Blood In, Blood Out. Lourdes had promised she was coming, but only Serena actually expected her. Coco surprised everyone by arriving on time with Mercedes and Nikki.

"Títi, look," Serena said, leading Coco into her room. She handed her aunt a school notebook opened to a page where the words *I wish* were followed by a blank, in which she'd written, "I wish there were no drug in the world, that would be nice."

"Thass good," Coco said, but she preferred to keep the day upbeat. Birthdays should be happy; they were the biggest events of the year. "Now, why don't ya'll sing me a song? Mercy, show your cousins the song I taught you. I sang it when I was your age, 'Kind Kind Mother.'"

The twins started, and Mercedes and Serena and Nikki joined in; Nikki's eagerness transformed her unintelligible words into a respectable gurgling sound. Coco clapped and nodded with each syllable of every plodding verse. It was a song that Foxy's older sister, Aida, had learned while she was in the youth house and had sung to Foxy, which Foxy had taught her daughter, in turn:

I had a kind kind mother
She was so kind to me
And when I got in trouble
She held me on her knee
That night when I was sleeping
Upon my mother's bed
An angel came down from heaven
And told me she was dead
That morning when I woke up
I found my dream come true
Now she's up in heaven
That's why the skies are blue
Now children obey they mother
Especially when they small
Cuz if you shall lose your mother
You lose the best of all!

Finally, the adults were ready. The children assembled in the hall. "Did Mommy close the window?" Serena asked Kevin, pushing the button to the elevator.

"I dunno," he said. The elevator door clunked open. Stephanie hopped over a puddle of urine. There were puddles in the lobby, too, but these were pungent with King Pine. The super was hosing down the walls for his morning mop-up. "Hello!" he called out to the train of children.

"Hello!" each one shouted, ducking through the missing panel at the base of the security entryway.

"*Dios bendiga tu barriga,*" he said to Coco. God bless your belly.

"Thank you," Coco said. She didn't speak Spanish, but she understood common phrases. The super wiped over a tattered copy of "Respect Thy Neighbor Commandments" stuck on the wall. "Help Thy Neighbor" and "Get to Know Thy Neighbor" were the only commandments not too pen-stabbed to be illegible. Outside, the sidewalk warmed. Angel pushed the cooler, which he'd strapped to a shopping cart, as far as the subway and said good-bye to the women and children.

At Coney Island, the wind made it too cold to swim, but the children ran in the sand and splashed their feet in the waves. The group trooped up to the boardwalk for lunch. On a picnic table outside the boarded-up Freak Show, everyone except Elaine's sons munched on Elaine's chicken and rice and beans. Her boys weren't hungry because Elaine had earlier spirited them away and treated them to McDonald's, on the sly.

Damp clothes made the children shiver. Their lips were blue. With the gusts of wind, it was impossible to light the candles on Serena's birthday cake, which was soon dusted with sand and ripped apart for a cake fight; Milagros tossed the remains in a garbage can. Serena spent the rest of her birthday lifting her sisters and cousins in and out of the seats of baby rides. For the long trip back to the Bronx, Serena, exhausted, sank into the sub-way seat next to Coco. Brooklyn passed in a rush. Serena watched the rooftops of the houses. "I want to live in a house," she said.

"Me, too, Mami," said Coco. "When I get my apartment, I want to get it big enough for Mommy Jessica to come and live."

Serena pointed out a fence. "A pregnant lady couldn't get over that fence," she observed. She distractedly brushed the sand from the soles of her sneakers. "My best birthday was my sixth birthday."

That was the summer before her mother went away. Jessica had rented a community center in the projects and threw Serena a big party. All of Serena's friends and family came for the celebration, said Serena, "even people from Florida." Streamers and balloons draped the tables and bags were stuffed with candy. Jessica had hired a DJ, and a clown who painted the children's faces. Even Lourdes showed. Serena still had the pictures of herself and her grandmother, cheeks pressed together, beside her layered Minnie Mouse birthday cake.

Two years later, Serena sat on the subway, contemplative and sticky with sand. Nikki sucked her thumb and leaned cautiously against Coco's big belly. Mercedes confidently plopped her head in what remained of Coco's lap.

"Old people should think like children," Serena whispered cryptically. Coco nodded. It was advice that, at nineteen, she easily took to heart. Coco covered Mercedes's shoulders with a towel and tightened her grip. The F train turned northward and jerked underground toward the Bronx.

Part 2

Lourdes was dressed like a schoolgirl the cold September morning in 1993 when she went to see her youngest son. She wore a green-and-cranberry-striped hoodie and matching green leggings. She sported canvas shoes. A gold scrunchie cinched her waist-length hair into a bun. Slender gold hoops dangled from her ears. She'd painted her lips summer pink. But by the time Lourdes laid eyes on the tree-lined drive of Coxsackie Correctional Facility, she looked as though she'd imploded. She hated prisons. "Because I feel the pain of the whole room, of the whole people in jail, and I can't take it," she said. She dragged behind Mercedes, who hopped toward the front gate, which was topped by tall loops of razor wire. Cows grazed in a nearby pasture. Lourdes kept her head down during the lengthy processing. When the guard asked her, "What's your relationship to the inmate?" Lourdes whispered, "Mother"—a word she usually proclaimed.

Across her belly, one arm rested in a sling. The stories of how she came to have a cast were lively and various: she preferred the tale about a trip she took with her man, Domingo, to buy chickens, his admirable intervention in someone else's domestic trouble, and her diving in front of him to block the bullet that the enraged husband had sent his way. For the prison visit, Lourdes had done her best to look buoyant, perhaps to minimize the wrath she anticipated from her son.

The guard assigned to the visiting room at Coxsackie was immersed in a book of word games. Lourdes, Coco, and Mercedes waited beside him to be acknowledged. Finally, pushing his chin in the general direction of their seat assignments, he said, "Sit second table, by the window," without lifting his head. Coco and Lourdes hesitated. They searched the room, perplexed. "Over there," he said impatiently, without offering further direction. They tiptoed uncertainly down several steps and to the center of the room. "See that black girl sitting with that white guy? NEAR HER!" the guard screamed.

Lourdes slid into a seat covered in greasy dirt so thick that other visitors had marked their presence in it with initials and hearts. The chair wobbled. "Can I switch chairs? Where do he come from?" she asked.

Mercedes pointed to a door. "*Abuela,* Daddy come out from there," she said. Lourdes tapped her left leg compulsively. When Cesar finally stepped through the inmate entrance, Mercedes bolted across the room; a guard removed his handcuffs just in time for him to catch her as she leaped into his arms. Cesar carried her to the desk guard, who took his ID number down, and he bounced Mercedes joyfully as he approached Lourdes and Coco. Lourdes stood. Cesar placed Mercedes down gently and hugged his mother, who sobbed. He kissed Coco's cheek softly. She was crying, too. "What are *you* crying for?" he asked. He smiled worriedly and regarded the women in his life, glancing back and forth—Coco with her belly and self-inflicted red spots; Lourdes, puffy-faced and sniffling; Mercedes peeking out happily beneath a head of perfect curls.

He dove straight into the heart of the trouble, staring directly into his mother's eyes: "So what's up with you? What's going on?" He knew most of it from Elaine, who believed that Domingo had beaten Lourdes for stealing his drugs. Elaine told Cesar about the resulting shoot-out between Domingo and her husband, Angel, how Domingo had threatened even Robert when he went to retrieve Lourdes's things. Elaine had called the police, and Domingo ended up in jail for carrying an unlicensed gun. Despite his family's posturing, Cesar knew the trouble—whatever it was—was his to fix. From prison, the business of fixing it was just that much harder. He'd already sent word to Rocco, who was back on the streets.

What Cesar didn't know was that, while Robert was making arrangements to get his mother to Florida, Lourdes had bailed Domingo out and returned to him. As Lourdes launched into her version of the story, Cesar's expression flattened. His body became taut as Lourdes went on about how Elaine just cared for herself, how Elaine's husband was a liar, how although Robert had invited Lourdes to stay with him and his wife, she couldn't stay as far away as Brooklyn, let alone survive their Jehovah's Witness rules.

Cesar turned to Coco, who sat quietly. He placed his large hand on her big belly. In one month, their baby was due. Cesar seemed steadied by his physical contact with the unborn baby. He asked his mother, "Where are you living?" She did not respond. He glanced at Coco. "Is she back with him?" he asked. Coco bit her lip and cast her eyes down. Lourdes re-launched an explanation that she'd gotten beaten up because of Angel, but Cesar's stare-down made her try another route. "Yes, I am back with my husband," she said. "We are back in the apartment—"

Cesar interrupted her. "He may give you food and he may give you clothes and he may give you shelter, but he did all that before without beating you and you gonna go back. And one day he's gonna beat you and you end up dead. What am I gonna do? Sit here?" Cesar crossed his legs and placed his chin in his hand like *The Thinker.* "What kind of man is he? I'm a violent person and I don't hit my girlfriend. Look at all I done to Coco, but I ain't never hit her." He fixed his eyes on the distance to control his rising anger, then noticed Lourdes's quivering cheeks. His voice softened. "I couldn't do nothing when I was a kid, but I can do something now. It's no death. But I'm gonna get every bone broke. I know you love him and that's your business, but this is out of your hands. Let it be." He placed his arms around Coco and pressed his face into her breasts.

Conversation meandered; Coco listened while Cesar and Lourdes discussed Cesar's discovery of his other daughter, Nikki. Mercedes padded over from across the room and presented Cesar with a car without a wheel. Hours passed. Cesar and Coco kissed; when Lourdes went to the bathroom, they necked. The food wrappers piled up. They caught up on family and friends. During a companionable lull, Cesar told Lourdes that he had recently tried heroin. He'd sniffed some with Tito, who was still at Coxsackie with him. Cesar didn't think he would use it again, although he admitted that the boredom of prison was killing him. "When somebody brings stuff in, and you get in prison and you be sitting here all day doing nothing, the programs—I hate that shit—and somebody says, 'You want to get high?' you get high," he said. Cesar instructed Coco to call Tito down the next time she came for a visit, so he could have visitors, too. She nodded, then excused herself, went into the bathroom, gripped the edge of the sink clogged with toilet paper and hair and cigarette butts, and cried. She never thought Cesar would try heroin. When he was out on the street, he had condemned every drug short of weed.

Meanwhile, Lourdes tucked stray strands of hair into her bun. "You'll fall in love again, it ain't the last man," Cesar assured his mother. Lourdes lifted her chin regally. A slat of afternoon sun pushed through the windows, which were so cloudy they looked as if they had been scrubbed with a giant Brillo pad.

"Time's up!" the droopy guard shouted. "Get out of here! Move it! Time to go!" Mercedes wanted more candy. There was no money, and only a Starburst left. "Can I have that?" she asked her father, who then popped it in his mouth. He exaggerated its deliciousness. "Bite it," he said, inviting her to sample the sticky gob on the tip of his tongue.

"Gim-*me!*" Mercedes cried. Cesar pulled out the gooey taffy and offered it to her, but just as she reached for it, he pulled it back. He teased her with the offer again, and just as she reached for it, he swallowed it and smacked his lips. He smothered her hurt feelings with hugs, making it into a game, drowning out her crying with laughter and kisses and silly smooching sounds. In the subtle tyranny of that moment beat the pulse of Cesar's neighborhood—the bid for attention, the undercurrent of hostility for so many small needs ignored and unmet, the pleasure of holding power, camouflaged in teasing, the rush of love. Then the moment passed, and Cesar's three-year-old daughter walked back out into the world and left him behind.

To Coco's relief, this time Mercedes didn't ask why Cesar wasn't coming home. Some parents lied to their children: they said the prison was a job or a hospital. Elaine used her brother as a lesson: she told her sons that Tío Cesar was paying the price for having done bad things. Coco thought it best to stay close to the truth while veering away from the harshness, so, whenever Mercedes asked, she assured her that Daddy would be home when he was done with being far away. When the guard ushered the visitors from the stuffy room, Coco did not turn back to Cesar. She said, "I get so much upset that I can't look back, then I miss him all the way home."

Coco and Mercedes searched for deer on the Thruway. Lourdes brooded, stoking her discontent: "George beat up Jessica with a two-by-four. Angel—am I right or am I wrong, Coco?—broke Elaine's jaw?" she exclaimed. In fact, it was George who broke Jessica's jaw. But there were so many fights and slights and brawls and arguments that it was hard to keep track of them. "Robert, now, he's a Jehovah's Witness and he is willing to let his younger brother get brought downstate and take care of this and get more time? He is a religious person, and that don't seem right to me. Did I tell them what to do when they get beaten up? Did I tell Jessica? Did I tell Elaine she had to leave Angel? Why do they get the right to tell me?" Coco and Mercedes fell asleep. Lourdes continued, "I told Cesar, 'Get out of that macho. Get out of that hoodlum! And get inside you the urge to freedom!'"

The anger gave way to sadness. Lourdes glanced over at a hill tapering up to a white colonial house. "One night in my life I want to sleep in a house like that, with a front porch, and all peace and quiet," she said. She rummaged through her purse for her cigarettes and searched for a Spanish station on the radio, which she finally found, over an hour later, after crossing the miraculous span of the Tappan Zee Bridge. She turned the volume up louder, then louder, the closer she got to the Bronx.

Part 3

One night, Coco, Mercedes, and Nautica, the new baby, waited at Columbus Circle in Manhattan for the Prison Gap, a bus to Southport. Coco had left Nikki with Foxy; when things were rocky between him and Coco, Coco knew it was best to bring only his girls. A stable of old buses idled. Transportation companies like Operation Prison Gap, some managed by ex-convicts, hauled families and friends of prisoners upstate to visit loved ones. Without them, the visits would have been impossible; few people had cars. Prisons dotted the huge state, and inmates moved among them, seemingly arbitrarily. The bus riders were almost always women and children. Except for special charters on Mother's Day or Family Day, the buses serviced primarily men's facilities. Women inmates, like Jessica, had a much harder time seeing family. Passengers often recognized one another—from other routes, the long hours spent together waiting in processing, or the neighborhood; the majority of state prisoners came from the same parts of New York City. Some of the women became friends.

At Southport, Cesar was allowed only three hours of exercise a week. For this, he would be led, shackled, to a cage in a cube of walled-in yard, where he could do sit-ups, push-ups, squat thrusts, and jumping jacks. Showers were timed and also limited to three a week. Like Jessica, Cesar was obsessive about cleanliness and he found this especially difficult. He had no books. He had no photographs to look at. Radios were forbidden. He reflected upon his life. It surprised him that he didn't miss the girls and parties as much as being able to open the door of a refrigerator, or play peekaboo with Mercedes on the floor. He said, "The street is like a scapegoat. You get in a fight with your mother and you go out and you get blasted and you have a beef with someone on the street—but two minutes later you don't even remember what's the beef about." He did, however, remember a time he and Rocco broke into an apartment to steal drugs and discovered the dealer, and his baby son, at home. The dealer cried, "Hold up, not my kid!" and Cesar took the boy and moved him. Even though they only beat the guy and tied him up, Cesar started thinking about how horrible it must have been for the boy to see his father so scared.

The isolation of the box made him feel, at turns, morose and hyperactive. He'd started suffering anxiety attacks. In his letter to Coco, he'd sounded desperate. "I'm in a real state of depression," he'd written. Coco fretted because Cesar—for all he'd been through—had never expressed himself in this way in letters before.

The bus dispatcher greeted the passengers warmly. "Welcome, everybody," he said. "There are some rules for you to follow. We don't allow drugs on the bus. Please don't be getting drunk. Be considerate to others, have a good visit tomorrow. Take the same seat when you come out of the facility, and come back next week and bring a friend."

Coco gave Mercedes some candy and spread out Mercedes's old black shearling along the backseat to make a bed. She held Nautica until she dozed off, then gently placed her beside Mercedes, who had quickly fallen asleep. Veteran visitors had equipped themselves with rolls of quarters and crisp dollars for the vending machines, clear plastic bags for locker keys and change. Some brought along pretty outfits whose perfection they preserved in dry-cleaning bags. The cost of the trip used up most of Coco's money. Lourdes's boyfriend, Domingo, had given Coco $20 to deposit in Cesar's commissary, and Coco had budgeted an additional $20 for the vending machines, so Cesar and the girls could eat. She opened a sandwich she'd made for the ride and offered half to the woman seated next to her.

The woman declined, but offered Coco some of her springwater. As Coco sipped, the woman said, "This is such a good bus, quiet, the people nice, you just don't know." She recounted less savory trips—loud music, dueling girlfriends, wailing children, drunks. She showed Coco a picture of her son. The boy had just received a scholarship to private school from a local youth group.

"God bless him, he's beautiful," Coco murmured. She appreciated anybody's good news. Mercedes curled close to her baby sister, and Coco covered them both with the coat she'd borrowed from Foxy. The bright city disappeared and the bus drove on in the companionable dark. Some of the riders spaced out, their Walkmans singing in their ears. The women chattered; two girls played clapping games. An old woman made her way slowly down the aisle, balancing on her cane. Her lopsided belly dragged beneath drooping breasts, but her spirits were high. "I had me a stroke right there at Rikers, right there in the visiting room," she said. The man she'd been visiting had become her husband. Tomorrow, she bragged, he'd sign their first joint tax forms.

The night stretched on. Conversation quieted. Legs and arms dusted the aisle floor, children coughed, braids came undone. Coco looked out the window. She couldn't imagine moving upstate, as Milagros planned to do, living out in the country, away from her family. The old bus creaked and rolled.

Nautica woke first; she spit up and cried at dawn. Coco covered her hairy head with a cotton cap. "You going to see your daddy. I'm getting butter-flies just thinking about seeing your daddy," Coco said. She raised Nautica up each time the bus bounced from a bump and smiled.

About a half hour from the prison, the bus pulled into a truck stop. The women gathered themselves and their dry cleaning and crowded into the cramped bathroom of the restaurant. There they tucked and scrutinized and tightened, sharing compliments and lipstick and complaints in the toasty bathroom air. They didn't want to dress in the bathroom at the prison, where they would lose precious minutes of their visits.

"I ain't never been to see my husband in nothing but a dress," said a young woman in a lime green sheath that showed her figure. An older woman gruffly forked her permed hair.

"Albany gave you the date?" one woman asked another. She was refer-ring to the official approval to marry an inmate; the headquarters of the De-partment of Corrections was in Albany.

"My friend is going to make my wedding dress. I already have it all de-signed," answered the bride-to-be.

Coco leaned against the wall and listened and waited for the one bath-room stall to clear; she felt too self-conscious to undress in front of the oth-ers. She snuck a look in the mirror: to save money, she'd trimmed her own bangs. She'd slicked them down with Vaseline, which emphasized the jaggedness. A fresh spray of red spots flecked her cheeks.

"Here, I'll hold her," a lady offered, reaching for Nautica. Coco slipped into the stall and stepped into a conservative outfit Elaine had loaned her—a beige turtleneck and matching skirt, topped by an embroidered vest. She wore sheer stockings beneath the slitted skirt, so she could show Cesar her tattoo. Her own style was more sporty, but she wanted Cesar to see that she had matured.

In the prison processing area, Mercedes sat beside Coco, legs swinging, humming to herself. "You been here before?" a woman asked, sounding concerned. Her eye makeup was a rainbow. The woman positioned herself over Mercedes's head and mouthed, so Mercedes couldn't hear, "Expect bars—you can only touch his hands." Coco's eyes filled with tears.

All the visitors were allowed to the next stage of processing except Coco. Coco waited. Nautica dozed. Mercedes doodled. Coco showed her how to draw "👁 ♥U." "Your Títi Jessica taught me that," Coco said.

After fifteen minutes, Coco hesitantly approached the guard at the desk. She hadn't filled out the forms correctly, and he hadn't bothered to tell her. Already, she'd lost an hour. Mercedes rested her nose on the counter. "What's in your lunch box?" she asked the guard as Coco struggled to hold Nautica and to write at the same time.

The guard pointed to a kitchenette. "That's where I heat up my food," he said. A woman emerged from the ladies' room, transformed. The guard bent forward and whispered, "Who is the painted lady?"

"What's in your lunch box? Tell me!" Mercedes said.

"You sure talk a lot. I bet you are a little flirt."

The guard stamped Coco's hand with invisible ink, then stamped Mercedes's, and finally directed them to a door.

The doors led out to a short walkway that led into another building, where Coco and her daughters waited twelve minutes for two guards to finish a conversation, after which one yelled at Coco for setting off the metal detector because she'd forgotten to remove her watch. When she cleared the detector, they were allowed into the visiting room. Carrying Nautica, Coco slowly wound her way to her seat assignment at the end of the S-shaped rows. Mercedes paraded through, initially oblivious to the shackled men behind the wire mesh.

She caused a little stir; her blond curls bounced as she searched eagerly for her father. Coco slid onto a chair, which was bound to three others by chains. She pretended to be absorbed by Nautica, who wobbled on her thighs. Cesar stood in the interior cage, waiting for a guard to spring the gate. At last, Mercedes spotted him. He shuffled toward them, barely able to move. He was shackled with leg irons, and in handcuffs, both of which were attached to a chain around his waist. Mercedes looked terrified. "Come out! Over here," she said desperately.

"I can't," Cesar mumbled.

"Teasing ain't nice, come out!" Mercedes said.

"Can't you see I'm chained up? I can't move, Mercy," he said, lifting his wrists slightly.

"Take them off. Take them off," she demanded. "Take them off!"

"I can't."

"Play patty-cake!"

"Mercedes," Coco chided.

"I can't take them off, Mercedes," Cesar said.

Mercedes determinedly outlined the invisible ink the guard had stamped on her hand. Soon her gesture became vague. "Daddy, you have money at your house?" she asked quietly.

"No, Mercedes," he said sadly.

Then Mercedes brightened. It was as though she'd grasped that her father couldn't tolerate the view of himself that her panic reflected. "We are going to get bunk beds and Nikki is going to be on the bottom, and I am going to be on the top!" she chattered. "You can come over and sleep with me on the top, and we can take a bubble bath."

Cesar squinted, as though he had suddenly recognized her voice from far away.

"Wanna hear a song?" Mercedes asked. Then she sang. Her father was smitten by her performance until she said, "That's Nikki's daddy's song," puncturing the moment. He glanced over his shoulder stonily. "Look at Mommy's face," Mercedes urged. "Mommy been messing with her face."

Cesar hadn't teased Coco or complimented her dressy outfit. He'd said nothing about the tattoo, or the special Weeboks Nautica wore. When he had been in Harlem Valley and Mercedes had worn the cheaper, no-name-brand sneakers called skippies, he'd removed them and tossed them across the visiting room. Since then, Coco had made sure Mercedes wore name-brand sneakers for visits, but it didn't seem to matter—all because of her face. "I'm sick of it; if that's the way you want it, fine," Cesar said to Coco. For the next three hours, they did not speak.

Coco busied herself with Nautica. Nautica grabbed on to the mesh cage, which was covered in lipstick. Mercedes explored the visiting room and collected compliments.

"Oh, that girl, she yours?" Cesar's neighbor asked, watching Mercedes pass.

"That's her," said Cesar.

"She look like Shirley Temple."

"These are my two girls. I got two other kids with other wives, four kids altogether. I'm nineteen. I got started young, right?"

Again, Mercedes asked Cesar, "Daddy, you wanna hear a song?" She performed "Kind Kind Mother" and got stuck on a verse. She kept repeating the start of the verse until she reached her aborted end, then began from the beginning again. "I had a kind kind mother . . ." Cesar teased her, "What about your father, too?"

Around noon, Cesar finally spoke to Coco: "Get me something to eat." She bought three packages of chicken wings from the vending machine and waited beside the microwave. She tore open the packets of sauce and silently passed them beneath the slot. Cesar hunched over the styrofoam tray. He pushed the wings into his mouth. The handcuffs dug into his wrists.

After he'd finished, Coco cleared the trays. Cesar carefully wiped his hands. He looked to the side and reached through the slot and held what he could of Coco. Touch did what only touch could do.

Coco's words poured out. She told him about a new girl at Thorpe who knew all about the trailer visits. The girl had had a prison wedding. She had told Coco about all the right things to bring—satin sheets, and cream and strawberries. Coco had been learning new things, too, from watching pornography.

Cesar watched Coco soberly. He waited for her to finish, then said tenderly, "Sex ain't everything." The box had forced him to do some thinking. If they were going to marry, they needed to communicate. Coco bit her lip. His hope came across as a reprimand. "I want it to be you love me and I love you. Where happiness comes in is when I'm making you happy and you do things to make me happy," Cesar said.

Meanwhile, Mercedes stared at the couple beside them, a young, skinny black man with a full set of gold teeth, and a large, middle-aged white woman in a modest silk dress. He was angry; she looked tired. He beckoned her closer, and she pressed her substantial bosom against the mesh. She bowed her head to listen. He cursed. Then, methodically, he smashed his handcuffed hands into her chest. He continued speaking in low tones as he punched her, and she held her body taut to receive him. Only her head jerked back. Coco furtively watched.

"They been having trailers for years," Cesar said, without irony.

A guard climbed to the top of what looked like a lifeguard chair, a signal to Cesar that they had less than an hour of visiting left.

"I'm starting to think about going back to that cell, and it's got me real depressed," Cesar said. Besides letters, chess was the only activity that helped him pass the time in solitary. He'd made a chessboard out of paper, and his opponent shouted out his plays from down the hall. The pending good-bye wedged between them. "You better come next week or I'll punch you in the face, you got my hopes up," he said miserably.

By the end of the hour, the couple beside them had reconciled. The young man pressed one ear to the counter, penitent, as the woman braided his hair. The guard called time. Chairs scraped the linoleum. The men tried to stretch. Children's hands clasped the grating like small claws. One mother yelled to her husband, who was talking to the other men, "Look at your boy! Look at your boy!" The man to whom she called hopped, as if shaking off the visit. She shoved her son closer to the cage her man was in. "Say good-bye to your daddy. Look at your boy! Look at your boy!" She pressed the boy against what divided them. "Get your father! Get your father!" The boy's thin fingers gripped the wire. His father swatted a good-bye and turned back to the protection of his friends.

"Mom, he said good-bye! Dad said bye!" the boy exclaimed.

Coco noticed Cesar eyeing a teenage girl who'd joined the line. Nautica slept, heavy in Coco's arms.

Coco was relieved to breathe the fresh, cold air outside. She paused, watching Mercedes energetically climb the stairs into the bus. The idea of staying with Cesar and the reality of it were different; he was more demanding in person than he was in her fantasies. She couldn't possibly afford to visit again any time soon—the girls' birthdays were coming. Yet she couldn't tell him no. Coco was glad to be heading home, even though home was Thorpe.

Shortly afterward, Cesar wrote and told her to limit the girls' visits to Southport; he didn't want them to see him caged in any more than necessary.

SEVEN

NEW GENERATIONS

I can't write the truth if I start inventing stuff for nonfiction.
—Tracy Kidder

When we look back at the journalism of the past century or more that remains informative and viable today, we generally discover that the leading texts are literary journalism.

We find Jack London writing about poverty, tramping, and Alaska. John Reed writing about wars in Mexico and Eastern Europe, or revolution in Russia. Ernest Hemingway, Reed, and John Dos Passos writing about World War I and its aftermath. James Agee, Edmund Wilson, Dos Passos, Martha Gellhorn, and George Orwell writing about the Great Depression. John Hersey on Hiroshima. Joseph Mitchell, A. J. Liebling, and Lillian Ross creating cultural portraits in *The New Yorker.* Tom Wolfe, Gay Talese, Truman Capote, Hunter S. Thompson, Michael Herr, and Joan Didion writing experimental narratives during the turbulent 1960s. And in recent years, Tracy Kidder, Susan Orlean, Mark Singer, Calvin Trillin, John McPhee, Jane Kramer, Ted Conover, Michael Paterniti, Doug Whynott, Adrian Nicole LeBlanc,

Jonathan Harr, and many others creating portraits of everyday life and of different cultural communities.

At the end of the last millennium, the New York University journalism department compiled a list of the one hundred best works of twentieth-century journalism; forty-one were works of literary journalism.[1] Though all the forms of journalism—including Muckraking, objective journalism, and investigative reporting—helped to create a representation of the world over the past hundred years, literary journalism is the form that has provided the intimacy, subtlety, and artistry we need to understand the times in which these journalists were writing.

Writers living and dead still pass along their knowledge to other writers today, sustaining the generational transfer that keeps literary journalism alive. Publishing opportunities are evolving, as are the elements that characterize literary journalism. Wolfe and others have described its identifying qualities, but new characteristics can be found, for example, in LeBlanc's connection with her subjects. A focus on the journalism of everyday life is as active today as it has been since literary journalism began. The younger generations of literary journalists maintain traditions that have passed from Agee to Mitchell to McPhee to Kidder, Conover, Whynott, Paterniti, and LeBlanc. They are bound together not by techniques but by a search for the true story. Sometimes that quest involves emotional truths that can be found within the writers themselves as well as in the people they portray. It's a craft that depends upon the excitement of good writing without abridging the fundamental power of facts and accuracy.

The metaphor of island biogeography—with magazines as safe islands where literary journalism can evolve in a larger world of uninhabitable media terrain—is correct, but it shifts over time. Now and then individual magazines find reason to focus on literary journalism, and they do become safe havens—*The Metropolitan* when John Reed was popular, *The New Yorker* under Ross and Shawn and arguably up until today, Willie Morris's *Harper's,* the early *Rolling Stone,* the early *New York Magazine,* and Harold Hayes's *Esquire* when this enriched nonfiction served as a way to compete with *Playboy* centerfolds during the New Journalism era.[2] A magazine can support a band of literary journalists for as long as circulation figures, advertisers, and editors remain sympathetic. The ecosystem changes through time. *Esquire* has seen high points, for example when Gay Talese wrote for *Esquire* in the sixties, and low points, for example when Michael Paterniti left to follow an editor to *GQ.* The history of literary journalism has played out among *The New Yorker*'s staff, with turnover eliminating some of the population of literary journalists. *Outside* magazine for a while hosted a raft-load of fine writers such as Tim Cahill, David Quammen, Jon Krakauer, and Sebastian Junger who could follow a topic until it reached several thousand words in print.

Nicholas Lemann, a *New Yorker* staff writer who has taken over Liebling's role as press critic, and dean of Columbia University's Graduate School of Journalism, feels that the magazine industry in recent years has become less of a haven for literary journalists. "Overall reality," Lemann said, "if you're a writer who wants to write in excess of ten thousand words, be somewhat experimental or novelistic in form without making things up and you want to have, at a crucial point, a lot of freedom as to subject matter, you're going to have a very hard time finding magazines that will publish your work."[3]

Magazines that once published literary journalism now contain more "Topic A" stories as opposed to stories of everyday life. Malcolm Gladwell, a *New Yorker* writer who published *The Tipping*

Point and *Blink,* almost perfectly defined "Topic A" when he told *The Observer* that "we live in a suddenly serious time, where people have an appetite for intelligent, thoughtful explanations of consequential topics."[4] Experiential profiles of truck drivers, carpenters, and innovative chefs lose out to seemingly consequential celebrity portraits or serious nonparticipatory essays on policy when a magazine concentrates on "Topic A" stories. "At places like *The New Yorker, The Atlantic,* the *New York Times Magazine,* and *Harper's* to a degree," Michael Paterniti told me, "I do think they are 'Topic A' magazines. When they do stories they want to do big stories and leave their mark on it. I love that ambition. But does it inhibit the ability of some writers to write a different kind of journalism? Yes, it does."[5]

Susan Orlean and other quality writers have struggled with the seemingly bottomless appetite of magazines for celebrity journalism. In 1992, Orlean was asked by the editors of *Esquire* to do a celebrity profile of Macaulay Culkin, the child star of the movie *Home Alone.* Orlean had suffered through celebrity interviews and wanted nothing to do with it. Instead, she agreed to write about a ten-year-old of her choosing, a boy with ordinary interests (if any ten-year-old's interests can be considered "ordinary"). The result was a spectacular article called "The American Man at Age Ten."[6] Orlean has since migrated to *The New Yorker.*

Lemann made the point that "market conditions shape what gets produced in journalism," but the details are not obvious. Lemann worked at the early *Texas Monthly,* which was created as a writers' magazine by Michael Levy and William Broyles Jr. Founded in 1972, by the mid-1970s it had become a thick magazine with a circulation of more than 200,000. At one point, Lemann said, the magazine had to *limit* the amount of advertising it would accept. Writers were asked to produce long pieces, he said, "just to fill the space to carry all that advertising. What a problem." Richard West, one of the founders, drove around Texas and filled a dozen magazine pages each month with reports on the people he encountered. Such conditions rarely last, and an editor's "subject matter filter" may push writers away from literary journalism about everyday life and toward serious essays or celebrity journalism. Eventually, such limitations drive highly qualified writers toward the freedom of book publishing.

In recent decades, the wider surrounding literary landscape has undermined the usefulness of the island biogeography metaphor, as applied to magazines, because the book publishing industry and even newspapers now sustain literary journalists.

After Truman Capote, John McPhee, Joan Didion, Tracy Kidder, and others demonstrated that literary journalists from the magazines could produce bestsellers, book publishers opened their arms. For a while, large book advances supported the labor-intensive reporting required to produce literary journalism. Writers needed big book advances to carry a project through two years or more of reporting and another year of full-time writing. After a substantial career at *The Atlantic,* Kidder's initial success with *The Soul of a New Machine,* which won the Pulitzer Prize and was reviewed on the front page of the *New York Times Book Review,* plus advances on his next books enabled him to spend years writing *House, Among Schoolchildren, Old Friends, Home Town,* and *Mountains beyond Mountains.*

Books are increasingly the choice of literary journalists who dedicate themselves to a major project. Unfortunately, even book publishing no longer offers the island of support that it once did, according to Lemann. "It is easier, much easier despite all the groaning, to get a book published than a magazine story published," Lemann said. "Much. Particularly if you're interested in the kind of thing we've been talking about. It's because, first of all, there are more outlets. And second of all, the financial onus is more on the writer. It's more self-financed. Book publishers are willing to make a social compact with you as a writer where they say, 'Look, if you're willing to essentially work for a $25,000 or $50,000 advance, and you're a pretty good writer, we'll publish anything.' It's a little better than the deal publishers offer academics but it's not a living wage. Nowhere close. But you get a lot of editorial freedom."

The key to the island biogeography metaphor comes from the fact that there's not often enough food—enough money. Looking for sustenance, the writers evolve, and so do art forms. For a time, *The New Yorker* and, particularly in the New Journalism era, other magazines represented a lush habitat. Then for a while book publishers gave six-figure advances. Later, as Lemann said, even writers with several published books like Doug Whynott could expect an advance of no more than $30,000 or $40,000—with only half, or less, paid before the manuscript was completed—to fund a four-year project. The risk has shifted from the publisher to the writer. "I'm willing to take the risk that something will happen," Whynott said. "And I've always felt that something would, and that I could work with whatever it was."[7] Even with reduced book advances, Lemann said, the main delivery system for literary journalism today is books, not magazines.

In other parts of the ecosystem, longer narrative stories have popped up at newspapers such as *The Oregonian,* the *St. Petersburg Times,* the *Philadelphia Inquirer,* the *Charlotte Observer,* and at long-standing weekly publications such as the *Chicago Reader.* Skilled staff reporters can make a career writing narrative journalism if they have enlightened editors such as Jack Hart at *The Oregonian.* The Internet has forced changes in newspapers, especially in the idea that the paper will record every detail of town government. The recipe for survival in a new digital age might include literary journalism as a means of attracting readers back to the newspaper.[8]

Internet sites such as Salon and Slate have published longer stories that could be classified as literary journalism, although most of the content runs toward personal essays and commentary. Lemann pointed out two problems with the idea of an Internet haven for literary journalism: first, though it is an inexpensive publishing method, it does not yet have a financial model to reward writers; and second, studies show that most readers will not go beyond three screens of content in reading a single story.

Documentary film took major steps toward literary journalism in Pare Lorentz's films during the Depression, and again in 1967 when Frederick Wiseman began his long career creating nonfiction documentaries, especially for the Public Broadcasting System, including *Titicut Follies, High School, Welfare, The Store,* and *Model.* Wiseman provides no narration as his films show ordinary people encountering institutions where they are molded and mauled, or where they struggle for their own identities.

Gloria Steinem, David Hayes, and Barbara Lounsberry, among others, have suggested that the graphic novel may be a new genre, one that might contain literary journalism or at least introduce younger readers to nonfiction reports. What to call it? *Graphic novel* as terminology may be nothing more than an attempt to get shelf space in Barnes and Noble; the *nonfiction graphic comic* seems redundant and weighty. Joe Sacco, in his monumental *Palestine* (2001), used the term *comics journalism* on the cover. It's hard to imagine the combination of a word like "comic" with a subject like Palestine, but his book was certainly journalism. Sacco portrays ordinary life and seeks cultural immersion, two qualities that characterize literary journalism. In his introduction, Edward Said drew attention to Sacco's perspective and stance in the book: "The un-hurried pace and the absence of a goal in his wanderings empha-sizes that he is neither a journalist in search of a story nor an ex-pert trying to nail down the facts in order to produce a policy. Joe is there to be in Palestine, and only that—in effect to spend as much time as he can sharing, if not finally living the life that Pales-tinians are condemned to lead."⁹ *Graphic journalism*—if we can set-tle on that term for a moment (and it is now preferred by Sacco)—tends toward memoirs, but a wide variety of nonfiction content can be found in books such as Harvey Pekar and Joyce Brabner's *Our Cancer Year* (1994), illustrated by Frank Stack; Joe Sacco's *The Fixer* (2003); Marjane Satrapi's memoirs of growing up in Iran dur-ing the Islamic revolution in *Persepolis* (2003) and *Embroideries* (2005); Art Spiegelman's *In the Shadow of No Towers* (2004); and French cartoonist David B.'s *Epileptic* (2005).

Environmental conditions change, but the essentials of the art of literary journalism have not changed much since the start of the twentieth century.

It seems to take forever—well, too many years—for a literary journalist to complete a book. Jonathan Harr spent seven years re-porting and writing *A Civil Action,* which was about a water pol-lution case, and four years working on *The Lost Painting.* Tracy Kidder sat for an entire year in a grade-school class in Holyoke, Massachusetts, before writing his book *Among Schoolchildren,* thus becoming possibly the only graduate of Harvard who ever re-peated the fifth grade. Ted Conover took New York State train-ing and worked for months as a prison guard before writing *New-jack: Guarding Sing Sing.* Adrian Nicole LeBlanc needed *twelve years* of "hanging around time" with the wives and girlfriends of drug dealers before she could write *Random Family: Love, Drugs, Trouble, and Coming of Age in the Bronx*. The time spent includes the kind of library and interview research that would constitute the core of a Ph.D. dissertation, which is just the start for most of these writers. They also live the story for months or years at a time.

Nothing seems to take longer than works that can be called the journalism of everyday life, an approach that forms a persistent theme in the history of literary journalism. One of the first works of literary journalism, the partially fictionalized *Journal of the Plague Year* by Daniel Defoe in 1722, focused on the impact of the disease on ordinary lives. Most of the sketches written in the nineteenth century by writers such as Mark Twain and Lafcadio Hearn concerned ordinary acts by common people. George Ade's columns were about roominghouse residents, market gardeners, and dwellers in the high-rise offices of Chicago. In 1902, Finley Peter Dunne's bartender character, Mr. Dooley, reflected on the same issue when he said:

> I know histhry isn't thrue, Hinnissy, because it ain't like what I see ivry day in Halsted Sthreet. If any wan comes along with a histhry iv Greece or Rome that'll show me th' people fightin,' gettin' dhrunk, makin' love, gettin' married, owin' th' grocery man an' bein' without hard-coal, I'll believe they was a Greece or Rome, but not befure. Historyans is like doctors. They are always lookin' f'r symptoms. Those iv them that writes about their own times examines th' tongue an' feels th' pulse an' makes a wrong dygnosis. Th' other kind iv histhry is a post-mortem examination. It tells ye what a counthry died iv. But I'd like to know what it lived iv.[10]

In the twentieth century, John Reed, James Agee, and Joseph Mitchell preferred everyday life to the celebrated or the aberrational. In his introduction to *My Ears Are Bent* (1938), Mitchell said:

The only people I do not care to listen to are society women, industrial leaders, distinguished authors, ministers, explorers, moving picture actors (except W. C. Fields and Stepin Fetchit), and
any actress under the age of thirty-five. I believe the most interesting human beings, so far as talk is concerned, are anthropologists, farmers, prostitutes, psychiatrists, and an occasional bartender. The best talk is artless, the talk of people trying to reassure
or comfort themselves, women in the sun, grouped around baby
carriages, talking about their weeks in the hospital or the way
meat has gone up, or men in saloons, talking to combat the loneliness everyone feels.[11]

A. J. Liebling's stories from World War II and from his native
New York City with only a few exceptions used central characters possessed of no particular fame. *The New Yorker* specialized in
portraits of everyday life, especially during William Shawn's editorship, ranging from Meyer Berger's "Sidewalk Fisherman" to
Ted Conover writing about riding with truckers along Africa's
AIDS highway. McPhee's glorious run of *New Yorker* articles included works on oranges, a canoe builder, settlers in the Alaskan
backwoods, market gardeners, and a game warden who happened
to be named John McPhee. He wrote in 2005 about train engi-
neers piloting extremely long cargoes of coal out of the Powder
River mines of Wyoming. In 2003 and 2005, McPhee contributed
to a *New Yorker* portfolio of trucking pieces with stories about a
driver named Don Ainsworth, who had driven "the world's most
beautiful truck"—a gleaming, stainless steel tanker—some three-
quarters of a million miles. Mark Murphy first did the long-
distance trucking story at *The New Yorker* in 1949, and Bryan Di
Salvatore wrote a classic piece of literary journalism about trucks
called "Large Cars" in 1988.[12] In book form, Kidder has written

about computer designers, carpenters building a new house, and two residents of a nursing home. Conover used techniques from anthropology in creating portraits of illegal Mexican agricultural workers in Arizona, of the working-class and the upper-class residents of Aspen, Colorado, and of prison guards at Sing Sing. Joe Mitchell would have loved talking to Ted Conover.

Since the sixties, ethnographers, historians, anthropologists, and even artists have found reason to focus on similar qualities. People writing in these disciplines have discovered that history, for example, can be written from the perspective of ordinary people, and that anthropology can concentrate on narrative rather than quantitative methodologies. Norman Rockwell, the great cover illustrator of the *Saturday Evening Post,* said in his autobiography, "I do ordinary people in everyday situations. . . . And I find that I can fit most anything into that frame, even fairly big ideas."[13] When he first arrived at *The New Yorker* in 1973, Mark Singer wrote "Talk of the Town" stories about ordinary people. "I decided the people I wanted to write about were not famous people because I wasn't going to ask a famous person a question he or she had not been asked before. I wasn't going to get an answer from a famous person that hadn't been published somewhere before."[14]

Writing about everyday life presents a literary journalist with surmountable hurdles. Since most of us live ordinary lives, we tend to think that such stories are boring. Ordinary lives do not carry the standard news values of prominence, conflict, aberration, and "Topic A" currency that dominate newspapers and magazines. The aberrational staples of death, sex, blood, and money do not occur in our ordinary lives with nearly the frequency that they appear in the press. Mitchell, who knew how to engage the commonplace, said, "To me ordinary lives, people who are 'boring,' are as filled with symbolism, ritual and myth as anybody else's life."

The literary journalist has to become immersed in characters and in the natural dramas that unfold in their lives. Having achieved that depth through extended reporting, the literary journalist can answer questions of the heart that reach beyond facts and events. Walt Harrington wrote:

> With notable exceptions, what passes for everyday-life journalism is too often a mishmash of superficial stories about Aunt Sadie cooking pies, unlikely heroes who save people from drowning or drag them from burning buildings, the nice kid next door who turns out to be a serial killer and poor people who, against the odds, make it to the top. There's nothing wrong with such stories, except that too often they are the end point of everyday-life coverage, reported and edited with the left hand by people unschooled and unaware of the intricate assumptions and techniques of intimate journalism, which results in stories made superficial by both accident and design.
>
> It's a failure of vision.[15]

Commentators on literary journalism who say that it "reads like a novel," while doing an injustice to the accuracy of the reporters, are correct in suggesting that fiction most often presents ordinary lives in a literary format. Lots of people say that fiction can be true because it has the feelings. The same can also be said of certain kinds of journalism, that it has the facts and the feelings, and that it can help us understand the truth.

An accomplished master of the literary journalism of everyday life is Douglas Whynott. He has written about beekeepers (*Following the Bloom*), fishermen (*Giant Bluefin*), a wooden boat builder in Maine (*A Unit of Water, A Unit of Time: Joel White's Last Boat*), and a veterinarian with a small practice in a tiny New Hampshire town

(*A Country Practice*). No one gets killed in these books. People don't commit crimes. They aren't celebrities. Why should we be interested in these lives? They aren't any different from our own lives. Well, exactly. Most journalists are attracted like iron filings to the magnet of famous, infamous, criminal, or well-connected characters. Interesting subjects, certainly, but their deviant behavior or attitudes rarely tell us much about our own lives.

Whynott said he first encountered the idea of writing about everyday life in John McPhee's work. "I remember what it was like to read McPhee," he said. "And to read *The Pine Barrens* or *Oranges* or to read *Giving Good Weight,* 'Travels in Georgia' with the e-shaped structure." He recalled:

> When I read McPhee, and Capote, too, it was like, 'Oh! Aha! You can write about people in *this* way. And if you do it well enough, if you do it the right way, then it is in the public eye. It is important.' I read the Lillian Ross *Reporting* book at about the same time. I was struggling to figure out how this is done. OK, I don't have to write about President Nixon. I don't have to write about Watergate or a murder. I can write about almost anything that interests me. If the people are interested in what they're doing and there's some multi-faceted elements in a social structure—although I didn't define it that way then—I can write about whatever interests me with length and with complexity. The deeper you get inside of it the better it will be.

Having grown up on Cape Cod, then spending his early years frequently changing his career plans, Whynott found that writing about "fishermen and beekeepers and piano players and veterinarians" was a way to explore alternate lives. "I was following my enthusiasm and my curiosity into a realm that I had been previously interested in—which I think was also the case with

McPhee." About 90 percent of McPhee's topics, he once told me, carried a link back to something that had interested him before he was twenty years old.

Context becomes part of the story in literary journalism. Writers put their characters into a social world. They cannot assume that all social worlds are the same. "Part of the challenge of writing this is to depict and create that social world and all of the influences coming into it," Whynott said. "It's a veterinarian within a community within a community. And it's a fisherman within a larger fishing community and an environmental community and a national and international community. To me that's part of the challenge. I read once that a novelist has to depict the great social world within which his characters are living, and it seemed to me that in this kind of journalism that's what you're doing, too. Whereas if I were to write about a celebrity . . ." Whynott's voice trailed off, as if the concept of portraying a celebrity with that sort of context was beyond comprehension.

Jack Hart, editor of *The Oregonian* and one of the best writing coaches in the country, has suggested a typology of four forms of narrative:

1. The story narrative: This is the classic protagonist-complication-resolution model. . . . Tom Hallman's "The Boy Behind the Mask" fits this form.

2. The explanatory narrative: This is the John McPhee/*New Yorker* model of an action line broken by segments of expository digression. . . . [or, as Hart explained another time, "a sequence of actions, coupled with abstract explanation, that helps us understand something about the world."]

3. The vignette: This is an action line that unfolds with neither a narrative arc nor explanatory digressions. I think "vignette" when Walt Harrington talks about "tone poems" and offers an evocative descriptive piece on a family shutting down the farm for winter as an example.

4. The narrative essay: Many personal essays open with a first-person narrative segment before negotiating a turn that leads up the ladder of abstraction to some cosmic conclusion.[16]

Whynott writes classic digressive narratives of the first two types in Hart's list. It's as if the story is a pickup truck that starts out relatively empty, but by the time we get to the end of the book the back of the pickup has acquired a load of information, understanding, and education. In the middle of scenes, we are carried into an explanation of how a vet determines if a cow is pregnant, or into theories of educational trends in veterinary medicine schools. In *Giant Bluefin,* Whynott's narrative carries explanations of the biology of the fish, the economics of the fishery, and the environmental movement, all within the vehicle of a book about fishermen's tales. Whynott's ordinary people have stories in their lives that make the information interesting. Narrative powers the vehicle. "Early on," Whynott said, "I've created a sense of suspense about what will become. It's a question I try to plant in the reader's mind. What will become of the fishermen, and of the fishery, and of the fish? I've tried to learn more and more about how to create narrative suspense without writing genre fiction. That narrative is what will draw the reader through."

McPhee once put a sign on his office wall in big letters that said: "HAVE THE COURAGE TO DIGRESS." He finds digression an opportunity to educate readers, especially about material they need to know later in the story. He described, for example, a "set piece" that might be inserted into a story. "You're on a lake in Maine. The narrative has brought you to a place where you're camped next to the lake and there's a loon on the water. You're entranced with loons and you always have been, so you take this opportunity to discuss loons before we come back to the narrative. A 'set piece' on loons." Nonfiction writing, McPhee said, is like cooking. You go to the market and come home with whatever looks interesting, and then you start dealing with the materials. "You'll go to Alaska. Sure, but *what* are you going to write about Alaska? You have a general idea but the *materials* start shaping *you*. If they don't, God help you." His goal has been to go into the field like a cook to the market and to come home with a potpourri of raw material: "sketches of characters—how many people can be developed as characters so they are really standing free, in the round?—places, the scenery, the science involved, the history, the landscape." Within those materials a structure will arise organically, and if the writer has the courage to digress, the story will be intensely flavorful for the reader.[17]

The keys to Whynott's reporting on everyday life include several elements that characterize contemporary literary journalism:

- *Immersion reporting*—His books required years of firsthand research. *Giant Bluefin* took two years aboard commercial fishing boats. His book on Joel White's last wooden boat required eighteen months in the field and more than eight months writing full time, with ten- or twelve-hour days. *A Country Practice* took four years from its inception to publication. Immersion reporting creates journalism with the authority of close contact. The length of time it takes

Whynott mirrors the time it takes Kidder or McPhee to write a
similar book. From conception to publication, four years is
about average for Kidder. Jonathan Harr, who spent more
than seven years on *A Civil Action,* explained why his next
book, *The Lost Painting: The Quest for a Caravaggio Masterpiece,*
took years longer than anticipated: "My first task was to learn
to speak Italian with some degree of fluency."[18] Harr considers
the time spent as a source of embarrassment, yet it contributes
to the depth and texture of the book.

• *Structure*—Longer literary narratives require different pacing,
character development, and structures than a newspaper
piece or even a magazine article. Whynott devotes serious
attention to structure and sequence. As someone who has
published anthologies of literary journalism, I can testify
that magazine articles are easier to anthologize. They have
compressed and self-contained structures. Books written by
Kidder, LeBlanc, or Whynott are particularly difficult to
excerpt because the scene at hand may have a structural
buildup that happened a chapter or two earlier. McPhee's
sense of structural architecture in writing exceeds that of
anyone I've met. When I first raised the subject, right off
the top of his head he said, "The juxtaposition of parts of a
piece of writing, the way in which two parts of a piece of
writing, merely by lying side by side, can comment on
each other without a word spoken. . . . The way in which
the thing is assembled, you can get much said, which can
be lying there in the structure of the piece rather than
being spelled out by this boring writer who's telling you
what you're supposed to be perceiving." He talked about
layers of meaning beneath a clear surface. But he
emphatically added that structure is not separate from the

material. The artistry comes from writing "with a structure that rises organically from the material as collected, not something imposed from outside."

- *Accuracy*—This is literary *journalism,* and in many cases it is more accurate and should be more complete than stories for dailies or even monthly magazines. A literary journalist writing a book may have years to get the details right, while other journalists may have only a couple days or a month for their stories. Whynott as an individual writer carries no institutional authority. He is not writing under the institutional banner of the *New York Times,* which automatically lends authority to a writer's voice. Nor does he have the confidence-building apparatus of the legendary *New Yorker* fact-checking department. Therefore, he has to create and maintain his own authority on the page. Nothing would undermine his authority faster than factual errors or misunderstandings of the world he portrays. Accuracy becomes a primary, daily, driving obsession for literary journalists. Those who abridge accuracy, as McPhee said, "hitchhike on the credibility of writers who don't." The liberties taken by some writers—such as John Berendt in *Midnight in the Garden of Good and Evil* (1994), originally published as nonfiction but best labeled a novel—have created a new standard practice among many literary journalists: they tell the reader directly that their work is real. Harr, in a foreword to the reader in *A Civil Action* (1995), said: "This is a work of nonfiction. All the characters and events depicted in this book are real."[19] Harr told an audience: "You never invent stuff. You put in details to provide texture only when you have the material."[20] Even Berendt, who helped create the problem by fictionalizing parts of *Midnight in the Garden,* has faced this problem. Berendt is a wonderful journalist whose career reaches back to *Esquire* magazine during the Vietnam War. In 2005, he published *The City of Falling Angels* about Venice. His "author's note" at the start said: "This is a work of nonfiction. All the people in it are real and are identified by their real names. There are no composite characters." Nonfiction that takes care to be accurate is not new, of course; what's new is the need to explain that to readers.

- *Voice*—Whether he's writing in first or third person, Whynott creates a voice and a personality for his narrator. The narrator has the ability to notice or comment on things the characters themselves would not know and to interpret the world. Mark Kramer, a literary journalist and founding director of the Nieman narrative conferences at Harvard, said that the personality of the writer is the defining mark of literary journalism.[21] When I asked John McPhee about his voice, he laughed. He said that one college class had been assigned to write in his—McPhee's—voice, but he felt the outcome was merely in his style. He wasn't sure what "voice" meant as distinct from style. Ben Yagoda acknowledged this overlap. "*Voice* is not a perfect metaphor for writing style, which is why it's just a metaphor," Yagoda said. "Writing is much more premeditated than speaking: we are allowed to mull over our words for an awfully long time before setting them down, and once they are down, on the page or screen, we can look at them, puzzle over them, revise them."[22] There may be a fine line between, say, Joan Didion's style and her voice, but either way the end result is a felt presence of the author on the page. Even newspapers—the bastions of institutional, impersonal, objective prose—have started injecting more personal qualities. Amanda Bennett, former editor of the *Philadelphia Inquirer,* when forced to remake the paper in the face of financial pressures in 2006, chose to abandon the bland newspaper-of-record model in favor of more storytelling and a voice for the paper. Bennett's background was at *The Oregonian* and the *Wall Street Journal,* two of the premier American newspapers with distinctive voices.[23] Voice and style can be contagious. Editor Richard Todd told Whynott to avoid reading contemporary nonfiction writers for fear he would fall into the trap of copying their style and techniques. "He said to read fiction—read *Moby-Dick,* he said. I did that, and then have continued to read novels, often with some intensity, and especially after finishing a project," Whynott said.

- *Access*—Subjects who are not celebrities may be cautious around the exotic species of human known as a writer. But they are not manipulative in the way that celebrities and politicians often are. Literary journalism can be done about celebrities, but access always remains the main issue. In "Frank Sinatra Has a Cold,"[24] which the editors of *Esquire* magazine called the best article ever published in the magazine, Gay Talese set out to interview Sinatra but ended up gaining access only to the handlers who surrounded and protected him. In Talese's case, lack of access made the piece, but for other writers it is simply frustrating. Using veterinarians, fishermen, beekeepers, schoolteachers, or truck drivers as subjects allows a writer nearly unfettered access and opens new dimensions for intimate, emotional portraits.

Whynott lives in Langdon, New Hampshire, only a few miles from the veterinary clinic at the center of *A Country Practice.* On my drive up there, I left behind any sense of the urban. Bridges were washed out from a recent flood. The road climbed up to Whynott's modest house where a spectacular view opened. In this rural world, the drama of everyday life can be felt everywhere in stories of bears wandering through the yard, chimney fires, and the new vet down at the clinic. We all live within our own private narratives, but no one comes along to learn about our stories and write them down over a two-year period. Whynott spends a great deal of time with people, discovers their narratives, and then structures his stories so readers can identify with the characters. In *A Country Practice,* for example, the young vet Erika Bruner represents the new person struggling to acquire knowledge and a workable attitude, then working hard to overcome her challenges. Each of us in our own way can identify with her feelings.

Literary journalists work in a lengthy cycle of production. It's an expensive and emotional gamble for a writer without an institutional safety net.

The dozen years Adrian Nicole LeBlanc spent reporting for her book *Random Family* taught her about another quality of literary journalism that might be called the writer's connection with her subjects. LeBlanc once called it "emotional reporting," but she's moving away from that description, and she's not sure that Ted Conover's term "empathy" describes it either. I had imagined the long process of reporting as an extended conversation with her subjects, but LeBlanc told me that's not it, either.

Whatever "it" is, it takes time. "I've never understood what you get from a conversation anyway," she said.[25] "It's not the time to think about the conversation, it's the time to think about the details and images that strike me. They can often not make sense immediately."

For her, the value of immersion reporting, as compared to standard celebrity interviews, extends beyond the notes taken or the conversations. LeBlanc said:

I think seeing subjects in their environment again and again and again contributes to confidence in my perceptions, which probably comes out in the kind of details I select. It's not necessarily that if you spend two hours with someone that you don't have a lot of great detail. But if you spend twenty-five hours with them there's something about the details you choose that have a granular quality. They're like the difference between that cheap mustard on the boardwalk and that nice French mustard. That part is instinctive, but I think it has something to do with confidence.

I used to think it was just having more details to choose from, and I'm not saying that doesn't help. But I think it's a measure of feeling as though you know them in their situation that makes it easier to be selective in a way that reveals them.

The writer's connection also includes the time spent away from subjects with the option of coming back. In those breaks during a long immersion, visual details that can symbolize larger qualities sometimes start to make sense.

In 2004, LeBlanc published an article in *The New Yorker* about young comedians in New York struggling to get time on stage in front of an audience. They "bark" tickets to the comedy club on the street, act as janitors in the club, and hope for a break. LeBlanc explained a moment of connection with comic Greg Barris that gave her the key detail in that article. "There's one scene toward the end where Greg Barris is in Times Square and it's snowing," she said. Explaining that moment, she added:

He slides in the snow and then he gets back into character and starts barking, "Hey lady! Free comedy." He starts to do his thing again. It's a moment where I've been with that guy for a real long time and I saw how hard it was. I saw how degrading it was to clear the empty bottles when he was sent to the basement of the club. How difficult it was to get on stage and he was living with his grandmother. It was a little moment of magic. Pretty clichéd magic—Times Square in New York—but revealing of the magic the city held for him and why he was even there. I thought of him sliding in the snow probably for two days after it happened. I thought, "Am I noticing him sliding in the snow because I used to love that as a kid? Am I noticing it because it was such a relief to have a little bit of fun because he's such a depressive?" I keep it in my head a lot. My ears are up for more moments with him that echo whatever that thing was. It's a little moment that, after I noticed it and got to think about it, I became more alert to other moments like it. That's what I mean about picking detail.

Sometimes the connection with her subject creates an emotional responsiveness to cues, usually something visual in LeBlanc's case. Her connection seems remarkably close to the connections of friendship that standard reporters avoid forming. Details that are important in standard journalism—ages, names, features of how an apartment is decorated—never naturally settle on LeBlanc's attention. She makes notes about them, of course. But she knows a lot more about a person's cares, vulnerabilities, and feelings about other people from moment to moment.

Such connectedness grows from immersion and from a willingness to enter into emotional intimacies with subjects. Like voice, immersion reporting, accuracy, access, and complicated structures, this connectedness that permits the writer to examine her own emotional perspective seems a characteristic of contemporary literary journalism.

• • •

Most of the literary journalists mentioned in this book have shown a remarkable consistency in attitude and approach to their journalism. In a century of work, they have shared much with writers from other generations. Dos Passos, railing about the personages he called "bigbugs" while fighting malaria in a godforsaken hotel in Baghdad, was temperamentally a cousin of Ted Conover following the AIDS highway in Africa nearly eighty years later. Edmund Wilson could arrange the facts in San Diego to make a point about culture in the Depression as well as Joan Didion could put her finger on the heart of California decades later. They shared something. An approach. A perspective. A sense of the power of journalism to portray the world and spark our imaginations.

In the late eighties, when I interviewed Joe Mitchell, who was born in 1908, I realized that his experiences reached as far back into the history of literary journalism as anyone I would ever meet. His approach was inherently literary.

"I had been trying to write this thing about the Fulton Fish Market in a kind of Melvillean way," Mitchell told me. "I feel funny to say such a thing. I read *Moby-Dick* in college and it had a great effect on me. I had often thought about a Melvillean background with the Fulton Fish Market. For one thing, Melville worked as a customs agent in the Gansevoort market. It had to be factual, completely."[26] Melville may have been Mitchell's second favorite writer. Jim Rogers noted that *Joe Gould's Secret* has a thematic antecedent in Melville's "Bartleby the Scrivener." Rogers wrote, "My inclination is to say that Mitchell saw himself not as reworking Bartleby's story, but as standing in a particular historical line of descent from Melville. I would suggest, too, that the relationship Mitchell felt would probably find an analog in the passing-on of stories in oral tradition." Mitchell's favorite writer was James Joyce, and Rogers has argued that Mitchell's work as a whole can be seen as "an attempt to do for New York what *Ulysses* had done for Dublin."[27] In his fantasy about writing a novel of the city, Mitchell in *Joe Gould's Secret* admits as much.

Like a psychoanalyst, Mitchell always sought the "revealing remark" from his subjects, the remark that would uncover the "unconscious as well as the consciousness of a man or woman." Once he discovered the revealing remark, he would encourage people to talk more and more about that aspect of their lives. "That way I could go far deeper into the man's life than I could any other way. It isn't necessary to fabricate anything if you have patience. In my case, it wasn't patience because I was genuinely interested in finding out these things." Factual and accurate. That theme pervades every interview I have done with writers.

John McPhee, who was born in 1931, about a generation after Mitchell, has inspired during his forty years of work as many literary journalists as Tom Wolfe has. He emphasizes accuracy when he talks about his work.

"You've got a professional writer," he said, referring to himself, "whose milieu seems to be real people, real places, factual writing, who is always looking for a new project." When I first met him in his office at Princeton University in 1982, he wore dark-rimmed glasses, a beard, an outdoorsy sweater, and work boots. In person, he was as casual, precise, and articulate as the personality of the narrator that we find in his books. McPhee wrote his early, wonderful articles on the basketball player Bill Bradley, oranges, the Pine Barrens of New Jersey, and the Grand Canyon during the heart of the New Journalism era, yet as a *New Yorker* writer he was almost never mentioned as a New Journalist. He recognizes a longer sense of tradition. "With time, I think the so-called New Journalism that came along in the sixties will seem less of a dramatic feature on the landscape," he said. "It was interesting but it wasn't as revolutionary or mountainous as it was made out to be by its own practitioners. There were plenty of very good people around for a long time. I think all this should fit into some continuum that wasn't invented by Jimmy Breslin." *The New Yorker,* where so many of those good people had worked, was McPhee's seedbed.

"One characteristic of the so-called New Journalism was that it seemed to attract writers who wanted to go into great detail about their own reactions to things," McPhee said. "I prefer to do that indirectly. You cannot help but present your own reactions. The subjective moment is always there, and importantly there. Every word you chose in lieu of ten thousand words you might have chosen, the very subjects you choose, they're all subjective." He felt that in his case there were better ways to get such ideas and reactions across than in a personal statement.

"Remember the possibilities in nonfiction writing," McPhee said. "The character sketching that stops well short of illegitimate invention. There's plenty of room for invention, for 'creativity' and so forth in this field. These possibilities, stopping well short of invading a number of things that only fiction can do—you can use fictional techniques: narrative, dialogue, character sketching, absolutely legitimate. Why do I make those trips with those people participating? I make them so I'll have something to describe. Sitting here like this, you don't have the matrix of a narrative. Sitting in a canoe for two weeks, you've got the narrative." He added, "Things that are cheap and tawdry in fiction work beautifully in nonfiction because they are *true.* That's why you should be careful not to abridge it, because it's the fundamental power you're dealing with. You arrange it and present it. There's lots of artistry. But you don't make it up."

Although he criticized New Journalism and Tom Wolfe's "Tiny Mummies!" article, McPhee ultimately paid Wolfe a compliment. "I think *The Right Stuff* is a marvel," McPhee said, referring to Wolfe's book about the early space program pilots. "I have asked lots of . . . well, ten . . . military pilots of bygone days, people who were good, what they think of that book. To a man they've said it's right on; that's the talk; that's the stuff. The believability is pretty high. It's a wonderful book to read. I've given it as presents to lots of people." Wolfe was accurate—the essential quality that generates respect.

The same concerns about accuracy characterize younger generations of literary journalists. Tracy Kidder, who was born in 1946, is chronologically not quite a generation younger than McPhee but culturally so because McPhee was born during the Depression and Kidder is a Baby Boomer. The author of *The Soul of a New Machine* (1981), *House* (1985), *Among Schoolchildren* (1989), *Old Friends* (1993), *Home Town* (1999), *Mountains beyond Mountains* (2003), and *My Detachment: A Memoir* (2005), Kidder has always been a big fan of McPhee's work. McPhee's precise, casual, and authoritative voice can be contagious, and for that reason Kidder does not read McPhee while he's writing. But he follows McPhee's pathway on accuracy. It was among the first things he said when I talked to him shortly after he won the Pulitzer Prize for *Soul of a New Machine.*

"At rock bottom, I'm trying to write accurately," Kidder said. "But it's more than taking a pile of good notes. You can't define good writing by ingredients. There are new ways to do things all the time. There may not be good and evil in the world, but there's good and bad writing and shades in between. Laying down rules doesn't matter. I have the awful fear that if I did something I called nonfiction and began making stuff up, I'd stop believing it myself.

Believability is an interesting ingredient. There's stuff that's true but it's written so I don't believe it. I can't write the truth if I start inventing stuff for nonfiction."

Moving nearly another generation younger in the ranks of literary journalists, we come to Ted Conover, born in 1958 and author of *Rolling Nowhere* (1984), *Coyotes* (1987), *Whiteout: Lost in Aspen* (1991), and *Newjack: Guarding Sing Sing* (2000). Conover uses techniques from anthropology, particularly participant observation, to create his portraits of cultural communities. In *Rolling Nowhere,* he traveled and lived with hobos who were riding the rails. *Coyotes* dealt with illegal immigrants from Mexico who worked in the citrus groves of Arizona. Conover picked oranges, traveled to California and Florida, and even migrated across the border with them. In *Newjack,* he trained as a New York State prison guard and worked at Sing Sing prison.

Conover's ease and friendliness make me feel more comfortable with him than with any other writer I've known. His penetrating gaze can be unnerving, but he tries to avoid that. With the eye of an anthropologist, he sees all the relationships at work in a room.

Conover echoes the comments about accuracy that can be heard from any of the best literary journalists—and he considers Tom Wolfe, Stanley Booth (author of a participant report on the Rolling Stones called *Dance with the Devil*), John Steinbeck, George Orwell, Nels Anderson, John Reed, Joan Didion, Hunter S. Thompson, Herman Melville, and Jack London the main influences on his writing. "I believe strongly that nonfiction writers can use only the truth," Conover said, "but I also think that the story you find in the facts is your paramount consideration, once you've decided to write about the truth. The story you can tell, and who you find to tell that story—those are the main things for me."[28]

Conover's use of participant observation techniques puts him in a special category among literary journalists. He was attracted to Stanley Booth's book (now retitled as *The True Adventures of the Rolling Stones*) because Booth's style of research, Conover said, "seemed similar to what I had in mind with Mexican migrants: participate and immerse rather than simply interview and observe."[29]

By living, working, and traveling with the subjects of his journalism, Conover creates a surface tension between himself and his subject. He also gains a knowledge that is not available either to the participant or to the observer. "That is," he explained, "a hobo riding on the freights is not going to understand what's interesting about his life in the way you do, if you still talk to people who are not hobos. At the same time, you could go down to the freight yard every weekend for a year and not begin to understand the desolate feeling you have when your partners steal your stuff, when the police look at you as one of *them,* when your friends don't recognize you on the street. That sort of thing is the gold mine. That comes only through a commitment to living in a different way, to putting yourself on the line in that very immediate way." Jack London made similar criticisms a century earlier about greenhorn journalists who wrote about hobos and trains.

Conover could empathize with Booth's risk-taking in living with the Rolling Stones—risks that largely involved the use of drugs. In Conover's case, not only has he ridden the rails with hobos, migrated across a dangerous border with Mexican workers, and been a guard at Sing Sing, he also followed the AIDS highway in Africa with truck drivers who were the mechanism by which the disease moved from central Africa to the coast—not to mention being in Rwanda during a bloody civil war.[30] "I think a degree of risk-taking both makes the material richer—you find out things other writers won't learn—and it adds excitement to the narrative. If we are, after all, writing narrative nonfiction, there will be an interest in things going wrong. That's always been my compensation when disaster strikes. I've thought, 'Well, this will be interesting to write about.' But I'm not insane. I don't seek out the overloaded ferry that's going to sink on its next crossing. But at the same time I'm not traveling for my amusement so much as to see things that interest me and to bear witness to them in some way. I see the distinction as between being a tourist and being a witness. It's a posture not just for a writer but for how you live your life." Dos Passos would have understood completely, and John Reed said he had similar thoughts as he ran from the *colorados'* bullets in Mexico: "I kept thinking to myself: 'Well, this is certainly an experience. I'm going to have something to write about.'"[31]

If the greatest achievement of the New Journalists of the sixties was a sense of experimentation, then Conover owes them a debt as well. In discussing Booth's book on the Rolling Stones, which was researched in 1969 and laden with accounts of drug addiction and an unfortunate death at Altamont, Conover wrote in the *Columbia Journalism Review,* "There's a sense of experimentation under way. And in that, *True Adventures* achieves true oneness with its subject: like the Stones, Booth is full of aspiration, trying something new, unsure where it will take him. And that, in retrospect, is I think the book's great resonance for me, and its promise for any young writer: take these chances, it has continued to tell me, and some of them will pay off."[32]

In Mitchell's and Liebling's literary journalism, we often find people who are labeled by others as "lowlife" characters, although neither writer approved of the term. Comparing that era to recent times, Christopher Carduff said that "'low life' is no longer amusingly raffish; the Commodore Dutches and Telephone Booth Indians have devolved into abject beggars and crack-cocaine dealers."[33] Undaunted, writers such as LeBlanc, who spent twelve

years writing about the wives and girlfriends of Bronx drug dealers, take their chances by crossing the uncomfortable cultural
boundaries between social groups. The experimentation of the
sixties has adapted to an age of diversity and internationalism.

Accuracy and what could be called the "fictive" quality of literary
journalism make uneasy partners. When a writer seeks a powerful
narrative, the facts do not always cooperate. Reporters of every
type sometimes discover a moment when skipping over the facts,
or not bothering to pursue more facts, would make the story less
complicated and easier to write. The same can happen with literary journalists, and sometimes they succumb to temptation—but
probably no more frequently than other kinds of reporters. I have
heard writers argue that literary journalism can be tougher to write
than fiction because you cannot change your facts to make the
story work better. Jonathan Harr joked about the difficulty of following people around and trying to create a narrative that is elegant and conforms to actual events, in contrast to the work of a
novelist friend who could make things up. Harr believes in absolute accuracy.

It's a tangled issue, but for a writer such as Kidder, who studied
fiction writing at Harvard and the University of Iowa, the standard
is clear. Referring to the term "nonfiction novel"—as in Capote's
In Cold Blood and Mailer's *The Executioner's Song*—Kidder said,
"That's not a paradox, you know. A paradox is an apparent con-
tradiction. That's just plain nonsense as far as I'm concerned. If it's
a novel then it's invented." He wants character, event, and narrative from a piece of writing, but fiction and literary journalism
have different qualities. "The beauty of a novel is that evil seems
explicable, and you should get the feeling of seeing a character in
the round. Life as you encounter it as a journalist is a lot messier

than you'd want it in a novel and evil isn't always explicable. It's a little frustrating." A lack of accuracy, however, is almost always inexcusable for Kidder. "I hate to sit down with a book that purports to be nonfiction," he said, "and discover inside that I just can't believe it. Whether it's true or not. With the one exception to that being *Fear and Loathing in Las Vegas,* which I loved."[34]

Joe Mitchell said he had a similar feeling in writing about real people. "In the beginning, the idea of a literary journalism scared me because I thought the readers would expect too much," he said. "But then when I began to realize the deeper you went into these people's lives, they were just as complex as people in novels." Mitchell made constant references to William Butler Yeats—how Yeats's older poems would contain a sudden and revealing remark—as well as Ivan Turgenev's *A Sportsman's Notebook,* Stephen Crane, Sherwood Anderson, *The Arabian Nights,* D. H. Lawrence, Rabelais, Melville, and Joyce. At *The New Yorker,* Harold Ross insisted on a traditional newspaper lead with the most important information at the top of the story. Mitchell and A. J. Liebling argued for more literary structures that created a background before the primary action arrived. "I was looking at my piece about the people who lived in the cave, in the McSorley's book," Mitchell said in a musing tone of voice. "I thought if I lopped off a little in the beginning and a little at the end, that would be just a short story. Out of a great many instances you run into as a reporter, you begin to pick up on the things you can turn into a narrative. Narrative is all-important. It was a constant fight here with Mr. Ross, and his concept of the newspaper lead, which he thought was the greatest thing in the world. You've got to fight, and in doing so you learn what is, for you, a new technique. We all discover over and over things that have been there all the time."

In slightly different form, the distinctions that Kidder and Mitchell talked about go back as far as Aristotle. In *Poetics,* Aristotle wrote, "The poet and the historian differ not by writing in verse or in prose. The work of Herodotus might be put into verse, and it would still be a species of history, with meter no less than without it. The true difference is that one relates what has happened, the other what may happen. Poetry, therefore, is a more philosophical and a higher thing than history: for poetry tends to express the universal, history the particular. By the universal I mean how a person of a certain type on occasion speak or act, according to the law of probability or necessity; and it is this universality at which poetry aims in the names she attaches to the personages."[35] We could just as easily substitute "journalism" for "history" and "the novel" for "poetry" in Aristotle's passage, as the perceived differences between the two follow similar patterns even today. Journalism, tied to the particular, seems natively restricted in its ability to fly into the future on wings of poetry. Yet literary journalists have challenged such assumptions since the dawn of the age of prose.

My first reaction to Michael Paterniti's article "The Long Fall of One-Eleven Heavy" was awe. My second reaction was that it might be fictionalized.

I saw it as reprinted in this volume without the pictures that appeared in *Esquire,* a special issue in July 2000 devoted to "True Stories of Men & Disaster." Although people spoke, their words were not in quotation marks. The main characters had no names, and even the place, Peggy's Cove, Nova Scotia, gained only one mention. Somehow the author knew what was said on the plane, which passengers were drinking soda and wine, and that someone was writing a postcard on an airplane where all 229 passengers were killed seventy-four minutes into their flight from New York to Geneva.

I once asked a graduate English class to read Paterniti's article alongside Michael Finkel's cover story, "Is Youssouf Malé a Slave?" from the *New York Times Magazine* of November 18, 2001. Finkel told a story without quotation marks about a child from Mali in West Africa who was deceived into a period of agricultural servitude in hopes of acquiring a pair of shoes. It was a well-written article, but the *Times* fired Finkel as a contributing editor when they learned it was an unacknowledged composite. He combined the stories of several young boys into the tale.

The students in the English class guessed, incorrectly, that Paterniti's *Esquire* article was fictionalized. Finkel, needing to conceal his secret, had to make sure the reader never asked if anything was made up. Paterniti turned "Long Fall" into an archetypal narrative of grief, and he consciously used the techniques associated with fiction to give the reader a closer connection with the grieving characters.

I went to Portland, Maine, to ask Paterniti about it. He's trim and energetic, with close-cropped hair and a smiling, open manner of conversation. In his early forties, he has worked for *Outside, Esquire,* and *GQ* magazines, all fine places for good writers. It may have been his earlier experience at *Story* magazine—which publishes fictional short stories—that gave him the most preparation for "Long Fall."[36]

"With the characters," he told me, "if you're a father you're going to be with the father in this story. If you don't get too deeply into who the medical examiner is—his name and all that stuff—you're going to be able to see him as an archetypal character rather than a particular character. His journey you will take on as your own because he hasn't been named. You're participating vicariously anyway when you're reading. It depends how thick that wall is, or how thick that wall has been built by the writer, between the story and you. You either get closer or you get farther. I wanted it to be right there. I wanted it to be very graphic."

He felt the techniques of standard journalism—attribution, quotation, identification—would drive the reader out of the piece. "You have to cite the source, their title, by the time you get to the end of the sentence you're exhausted having read who that person was who said this, rather than just having what they said." Paterniti wrote the factual piece with a rhythmic literary style, the green light over the sea, revolving, the waves hitting the rocks, the clothes on the line that looked like bodies. While graphic in its descriptions—can "degloved" ever leave your mind?—it became a story of grief more than of death.

But was it real?

Paterniti showed up in Peggy's Cove eighteen months after the crash. The coroner was finishing his work. Crews were still reassembling millions of airplane parts in a hangar. Most of what remained was grief and a peculiar feeling. He talked to everyone—the coroner, the father of the woman with Persian eyes, the boxer, the Boston lawyer for the family of four that were killed. The lawyer showed him photos of the family and after a while asked if he'd like to see what was left of them. Paterniti did not want to see but he said yes. The lawyer slid over a manila envelope. Inside was a single photograph of an ankle. He said, "That's the family. That's what's left."

"Sometimes this work feels like method acting," Paterniti said. "You attempt to live so completely inside of your characters and their stories that it becomes part of you. I've often dreamt a story many times over the course of weeks, in different variations, before committing to a set of sentences, to the first notes. But the dreaming, like dreaming in a foreign language, is part of the process: it means you're approaching fluency."

All the details were accurate in "Long Fall." "It's all my job," Paterniti said. "It went through a fact check. This is all reported. In the case of Flight One-Eleven, it was exhaustive—the work it took to get some of the details. Some of it existed, like what was going on in the cockpit. The black box had that. Actually all of the dialogue in here was recorded. The theory that they caught fire was one that investigators had put forth. They really thought the pilot and copilot had caught fire." He continued:

> The drink orders raised an interesting challenge. Peter Griffin [his editor] and I went back and forth about that. I knew it was a full flight—and knew, too, where the investigators thought everyone had been sitting. And I had interviewed the families. I knew what they did on that flight traditionally. I knew the procedures on that flight, when the drinks would have been served, what exactly would have been happening as the plane flew north of Boston, headed Downeast, and then to Nova Scotia. I took what I knew to be the schedule on the best airline in the world at that time, one that ran like clockwork, and assumed that on this flight, with no sign of anything wrong, that the drinks were served and the entertainment system had been cued. I named two seat numbers, and there was some controversy about that. It's possible that no one was sitting in one of those seats, but again, I went with what the investigators said—and then also the coroner. He had a schematic of the plane on the wall in the hangar where they had the bodies, and they put up blue dots with names on each seat for each person they found. I went with that, but I also wrote it broadly enough so that I wasn't speaking for any one person's ac-

tions on that plane before it crashed. This was probably the only detail in the story where I might have used the evidence more conjecturally, but in the end, we felt pretty solid about it.

The postcard was found on the surface of the water. It had been written on the plane and ended up floating in the ocean. "There's a little detail about all the currencies floating on the water, and the purses," Paterniti said. "They'd fish the purse out and go to look for a wallet or lipstick or something, and it would be empty. There were hundreds of shoes on the surface of the water. In the end, I used the postcard, found on the water, but I put it on the plane." He hid all his deep reporting behind the narrative so it would not intrude.

Paterniti said the evolution of narrative nonfiction requires a commitment to the "metaphysical details"—to the mystery of what it means—and sometimes it requires narrative forms that can change from story to story. He explained how this principle worked for him in "Long Fall":

> When I went to Peggy's Cove, I arrived as a reporter, having already done months of research, toting file folders and phone numbers, with the usual docket of interviews. But then, as always, I tried not to forget that I was there as a human being, too. That I was feeling something—lost, haunted, starkly alive in the face of so much death—and searching for something. I went looking for the finest details of grief, and how one survives that kind of grief. And I went looking for those irrevocable moments of change: the coroner, in a state of blithe frustration at his long day, eating a TV dinner just as the phone first rang with news of the crash; the father staring at the river with an idea of suicide just before saving himself by leaving Switzerland and opening a

restaurant on the shore near the crash site, in order to be near his dead daughter. From those moments came the molecules of thought and feeling that, for me, provided some sort of edification. What's truest about the story, though, is that the edification never rose to an epiphany, rather was defined by that electrical current of loss that ran all the way to the end.

Paterniti's personal connection to the event originally grew from the unrelated death of his wife's mother, Peggy, in a scuba-diving accident. His connection deepened and became personal in Peggy's Cove. He said:

I walked into this, into a landscape where I hadn't been before. My grief was projected from all the people I met. I put it on this place, but I had a certain freedom to use fictive and poetic devices or to employ some sort of lyricism. Although I think that's a dangerous word. When overdone or in the wrong hands I don't like it. I don't like it when someone's really forcing it in. But I think if it rises out of the piece it can be a powerful thing.

To my mind, going to Nova Scotia to write about grief wasn't all that different from John McPhee going to write about the Mississippi River or Ted Conover trucking Africa. Human thought and feeling reflected brightly in those stories. The more radical notion, I think, is if a journalist chooses to write in the name of an emotion first, then uses one's reporting and language to find that seam in the tonnage of facts, the one that suddenly accesses a secret world that moves us in strange ways.

Fiction might be easier, but Paterniti said he could not do it. Having made the decision to write nonfiction, it had to be done right. "I didn't have any last words that anyone said," he told me:

The guy who had the postcard of Peggy's Cove on his refrigerator. How ironic that he would look at Peggy's Cove every day of his living life, and then die there on a plane to Switzerland. Unbelievable. I wish I had him, all alone, his last words. That would have been powerful. But I didn't. So I thought I'd let the voice carry that. Do you remember the last time your lips touched the head of your child? Do you remember the last thing she said when she left with her ticket in hand? These are common, everyday moments when suddenly you think, "Whoa, what's happening here?" You're implicated. You can't really get out of it. I'm saying that's the goal of what I'm writing.

Paterniti described a sacred undoing of the body. How do you write that? Facts help. But language is more powerful than facts, if we can control it. He said the rhythm came first in the piece, almost like music, when he was driving out of town and saw the clothes billowing on the line like bodies. Then the language of the piece suggested itself to him. He found the words to report the event and the feelings and the lives that were involved.

This is tough. It takes a literary sensibility. And at the same time, it takes a commitment to the facts. Paterniti could not cut corners and make things up. Because this was real life. He simply had to find a way to convey its true story.

NOTES

◈

PREFACE

1. Jane Kramer, "Cowboy," *The New Yorker,* 30 May and 6 June 1977, later published in book form as *The Last Cowboy* (New York: Harper and Row, 1977).

2. Tom Connery, "Research Review: Magazines and Literary Journalism, an Embarrassment of Riches," in David Abrahamson, ed., *The American Magazine: Research Perspectives and Prospects* (Ames: Iowa State University Press, 1995), p. 208.

CHAPTER ONE

1. Michael Robertson, *Stephen Crane, Journalism, and the Making of Modern American Literature* (New York: Columbia University Press, 1997), pp. 3–6.

2. Personal interview with Tracy Kidder, 1982.

3. Todd's comments were made in a speech at Mt. Holyoke College, 30 April 1986.

4. Quoted in Michael Depp, "What Happened to the Revolution? The Legacy of New Journalism," *Poets & Writers,* May/June 2004.

5. Personal interview with John McPhee, 1982.

6. Details taken from a Salon article by Allen Barra, "The Education of Little Fraud," at http://archive.salon.com/books/feature/2001/12/20/carter/index.html.

7. Francine Prose, "The Lost Boy," *New York Times Book Review,* 24 December 2006.

8. Andrew Chaikivsky, "Nasdijj—Seven Years Ago, He Was Born in This Magazine as a Significant New Navajo Writer. The Story of a Fraud," *Esquire,* May 2006.

9. The Smoking Gun website, "A Million Little Lies," 8 January 2006. See http://www.thesmokinggun.com/archive/0104061jamesfrey1.html. See also the journal *Creative Nonfiction,* no. 29 (2006), including Daniel Nester's article "Notes on Frey," which attempts to defend Frey.

10. Mark Kramer, "Breakable Rules for Literary Journalists," in Norman Sims and Mark Kramer, eds., *Literary Journalism* (New York: Ballantine, 1995), pp. 21–34.

11. Mark Kramer, "Reporting for Narrative: Ten Tips," in Mark Kramer and Wendy Call, eds., *Telling True Stories: A Nonfiction Writer's Guide from the Nieman Foundation at Harvard University* (New York: Plume, 2007).

12. *Creative Nonfiction,* no. 29 (2006), p. 24.

13. Sherwin Cody, whom Edwin Ford included in his bibliography as the author of a book "on essayists, prose writers and journalists," wrote a book in 1894 called *The Art of Writing and Speaking the English Language: Story-Writing and Journalism.* Part I of that text is titled "Literary Journalism"; Cody's sense of literary journalism was not modern; it was somewhat closer to the definition of literary journalism as a form of journalism that deals with literature, such as book reviewing. Cody included comments on writing as a profession, the news sense, how to write news and magazine features, book reviewing, juvenile fiction, and advertising. It's a revealing document that exposes how much of standard news was actually made up at the time. Cody believed that journalism was superficial and temporary when compared to real literature, and judging from his treatment of journalistic features, it certainly would be. The early twentieth-century writer Hutchins Hapgood used the term in his 1939 memoir, *A Victorian in the Modern World,* but early in the century he advocated for a "new form of literature" based on extensive interviewing. At that time he did not use the term *literary journalism.* See Tom Connery, "Hutchins Hapgood and the Search for a 'New Form of Literature,'" *Journalism History* 1, no. 13 (Spring 1986), pp. 2–9. Van Wyck Brooks used a different sense of the term in 1954 when describing Max Perkins's experiences in New York following World War I. Brooks wrote: "Copey, no doubt, the old newspaperman, had worked on Max's imagination; and had not Pendennis been a literary journalist before he became a novelist in London?" Pendennis, a character in William Make-

peace Thackeray's 1848 novel by the same name, published literary verses in a newspaper, and thus the term "literary journalist." See Van Wyck Brooks, *An Autobiography* (New York: E. P. Dutton, 1965), which contains "Scenes and Portraits," written in 1954, p. 129.

14. Edwin H. Ford, "Foreword," *A Bibliography of Literary Journalism in America* (Minneapolis: Burgess, 1937).

15. Ibid.

16. Quoted from a presentation by Joseph North at the American Writers' Congress of 1935 in James Boylan, "Publicity for the Great Depression: Newspaper Default and Literary Reportage," in Catherine L. Covert and John D. Stevens, eds., *Mass Media between the Wars: Perceptions of Cultural Tension, 1918–1941* (Syracuse, N.Y.: Syracuse University Press, 1984), p. 165.

17. According to its website, "The *Lettre Ulysses Award* is the only world prize for the genre of literary reportage. The award was initiated by the cultural journal *Lettre International* in association with the *Aventis Foundation,* and in partnership with the *Goethe-Institut.*" See http://www.lettre-ulysses-award.org/about.html.

18. Lillian Ross, *Reporting Back: Notes on Journalism* (Washington, D.C.: Counterpoint, 2002), p. 9.

19. Tom Wolfe, "The New Journalism," in Tom Wolfe and E. W Johnson, eds., *The New Journalism with an Anthology* (New York: Harper & Row, 1973), pp. 31–32.

20. Sarah R. Shaber, "Hemingway's Literary Journalism: The Spanish Civil War Dispatches," *Journalism Quarterly* 57, no. 3 (Autumn 1980), p. 420. Harold Hayes had also used the term with its contemporary meaning in 1972; see Chapter 7.

21. Quoted from the Nieman Program website, http://www.nieman.harvard.edu/narrative/what_is.html.

22. Paul Many, "Literary Journalism: Newspapers' Last, Best Hope," *Connecticut Review* 18, no. 1 (Spring 1996), pp. 59–69.

23. Norman Sims, *The Literary Journalists* (New York: Ballantine, 1984), pp. 3–27.

24. Todd, Mt. Holyoke College speech, 30 April 1986.

25. James Agee and Walker Evans, *Let Us Now Praise Famous Men* (Boston: Houghton Mifflin, 1941), p. 234.

26. Ibid., pp. 235–236.

27. Works that include more theoretical perspectives on literary journalism include John Hartsock, *A History of American Literary Journalism: The Emergence of a Modern Narrative Form* (Amherst: University of Massachusetts Press, 2000); Phyllis Frus, *The Politics and Poetics of Journalistic Narrative: The Timely and the Timeless* (Cambridge: Cambridge University Press, 1994); Barbara Lounsberry, *The Art of Fact: Contemporary Artists of Nonfiction* (Westport, Conn.: Greenwood Press, 1990); Chris Anderson, ed., *Literary Nonfiction: Theory, Criticism, Pedagogy* (Carbondale: Southern Illinois University Press, 1989); and Mas'ud Zavarzadeh, *The Mythopoeic Reality: The Postwar American Nonfiction Novel* (Urbana: University of Illinois Press, 1976).

28. Michael P. Lynch, "Who Cares about the Truth?" *Chronicle of Higher Education,* 10 September 2004.

29. Robert S. Feldman, J. A. Forrest, and B. R. Happ, "Self-Presentation and Verbal Deception: Do Self-Presenters Lie More?" *Basic and Applied Social Psychology* 24 (2002), pp. 163–170; David Hayes, "The Truth about Lying," *enRoute,* the Air Canada in-flight magazine, July 2005.

30. John Pauly, private e-mail correspondence, 2005.

31. Ralph Keyes, *The Post-Truth Era: Dishonesty and Deception in Contemporary Life* (New York: St. Martin's Press, 2004), p. 169.

32. *Creative Nonfiction,* no. 29 (2006), p. 77.

33. Kramer, "Breakable Rules," p. 29.

34. Ben Yagoda, *The Sound on the Page: Style and Voice in Writing* (New York: HarperCollins, 2004), pp. xi–xiv.

35. Ibid., p. xviii.

36. Ross, *Reporting Back,* pp. 5–6.

CHAPTER TWO

1. John F. Finerty, *War-Path and Bivouac, or The Conquest of the Sioux* (Norman: University of Oklahoma Press, 1994; originally published 1890).

2. For a longer treatment of Twain's book as literature, see Paul Many,

"Extraordinary Voyage: The Journey from Journalism to Literature of Mark Twain's *The Innocents Abroad*," paper presented at the annual meeting of the American Journalism Historians Association, October 1996, London, Ontario.

3. Twain's early writing, when collected now, frequently carries the term *sketch*. For example: *California Sketches: Mark Twain and Bret Harte* (New York: Dover, 1991)*; The Works of Mark Twain: Early Tales and Sketches,* covering 1851–1865 in two volumes, edited by Edgar Marquess Branch and Robert H. Hirst (Berkeley: University of California Press, 1979); and *The Complete Humorous Sketches and Tales of Mark Twain,* edited with an introduction by Charles Neider (Garden City, N.Y.: Doubleday, 1961). See also Martina Lauster, *Sketches of the Nineteenth Century.*

4. Roger Fowler, ed., *A Dictionary of Modern Critical Terms,* rev. ed. (London: Routlege and Kegan Paul, 1987).

5. H. W. Fowler, ed., *A Dictionary of Modern English Usage,* 2d ed. (Oxford: Oxford University Press, 1965).

6. Twain, *The Works of Mark Twain,* vol. 1, pp. 2–3.

7. Franklin J. Meine, "Preface," in *Tall Tales of the Southwest* (New York: Alfred A. Knopf, 1930).

8. Personal interview with Michael Paterniti, 2004.

9. Quoted by Jim Romenesko, 14 November 2006, from a *New York Times* memo.

10. Twain, *Early Tales and Sketches,* vol. 1, pp. 15, 18.

11. Ibid., p. 159.

12. Reprinted in the *Marysville* (Calif.) *Appeal,* 9 January 1863, p. 2, which attributes the story to the *Enterprise* of 6 January. Quoted on p. 20 of Branch's introduction to Twain, *Early Tales and Sketches,* vol. 1.

13. Mark Twain, "My Bloody Massacre," in *The Complete Humorous Sketches.*

14. Twain, *Early Tales and Sketches,* vol. 1, pp. 320–330.

15. Twain, "My Bloody Massacre."

16. Ibid.

17. Harry P. Harrison, *Culture under Canvas: The Story of Tent Chautauqua* (New York: Hastings House, 1958), p. xiii.

18. See, for example, Elia Peattie of Omaha writing about riding the

trolley in *Impertinences: Selected Writings of Elia Peattie, A Journalist in the Gilded Age,* edited and with a biography by Susanne George Bloomfield (Lincoln: University of Nebraska Press, 2005).

19. Maurice Elfer, *Opie Read* (Detroit: Boyten Miller, 1940), p. 178.

20. Opie Read, *I Remember* (New York: Richard R. Smith, 1930), pp. 108–109.

21. Read, presumably, *Daily Arkansas Gazette,* 17 April 1880.

22. Read, *I Remember,* p. 173.

23. For an account of how these conflicts played out in New York, see W. Joseph Campbell, *The Year That Defined American Journalism: 1897 and the Clash of Paradigms* (New York: Routledge, 2006). He identified three paradigms; Lincoln Steffens as city editor at the *Commercial Advertiser* represented literary journalism.

24. Forman, "The Line of Improvement," *Journalist,* 27 August 1887, p. 8, quoted in Christopher P. Wilson, *The Labor of Words: Literary Professionalism in the Progressive Era* (Athens: University of Georgia Press, 1985), pp. 22–23.

25. Christopher P. Wilson, "The Era of the Reporter Reconsidered: The Case of Lincoln Steffens," *Journal of Popular Culture* 15, no. 2 (Fall 1981), pp. 41–49.

26. Ronald Weber, *Hired Pens: Professional Writers in America's Golden Age of Print* (Athens: Ohio University Press, 1997), p. 112.

27. James Carey, "The Communications Revolution and the Professional Communicator," in Eve Stryker Munson and Catherine A. Warren, eds., *James Carey: A Critical Reader* (Minneapolis: University of Minnesota Press, 1997), pp. 136–137.

28. George Ade to Josh Hilderbrand, August 1890, in Fred C. Kelly, *George Ade: Warmhearted Satirist* (Indianapolis: Bobbs-Merrill, 1947), p. 81.

29. Larzer Ziff, *The American 1890s: Life and Times of a Lost Generation* (New York: Viking Press, 1966).

30. Charles H. Dennis to F. J. Meine, 2 July 1940, quoted in George Ade, *Stories of the Streets and of the Town from the* Chicago Record, *1893–1900,* edited by Franklin Meine (Chicago: Caxton Club, 1941), p. xii.

31. *Chicago Record,* 17 November 1893.

32. Kelly, *George Ade,* p. 109.

33. George Ade, *Fables in Slang and More Fables in Slang* (New York: Dover, 1960; reprinted from Herbert S. Stone, 1899 and 1900), p. 70.

34. Jack London, *Jack London on the Road: The Tramp Diary and Other Hobo Writings,* edited by Richard W. Etulain (Logan: Utah State University Press, 1979), pp. 81, 95.

35. George Ade, *Chicago Record,* 5 October 1894, and in Ade, *Stories of the Streets,* pp. 114–118.

36. Wilson, *The Labor of Words,* p. 12.

37. Quoted in Phillip B. Nordhus, "George Ade: A Critical Study" (Ph.D. dissertation, State University of Iowa, 1957), p. 41.

38. Quoted in Kelly, *George Ade,* p. 144, from Howells' "Editor's Easy Chair" column in *Harper's.*

39. Michael Schudson, *Discovering the News: A Social History of American Newspapers* (New York: Basic Books, 1978), p. 74.

40. For more on the Whitechapel Club, see Norman Sims, "The Chicago Style of Journalism" (Ph.D. dissertation, University of Illinois, 1979), chapter 5.

41. Finley Peter Dunne, "The Chinese Situation," in *Mr. Dooley on Ivrything and Ivrybody* (New York: Dover, 1963), pp. 120–123.

42. Ziff, *The American 1890s,* p. 165.

43. Wolfe, "The New Journalism," p. 3.

44. Read, *I Remember,* p. 207.

45. Opie Read, "Hanging Is Serious," *Arkansaw Traveler,* 12 November 1887. Published the day after four of the Chicago anarchists from the Haymarket bombing were hanged.

46. Elfer, *Opie Read,* p. 126. Interior quote is from Elmer Ellis, *Mr. Dooley's America* (New York: Alfred A. Knopf, 1941), p. 52.

47. Jane Benardete, ed., *American Realism* (New York: G. P. Putnam's Sons, 1972), p. 9.

48. Read, *I Remember,* p. 320.

49. Hugh Kenner, "The Politics of the Plain Style," *New York Times Book Review,* 15 September 1985; reprinted in Norman Sims, ed., *Literary Journalism in the Twentieth Century* (New York: Oxford University Press, 1990); see also Ben Yagoda, *The Sound on the Page.*

50. Hartsock, *A History of American Literary Journalism,* pp. 94, 102–104.

51. Kenner, "The Politics of the Plain Style," pp. 186–187.

52. Roger Angell, "Personal History: Andy," *The New Yorker,* 14 February 2005, p. 142.

53. Theodore Peterson, *Magazines in the Twentieth Century* (Urbana: University of Illinois Press, 1956), pp. 3, 13–14, 56.

54. Ibid., p. 14.

55. Schudson, *Discovering the News,* chapter 3, "Stories and Information: Two Journalisms in the 1890s."

56. David L. Eason, "Telling Stories and Making Sense," *Journal of Popular Culture* 15, no. 2 (Fall 1981), p. 125.

CHAPTER THREE

1. Donald J. Adams, "Prologue," in *Copey of Harvard: A Biography of Charles Townsend Copeland* (Boston: Houghton Mifflin, 1960).

2. Ibid., p. 150.

3. Ibid., pp. 153–155, 166.

4. Brooks, *An Autobiography,* pp. 122–123, 128–129.

5. Daniel W. Lehman, *John Reed and the Writing of Revolution* (Athens: Ohio University Press, 2002), pp. 8–9.

6. Ibid., p. 131.

7. Dedication (dated 3 July 1914), in John Reed, *Insurgent Mexico* (New York: D. Appleton, 1914; reprint, New York: Greenwood Press, 1969).

8. Lehman, *John Reed,* pp. 65, 106.

9. Quoted in Yagoda, *The Sound on the Page,* p. xxxi.

10. Martha Gellhorn, *Travels with Myself and Another: A Memoir* (New York: Putnam, 2001), p. xx; Neil Sheehan, "Life during Wartime: Vietnam, 1966," *The New Yorker,* 12 June 2006, p. 52.

11. Patrick Holland and Graham Huggan, *Tourists with Typewriters: Critical Reflections on Contemporary Travel Writing* (Ann Arbor: University of Michigan Press, 1998), pp. viii, 8–9.

12. Jonathan Raban, *For Love and Money: A Writing Life, 1969–1989* (New York: Harper & Row, 1989), p. 224.

13. Reed, *Insurgent Mexico*, p. 88; for this episode, see the chapters entitled "The Coming of the Colorados" and "Meester's Flight."

14. Lehman, *John Reed*, p. 135.

15. Adams, *Copey of Harvard*, p. 190.

16. Ibid., pp. 207–209.

17. John Dos Passos, *The Best Times: An Informal Memoir* (New York: New American Library, 1966), p. 55.

18. Thomas D. Snyder, ed., *120 Years of American Education: A Statistical Portrait* (Washington, D.C.: National Center for Education Statistics, January 1993), pp. 72–74.

19. Michael Reynolds, *The Young Hemingway* (Oxford: Basil Blackwell, 1986), p. 14.

20. Anthony Burgess, *Ernest Hemingway and His World* (New York: Charles Scribner's Sons, 1978), pp. 20, 24; Stephen Koch, *The Breaking Point: Hemingway, Dos Passos, and the Murder of Jose Robles* (New York: Counterpoint, 2005), p. 11.

21. Adams, *Copey of Harvard*, p. 213.

22. Ibid., p. 215.

23. Quoted from John Reed, *The Education of John Reed: Selected Writings* (New York: International Publishers, 1955), pp. 147–150. "Magnots" and "entanged" are from the passage.

24. "Publisher's Note," in John Reed, *The War in Eastern Europe* (New York: Charles Scribner's Sons, 1918), p. v.

25. Donald Pizer, *American Expatriate Writing and the Paris Moment: Modernism and Place* (Baton Rouge: Louisiana State University Press, 1996), p. 1.

26. Ronald Weber, *News of Paris: American Journalists in the City of Light between the Wars* (Chicago: Ivan R. Dee, 2006), p. 5.

27. See Charles A. Fenton, "Ambulance Drivers in France and Italy: 1914–1918," *American Quarterly* 3 (Winter 1951), pp. 326–343.

28. Pizer, *American Expatriate Writing*, p. 4, quoting Ezra Pound's "Hugh Selwyn Mauberly."

29. Shelley Fisher Fishkin, *From Fact to Fiction: Journalism and Imaginative Writing in America* (Baltimore: Johns Hopkins University Press, 1985; Oxford: Oxford University Press, 1988), pp. 167, 174.

30. Fenton, *The Apprenticeship of Ernest Hemingway,* p. vii. See also a counterview in Barbie Zelizer, *Taking Journalism Seriously: News and the Academy* (Thousand Oaks, Calif.: Sage, 2004), p. 1.

31. John Dos Passos to Robert Hillyer, October 1921, in Dos Passos, *The Fourteenth Chronicle: Letters and Diaries of John Dos Passos,* edited and with a biographical narrative by Townsend Ludington (Boston: Gambit, 1973), p. 321.

32. Dos Passos, *The Best Times,* p. 85.

33. Dos Passos to Rumsey Marvin, October 1921, from Teheran, in Dos Passos, *Fourteenth Chronicle,* p. 319.

34. Dos Passos to John Howard Lawson, 23 October 1921, from Baghdad, in Dos Passos, *Fourteenth Chronicle,* p. 323.

35. Dos Passos to Thomas P. Cope, 13 November 1921, from Baghdad, in Dos Passos, *Fourteenth Chronicle,* p. 327.

36. Dos Passos to Marvin, 5 November 1921, from Baghdad, in Dos Passos, *Fourteenth Chronicle,* pp. 324, 326.

37. Ernest Hemingway, "A Silent, Ghastly Procession," *Toronto Daily Star,* 20 October 1922, in *Dateline: Toronto. The Complete Toronto Star Dispatches, 1920–1924,* edited by William White (New York: Charles Scribner's Sons, 1985), p. 232.

38. Fishkin, *From Fact to Fiction,* p. 168.

39. Raban, *For Love and Money,* p. 226.

40. Ibid., p. 85.

41. Ibid., pp. 225–226.

42. Gellhorn, *Travels with Myself and Another,* p. 4.

43. Raban, *For Love and Money,* p. 236.

44. Ibid.

45. Gellhorn, *Travels with Myself and Another,* p. 14.

46. Peter Griffin, *Less Than a Treason: Hemingway in Paris* (New York: Oxford University Press, 1990), p. 75.

47. Ibid., p. 168.

48. Virginia Spencer Carr, *Dos Passos: A Life* (Garden City, N.Y.: Doubleday, 1984), p. 451.

49. John Dos Passos, "Madrid under Siege," in *Journeys between Wars* (New York: Harcourt, Brace, 1938), republished in Valentine Cunning-

ham, ed., *Spanish Front:Writers on the Civil War* (Oxford: Oxford University Press, 1986).

50. Carr, *Dos Passos,* pp. 367, 369, 372; Koch, *The Breaking Point.* See also, for example, Elizabeth Kolbert, "Looking for Lorca," *The New Yorker,* 22 and 29 December 2003, pp. 64–75.

CHAPTER FOUR

1. *The New Republic,* 27 July 1932.

2. Dos Passos, *The Best Times,* p. 205.

3. James Boylan, "Publicity for the Great Depression," p. 175.

4. My comments on newspaper failure during the Depression are based primarily on Boylan's "Publicity for the Great Depression."

5. Jonathan Clements, "Four Key Investment Implications of the Changing Interest-Rate Picture," *Wall Street Journal,* 5 January 2005, p. D1.

6. Boylan, "Publicity for the Great Depression," p. 162.

7. John F. Bauman and Thomas H. Coode, *In the Eye of the Great Depression: New Deal Reporters and the Agony of the American People* (Dekalb: Northern Illinois University Press, 1988), p. 5.

8. Boylan, "Publicity for the Great Depression," p. 160, citing William E. Leuchtenburg, *The Perils of Prosperity, 1914–1932* (Chicago: University of Chicago Press, 1958), p. 248; Boylan, pp. 159, 162.

9. Quoted in Bauman and Coode, *In the Eye of the Great Depression,* p. 1.

10. Ibid., pp. 19, 27–29; Gellhorn, *Travels with Myself and Another.*

11. Bauman and Coode, *In the Eye of the Great Depression,* p. 191.

12. Boylan, "Publicity for the Great Depression," p. 166.

13. Edmund Wilson, "Communists and Cops," *The New Republic,* 11 February 1931; reprinted in Edmund Wilson, *The American Earthquake:A Documentary of the Jazz Age, the Great Depression, and the New Deal* (New York: Doubleday, 1958).

14. See Edmund Wilson, *The Thirties: From Notebooks and Diaries of the Period,* edited and with an introduction by Leon Edel (New York: Farrar, Straus & Giroux, 1980), pp. 130–132.

15. Boylan, "Publicity for the Great Depression," p. 170.

16. Trachtenberg, "Foreword," in Erskine Caldwell and Margaret Bourke-White, *You Have Seen Their Faces* (1937; reprint, Athens: University of Georgia Press, 1995), p. viii.

17. See William Stott, *Documentary Expression and Thirties America* (New York: Oxford University Press, 1973), chapter 12.

18. Ibid., p. 216.

19. William Howarth, "The Mother of Literature: Journalism and *The Grapes of Wrath*," in Norman Sims, ed., *Literary Journalism in the Twentieth Century* (New York: Oxford University Press, 1990), p. 58.

20. Ibid., p. 60.

21. Stott, *Documentary Expression*, p. 294.

22. Agee and Evans, *Let Us Now Praise Famous Men*, p. 101.

23. Stott, *Documentary Expression*, p. 281.

24. Jeff L. Rosenheim, "'The Cruel Radiance of What Is': Walker Evans and the South," in Jeff L. Rosenheim, Maria Morris Hambourg, Douglas Eklund, and Mia Fineman, *Walker Evans* (New York: Metropolitan Museum of Art, 2000), p. 86.

25. Genevieve Moreau, *The Restless Journey of James Agee*, translated from the French by Miriam Kleiger with the assistance of Morty Schiff (New York: William Morrow, 1977), chapters 4 and 5. Many of Agee's articles are reprinted in *James Agee: Selected Journalism*, edited by Paul Ashdown (Knoxville: University of Tennessee Press, 1985).

26. Rosenheim, "'The Cruel Radiance of What Is,'" pp. 86–87.

27. Agee, "Preface," *Let Us Now Praise Famous Men*.

28. Quoted in Stott, *Documentary Expression*, pp. 261–266.

29. Agee, *Let Us Now Praise Famous Men*, p. 7.

30. Ronald Weber, *The Literature of Fact: Literary Nonfiction in American Writing* (Athens: Ohio University Press, 1980), pp. 62–63.

31. Quoted from a conversation with Evans in Stott, *Documentary Expression*, pp. 222–223.

32. Agee, *Let Us Now Praise Famous Men*, p. 80.

33. Stott, *Documentary Expression*, pp. 297–298.

34. Agee, "Havana Cruise," *Fortune*, September 1937, p. 117. Reprinted in *James Agee: Selected Journalism*, edited by Paul Ashdown, p. 139.

35. Rosenheim, "'The Cruel Radiance of What Is,'" p. 105, n214. In 1958 a vice president of Houghton Mifflin told *The New Yorker* that the book remained in print until 1948.

CHAPTER FIVE

1. Wolfe, "The New Journalism," p. 8.

2. Ibid., pp. 45–46.

3. All quotations from Mitchell, unless otherwise identified, are from our private interviews and conversations between 1988 and the day before he entered the hospital, for the last time, in 1996. Mitchell died 24 May 1996.

4. The group is portrayed in a movie starring Jennifer Jason Leigh titled *Mrs. Parker and the Vicious Circle* (1994). An Academy Award–winning documentary film about the Round Table members was called *The Ten-Year Lunch* (1987).

5. Molly Ivins, 18 January 2005, syndicated column; Gigi Mahon, *The Last Days of* The New Yorker (New York: McGraw-Hill, 1988), pp. 9–10. Among the books that contain histories of *The New Yorker* are James Thurber, *The Years with Ross* (Boston: Little, Brown, 1959); Jane Grant, *Ross,* The New Yorker *and Me* (New York: Reynal, 1968); Brendan Gill, *Here at* The New Yorker (New York: Random House, 1975); E. J. Kahn Jr., *About* The New Yorker *and Me: A Sentimental Journal* (New York: G. P. Putnam's Sons, 1979); Mahon, *The Last Days of* The New Yorker; Renata Adler, *Gone: The Last Days of* The New Yorker (New York: Simon & Schuster, 1999); and Ben Yagoda, *About Town:* The New Yorker *and the World It Made* (New York: Scribner, 2000).

6. Mahon, *The Last Days,* pp. 13–35; Value comparisons from Samuel H. Williamson, "What Is the Relative Value?" Economic History Services, June 2005, http://www.eh.net/hmit/compare.

7. Leslie D. Sillars, "Reporter at Large: Morris Markey's Literary Journalism in *The New Yorker,*" paper delivered at the annual meeting of the Association for Education in Journalism and Mass Communication, 2001.

8. Gill, *Here at* The New Yorker, p. 48.

9. See Angell, "Personal History."

10. For more on McKelway, see Ben Yagoda, "Benevolent Dreamer: Ben Yagoda on St. Clair McKelway, Who Wrote with Lucidity about His Own Mental Illness," *Columbia Journalism Review,* January/February 2007, pp. 52–55.

11. Quoted in Raymond Sokolov, *Wayward Reporter: The Life of A. J. Liebling* (New York: Harper & Row, 1980), p. 105. The easiest access to the work of writers such as Berger, McKelway, Johnston, and Sayre is via the searchable database in *The Complete* New Yorker: *Eighty Years of the Nation's Greatest Magazine with DVD-ROMs* (New York: Random House, 2005).

12. Yagoda, *About Town,* p. 103.

13. Paul Bush, "The Use of Fiction Elements in Nonfiction: Proving the Existence of a New Genre" (Master's thesis, Vermont College of Norwich University, 1989), chapter 3.

14. Joseph Mitchell, *My Ears Are Bent* (New York: Sheridan House, 1938; reprint, New York: Pantheon Books, 2001), p. 3.

15. Personal interview with Calvin Trillin, 14 December 1989; Stanley Edgar Hyman, "The Art of Joseph Mitchell," in *The Critic's Credentials* (New York: Atheneum, 1978), p. 79.

16. Mitchell said this to me in a 1988 interview and also wrote the same in *Up in the Old Hotel* (New York: Pantheon Books, 1992), p. 373.

17. Alec Wilkinson, "Setting the Standard," *Vogue,* August 1992, p. 154.

18. Hyman, "The Art of Joseph Mitchell," p. 83.

19. Sokolov, *Wayward Reporter,* p. 252.

20. Mitchell, *Up in the Old Hotel,* pp. 52–70.

21. Ibid., p. 644.

22. Noel Perrin, "A Kind of Writing for Which No Name Exists," in *A Reader's Delight* (Hanover, N.H.: University Press of New England, 1988), p. 21.

23. Mitchell, *Up in the Old Hotel,* p. 689.

24. Ibid., pp. 690–693.

25. Ibid., p. 698.

26. Hyman, "The Art of Joseph Mitchell," pp. 84–85. On Mitchell's symbolism, see also James Rogers, "Making Sense of *Joe Gould's Secret*" (Master's thesis, University of St. Thomas, 1999); "Seumas O'Kelly's *The Weaver's Grave* and Joseph Mitchell's 'Mr. Hunter's Grave'" (delivered to the American Conference for Irish Studies, University of Wisconsin–Milwaukee, 15 October 2004); and "Joseph Mitchell's Invention of History" (delivered at the NonfictionNow Conference, University of Iowa, 12 November 2005).

27. Mitchell, *Up in the Old Hotel,* pp. 624, 657.

28. Ibid., pp. 708–709.

29. James Rogers, "Joseph Mitchell's Irish Imagination," in Charles Fanning, ed., *New Perspectives on the Irish Diaspora* (Carbondale: Southern Illinois University Press, 2000), p. 52.

30. Sokolov, *Wayward Reporter,* p. 89.

31. Remnick, "Introduction," in A. J. Liebling, *Just Enough Liebling: Classic Work by the Legendary* New Yorker *Writer* (New York: North Point Press, 2004), pp. xvii–xviii.

32. Ross, *Reporting Back,* pp. 158–159.

33. Ibid., p. 1.

34. Lillian Ross, "Introduction," in *Reporting* (New York: Dodd, Mead, 1981).

35. Ross, *Reporting Back,* p. 12.

36. Mahon, *The Last Days,* pp. 3–36.

37. For sources of these casualty statistics, see *Wall Street Journal,* 4 March 2005, citing the U.S. Centers for Disease Control and Prevention in Atlanta; Felicia McCrary and Mona Baumgarten, "Casualties of War: The Short- and Long-Term Effects of the 1945 Atomic Bomb Attacks on Japan," Young Epidemiology Scholars Program (2004), available at http://www.collegeboard.com/prod_downloads/yes/4297_MODULE _20.pdf, p. 10.

38. David Sanders, *John Hersey* (New Haven, Conn.: College and University Press, 1967), p. 41.

39. On the controversy over use of The Bomb, see, for example, the final chapters in Richard Rhodes, *The Making of the Atomic Bomb* (New York: Simon & Schuster, 1987), which won the Pulitzer Prize.

40. Alistair Horne, "Battle in the Pacific," *Wall Street Journal,* 16–17 December 2006, p. P11.

41. John Hersey, *Hiroshima* (New York: Alfred A. Knopf, 1946), p. 37.

42. Stanley Weintraub, *Wall Street Journal,* 12–13 August 2006, p. P8.

CHAPTER SIX

1. "Redpants and Sugarman" was Part II of a piece by Sheehy titled "Wide Open City" in the 26 July 1971 *New York* magazine. Part I was "The New Breed." She later published a book called *Hustling: Prostitution in Our Wide-Open Society* (New York: Delacorte Press, 1973) in which she thanked New York Mayor John Lindsay and Chief Corporation Counsel Norman Redlich for inviting her "cooperation in finding old laws and formulating new ones to inhibit criminal profit-makers at every level of prostitution," p. x.

2. Sarah Harrison Smith, *The Fact Checker's Bible: A Guide to Getting It Right* (New York: Anchor Books, 2004), p. 97.

3. Norman Mailer, *The Armies of the Night: History as a Novel. The Novel as History* (New York: New American Library, 1968), p. 14; Thompson, *Fear and Loathing: On the Campaign Trail '72* (New York: Simon & Schuster, 1973), p. 48.

4. See the chart of birth years for New Journalists in John Pauly, "The Politics of the New Journalism," in Norman Sims, ed., *Literary Journalism in the Twentieth Century* (New York: Oxford University Press, 1990), p. 117; Norman Mailer, *Some Honorable Men: Political Conventions, 1960–1972* (Boston: Little, Brown, 1976), p. vii.

5. Harold Hayes, "Editor's Note," *Esquire,* January 1972, reprinted in Ronald Weber, ed., *The Reporter as Artist: A Look at the New Journalism Controversy* (New York: Hastings House, 1974), pp. 260–262; Thomas Connery, "Research Review," p. 210.

6. Mailer, *Some Honorable Men,* pp. 15–16.

7. Ibid., pp. 23–24.

8. Ibid., p. ix.

9. See also Eason, "Telling Stories and Making Sense," 125–129.

10. Tom Wolfe, "King of the Status Dropouts," in *The Pump House Gang* (New York: Farrar, Straus & Giroux, 1968), p. 49.

11. Tom Wolfe to Henry Robbins at Farrar, Straus & Giroux, 26 April 1967, New York Public Library, Manuscripts and Archives Division; Norman Podhoretz, "The Article as Art," in Ronald Weber, *The Reporter as Artist: A Look at the New Journalism Controversy* (New York: Hastings House, 1974), p. 129.

12. Sales figures from 4 April 2006 issue of "The Writing Life," by Terry Whalin, a fiction acquisitions editor at Howard Books, an imprint of Simon and Schuster, http://terrywhalin.blogspot.com/2006/04/truth-sells-books.html. Whalin cites *Publishers Weekly* as the source of the sales figures.

13. William Shawn to John Whitney, 9 April 1965, New York Public Library, Manuscripts and Archives Division.

14. Wolfe, "The New Journalism," p. 16.

15. Walter Lippmann to Ted Weeks, editor of *The Atlantic Monthly,* 16 March 1965 (misdated on the letter), New York Public Library, Manuscripts and Archives Division.

16. Wolfe, "The New Journalism," p. 12.

17. Leonard C. Lewin, "Is Fact Necessary?" *Columbia Journalism Review* (Winter 1966), pp. 32–34.

18. "Parajournalism, or Tom Wolfe and His Magic Writing Machine," *New York Review of Books,* 26 August 1965, reprinted in Ronald Weber, ed., *The Reporter as Artist: A Look at the New Journalism Controversy* (New York: Hastings House, 1974), pp. 223–233.

19. Ved Mehta to Walter Lippmann, 5 May 1965, New York Public Library, Manuscripts and Archives Division.

20. Tom Wolfe, "Lost in the Whichy Thicket: *The New Yorker II,*" *New York* magazine of the *Herald Tribune,* 18 April 1965, p. 24. Reprinted in Tom Wolfe, *Hooking Up* (New York: Farrar, Straus, & Giroux, 1980), p. 281.

21. Lewin, "Is Fact Necessary?" pp. 29–34.

22. Wolfe, *Hooking Up,* p. 292; Wolfe, "The New Journalism," p. 24.

23. Hersey, "The Legend on the License," *Yale Review* 70 (Autumn 1980), pp. 5, 8.

24. Wolfe, "The New Journalism," pp. 31–32. Wolfe published an earlier and slightly different draft of his essay in *The Bulletin* of the American Society of Newspaper Editors in September 1970.

25. Truman Capote, *In Cold Blood: A True Account of a Multiple Murder and Its Consequences* (New York: Random House, 1965), p. 331.

26. Madeleine Blais, personal correspondence with author.

27. Harry Gilroy, "A Book in a New Form Earns $2-Million for Truman Capote," *New York Times Book Review,* 31 December 1965; economic values from Samuel H. Williamson, "What Is the Relative Value?" Economic History Services, June 2005, http://www.eh.net/hmit/compare; Steinbeck sales from George Will column, 26 June 2006.

28. Capote, *In Cold Blood,* p. 3.

29. Robert McCrum, review of George Plimpton's *Truman Capote* in *The Observer* (London), 22 February 1998, p. 14.

30. Gerald Clarke, *Capote: A Biography* (New York: Simon & Schuster, 1988), pp. 358–359.

31. Kenneth Tynan, "The Kansas Farm Murders," in *The Observer* (London), 13 March 1966, p. 21; Joseph J. Waldmeir and John C. Waldmeir, eds., *The Critical Response to Truman Capote* (Westport, Conn.: Greenwood Press, 1999), p. 130.

32. Waldmeir and Waldmeir, *Critical Response,* pp. 133–134.

33. Blais, personal correspondence with author.

34. David Hayes, personal correspondence with author; Janet Malcolm, "The Journalist and the Murderer," *The New Yorker,* 13 March 1989, p. 38; Joan Didion, *Slouching towards Bethlehem* (New York: Farrar, Straus & Giroux, 1968), p. xiv.

35. Eason, "Telling Stories and Making Sense," p. 125.

36. Blais, personal correspondence.

37. Capote, *In Cold Blood,* p. 247; Waldmeir and Waldmeir, *Critical Response,* p. 133.

38. George Plimpton, "The Story behind a Nonfiction Novel," *New York Times Book Review,* 16 January 1966.

39. Terry Whalen, "The Writing Life," 4 April 2006, http://terrywhalin.blogspot.com/2006/04/truth-sells-books.html.

40. David Eason, "The New Journalism and the Image-World," in Norman Sims, ed., *Literary Journalism in the Twentieth Century* (New York: Oxford University Press, 1990).

41. Joan Didion, *The White Album* (New York: Simon & Schuster, 1979), p. 12.

42. See Norman Sims, "Conversations with Tracy Kidder," *Points of Entry: Cross-Currents in Storytelling,* no. 3 (2005), pp. 175–181.

43. David Eason, personal correspondence with author.

44. Fishkin, "The Borderlands of Culture," in Norman Sims, ed., *Literary Journalism in the Twentieth Century* (New York: Oxford University Press, 1990), pp. 153, 164.

45. Michael Herr to Harold Hayes, 1 June 1967. Unless otherwise noted, quotations are from Herr's letters, Rare Books and Manuscripts, Special Collections Department, Z. Smith Reynolds Library, Wake Forest University, Winston-Salem, North Carolina.

46. Herr to Hayes, 7 January 1968.

47. Herr to Hayes, 1 June 1967.

48. Marc Weingarten, *The Gang That Wouldn't Write Straight: Wolfe, Thompson, Didion, and the New Journalism Revolution* (New York: Crown, 2006), p. 168; voices quotation from Eric James Schroeder, *Vietnam, We've All Been There: Interviews with American Writers* (Westport, Conn.: Praeger, 1992), p. 43; "straight reporting" quoted in W. Stewart Pinkerton Jr., "'New Journalism': Believe It or Not," in A. Kent MacDougall, ed., *The Press: A Critical Look from the Inside* (Princeton, N.J.: Dow Jones Books, 1972), pp. 162–163.

49. Michael Herr, *Dispatches* (New York: Alfred A. Knopf, 1977), p. 133.

50. Ibid., p. 20.

51. Ibid., p. 22.

52. Schroeder, *Vietnam,* pp. 35, 40; Weingarten, *The Gang That Wouldn't Write Straight,* p. 173.

53. Didion, "Slouching towards Bethlehem," *Saturday Evening Post,* 23 September 1967, p. 26, reprinted in *Slouching towards Bethlehem.*

54. "Notebook" was originally in *Holiday* and reprinted in *Slouching towards Bethlehem,* p. 133; italics in original. See, for example, Martin Kasindorf, "New Directions for the First Family of Angst," *Saturday Review,* April 1982, pp. 15–18.

55. Joan Didion, *Salvador* (New York: Simon & Schuster, 1983), p. 26.

56. Blais, personal correspondence with author; "Truth and Memoir: A Conversation with William Zinsser," *Authors Guild Bulletin,* Spring 2006, p. 9; Walt Harrington, "What Journalism Can Offer Ethnography," *Qualitative Inquiry,* February 2003, pp. 98–99.

57. Walt Harrington, ed., *The Beholder's Eye: A Collection of America's Finest Personal Journalism* (New York: Grove Press, 2005), pp. xxi–xxii.

58. Didion, *White Album,* pp. 14–15.

59. Rich Cohen, "Gonzo Nights," *New York Times,* 17 April 2005.

60. Ibid.

61. Hunter S. Thompson to Ted Sorenson, 28 March 1968, John F. Kennedy Library.

62. Hunter S. Thompson, *Fear and Loathing in Las Vegas: A Savage Journey in the Heart of the American Dream* (New York: Popular Library, 1971), p. 38.

63. Joseph Nocera, "How Hunter Thompson Killed New Journalism," *Washington Monthly,* April 1981, p. 50.

CHAPTER SEVEN

1. The NYU list compiled by project editor Mitchell Stephens is available at http://www.nyu.edu/classes/stephens/Top%20100%20page.htm.

2. See Joan Acocella, "The Girls Next Door," *The New Yorker,* 20 March 2006, p. 144. Also S. M. W. Bass and Joseph Rebello, "The Appearance of New Journalism in the Sixties. *Esquire:* A Look at the Editorial Marketplace," a paper delivered at the American Journalism Historians Association convention, St. Paul, Minn., Fall 1987.

3. All quotations from Lemann come from personal interviews.

4. *The Observer,* Sunday, 10 September 2006.

5. All quotations from Paterniti come from a personal interview or e-mail correspondence with the author.

6. Reprinted in Sims and Kramer, eds., *Literary Journalism.*

7. All quotations from Whynott come from a personal interview or e-mail correspondence with the author.

8. See, for example, Many, "Literary Journalism: Newspapers' Last, Best Hope."

9. Edward Said, in Joe Sacco, *Palestine* (Seattle: Fantagraphics Books, 2001), p. iv.

10. Finley Peter Dunne, *Observations by Mr. Dooley* (London: William Heinemann, 1902).

11. Mitchell, *My Ears Are Bent,* p. 19.

12. McPhee, "Land of the Diesel Bear," *The New Yorker,* 28 November 2005, p. 86, reprinted in *Uncommon Carriers* (New York: Farrar, Straus & Giroux, 2006); Mark Murphy, "Over the Road, Legal," *The New Yorker,* 19 November 1949; Bryan Di Salvatore, "Large Cars," *The New Yorker,* 12 and 19 September 1988.

13. Norman Rockwell, as told to Tom Rockwell, *My Adventures as an Illustrator* (New York: Harry Abrams, 1994).

14. Personal interview with Mark Singer.

15. Walt Harrington, *Intimate Journalism: The Art and Craft of Reporting Everyday Life* (Thousand Oaks, Calif.: Sage, 1997), p. xv.

16. WriterL listserv posting, 7 June 2004, used by permission of Jack Hart.

17. All quotations from McPhee come from personal interviews starting in 1982.

18. Jonathan Harr, *The Lost Painting: The Quest for a Caravaggio Masterpiece* (New York: Random House, 2005), p. 265.

19. Jonathan Harr, "Foreword," in *A Civil Action* (New York: Random House, 1995).

20. Jonathan Harr, 3 April 2006, speech at the University of Massachusetts.

21. Kramer, "Breakable Rules," p. 29.

22. Yagoda, *The Sound on the Page,* p. xxxi.

23. Michael Shapiro, "Looking for Light: *The Philadelphia Inquirer* and the Fate of American Newspapers," *Columbia Journalism Review,* March/April 2006, pp. 25–37.

24. Gay Talese, "Frank Sinatra Has a Cold," *Esquire,* April 1966.

25. All quotations from LeBlanc come from personal interviews starting in 1994 and from e-mail correspondence with the author.

26. All quotations from Mitchell come from personal interviews.

27. Rogers, "Making Sense of *Joe Gould's Secret.*"

28. Except as otherwise noted, all quotations from Conover come from personal interviews.

29. Conover, "Backstage Man," *Columbia Journalism Review,* January/February 2006, p. 52.

30. Conover, "The Road Is Very Unfair: Trucking across Africa in the Age of AIDS," in Norman Sims and Mark Kramer, eds., *Literary Journalism* (New York: Ballantine, 1995); originally published in *The New Yorker* in different form.

31. Reed, *Insurgent Mexico,* p. 88.

32. Conover, "Backstage Man," p. 54.

33. Christopher Carduff, "Fish-Eating, Whiskey, Death and Rebirth," *The New Criterion,* November 1992, p. 21.

34. All quotations from Kidder come from personal interviews beginning in 1982.

35. Aristotle, *Poetics,* Sect. 1, Part 9, c. 350 B.C.E., translated by S. H. Butcher (New York: Hill and Wang, 1961).

36. All quotations from Michael Paterniti come from personal interviews or e-mails with the author.

BIBLIOGRAPHY

◈

Abrahamson, David, ed. *The American Magazine: Research Perspectives and Prospects.* Ames: Iowa State University Press, 1995.

Acocella, Joan. "The Girls Next Door." *The New Yorker,* 20 March 2006.

Adams, J. Donald. *Copey of Harvard: A Biography of Charles Townsend Copeland.* Boston: Houghton Mifflin, 1960.

Ade, George. *Fables in Slang and More Fables in Slang.* Herbert S. Stone, 1899 and 1900; reprint, New York: Dover, 1960.

———. *Stories of the Streets and of the Town from the* Chicago Record, *1893–1900.* Edited by Franklin Meine. Chicago: Caxton Club, 1941.

Adler, Renata. *Gone: The Last Days of* The New Yorker. New York: Simon & Schuster, 1999.

Agee, James. *James Agee: Selected Journalism.* Edited by Paul Ashdown. Knoxville: University of Tennessee Press, 1985.

Agee, James, and Walker Evans. *Let Us Now Praise Famous Men.* Boston: Houghton Mifflin, 1941; paperback, 1980.

Anderson, Chris, ed. *Literary Nonfiction: Theory, Criticism, Pedagogy.* Carbondale: Southern Illinois University Press, 1989.

Anderson, Nels. *The Hobo: The Sociology of the Homeless Man.* Chicago: University of Chicago Press, 1923; Phoenix ed., 1961.

Angell, Roger. "Personal History: Andy." *The New Yorker.* 14 February 2005, pp. 132–148.

Applegate, Edd. *Literary Journalism: A Biographical Dictionary of Writers and Editors.* Westport, Conn.: Greenwood Press, 1996.

Baker, Carlos. *Ernest Hemingway: A Life Story.* New York: Charles Scribner's Sons, 1969.

Baritz, Loren, ed. *The Culture of the Twenties.* Indianapolis: Bobbs-Merrill Educational Publishing, 1970.

Barnouw, Erik. *Documentary: A History of the Non-Fiction Film.* New York: Oxford University Press, 1974.

Barra, Allen. "The Education of Little Fraud." Salon, http://archive
.salon.com/books/feature/2001/12/20/carter/index.html.

Baskin, Alex. *John Reed: The Early Years in Greenwich Village.* New York:
Archives of Social History, 1990.

Bauman, John F., and Thomas H. Coode. *In the Eye of the Great Depression: New Deal Reporters and the Agony of the American People.* Dekalb:
Northern Illinois University Press, 1988.

Becker, George J. *John Dos Passos.* New York: Frederick Ungar, 1974.

Benardete, Jane, ed. *American Realism.* New York: G. P. Putnam's Sons,
1972.

Booth, Wayne C. *The Rhetoric of Fiction,* 2d ed. Chicago: University of
Chicago Press, 1983; originally published 1961.

Boylan, James. "Publicity for the Great Depression: Newspaper Default
and Literary Reportage." In *Mass Media between the Wars: Perceptions
of Cultural Tension, 1918–1941.* Edited by Catherine L. Covert and
John D. Stevens. Syracuse, N.Y.: Syracuse University Press, 1984.

Boynton, Robert S. *The New New Journalism: Conversations with America's
Best Nonfiction Writers on Their Craft.* New York: Vintage Books, 2005.

Brooks, Van Wyck. *An Autobiography.* New York: E. P. Dutton, 1965.

Burgess, Anthony. *Ernest Hemingway and His World.* New York: Charles
Scribner's Sons, 1978; paperback, 1985.

Bush, Paul. "The Use of Fiction Elements in Nonfiction: Proving the
Existence of a New Genre." Master's thesis, Vermont College of
Norwich University, 1989.

Caldwell, Erskine, and Margaret Bourke-White. *Say, Is This the U.S.A.*
Reprint, New York: Da Capo Press, 1977; originally published
1941.

———. *You Have Seen Their Faces.* Reprint, Athens: University of Georgia Press, 1995; originally published 1937.

Campbell, W. Joseph. *The Year That Defined American Journalism: 1897 and
the Clash of Paradigms.* New York: Routledge, 2006.

Capote, Truman. *In Cold Blood: A True Account of a Multiple Murder and Its
Consequences.* New York: Random House, 1965.

———. *The Muses Are Heard.* New York: Random House, 1956.

———. *Truman Capote: Conversations.* Edited by M. Thomas Inge. Jackson, Miss.: University Press of Mississippi, 1987.

Carduff, Christopher. "Fish-Eating, Whiskey, Death and Rebirth." *The New Criterion,* November 1992.

Carey, James. "The Communications Revolution and the Professional Communicator." In *James Carey: A Critical Reader.* Edited by Eve Stryker Munson and Catherine A. Warren. Minneapolis: University of Minnesota Press, 1997.

Carr, Virginia Spencer. *Dos Passos: A Life.* Garden City, N.Y.: Doubleday, 1984.

Chaikivsky, Andrew. "Nasdijj—Seven Years Ago, He Was Born in This Magazine as a Significant New Navajo Writer. The Story of a Fraud." *Esquire,* May 2006.

Clarke, Gerald. *Capote: A Biography.* New York: Simon & Schuster, 1988.

Cody, Sherwin. *The Art of Writing and Speaking the English Language: Story-Writing and Journalism.* Chicago: Old Greek Press, 1894; rev. eds., 1903, 1905.

Cohen, Rich. "Gonzo Nights." *New York Times,* 17 April 2005.

The Complete New Yorker: *Eighty Years of the Nation's Greatest Magazine with DVD-ROMs.* New York: Random House, 2005.

Connery, Thomas B. "Hutchins Hapgood and the Search for a 'New Form of Literature.'" *Journalism History* 1, no. 13 (Spring 1986), pp. 2–9.

———. "Research Review: Magazines and Literary Journalism, an Embarrassment of Riches." In *The American Magazine: Research Perspectives and Prospects.* Edited by David Abrahamson. Ames: Iowa State University Press, 1995.

———, ed. *A Sourcebook of American Literary Journalism: Representative Writers in an Emerging Genre.* New York: Greenwood Press, 1992.

Conover, Ted. "Backstage Man." *Columbia Journalism Review,* January/February 2006, pp. 52–55.

———. "The Road Is Very Unfair: Trucking across Africa in the Age of AIDS." In *Literary Journalism.* Edited by Norman Sims and Mark Kramer. New York: Ballantine Books, 1995.

Conrow, Robert. *Field Days: The Life, Times and Reputation of Eugene Field.* New York: Charles Scribner's Sons, 1974.

Creative Nonfiction, no. 29. (2006). A special issue of the journal containing "A Million Little Choices: The ABCs of CNF."

Cunningham, Valentine, ed. *Spanish Front: Writers on the Civil War.* Oxford: Oxford University Press, 1986.

Dennis, Everette E., and William L. Rivers. *Other Voices: The New Journalism in America.* San Francisco: Canfield Press, 1974.

Depp, Michael. "What Happened to the Revolution? The Legacy of New Journalism." *Poets & Writers,* May/June 2004.

Di Salvatore, Bryan. "Large Cars." *The New Yorker,* 12 and 19 September 1988.

Didion, Joan. *Salvador.* New York: Simon & Schuster, 1983.

———. *Slouching towards Bethlehem.* New York: Farrar, Straus & Giroux, 1968.

———. *The White Album.* New York: Simon & Schuster, 1979.

Dos Passos, John. *The Best Times: An Informal Memoir.* New York: New American Library, 1966.

———. *The Fourteenth Chronicle: Letters and Diaries of John Dos Passos.* Edited and with a biographical narrative by Townsend Ludington. Boston: Gambit, 1973.

———. *John Dos Passos: The Major Nonfictional Prose.* Edited by Donald Pizer. Detroit: Wayne State University Press, 1988.

———. *John Dos Passos' Correspondence with Arthur K. McComb, or "Learn to Sing the Carmagnole."* Narrative and editing by Melvin Landsberg. Niwot, Colo.: University Press of Colorado, 1991.

———. *Journeys between Wars.* New York: Harcourt, Brace, 1938.

———. *Orient Express.* New York: Harper & Brothers, 1927.

———. *Rosinante to the Road Again.* New York: George H. Doran, 1922.

———. *Travel Books and Other Writings, 1916–1941.* Edited by Townsend Ludington. New York: Library of America, 2003.

———. *U.S.A.* Notes by Daniel Aaron and Townsend Ludington. New York: Library of America, 1996. Contains *The 42nd Parallel* (1930), *1919* (1932), and *The Big Money* (1933).

Dreiser, Theodore. *Dawn: His Autobiography 1: The Early Years.* Reprint, New York: Premier Books, 1965; originally published 1931.

Dunne, Finley Peter. *Mr. Dooley on Ivrything and Ivrybody.* Selected by Robert Hutchinson from Dunne's columns, 1898–1906. New York: Dover, 1963.

———. *Observations by Mr. Dooley.* London: William Heinemann, 1903.

Eason, David L. "Telling Stories and Making Sense." *Journal of Popular Culture* 15, no. 2 (Fall 1981), pp. 125–129.

———. "The New Journalism and the Image-World." In *Literary Journalism in the Twentieth Century.* Edited by Norman Sims. New York: Oxford University Press, 1990.

Elfer, Maurice. *Opie Read.* Detroit: Boyten Miller, 1940.

Ellis, Elmer. *Mr. Dooley's America.* New York: Alfred A. Knopf, 1941.

Feied, Frederick. *No Pie in the Sky: The Hobo as American Cultural Hero in the Works of Jack London, John Dos Passos, and Jack Kerouac.* New York: Citadel Press, 1964.

Feldman, Robert S., J. A. Forrest, and B. R. Happ. "Self-Presentation and Verbal Deception: Do Self-Presenters Lie More?" *Basic and Applied Social Psychology* 24 (2002), pp. 163–170.

Fenton, Charles A. "Ambulance Drivers in France and Italy: 1914–1918." *American Quarterly* 3 (Winter 1951), pp. 326–343.

———. *The Apprenticeship of Ernest Hemingway: The Early Years.* New York: Farrar, Straus & Cudahy, 1954; reprint, New York: Mentor Books, 1961.

Finerty, John F. *War-Path and Bivouac, or The Conquest of the Sioux.* Norman: University of Oklahoma Press, 1994; originally published 1890.

Fishkin, Shelley Fisher. *From Fact to Fiction: Journalism and Imaginative Writing in America.* Baltimore: Johns Hopkins University Press, 1985; Oxford: Oxford University Press, 1988.

Foner, Philip S., ed. *Jack London, American Rebel.* New York: Citadel Press, 1947.

Ford, Edwin H. *A Bibliography of Literary Journalism in America.* Minneapolis: Burgess, 1937.

Fowler, H. W., ed. *A Dictionary of Modern English Usage,* 2d ed. Oxford: Oxford University Press, 1965.

Fowler, Roger, ed. *A Dictionary of Modern Critical Terms,* rev. ed. London: Routledge and Kegan Paul, 1987.

Frus, Phyllis. *The Politics and Poetics of Journalistic Narrative: The Timely and the Timeless.* Cambridge: Cambridge University Press, 1994.

Fussell, Paul. *Abroad: British Literary Traveling between the Wars.* Oxford: Oxford University Press, 1980.

Gellhorn, Martha. *Travels with Myself and Another: A Memoir.* Foreword by Bill Buford. New York: Putnam, 2001; originally published 1978.

Gill, Brendan. *Here at* The New Yorker. New York: Random House, 1975.

Gilroy, Harry. "A Book in a New Form Earns $2-Million for Truman Capote." *New York Times Book Review,* 31 December 1965.

Grant, Jane. *Ross,* The New Yorker *and Me.* New York: Reynal, 1968.

Griffin, Peter. *Less Than a Treason: Hemingway in Paris.* New York: Oxford University Press, 1990.

Grobel, Lawrence. *Conversations with Capote.* Foreword by James A. Michener. New York: New American Library, 1985.

Harr, Jonathan. *A Civil Action.* New York: Random House, 1995.

———. *The Lost Painting: The Quest for a Caravaggio Masterpiece.* New York: Random House, 2005.

Harrington, Walt, ed. *The Beholder's Eye: A Collection of America's Finest Personal Journalism.* New York: Grove Press, 2005.

———. *Intimate Journalism: The Art and Craft of Reporting Everyday Life.* Thousand Oaks, Calif.: Sage, 1997.

———. "What Journalism Can Offer Ethnography." *Qualitative Inquiry,* February 2003, pp. 98–99.

Harrison, Harry P. *Culture under Canvas: The Story of Tent Chautauqua.* New York: Hastings House, 1958.

Hartsock, John. *A History of American Literary Journalism: The Emergence of a Modern Narrative Form.* Amherst: University of Massachusetts Press, 2000.

Hayes, David. "The Truth about Lying." In *enRoute,* the Air Canada in-flight magazine, July 2005.

Hemingway, Ernest. *The Dangerous Summer.* Introduction by James A. Michener. Thorndike, Maine: Thorndike Press, 1985; originally published 1960.

———. *Dateline: Toronto: The Complete Toronto Star Dispatches, 1920–1924.* Edited by William White. New York: Charles Scribner's Sons, 1985.

———. *Death in the Afternoon.* New York: Charles Scribner's Sons, 1932.

———. *Ernest Hemingway: Selected Letters, 1917–1961.* Edited by Carlos Baker. New York: Charles Scribner's Sons, 1981.

————. *Green Hills of Africa.* New York: Charles Scribner's Sons, 1935; reprint, New York: Macmillan, 1987.

————. *A Moveable Feast.* New York: Charles Scribner's Sons, 1964.

Herr, Michael. *Dispatches.* New York: Alfred A. Knopf, 1977.

Hersey, John. *Hiroshima.* New York: Alfred A. Knopf, 1946.

————. "Joe Is Home Now." In *Here to Stay.* New York: Alfred A. Knopf, 1963; New York: Paragon House, 1988.

————. "The Legend on the License." *Yale Review* 70 (Autumn 1980), 1–25.

Holland, Patrick, and Graham Huggan. *Tourists with Typewriters: Critical Reflections on Contemporary Travel Writing.* Ann Arbor: University of Michigan Press, 1998.

Hollowell, John. *Fact and Fiction: The New Journalism and the Nonfiction Novel.* Chapel Hill: University of North Carolina Press, 1977.

Hovey, Tamara. *John Reed: Witness to Revolution.* Los Angeles: George Sand Books, 1975.

Howarth, William. "The Mother of Literature: Journalism and *The Grapes of Wrath.*" In *Literary Journalism in the Twentieth Century.* Edited by Norman Sims. New York: Oxford University Press, 1990.

Hyman, Stanley Edgar. "The Art of Joseph Mitchell." In *The Critic's Credentials.* New York: Atheneum, 1978.

Johnson, Michael L. *The New Journalism: The Underground Press, the Artists of Nonfiction, and Changes in the Established Media.* Lawrence: University Press of Kansas, 1971.

Kahn, E. J., Jr. *About* The New Yorker *and Me: A Sentimental Journal.* New York: G. P. Putnam's Sons, 1979.

Kasindorf, Martin. "New Directions for the First Family of Angst." *Saturday Review,* April 1982, pp. 15–18.

Kelly, Fred C. *George Ade: Warmhearted Satirist.* Indianapolis: Bobbs-Merrill, 1947.

Kenner, Hugh. "The Politics of the Plain Style." In the *New York Times Book Review,* 15 September 1985; reprinted in Norman Sims, ed., *Literary Journalism in the Twentieth Century.* New York: Oxford University Press, 1990.

Kerrane, Kevin, and Ben Yagoda. *The Art of Fact: A Historical Anthology of Literary Journalism.* New York: Scribner, 1997.

Keyes, Ralph. *The Post-Truth Era: Dishonesty and Deception in Contemporary Life.* New York: St. Martin's Press, 2004.

Kimbrel, William W., Jr. "Necessary Illusions: Biography and the Problem of Narrative Truth." Ph.D. dissertation, University of Massachusetts, 1992.

Koch, Stephen. *The Breaking Point: Hemingway, Dos Passos, and the Murder of Jose Robles.* New York: Counterpoint, 2005.

Kolbert, Elizabeth. "Looking for Lorca." *The New Yorker,* 22 and 29 December 2003, pp. 64–75.

Kramer, Mark. "Breakable Rules for Literary Journalists." In *Literary Journalism.* Edited by Norman Sims and Mark Kramer. New York: Ballantine, 1995.

Kramer, Mark, and Wendy Call, eds. *Telling True Stories: A Nonfiction Writer's Guide from the Nieman Foundation at Harvard University.* New York: Plume, 2007.

Lange, Dorothea, and Paul Taylor. *An American Exodus: A Record of Human Erosion.* New York: Reynal & Hitchcock, 1939.

Lauster, Martina. *Sketches of the Nineteenth Century: European Journalism and Its Physiologies, 1830–50.* New York: Palgrave Macmillan, 2007.

LeBlanc, Adrian Nicole. *Random Family: Love, Drugs, Trouble, and Coming of Age in the Bronx.* New York: Scribner, 2003.

Lehman, Daniel W. *John Reed and the Writing of Revolution.* Athens: Ohio University Press, 2002.

———. *Matters of Fact: Reading Nonfiction over the Edge.* Columbus: Ohio State University Press, 1997.

Lemann, Nicholas. *Out of the Forties.* Austin: Texas Monthly Press, 1983.

Lewin, Leonard C. "Is Fact Necessary?" *Columbia Journalism Review* (Winter 1966), pp. 29–34.

Liebling, A. J. *Between Meals: An Appetite for Paris.* Introduction by James Salter. New York: North Point Press, 1986.

———. *The Honest Rainmaker: The Life and Times of Colonel John R. Stingo.* Foreword by Garrison Keillor and Mark Singer. San Francisco: North Point Press, 1989; originally published 1953.

———. *Just Enough Liebling: Classic Work by the Legendary* New Yorker *Writer.* Introduction by David Remnick. New York: North Point Press, 2004.

―――. *Liebling Abroad*. Introduction by Raymond Sokolov. New York: Playboy Press, 1981. Contains *The Road Back to Paris; Mollie and Other War Pieces; Normandy Revisited;* and *Between Meals: An Appetite for Paris.*

―――. *Liebling at Home*. Introduction by Herbert Mitgang. New York: Wideview Books, 1982. Contains *The Telephone Booth Indian; Chicago: The Second City; The Honest Rainmaker: The Life and Times of Colonel John R. Stingo; The Earl of Louisiana;* and *The Jollity Building.*

―――. *Liebling at* The New Yorker: *Uncollected Essays*. Edited by James Barbour and Fred Warner. Albuquerque: University of New Mexico Press, 1994.

―――. *The Press*. Introduction by Jean Stafford. New York: Pantheon Books, 1981; originally published 1964.

―――. *The Sweet Science*. New York: Viking Press, 1956.

London, Jack. *Jack London: Novels and Social Writings*. Selected by Donald Pizer. New York: Literary Classics of the United States, 1982. Contains *The People of the Abyss; The Road; The Iron Heel; Martin Eden; John Barleycorn;* and *Essays.*

―――. *Jack London on the Road: The Tramp Diary and Other Hobo Writings*. Edited by Richard W. Etulain. Logan: Utah State University Press, 1979.

Lorentz, Pare. *The Plow That Broke the Plains*. Washington, D.C.: Resettlement Administration, 1936.

―――. *The River*. Washington, D.C.: Farm Security Administration, 1937.

Lounsberry, Barbara. *The Art of Fact: Contemporary Artists of Nonfiction*. Westport, Conn.: Greenwood Press, 1990.

Ludington, Townsend. *John Dos Passos: A Twentieth Century Odyssey*. New York: E. P. Dutton, 1980.

Lynch, Michael P. "Who Cares about the Truth?" *Chronicle of Higher Education,* 10 September 2004.

Maharidge, Dale, and Michael Williamson. *And Their Children After Them*. New York: Pantheon, 1989.

Mahon, Gigi. *The Last Days of* The New Yorker. New York: McGraw-Hill, 1988.

Mailer, Norman. *The Armies of the Night*. New York: New American Library, 1968.

———. "Superman Comes to the Supermarket." In *Some Honorable Men: Political Conventions, 1960–1972*. Boston: Little, Brown, 1976.

Malcolm, Janet. "The Journalist and the Murderer." *The New Yorker,* 13 March 1989.

Many, Paul. "Extraordinary Voyage: The Journey from Journalism to Literature of Mark Twain's *The Innocents Abroad.*" Paper presented at the annual meeting of the American Journalism Historians Association, October 1996, London, Ontario.

———. "Literary Journalism: Newspapers' Last, Best Hope." *Connecticut Review* 18, no. 1 (Spring 1996), pp. 59–69.

———. "Toward a History of Literary Journalism." *Michigan Academician* 24, (1992), 559–569.

Massé, Mark H. "Capote's Legacy: The Challenge of Creativity and Credibility in Literary Journalism." Paper delivered at the Association for Education in Journalism and Mass Communication annual convention in Phoenix, Arizona, August 2000.

McCrum, Robert. Review of George Plimpton's *Truman Capote,* in *The Observer* (London), 22 February 1998.

Meine, Franklin J. *Tall Tales of the Southwest*. New York: Alfred A. Knopf, 1930.

Mitchell, Joseph. *The Bottom of the Harbor*. Boston: Little, Brown, 1960.

———. *Joe Gould's Secret*. New York: Viking Press, 1965.

———. *McSorley's Wonderful Saloon*. New York: Duell, Sloan and Pearce, 1943.

———. *My Ears Are Bent*. New York: Sheridan House, 1938; reprint, New York: Pantheon Books, 2001, with a foreword by Sheila McGrath and Dan Frank.

———. *Old Mr. Flood*. New York: Duell, Sloan and Pearce, 1948.

———. *Up in the Old Hotel*. New York: Pantheon Books, 1992.

Mitchell, Joseph, with Edmund Wilson. *Apologies to the Iroquois with a Study of the Mohawks in High Steel*. New York: Farrar, Straus, 1960.

Moreau, Genevieve. *The Restless Journey of James Agee*. Translated from the French by Miriam Kleiger with the assistance of Morty Schiff. New York: William Morrow, 1977.

Murphy, James E. "The New Journalism: A Critical Perspective." *Journalism Monographs,* No. 34, May 1974.

Murphy, Mark. "Over the Road, Legal." *The New Yorker,* 19 November 1949.

Nanney, Lisa. *John Dos Passos.* New York: Twayne, 1998.

Nelson, William. *Fact or Fiction: The Dilemma of the Renaissance Storyteller.* Cambridge: Harvard University Press, 1973.

The New Yorker *Book of War Pieces: London, 1939, to Hiroshima, 1945.* New York: Reynal & Hitchcock, 1947; reprint, New York: Schocken Books, 1988.

Nocera, Joseph. "How Hunter Thompson Killed New Journalism." *Washington Monthly,* April 1981, pp. 44–50.

Nordhus, Phillip B. "George Ade: A Critical Study." Ph.D. dissertation, State University of Iowa, 1957.

Paterniti, Michael. "The Great Fuel-Injected Leap Forward." *GQ,* March 2006.

———. "The Long Fall of One-Eleven Heavy." *Esquire,* July 2000.

Pauly, John. "The Politics of the New Journalism." In *Literary Journalism in the Twentieth Century.* Edited by Norman Sims. New York: Oxford University Press, 1990.

Peattie, Elia. *Impertinences: Selected Writings of Elia Peattie, A Journalist in the Gilded Age.* Edited and with a biography by Susanne George Bloomfield. Lincoln: University of Nebraska Press, 2005.

Perrin, Noel. "A Kind of Writing for Which No Name Exists." In *A Reader's Delight.* Hanover, N.H.: University Press of New England, 1988.

Peterson, Theodore. *Magazines in the Twentieth Century.* Urbana: University of Illinois Press, 1956.

Pinkerton, W. Stewart, Jr. "'New Journalism': Believe It or Not." In *The Press: A Critical Look from the Inside.* Edited by A. Kent MacDougall. Princeton, N.J.: Dow Jones Books, 1972.

Pizer, Donald. *American Expatriate Writing and the Paris Moment: Modernism and Place.* Baton Rouge: Louisiana State University Press, 1996.

———. *Twentieth-Century American Literary Naturalism: An Interpretation.* Carbondale: Southern Illinois University Press, 1982.

Plimpton, George. "The Story behind a Nonfiction Novel." *New York Times Book Review,* 16 January 1966.

———. *Truman Capote: In Which Various Friends, Enemies, Acquaintances, and Detractors Recall His Turbulent Career.* New York: Doubleday, 1997.

Prose, Francine. "The Lost Boy." *New York Times Book Review,* 24 December 2006.

Raban, Jonathan. *For Love & Money: A Writing Life, 1969–1989.* New York: Harper & Row, 1989.

Read, Opie. "Hanging Is Serious." *Arkansaw Traveler,* 12 November 1887.

———. *I Remember.* New York: Richard R. Smith, 1930.

Reed, John. *The Education of John Reed: Selected Writings.* Introductory essay by John Stuart. New York: International Publishers, 1955.

———. *Insurgent Mexico.* New York: D. Appleton, 1914; reprint, New York: Greenwood Press, 1969.

———. *The War in Eastern Europe.* New York: Charles Scribner's Sons, 1918.

Remnick, David. "Introduction." *The Complete* New Yorker: *Eighty Years of the Nation's Greatest Magazine with DVD-ROMs.* New York: Random House, 2005.

Reynolds, Michael. *Hemingway: The Paris Years.* Oxford: Basil Blackwell, 1989.

———. *The Young Hemingway.* Oxford: Basil Blackwell, 1986.

Rhodes, Richard. *The Making of the Atomic Bomb.* New York: Simon & Schuster, 1987.

Riis, Jacob A. *How the Other Half Lives: Studies among the Tenements of New York.* New York: Charles Scribner's Sons, 1890; reprint, New York: Dover, 1971.

Roberts, Arthur W. "Lillian Ross." In *A Sourcebook of American Literary Journalism: Representative Writers in an Emerging Genre.* Edited by Thomas B. Connery. New York: Greenwood Press, 1992, pp. 231–237.

Robertson, Michael. *Stephen Crane, Journalism, and the Making of Modern American Literature.* New York: Columbia University Press, 1997.

Rogers, James. "Joseph Mitchell's Irish Imagination." In *New Perspectives on the Irish Diaspora*. Edited by Charles Fanning. Carbondale: Southern Illinois University Press, 2000, pp. 52–62.

———. "Making Sense of *Joe Gould's Secret*." Master's thesis, University of St. Thomas, 1999.

Rosenheim, Jeff L., Maria Morris Hambourg, Douglas Eklund, and Mia Fineman. *Walker Evans*. New York: Metropolitan Museum of Art, 2000.

Rosenstone, Robert A. *Romantic Revolutionary: A Biography of John Reed*. New York: Alfred A. Knopf, 1975.

Ross, Lillian. *Reporting*. New York: Dodd, Mead, 1964; reprint, with a new introduction, New York: Simon & Schuster, 1981.

———. *Reporting Back: Notes on Journalism*. Washington, D.C.: Counterpoint, 2002.

Sacco, Joe. *Palestine*. Introduction by Edward Said. Seattle: Fantagraphics Books, 2001.

Sanders, David. *John Hersey*. New Haven, Conn.: College and University Press, 1967.

Schroeder, Eric James. *Vietnam, We've All Been There: Interviews with American Writers*. Westport, Conn.: Praeger, 1992.

Schudson, Michael. *Discovering the News: A Social History of American Newspapers*. New York: Basic Books, 1978.

Shaber, Sarah R. "Hemingway's Literary Journalism: The Spanish Civil War Dispatches." *Journalism Quarterly* 57, no. 3 (Autumn 1980), pp. 420–424, 535.

Shapiro, Michael. "Looking for Light: *The Philadelphia Inquirer* and the Fate of American Newspapers." *Columbia Journalism Review*, March/April 2006, pp. 25–37.

Sheehan, Neil. "Life during Wartime: Vietnam, 1966." *The New Yorker*, 12 June 2006.

Sheehy, Gail. *Hustling: Prostitution in Our Wide-Open Society*. New York: Delacorte Press, 1973.

Sillars, Leslie D. "Reporter at Large: Morris Markey's Literary Journalism in *The New Yorker*." Paper delivered at the annual meeting of the Association for Education in Journalism and Mass Communication, 2001.

Sims, Norman. "The Chicago Style of Journalism." Ph.D. dissertation, University of Illinois, 1979.

———. "Conversations with Tracy Kidder." *Points of Entry: Cross-Currents in Storytelling,* no. 3 (2005), pp. 175–181.

———. "Joseph Mitchell and *The New Yorker* Nonfiction Writers." In *Literary Journalism in the Twentieth Century.* New York: Oxford University Press, 1990.

———, ed. *Literary Journalism in the Twentieth Century.* New York: Oxford University Press, 1990.

———, ed. *The Literary Journalists.* New York: Ballantine, 1984.

Sims, Norman, and Mark Kramer, eds. *Literary Journalism.* New York: Ballantine, 1995.

Sims, Norman, and James Rogers. "Joseph Mitchell." In *Dictionary of Literary Biography: American Literary Journalists.* Edited by Arthur Kaul. Detroit: Gale Research, 1997.

Smith, Sarah Harrison. *The Fact Checker's Bible: A Guide to Getting It Right.* New York: Anchor Books, 2004.

Sokolov, Raymond. *Wayward Reporter: The Life of A. J. Liebling.* New York: Harper & Row, 1980.

Stanton, Edward F. *Hemingway and Spain: A Pursuit.* Seattle: University of Washington Press, 1989.

Stephens, Robert O. *Hemingway's Nonfiction: The Public Voice.* Chapel Hill: University of North Carolina Press, 1968.

Stott, William. *Documentary Expression and Thirties America.* New York: Oxford University Press, 1973.

Talese, Gay. "Frank Sinatra Has a Cold." *Esquire,* April 1966.

Thompson, Hunter S. *Fear and Loathing in Las Vegas: A Savage Journey to the Heart of the American Dream.* Illustrated by Ralph Steadman. New York: Random House, 1972; reprint, New York: Vintage Books, 1989. First published in *Rolling Stone,* November 1971.

———. *Fear and Loathing on the Campaign Trail '72.* New York: Simon & Schuster, 1973.

Thurber, James. *The Years with Ross.* Boston: Little, Brown, 1959.

Tompkins, Phillip K. "In Cold Fact." *Esquire,* June 1966, p. 125.

"Truth and Memoir: A Conversation with William Zinsser." *Authors Guild Bulletin,* Spring 2006.

Twain, Mark. "My Bloody Massacre." In *The Complete Humorous Sketches and Tales of Mark Twain*. Edited and with an introduction by Charles Neider. Garden City, N.Y.: Doubleday, 1961, p. 143.

———. *Tales, Speeches, Essays, and Sketches*. Edited and with an introduction by Tom Quirk. New York: Penguin Books, 1994.

———. *The Works of Mark Twain: Early Tales and Sketches,* Vol. 1, *1851–1864*. Edited by Edgar Marquess Branch and Robert H. Hirst. Berkeley: University of California Press, 1979.

Twain, Mark, and Bret Harte. *California Sketches*. New York: Dover, 1991; reprint of *Sketches of the Sixties: Being Forgotten Material Now Collected for the First Time from "The Californian," 1864–67*. San Francisco: John Howell, 1926.

Tynan, Kenneth. "The Kansas Farm Murders." *The Observer* (London), 13 March 1966.

Wain, John, ed. *Edmund Wilson: The Man and His Work*. New York: New York University Press, 1978.

Waldmeir, Joseph J., and John C. Waldmeir, eds. *The Critical Response to Truman Capote*. Westport, Conn.: Greenwood Press, 1999.

Weber, Ronald. *Hired Pens: Professional Writers in America's Golden Age of Print*. Athens: Ohio University Press, 1997.

———. *The Literature of Fact: Literary Nonfiction in American Writing*. Athens: Ohio University Press, 1980.

———. *News of Paris: American Journalists in the City of Light between the Wars*. Chicago: Ivan R. Dee, 2006.

———. *The Reporter as Artist: A Look at the New Journalism Controversy*. New York: Hastings House, 1974.

Weingarten, Marc. *The Gang That Wouldn't Write Straight: Wolfe, Thompson, Didion, and the New Journalism Revolution*. New York: Crown, 2006.

Whynott, Douglas. *A Country Practice: Scenes from the Veterinary Life*. New York: North Point Press, 2004.

———. *Following the Bloom: Across America with the Migratory Beekeepers*. Mechanicsburg, Penn.: Stackpole Books, 1991; reprint, New York: Penguin/Tarcher, 2004.

———. *Giant Bluefin*. New York: Farrar, Straus & Giroux, 1995.

———. *A Unit of Water, A Unit of Time: Joel White's Last Boat.* New York: Doubleday, 1999; paperback, New York: Washington Square Press, Pocket Books, 2000.

Wilkinson, Alec. "Setting the Standard." *Vogue,* August 1992.

Wilson, Christopher P. "The Era of the Reporter Reconsidered: The Case of Lincoln Steffens." *Journal of Popular Culture* 15, no. 2 (Fall 1981), pp. 41–49.

———. *The Labor of Words: Literary Professionalism in the Progressive Era.* Athens: University of Georgia Press, 1985.

Wilson, Edmund. *The American Earthquake: A Documentary of the Jazz Age, the Great Depression, and the New Deal.* New York: Doubleday, 1958.

———. *The Thirties: From Notebooks and Diaries of the Period.* Edited and with an introduction by Leon Edel. New York: Farrar, Straus & Giroux, 1980.

Wolfe, Tom. *Hooking Up.* New York: Farrar, Straus & Giroux, 2000.

———. "The New Journalism." In *The New Journalism with an Anthology.* Edited by Tom Wolfe and E. W. Johnson. New York: Harper & Row, 1973.

———. "The New Journalism." *The Bulletin* of the American Society of Newspaper Editors, September 1970.

———. *The Pump House Gang.* New York: Farrar, Straus & Giroux, 1968.

———. *Radical Chic and Mau-Mauing the Flak Catchers.* New York: Farrar, Straus & Giroux, 1970.

———. "Tiny Mummies! The True Story of The Ruler of 43d Street's Land of the Walking Dead!" and "Lost in the Whichy Thicket: The New Yorker-II." *New York* magazine, 11 and 18 April 1965, then the Sunday supplement of the *New York Herald Tribune.* Reprinted in Tom Wolfe, *Hooking Up* (New York: Farrar, Straus and Giroux, 2000).

Yagoda, Ben. *About Town:* The New Yorker *and the World It Made.* New York: Scribner, 2000.

———. "Benevolent Dreamer: Ben Yagoda on St. Clair McKelway, Who Wrote with Lucidity about His Own Mental Illness." *Columbia Journalism Review,* January/February 2007, pp. 52–55.

―――. *The Sound on the Page: Style and Voice in Writing*. New York: HarperCollins, 2004.

Zavarzadeh, Mas'ud. *The Mythopoeic Reality: The Postwar American Nonfiction Novel*. Urbana: University of Illinois Press, 1976.

Zelizer, Barbie. *Taking Journalism Seriously: News and the Academy*. Thousand Oaks, Calif.: Sage, 2004.

Ziff, Larzer. *The American 1890s: Life and Times of a Lost Generation*. New York: Viking Press, 1966.

―――. *Return Passages: Great American Travel Writing, 1780–1910*. New Haven, Conn.: Yale University Press, 2000.

APPENDIX: A SELECTED HISTORICAL BIBLIOGRAPHY OF LITERARY JOURNALISM

◈

This bibliography is more suggestive than complete. It contains a range of books, some that are considered classic works and others that are much less known. These works are not infallible; some may contain fictionalized stories or elements. Mark Twain encouraged readers to exercise judgment, and that advice remains valid today.

With a few exceptions, autobiographies, memoirs, and newspaper stories have been excluded, as have criticism and books about literary journalism. Most of the works were written during the twentieth century, although a few nineteenth-century classics are included. Often only a few works by an author are mentioned. For example, John McPhee has more than thirty books of literary journalism in print, all worth reading, but only a few are listed here. This list is intended as a starting point for further reading and research.

Works are arranged in three categories according to date of publication; sometimes the same author appears in two sections.

BEFORE 1915

Ade, George. *Chicago Stories.* Edited by Franklin J. Meine; illustrated by John T. McCutcheon and others. Chicago: Henry Regnery, 1963.

Baker, Ray Stannard. *Following the Color Line.* New York: Doubleday, Page, 1908; reprint, New York: Harper Torchbooks, 1964.

Banks, Elizabeth L. *Campaigns of Curiosity: Journalistic Adventures of an American Girl in Late Victorian London.* Introduction by Mary Suzanne Schriber and Abbey Zink. Reprint, Madison: University of Wisconsin Press, 2003; originally published 1894.

Berkman, Alexander. *Prison Memoirs of an Anarchist.* Introduction by Hutchins Hapgood; new introduction by Paul Goodman. New York: Schocken Books, 1970; originally published 1912.

Bierce, Ambrose. *The Collected Writings of Ambrose Bierce.* Introduction by Clifton Fadiman. Secaucus, N.J.: Citadel Press, 1946.

Borrow, George. *The Bible in Spain.* New York: G. P. Putnam's Sons, 1899.

———. *The Zincali: An Account of the Gypsies of Spain.* London: John Murray, 1923.

Cahan, Abraham. *Grandma Never Lived in America: The New Journalism of Abraham Cahan.* Edited with an introduction by Moses Rischin. Bloomington: Indiana University Press, 1985.

Crane, Stephen. *Tales, Sketches, and Reports,* vol. 7 of *The Works of Stephen Crane.* Edited by Fredson Bowers. Charlottesville: University Press of Virginia, 1973.

Davis, Richard Harding. *The Red Cross Girl.* New York: Charles Scribner's Sons, 1916.

———. *A Year from a Reporter's Note-Book.* New York: Harper & Brothers, 1897.

Dreiser, Theodore. *Selected Magazine Articles of Theodore Dreiser: Life and Art in the American 1890s.* Edited with an introduction and notes by Yoshinobu Hakutani. Rutherford, N.J.: Fairleigh Dickinson University Press, 1985.

DuBois, W. E. B. *The Souls of Black Folk.* Edited by Saunders Redding. New York: Fawcett, 1961; originally published 1903.

———. *W. E. B. DuBois: Writings.* Edited by Nathan Huggins. New York: Library of America, 1986.

Dunne, Finley Peter. *Mr. Dooley at His Best.* Edited by Elmer Ellis. New York: Scribner's, 1943.

Durland, Kellogg. *The Red Reign: The True Story of an Adventurous Year in Russia.* New York: Century, 1907.

Finerty, John F. *War-Path and Bivouac, or The Conquest of the Sioux*. Norman: University of Oklahoma Press, 1994; originally published 1890.

Flynt, Josiah. *Tramping with Tramps: Studies and Sketches of Vagabond Life*. New York: Century, 1899.

Hapgood, Hutchins. *An Anarchist Woman*. New York: Duffield, 1909.

———. *The Spirit of the Ghetto: Studies of the Jewish Quarter in New York*. Introduction by Moses Rischin. Cambridge: Harvard University Press, 1967; originally published 1902.

———. *The Spirit of Labor*. New York: Duffield, 1907.

———. *Types from City Streets*. New York: Funk & Wagnalls, 1910.

Hearn, Lafcadio. *Creole Sketches*. Edited by Charles Woodward Hutson. Boston: Houghton Mifflin, 1924.

———. *Fantastics and Other Fancies*. Boston: Houghton Mifflin, 1914.

———. *Lafcadio Hearn's America: Ethnographic Sketches and Editorials*. Edited by Simon J. Bronner. Lexington: University Press of Kentucky, 2002.

London, Jack. *Jack London on the Road: The Tramp Diary and Other Hobo Writings*. Edited by Richard W. Etulain. Logan: Utah State University Press, 1979.

———. *The People of the Abyss*. New York: Grosset & Dunlap, 1903.

———. *The Road*. New York: Macmillan, 1907.

Reed, John. *Insurgent Mexico*. New York: D. Appleton, 1914; reprint, New York: Greenwood Press, 1969.

Riis, Jacob A. *How the Other Half Lives: Studies among the Tenements of New York*. New York: Charles Scribner's Sons, 1890.

Schuyler, Eugene. *Turkistan: Notes of a Journey in Russian Turkistan, Kokand, Bukhara and Kuldja*. Edited and with an introduction by Geoffrey Wheeler; abridged by K. E. West. New York: Frederick A. Praeger, 1966; originally published in two volumes, New York: Scribner, Armstrong, 1877.

Turgenev, Ivan. *A Sportsman's Notebook*. New York: Viking, 1950; originally published 1852.

Twain, Mark. *The Complete Humorous Sketches and Tales of Mark Twain*. Edited with an introduction by Charles Neider. Garden City, N.Y.: Doubleday, 1961.

————. *Early Tales and Sketches.* Vols. 1 (1851–1864) and 2 (1864–1865). Edited by Edgar Marquess Branch and Robert H. Hirst with the assistance of Harriet Elinor Smith. Berkeley: University of California Press, 1979.

————. *Innocents Abroad: or, The New Pilgrim's Progress.* New York: Signet Classics, 1966; originally published 1869.

————. *Life on the Mississippi.* New York: New American Library, 1980; originally published 1883.

————. *Roughing It.* Hartford, Conn.: American Publishing, 1895; originally published 1871.

West, Rebecca. *The Young Rebecca: Writings of Rebecca West, 1911–17.* Selected and introduced by Jane Marcus. New York: Viking, 1982.

Wyckoff, Walter A. *A Day with a Tramp, and Other Days.* New York: Benjamin Blom, 1971; originally published 1901.

1915–1960

Adamic, Louis. *My America, 1928–1938.* New York: Harper & Brothers, 1938.

Ade, George. *The Old Time Saloon.* New York: R. Long & R. R. Smith, 1931.

Agee, James. *James Agee: Selected Journalism.* Edited with an introduction by Paul Ashdown. Knoxville: University of Tennessee Press, 1985.

————. *Let Us Now Praise Famous Men.* Photos by Walker Evans with an introduction by John Hersey. Boston: Houghton Mifflin, 1988; originally published 1941.

Berger, Meyer. *The Eight Million: Journal of a New York Correspondent.* New York: Simon & Schuster, 1942; reprint, New York: Columbia University Press, 1983.

————. *Meyer Berger's New York.* New York: Random House, 1960.

Bolitho, William. *Camera Obscura.* New York: Simon & Schuster, 1930.

Caldwell, Erskine, and Margaret Bourke-White. *You Have Seen Their Faces.* New York: Modern Age Books, 1937.

Capote, Truman. *The Muses Are Heard.* New York: Random House, 1956.

Dorr, Rheta Childe. *Inside the Russian Revolution.* New York: Macmillan, 1918; reprint, New York: Arno Press, 1970.

Dos Passos, John. *In All Countries.* New York: Harcourt, Brace, 1934.

———. *Orient Express.* New York: Harper & Brothers, 1927.

Dreiser, Theodore. *The Color of a Great City.* New York: Boni and Liveright, 1923.

———. *Theodore Dreiser: A Selection of Uncollected Prose.* Detroit: Wayne State University Press, 1977.

Flanner, Janet (Genêt). *Paris Journal, 1944–1965.* Edited by William Shawn. New York: Atheneum, 1965.

———. *Paris Was Yesterday (1925–1939).* New York: Popular Library, 1972.

Gellhorn, Martha. "The Third Winter." In *The Face of War.* New York: Simon & Schuster, 1959; reprint, New York: Atlantic Monthly Press, 1988.

———. *Travels with Myself and Another.* Foreword by Bill Buford. New York: Putnam, 2001; originally published 1978.

———. *The Trouble I've Seen.* New York: William Morrow, 1936.

Hecht, Ben. *1001 Afternoons in Chicago.* Chicago: Pascal Covici, 1922.

Hemingway, Ernest. *By-Line: Ernest Hemingway.* Edited by William White. New York: Scribner's, 1967.

———. *The Dangerous Summer.* New York: Scribner's, 1985; originally published 1960.

———. *Dateline: Toronto. The Complete Toronto Star Dispatches, 1920–1924.* Edited by William White. New York: Charles Scribner's Sons, 1985.

———. *Death in the Afternoon.* New York: Scribner's, 1932.

———. *Green Hills of Africa.* New York: Scribner's, 1935.

———. *A Moveable Feast.* New York: Scribner's, 1964.

Hersey, John. *Here to Stay.* New York: Alfred A. Knopf, 1963.

———. *Hiroshima.* New York: Alfred A. Knopf, 1946.

Lange, Dorothea, and Paul S. Taylor. *An American Exodus: A Record of Human Erosion.* New York: Reynal & Hitchcock, 1939.

Liebling, A. J. *Back Where I Came From.* New York: Sheridan House, 1938.

———. *Just Enough Liebling: Classic Work by the Legendary* New Yorker *Writer.* Introduction by David Remnick. New York: North Point Press, 2004.

———. *Liebling Abroad.* Introduction by Raymond Sokolov. New York: Playboy Press, 1981. Contains *The Road Back to Paris; Mollie and*

Other War Pieces; Normandy Revisited; Between Meals: An Appetite for Paris.

————. *Liebling at Home.* Introduction by Herbert Mitgang. New York: Wideview Books, 1982. Contains *The Telephone Booth Indian; Chicago: The Second City; The Honest Rainmaker; The Earl of Louisiana; The Jollity Building.*

————. *The Sweet Science.* New York: Viking, 1956.

Márquez, Gabriel García. *The Story of a Shipwrecked Sailor.* New York: Alfred A. Knopf, 1986; originally published 1955.

McCarthy, Mary. *On the Contrary.* New York: Farrar, Straus & Cudahy, 1961.

McKelway, St. Clair. *True Tales from the Annals of Crime and Rascality.* New York: Random House, 1951.

McNulty, John. *A Man Gets Around.* Boston: Little, Brown, 1951.

————. *Third Avenue, New York.* Boston: Little, Brown, 1946.

————. *The World of John McNulty.* With an appreciation by James Thurber. Garden City, N.Y.: Doubleday, 1957.

Mitchell, Joseph. *The Bottom of the Harbor.* Boston: Little, Brown, 1960.

————. *McSorley's Wonderful Saloon.* New York: Duell, Sloan and Pearce, 1943.

————. "The Mohawks in High Steel." In *Apologies to the Iroquois,* with Edmund Wilson. New York: Farrar, Straus, 1960.

————. *My Ears Are Bent.* New York: Sheridan House, 1938.

————. *Up in the Old Hotel.* New York: Random House, 1992.

Orwell, George. *Down and Out in Paris and London.* London: Gollancz, 1933.

————. *Homage to Catalonia.* London: Secker & Warburg, 1938.

————. *The Road to Wigan Pier.* London: Gollancz, 1937.

Paul, Elliot. *The Last Time I Saw Paris.* New York: Random House, 1942.

————. *The Life and Death of a Spanish Town.* New York: Random House, 1937; reprint, Westport, Conn.: Greenwood Press, 1971.

Reed, John. *Adventures of a Young Man: Short Stories from Life.* San Francisco: City Lights Books, 1975; originally published 1963.

————. *The Education of John Reed.* Introductory essay by John Stuart. New York: International Publishers, 1955.

―――. *Ten Days That Shook the World.* Foreword by V. I. Lenin. New York: Vintage Books, 1960; originally published 1919.

―――. *The War in Eastern Europe.* New York: Charles Scribner's Sons, 1918.

Ross, Lillian. *Picture: John Huston, M.G. M., and the Making of* The Red Badge of Courage. New York: Limelight Editions, 1984; originally published 1952.

―――. *Reporting.* New York: Dodd, Mead, 1964; reprint, with a new introduction, New York: Simon & Schuster, 1981.

Shirer, William L. *Berlin Diary.* New York: Alfred A. Knopf, 1941.

Steinbeck, John. *Bombs Away: The Story of a Bomber Team.* New York: Viking, 1942.

―――. *Once There Was a War.* New York: Viking, 1958; originally published 1943.

―――. *A Russian Journal.* With pictures by Robert Capa. New York: Viking, 1948.

West, Rebecca. *Black Lamb and Grey Falcon: A Journey through Yugoslavia.* New York: Viking, 1941.

―――. *The New Meaning of Treason.* New York: Viking, 1964.

―――. *Rebecca West—A Celebration.* Selected from her writings, with a critical introduction by Samuel Hynes. New York: Penguin Books, 1978.

Wilson, Edmund. *The American Earthquake.* Garden City, N.Y.: Doubleday, 1958.

White, E. B. *Essays of E. B. White.* New York: Harper Colophon Books, 1977.

―――. *Here Is New York.* New York: Harper & Brothers, 1949.

―――. *The Second Tree from the Corner.* New York: Harper & Bros., 1954.

SINCE 1960

Alvarez, A. *Feeding the Rat: Profile of a Climber.* New York: Atlantic Monthly Press, 1988.

―――. *Offshore: A North Sea Journey.* Boston: Houghton Mifflin, 1986.

Anzaldúa, Gloria. *Borderlands/La Frontera: The New Mestiza.* San Francisco: Spinsters/Aunt Lute, 1987.

Arlen, Michael J. *Thirty Seconds.* New York: Farrar, Straus & Giroux, 1980.

Bangs, Lester. *Psychotic Reactions and Carburetor Dung.* New York: Alfred A. Knopf, 1987.

Barich, Bill. *A Fine Place to Daydream: Racehorses, Romance, and the Irish.* New York: Alfred A. Knopf, 2005.

————. *Laughing in the Hills.* New York: Viking Penguin, 1980.

Bedford, Sybille. *The Faces of Justice: A Traveller's Report.* New York: Simon & Schuster, 1961.

Bissinger, H. G. "Buzz." *Friday Night Lights: A Town, a Team, and a Dream.* Reading, Mass.: Addison Wesley, 1990.

————. *A Prayer for the City.* New York: Random House, 1997.

————. *Three Nights in August: Strategy, Heartbreak, and Joy Inside the Mind of a Manager.* Boston: Houghton Mifflin, 2005.

Blais, Madeleine. *The Heart Is an Instrument: Portraits in Journalism.* Foreword by Geneva Overholser. Amherst: University of Massachusetts Press, 1992.

————. *In These Girls, Hope Is a Muscle.* New York: Atlantic Monthly Press, 1995.

Booth, Stanley. *The True Adventures of the Rolling Stones.* Chicago: A Cappella Books, 2000; originally published as *Dance with the Devil* in 1984.

Bowden, Mark. *Black Hawk Down: A Story of Modern War.* New York: Atlantic Monthly Press, 1999.

Breslin, Jimmy. *The World of Jimmy Breslin.* New York: Viking, 1967.

Bryan, C. D. B. *Friendly Fire.* New York: G. P. Putnam's Sons, 1976.

Buford, Bill. *Among the Thugs.* New York: W. W. Norton, 1992.

Cahill, Tim. *Jaguars Ripped My Flesh: Adventure Is a Risky Business.* New York: Bantam Books, 1987.

————. *Lost in My Own Backyard: A Walk in Yellowstone National Park.* New York: Crown, 2004.

————. *A Wolverine Is Eating My Leg.* New York: Vintage, 1989.

Capote, Truman. *In Cold Blood.* New York: Random House, 1965.

Carr, Cynthia. *On Edge: Performance at the End of the Twentieth Century.* Hanover, N.H.: University Press of New England, 1993.

Carson, Rachel. *Silent Spring.* Boston: Houghton Mifflin, 1962.

Conaway, James. *Napa: The Story of an American Eden*. Boston: Houghton Mifflin, 1990.

———. *The Texans*. New York: Alfred A. Knopf, 1976.

Conover, Ted. *Coyotes: A Journey across Borders with America's Illegal Migrants*. New York: Vintage Books, 1987.

———. *Newjack: Guarding Sing Sing*. New York: Random House, 2000.

———. *Rolling Nowhere: Riding the Rails with America's Hoboes*. New York: Viking, 1984.

———. *Whiteout: Lost in Aspen*. New York: Random House, 1991.

Cramer, Richard Ben. *Joe DiMaggio: The Hero's Life*. New York: Simon & Schuster, 2000.

Dash, Leon. *Rosa Lee: A Mother and Her Family in Urban America*. New York: Basic Books, 1996.

Davidson, Sara. *Loose Change: Three Women of the Sixties*. Garden City, N.Y.: Doubleday, 1977.

———. *Real Property*. Garden City, N.Y.: Doubleday, 1980.

Didion, Joan. *Miami*. New York: Simon & Schuster, 1987.

———. *Salvador*. New York: Simon & Schuster, 1983.

———. *Slouching towards Bethlehem*. New York: Farrar, Straus & Giroux, 1968.

———. *The White Album*. New York: Simon & Schuster, 1979.

Dunne, John Gregory. *Vegas: A Memoir of a Dark Season*. New York: Random House, 1974.

Ehrenreich, Barbara. *Nickel and Dimed: On (Not) Getting By in America*. New York: Henry Holt, 2001.

Ehrlich, Gretel. *The Solace of Open Spaces*. New York: Viking, 1985.

Fadiman, Anne. *The Spirit Catches You and You Fall Down: A Hmong Child, Her American Doctors, and the Collision of Two Cultures*. New York: Farrar, Straus & Giroux, 1997.

Finnegan, William. *Dateline Soweto: Travels with Black South African Reporters*. New York: HarperCollins, 1988.

Fitzgerald, Frances. *Cities on a Hill: A Journey through Contemporary American Cultures*. New York: Simon & Schuster, 1986.

Frady, Marshall. *Southerners: A Journalist's Odyssey*. New York: New American Library, 1980.

Franklin, Jon. "Mrs. Kelly's Monster." In *Writing for Story: Craft Secrets of Dramatic Nonfiction by a Two-Time Pulitzer Prize Winner.* New York: Atheneum, 1986; originally published in the *Baltimore Evening Sun,* 1978.

———. *Shocktrauma.* New York: St. Martin's Press, 1980.

Frazier, Ian. *Great Plains.* New York: Farrar, Straus & Giroux, 1989.

———. *On the Rez.* New York: Farrar, Straus & Giroux, 2000.

Frey, Darcy. *The Last Shot: City Streets, Basketball Dreams.* Boston: Houghton Mifflin, 1994.

Goldstein, Richard. *Reporting the Counterculture.* Boston: Unwin Hyman, 1989.

Gorney, Cynthia. *Articles of Faith: A Frontline History of the Abortion Wars.* New York: Simon & Schuster, 1998.

Gray, Francine du Plessix. *Adam and Eve and the City: Selected Nonfiction.* New York: Simon & Schuster, 1987.

Greene, Melissa Fay. *Praying for Sheetrock: A Work of Nonfiction.* Reading, Mass.: Addison-Wesley, 1991.

Halberstam, David. *The Amateurs.* New York: William Morrow, 1985.

———. *The Breaks of the Game.* New York: Alfred A. Knopf, 1981.

Hamburger, Robert. *All the Lonely People: Life in a Single Room Occupancy Hotel.* New Haven, Conn.: Ticknor & Fields, 1983.

Hamill, Pete. *The Invisible City: A New York Sketchbook.* Drawings by Susan Stillman. New York: Random House, 1980.

Harr, Jonathan. *A Civil Action.* New York: Random House, 1995.

———. *The Lost Painting: The Quest for a Caravaggio Masterpiece.* New York: Random House, 2005.

Harrington, Walt. *At the Heart of It: Ordinary People, Extraordinary Lives.* Columbia: University of Missouri Press, 1996.

———. *Crossings: A White Man's Journey into Black America.* New York: HarperCollins, 1993.

Hayes, David. *No Easy Answers: The Trial and Conviction of Bruce Curtis.* New York: Viking, 1986.

———. *Power and Influence: The Globe and Mail and the News Revolution.* Toronto: Key Porter Books, 1992.

Herr, Michael. *Dispatches.* New York: Alfred A. Knopf, 1977.

Hoagland, Edward. *The Edward Hoagland Reader.* Edited and with an introduction by Geoffrey Wolff. New York: Random House, 1979.

Hubbell, Sue. A *Book of Bees.* New York: Random House, 1988.

Junger, Sebastian. *A Death in Belmont.* New York: W. W. Norton, 2006.

———. *The Perfect Storm: A True Story of Men against the Sea.* New York: W. W. Norton, 1997.

Kapuściński, Ryszard. *Another Day of Life.* New York: Harcourt Brace Jovanovich, 1987; Vintage International Edition, 2001.

———. *The Shadow of the Sun.* New York: Alfred A. Knopf, 2001.

Kidder, Tracy. *Among Schoolchildren.* Boston: Houghton Mifflin, 1989.

———. *Home Town.* New York: Random House, 1999.

———. *House.* Boston: Houghton Mifflin, 1985.

———. *Mountains beyond Mountains.* New York: Random House, 2003.

———. *Old Friends.* Boston: Houghton Mifflin, 1993.

———. *The Soul of a New Machine.* Boston: Little, Brown, 1981.

Klinkenborg, Verlyn. *The Last Fine Time.* New York: Alfred A. Knopf, 1991.

———. *Making Hay.* New York: Lyons Books, 1986.

Krakauer, Jon. *Into Thin Air: A Personal Account of the Mt. Everest Disaster.* New York: Villard,1997.

———. *Under the Banner of Heaven: A Story of Violent Faith.* New York: Doubleday, 2003.

Kramer, Jane. *Europeans.* New York: Farrar, Straus & Giroux, 1988.

———. *The Last Cowboy.* New York: Harper & Row, 1977.

———. *Lone Patriot: The Short Career of an American Militiaman.* New York: Pantheon, 2002.

———. *Unsettling Europe.* New York: Random House, 1980.

Kramer, Mark. *Invasive Procedures: A Year in the World of Two Surgeons.* New York: Harper & Row, 1983.

———. *Three Farms: Making Milk, Meat and Money from the American Soil.* Boston: Little, Brown, 1980.

———. *Travels with a Hungry Bear: A Journey to the Russian Heartland.* Boston: Houghton Mifflin, 1996.

Langewiesche, William. *American Ground: Unbuilding the World Trade Center.* New York: North Point Press, 2002.

LeBlanc, Adrian Nicole. *Random Family: Love, Drugs, Trouble, and Coming of Age in the Bronx*. New York: Scribner, 2003.

Lemann, Nicholas. *The Big Test: The Secret History of the American Meritocracy*. New York: Farrar, Straus & Giroux, 1999.

———. *The Promised Land: The Great Black Migration and How It Changed America*. New York: Alfred A. Knopf, 1991.

Lernoux, Penny. *Cry of the People*. Garden City, N.Y.: Doubleday, 1982.

Levine, Richard M. *Bad Blood: A Family Murder in Marin County*. New York: Random House, 1982.

Lewis, Michael. *Liar's Poker: Rising through the Wreckage on Wall Street*. New York: W. W. Norton, 1989.

———. *The New New Thing: A Silicon Valley Story*. New York: W. W. Norton, 1999.

———. *Moneyball: The Art of Winning an Unfair Game*. New York: W. W. Norton, 2003.

Lopez, Barry. *Arctic Dreams: Imagination and Desire in a Northern Landscape*. New York: Charles Scribner's Sons, 1986.

Lukas, J. Anthony. *Common Ground: A Turbulent Decade in the Lives of Three American Families*. New York: Alfred A. Knopf, 1985.

Maclean, Norman. *Young Men and Fire*. Chicago: University of Chicago Press, 1992.

Mahoney, Rosemary. *Whoredom in Kimmage: Irish Women Coming of Age*. Boston: Houghton Mifflin, 1993.

Mailer, Norman. *The Armies of the Night: History as a Novel, the Novel as History*. New York: New American Library, 1968.

———. *The Executioner's Song*. Boston: Little, Brown, 1979.

———. *Some Honorable Men: Political Conventions, 1960–1972*. Boston: Little, Brown, 1976. Contains "Superman Comes to the Supermarket."

Marcus, David L. *What It Takes to Pull Me Through*. Boston: Houghton Mifflin, 2005.

Massé, Mark H. *Inspired to Serve: Today's Faith Activists*. Bloomington: Indiana University Press, 2004.

Matthews, Anne. *Wild Nights: Nature Returns to the City*. New York: North Point Press, 2001.

Matthiessen, Peter. *The Snow Leopard*. New York: Viking, 1978.

McCarthy, Mary. *Hanoi.* London: Weidenfeld and Nicholson, 1968.

———. *Vietnam.* New York: Harcourt, Brace & World, 1967.

McGinniss, Joe. *Fatal Vision.* New York: Putnam, 1983.

———. *The Selling of the President 1968.* New York: Trident Press, 1969.

McKelway, St. Clair. *The Big Little Man from Brooklyn.* Boston: Houghton Mifflin, 1969.

———. *The Edinburgh Caper: A One-Man International Plot.* New York: Holt, Rinehart and Winston, 1962.

McPhee, John. *Annals of the Former World.* New York: Farrar, Straus & Giroux, 1998.

———. *Coming Into the Country.* New York: Farrar, Straus & Giroux, 1977.

———. *The Control of Nature.* New York: Farrar, Straus & Giroux, 1989.

———. *Encounters with the Archdruid.* New York: Farrar, Straus, & Giroux, 1971.

———. *The John McPhee Reader.* Edited with an introduction by William Howarth. New York: Farrar, Straus, & Giroux, 1976.

———. *Oranges.* New York: Farrar, Straus & Giroux, 1966.

———. *Uncommon Carriers.* New York: Farrar, Straus & Giroux, 2006.

Mitchell, Joseph. *Joe Gould's Secret.* New York: Viking, 1965.

———. *Up in the Old Hotel.* New York: Pantheon Books, 1992.

Morgan, Dan. *Merchants of Grain.* New York: Viking, 1979.

Naipaul, Shiva. *Journey to Nowhere: A New World Tragedy.* New York: Simon & Schuster, 1981; originally published in Great Britain as *Black and White,* 1980.

Naipaul, V. S. *A Turn in the South.* New York: Alfred A. Knopf, 1989.

Okrent, Daniel. *Nine Innings.* New York: Ticknor & Fields, 1985.

Olsen, Tillie. *Silences.* New York: Delta/Seymour Lawrence, 1989; originally published 1978.

Orlean, Susan. *The Bullfighter Checks Her Makeup: My Encounters with Extraordinary People.* New York: Random House, 2001.

———. *The Orchid Thief.* New York: Random House, 1998.

Paterniti, Michael. *Driving Mr. Albert: A Trip across America with Einstein's Brain.* New York: Dial Press, 2000.

———. "The Long Fall of One-Eleven Heavy." *Esquire,* July 2000.

Plimpton, George. *Paper Lion.* New York: Harper & Row, 1966.

Preston, Richard. *The Demon in the Freezer: A True Story.* New York: Random House, 2002.

———. *First Light: The Search for the Edge of the Universe.* New York: Atlantic Monthly Press, 1987.

———. *The Hot Zone.* New York: Random House, 1994.

Quammen, David. *Natural Acts: A Sidelong View of Science and Nature.* New York: Schocken Books, 1985.

———. *The Song of the Dodo: Island Biogeography in an Age of Extinctions.* New York: Scribner, 1996.

Raban, Jonathan. *Bad Land: An American Romance.* New York: Pantheon, 1996.

———. *Old Glory: A Voyage down the Mississippi.* New York: Vintage Reprint, 1998.

Rhodes, Richard. *Farm: A Year in the Life of an American Farmer.* New York: Simon & Schuster, 1989.

———. *The Making of the Atomic Bomb.* New York: Simon & Schuster, 1986.

Sacco, Joe. *Palestine.* Introduction by Edward Said. Seattle: Fantagraphics Books, 2001.

Sager, Mike. *The Revenge of the Donut Boys: True Stories of Fame, Lust, Survival, and Multiple Personalities.* New York: Thunder's Mouth Press, 2007.

———. *Scary Monsters and Super Freaks: Stories of Sex, Drugs, Rock 'n' Roll and Murder.* New York: Thunder's Mouth Press, 2004.

Sanders, Ed. *The Family: The Story of Charles Manson's Dune Buggy Attack Battalion.* New York: Dutton, 1971.

Satrapi, Marjane. *Persepolis: The Story of a Childhood.* New York: Pantheon, 2003.

———. *Persepolis 2: The Story of a Return.* New York: Pantheon, 2004.

Sheehan, Neil. *A Bright Shining Lie: John Paul Vann and America in Vietnam.* New York: Random House, 1988.

Sheehan, Susan. *Is There No Place on Earth for Me?* Boston: Houghton Mifflin, 1982.

———. *Kate Quinton's Days.* Boston: Houghton Mifflin, 1984.

———. *A Welfare Mother.* New York: New American Library, 1976.

Sims, Patsy. *Can Somebody Shout Amen!: Inside the Tents and Tabernacles of American Revivalists.* Lexington: University Press of Kentucky, 1996; originally published 1988.

―――. *The Klan.* Lexington: University Press of Kentucky, 1996; originally published 1978.

Singer, Mark. *Character Studies: Encounters with the Curiously Obsessed.* Boston: Houghton Mifflin, 2005.

―――. *Funny Money.* New York: Alfred A. Knopf, 1985.

―――. *Mr. Personality: Profiles and Talk Pieces.* New York: Alfred A. Knopf, 1989.

Smith, Gary. "Crime and Punishment." *Sports Illustrated,* June 24, 1996.

Snow, Edgar. *Red China Today.* New York: Random House, 1970; originally published as *The Other Side of the River* in 1962.

Southern, Terry. *Red-Dirt Marijuana and Other Tastes.* New York: New American Library, 1967.

Spiegelman, Art. *In the Shadow of No Towers.* New York: Viking, 2004.

―――. *Maus II: A Survivor's Tale. And Here My Troubles Began.* New York: Pantheon, 1991.

Steinbeck, John. *Travels with Charley: In Search of America.* New York: Viking, 1962.

Talese, Gay. *Fame and Obscurity.* New York: Ivy Books, 1995; originally published 1970.

―――. *Honor Thy Father.* New York: Fawcett-World, 1972.

―――. *The Kingdom and The Power.* New York: World Publishing, 1966.

―――. *Thy Neighbor's Wife.* Garden City, N.Y.: Doubleday, 1980.

Thompson, Hunter S. *Fear and Loathing in Las Vegas: A Savage Journey to the Heart of the American Dream.* New York: Popular Library, 1971.

―――. *Fear and Loathing: On the Campaign Trail '72.* New York: Simon & Schuster, 1973.

―――. *The Great Shark Hunt.* New York: Fawcett, 1979.

―――. *Hell's Angels.* New York: Random House, 1967.

Tosches, Nick. *Where Dead Voices Gather.* Boston: Little, Brown, 2001.

Trillin, Calvin. *American Stories.* New York: Ticknor & Fields, 1991.

―――. *Killings.* New York: Ticknor & Fields, 1984.

―――. *U.S. Journal.* New York: Dutton, 1971.

Ungar, Sanford J. *Fresh Blood: The New American Immigrants.* New York: Simon & Schuster, 1995.

Wambaugh, Joseph. *The Onion Field.* New York: Delacorte Press, 1973.

Werth, Barry. *Damages: One Family's Legal Struggles in the World of Medicine.* New York: Simon & Schuster, 1998.

Weschler, Lawrence. *Shapinsky's Karma, Bogg's Bills: And Other True-Life Tales.* New York: North Point Press, 1988.

White, Theodore H. *The Making of the President 1960.* New York: Atheneum, 1961.

Whynott, Douglas. *A Country Practice: Scenes from the Veterinary Life.* New York: North Point Press, 2004.

———. *Following the Bloom: Across America with the Migratory Beekeepers.* Mechanicsburg, Penn.: Stackpole Books, 1991; reprint, New York: Penguin/Tarcher, 2004.

———. *Giant Bluefin.* New York: Farrar, Straus & Giroux, 1995.

———. *A Unit of Water, A Unit of Time: Joel White's Last Boat.* New York: Doubleday, 1999; paperback, New York: Washington Square Press, Pocket Books, 2000.

Wicker, Tom. *A Time to Die.* New York: Quadrangle, 1975.

Wideman, John Edgar. *Brothers and Keepers.* New York: Holt Rinehart and Winston, 1984.

Wilkinson, Alec. *Midnights: A Year with the Wellfleet Police.* New York: Random House, 1982.

———. *Moonshine: A Life in Pursuit of White Liquor.* New York: Alfred A. Knopf, 1985.

Winegardner, Mark. *Prophet of the Sandlots: Journeys with a Major League Scout.* Introduction by Daniel Okrent. New York: Prentice Hall, 1990.

Wolfe, Tom. *The Electric Kool-Aid Acid Test.* New York: Farrar, Straus & Giroux, 1970.

———. *The Kandy-Kolored Tangerine-Flake Streamline Baby.* New York: Farrar, Straus & Giroux, 1965.

———. *The Pump House Gang.* New York: Farrar, Straus & Giroux, 1968.

————. *Radical Chic and Mau-Mauing the Flak Catchers.* New York: Farrar, Straus & Giroux, 1970.

————. *The Right Stuff.* New York: Farrar, Straus & Giroux, 1979.

Zinsser, William. *Willie and Dwike: An American Profile.* New York: Harper & Row, 1984.

INDEX

◈

Norman Sims is a professor of journalism at the University of Massachusetts. He is the editor of *The Literary Journalists* and *Literary Journalism in the Twentieth Century* and coeditor, with Mark Kramer, of *Literary Journalism*.

Ted Conover is a Distinguished Writer in Residence at New York University, a winner of the National Book Critics Circle Award in Nonfiction, and the author of *Newjack: Guarding Sing Sing; Coyotes: A Journey Across Borders with America's Illegal Migrants; Rolling Nowhere;* and *Whiteout.*